Hans Christian Andersen

Danish Fairy Legends and Tales

Hans Christian Andersen

Danish Fairy Legends and Tales

ISBN/EAN: 9783743307520

Manufactured in Europe, USA, Canada, Australia, Japa

Cover: Foto ©ninafisch / pixelio.de

Manufactured and distributed by brebook publishing software (www.brebook.com)

Hans Christian Andersen

Danish Fairy Legends and Tales

THE GARDEN OF PARADISE. *Page* 119.

LIST OF THE FULL-PAGE ILLUSTRATIONS.

	PAGE
THE WILD SWANS	7
THE WILD SWANS	11
THE UGLY DUCKLING	22
THE LITTLE MERMAID	28
THE SWINEHERD	76
THE GARDEN OF PARADISE	119
TOMMELISE	194
GREAT CLAUS AND LITTLE CLAUS	208
THE FELLOW-TRAVELLERS	290
THE FELLOW-TRAVELLERS	297
LITTLE TUK	349
THE OLD HOUSE	373

CONTENTS.

	PAGE
THE WILD SWANS	1
THE UGLY DUCKLING	17
THE LITTLE MERMAID	27
THE STORKS	49
THE NIGHTINGALE	55
LITTLE IDA'S FLOWERS	65
THE SWINEHERD	73
OLE LUCKÖIE; OR, THE DUSTMAN	78
THE DAISY	92
THE BUCKWHEAT	97
THE EMPEROR'S NEW CLOTHES	99
THE REAL PRINCESS	105
THE TOP AND THE BALL	107
THE GARDEN OF PARADISE	110
THE FIR-TREE	124
MOTHER ELDER	133
ELFIN-MOUNT	142
THE SNOW QUEEN	150
HOLGER THE DANE	185
TOMMELISE	191
GREAT CLAUS AND LITTLE CLAUS	203
THE CONSTANT TIN-SOLDIER	215
THE NAUGHTY BOY	220
THE ANGEL	223
THE CLOGS OF FORTUNE	226

	PAGE
THE SHEPHERDESS AND THE CHIMNEY-SWEEPER	257
THE TINDER-BOX	262
THE RED SHOES	271
THE FELLOW-TRAVELLERS	278
THE LEAPING-MATCH	300
THE ROSE-ELF	308
THE FLYING TRUNK	309
THE OLD STREET LAMP	316
THE LITTLE MATCH-GIRL	324
THE NEIGHBOURS	327
THE BELL	338
THE DARNING-NEEDLE	344
LITTLE TUK	348
THE SHADOW	353
THE OLD HOUSE	367
THE FLAX	377
THE DROP OF WATER	383
THE HAPPY FAMILY	386
THE FALSE COLLAR	391
STORY OF A MOTHER	394
THE HISTORY OF THE YEAR	401
THE WORLD'S FAIREST ROSE	410
A PICTURE FROM THE CASTLE RAMPARTS	413
"QUITE TRUE!"	414
THE SWANS' NEST	417
GOOD HUMOUR	419
GRIEF OF HEART	423
"EVERYTHING IN ITS PLACE!"	425
THE NISSE AT THE GROCER'S	433
A THOUSAND YEARS HENCE	437
UNDER THE WILLOW-TREE	439
VISION OF THE LAST DAY	451

Memoir of the Author.

Hans Christian Andersen, the author of these tales, may not without reason call himself " the Child of Good Fortune." Born at Odense, an obscure town in the island of Funen, his father a shoemaker, his mother a poor woman, so poor, that in her childhood she was sent out to beg in the streets—intended by his parents to gain his livelihood as a tailor, and so uninstructed, that when at the age of eighteen he tried in Copenhagen to support himself by composing pieces for the theatre, he could not write and spell his own language correctly, he has yet attracted the sympathy and esteem of the noblest and choicest spirits of his own land, he has won friends in almost all countries of Europe, and by giving them hours of refreshment and pleasure has awakened kindly feelings in the hearts of thousands personally unknown to him. Envy, opposition, and misconstruction, he has had to encounter, both from those in whose rank he was born, and those to whose level he has raised himself; realising the dream of his youth, " he has gone through a great deal of adversity ere at last he became famous." But, indeed, as he says of the long-despised hero of the fable which shadows forth his own life-history, " It matters not to have been born in a duck-yard, when one has been hatched from a swan's egg."

Andersen's early years were, however, very happy; his parents, poor as they were, never suffered him to feel want, and indulged him in all his childish fancies. His father, an intelligent man, was the son of a country farmer, who, after sustaining severe misfortunes, finally lost his reason; and although some neighbours had half promised to send the son to a grammar-school, their good intentions had evaporated in talk, and he had instead been bound apprentice to a shoemaker. But he could never reconcile himself to this mechanical occupation, rarely associated with his equals, and spent all his leisure in reading aloud to little Hans Christian, especially from Holberg's Comedies, and the "Arabian Nights," or in taking long rambles with him through the pleasant beech-woods of the island. There, whilst the child ran about, threading strawberries, or making garlands of wild flowers, the father would sit down, silently brooding over the one great disappointment of his life. Sometimes he amused himself in making toys, amongst others a little puppet-theatre, with a whole dramatic corps of dolls, which his son took great delight in dressing, afterwards making them act the plays his father read to him. And though so dreamy a child that he continually walked about with his eyes shut, every slight incident and scene of his early life seems to have been deeply impressed on his memory. References to these constantly occur in his writings; his parents' humble garden, consisting of a few vegetables grown in a box filled with mould, and placed on the gutter between theirs and the neighbouring house, still blooms in his story of the "Snow-Queen;" a likeness of his half-witted grandfather, a harmless old man, who lived in a small house with his excellent, intelligent, industrious wife, spending his time in carving figures out of wood, may be found in the legend of "Holger the Dane;" and the pair of boots, the first he ever possessed, that were given him to wear at his confirmation, and so distracted his mind from his devotions, is immortalised in little Karen's "Red Shoes."

One anecdote of his childhood is worth preserving. He and his mother were gleaning in some fields where the bailiff had the reputation of being a savage, coarse-minded man.

Upon the appearance of this formidable personage, armed with a heavy whip, all the gleaners took flight, but little Hans Christian's clumsy wooden shoes fell off, the stubble pricked his bare feet, and he was unable to effect his escape. He saw the bailiff close behind him, brandishing the whip over his head, when with a sudden impulse of courage the child looked his pursuer steadily in the face, and exclaimed, " How dare you strike me when God can see you!" At this the man's rough visage softened at once; instead of hurting the boy he stroked his cheeks, asked his name, and even gave him some money.

When Hans Christian was about nine years old, his father, who had lately grown more and more restless and moody, enlisted among the troops preparing to join Napoleon, Denmark being then in league with France. However, peace having been concluded, the regiment advanced no farther than Holstein, and the soldier again became a shoemaker; but his health had suffered from the sudden change in his mode of life. One morning he awoke in feverish delirium, raving of his imaginary campaign-life, and his favourite hero, Napoleon. Conformably with the superstitious feeling of the place, his wife sent off little Hans Christian, not to a physician, but to a so-called wise-woman, who lived in a little village half a mile from Odense, to learn from her whether his father would live or die. The old dame questioned the boy, took the measure of his arm with a woollen thread, and after various other cabalistical manœuvres, laid a green bough on his breast, a bough off a tree of the same kind as that of which the cross of our Saviour was made,—so, at least, she assured him. She then bade him go home by the river-side, for that if his father were to die of this illness he would meet his ghost by the way. Poor child! a pleasant walk it must have been for him! "But thou hast not met any such thing, hast thou?" asked his mother, on his repeating to her the reply of the oracle. No, he had not. Unfortunately for the credit of the wise-woman, his father died three days after.

His mother married again, but the stepfather never interfered either with Hans Christian or his education. He was left for a long time to amuse himself with his little puppet-theatre, making clothes for his dolls out of all the bright-coloured pieces of silk and cloth he could procure. His mother was well pleased with this employment, thinking it a good preparation for the tailor-trade, for which she was convinced he had a decided vocation; but he, on the contrary, declared his full determination to be a play-actor and poet. This last desire had been awakened in him by his visits to a kind old lady, Madame Bunkeflod, the widow of a clergyman, of some poetical reputation, and whose sister, as well as his widow, opened house and heart to the tall yellow-haired youth. Hans Christian frequently heard Bunkeflod's sister talk of "my brother, the poet," with kindling eyes, and an enthusiasm which showed that the epithet "poet" had something sacred and glorious in it: here, too, he read a translation of Shakespeare, and while under these inspirations he wrote his first play.

This was, of course, a tragedy; the subject was Pyramus and Thisbe, all the dramatis personæ being killed off in the closing scene; for the greater the number of people dying, the more interesting our young aspirant thought the play must be. His second piece was still more ambitious; a king and queen were introduced: but now came this difficulty — how were they to speak? for he thought it would be undignified for their majesties to talk ordinary Danish. He asked his mother and several others how a king ought to speak, but unfortunately it was so long since any such exalted personage had visited Odense that no one could enlighten him on this point. All were agreed, however, that a king must speak some foreign language, so he procured himself a lexicon, and manufactured for the use of the royal pair a sort of Babel-like jargon, compounded of German, English, and French.

The young dramatist wished every one to hear his pieces, not merely for the sake of winning admiration, but for the pleasure he took in reading them aloud. But it was a great affliction to him, shy and sensitive as he was, when the boys in the street hooted him, and shouted, "There goes the play-writer!" However, the sort of reputation he acquired brought him happiness also, for some of the gentry of the place, struck by his passion for reading, his aptness for reciting whole scenes from plays, and his clear, beautiful voice, invited him to their houses, and lent him books. His mother sent him for a short period to a charity-school, but here he did not learn much, and at the age of fourteen, having been confirmed, it was settled that he should be apprenticed to a tailor.

And now came the great question! Should he yield to his mother's wishes, or satisfy his own indefinite longing for some career more refined and elevated? Probably the recollection of the unhappy life his father had led as a handicraftsman strengthened his resolution. He had carefully saved up his money during the past year, and now found it to amount to about thirty shillings. With this immense wealth at his disposal, he entreated his mother to allow him to journey to Copenhagen, "the greatest city in the world," according to his notions.

"What wouldest thou do there?" was her very natural question.

"I will become famous!" was the reply; and then he recounted to her all he had ever heard or read of great men who had risen from poverty, concluding invariably every history with the same moral, viz. that "People had a great deal of adversity to go through, and then at last they become famous."

His own vehement prayers and tears were probably more powerful arguments with his mother, ignorant as she was of the world and its ways. She consented to abide by the decision of a certain wise-woman from the hospital. This old lady, after consulting her coffee-grounds and her cards, announced that the lad would become a great man, and that some day Odense should be illuminated in his honour; and thus the matter was decided. The neighbours, however, who had no great opinion of young Andersen, and disliked his peculiarities, represented to the mother the folly of sending a boy of fourteen to lose himself in a great city where he knew no one; and to all they said his mother agreed; "but," she said, "he left her no peace:" besides, she felt sure that "when he got in sight of the sea he would be frightened and turn back again."

It must be confessed that our young hero had as yet a very vague notion how to commence the glorious career he felt himself destined to pursue. Some way or other connected with the stage he must be, but in what capacity, whether as play-writer or play-actor, singer or dancer, he was quite undetermined.

Andersen's little bundle of clothes was now made up, a bargain was struck with the driver of a postchaise, who was to take him back with him to Copenhagen, and his mother and grandmother took leave of him at the gates of Odense.

From Nyborg the ship bore him across the Belt. As soon as it anchored, and he set foot on the coast of Zealand, he stepped behind a shed, and there kneeling down prayed the God of the fatherless to help and guide him.

He now travelled a whole night and day without resting, and on the morning of September 5, 1819, got out of the carriage and, his bundle in his hand, entered the capital, where he immediately sought out a certain Madame Schall, to whom he had a letter of introduction. Upon this lady, who, it seems, was an opera-dancer of some repute, he does not appear to have made a favourable impression; but, nothing daunted, he next went to the manager of a theatre, and asked for an engagement. The reply was, that he was " too thin for the stage." " Oh no," returned the supplicant; " if you will but give me a salary of a hundred rix-dollars banco, I shall soon get fat." But the manager looked grave at this proposal, and told him he " never engaged any but people of education."

Poor Andersen! this repulse wounded him sore, and there was no one to whom he could go for counsel; his own words are, " I thought of death as the only help for me, but even amid this anguish my thoughts rose to God, resting upon Him with all the undoubting confidence of a child in his father. I wept bitterly; but still I said to myself, ' When all seems dark and hopeless, God always sends help; I have read so many times; people must suffer much, very much, before they can attain their heart's desire.' "

After paying his bill, he found he had only one rix-dollar left; it was clear, therefore, that something must be done at once. He offered himself to a cabinet-maker in want of an apprentice; one day, however, spent with the journeymen, who, in their master's absence, indulged in a great deal of coarse jesting, so disgusted him that he could not endure it longer. It then occurred to him, that no one in Copenhagen had heard his beautiful voice, so often praised in his own country, and as the name of the Italian director of the Academy of Music, Siboni, was familiar to him, he hastened in a state of great excitement to his house.

Siboni was at dinner with a large party; Andersen told his story to the housekeeper, who listened with interest, and then went and repeated it to the company. Presently the dining-room door opened, and all the guests came out to look at the young adventurer; he was called upon to sing and recite some scenes from Holberg, but in the midst of this declamation, the sense of his poverty and dependent situation so overcame him, that he could not restrain his tears. All present encouraged him, and, which was more to the purpose, Siboni, who had listened attentively to his singing, promised to cultivate his voice, and bring him out at the Theatre Royal.

He was now perfectly satisfied with the prospects opening before him, and sent a rapturous letter home to his mother. Professor Weyse, one of Siboni's guests, collected seventy rix-dollars for him; and Siboni himself received him into his house, gave him his board and instructed him. But this happiness was of short duration; in six months his voice broke, and Siboni told him he had better go back to Odense and learn a trade.

Return to Odense, and be the laughing-stock of the place! Better learn a trade in Copenhagen; however, he did neither. Professor Guldberg, a relation of one of his friends in Odense, gave him temporary assistance, and introduced him to one or two actors, from whom he received now a lesson in Latin, now in dancing, now in singing, now in recitation; he was even suffered to appear on the stage sometimes. Meanwhile he lived almost entirely on dry bread, and his clothes were nearly threadbare. Three years had he passed in this miserable manner when, one day, he received a letter from the directors of the theatre, dismissing him from the dancing and singing schools, and telling him that the instruction given there could be of no possible use to him, but that he ought to apply to some friends and endeavour to move them to bestow upon him a regular education, without which his talents would remain useless. The idea of becoming a student had been suggested to Andersen before, and in the hope of obtaining the necessary funds, he had composed and sent to the directors a tragedy, called " The Robbers of Wissenburg;" but as it was written in defiance of all the rules of grammar, it had, of course, been returned. Now, however, he set to work upon a new tragedy, to be entitled "Alfsol," and this, when finished, was also sent to the managers, accompanied by a letter from one Dean Gutfeldt. The whole summer was spent in anxious suspense; Scott's novels, with which he at that period became acquainted through a circulating library, formed his only pleasure, and even the consolation they afforded could only be obtained at the sacrifice of a dinner.

Yet this summer proved the turning point of Andersen's fortunes, it brought him a true and steady friend, one who became to him a second father, and in whose house he found a real home. This was the Conference-Councillor Collin. Some one mentioned Andersen's case to him, and he sent for the youth. His manner was grave and cold; he said little, and did not seem to admire the tragedy which had been shown him, consequently Andersen, who was accustomed to receive either injudicious praise or undiscriminating censure, went away chilled and disappointed. His tragedy, too, was in a few days finally rejected. It was, therefore, a most unexpected happiness when he received a letter informing him, that not only was he to receive from King Frederick VI. a small annual stipend, but that he was to be admitted free of expense into the Grammar-school at Slagelse. For this he was indebted to Collin, from Collin he was to receive the money every quarter, Collin was responsible for his diligence.

Alas, the poor shoemaker of Odense! Why had he not lived to see the joyful day when his son became a student! when his son should receive the education he so much coveted for himself!

However, Andersen did not find his school-life so particularly delightful. At the age of eighteen, after writing tragedies and poems numberless, he had to sit down on the lowest form, and learn to spell with the youngest boys in the school of Slagelse. It was not a pleasant situation by any means; and shy, awkward, and peculiarly sensitive to ridicule, he could not help feeling it acutely. The rector of the school appeared to take pleasure in tormenting him, he had little confidence in himself, and though resolute and persevering in his application, he could not make the progress he desired. Collin had charged his *protégé* to write to him without restraint and tell him everything; this permission was a great relief to Andersen, and he often availed himself of it. On one occasion he wrote to express his distress, because "very good" had been written in his character-book, instead of "particularly good," as was usual; "he could not," he said, "imagine what he had done, or left undone, to occasion the difference." Another time the rector had called him "stupid," and he feared he was so, and that he did not deserve all that was done for him. Collin alone could reassure and comfort him in all his troubles, and this he was never slow to do. Moreover, his old friend, Colonel Guldberg, during this period of his life, kindly furnished him with the means for revisiting his birthplace. He says, "When I came in sight of the tall, old church-tower of Odense, I felt more and more affected: I felt how God had cared for me, and I burst into tears. My mother rejoiced over me, the families of Iversen and Guldberg gave me a hearty welcome, and I saw windows opening in the street, and faces looking out at me, for all knew how well I had prospered."

After a time the rector, weary of his residence at Slagelse, applied for the appointment of rector in the grammar-school at Helsingör. He obtained it, and invited Andersen to remove with him thither, and lodge in his house, promising to give him private lessons in Latin and Greek. With Collin's approval, the invitation was accepted; his new home, however, did not prove a happy one, the rector's continual depreciation and sarcasm made him thoroughly miserable; and it was fortunate that one of the masters, when on a visit at Copenhagen, informed his patron of his uncomfortable position. Collin immediately recalled Andersen to Copenhagen; and, henceforth, he was to study under a private tutor.

In September, 1828, after passing his examination, he brought out his first book, entitled "A Journey on Foot to Amager;" and also a play, which this time was accepted and actually performed; but these trifles did not divert him from severer studies, and in the following year he passed his Examen Philologicum et Philosophicum,—an examination which, notwithstanding its high-sounding title, we may presume, was not a very awful affair.

From this period the course of his life seems to have flowed smoothly enough, his chief, if not only trouble being the ill-natured satire of some of his critics, an annoyance, however, which must have been very light when weighed in the balance with the attachment of those warm and steady friends he had won among all ranks, and in different countries.

In 1831 he made a tour of Germany, and there became acquainted with Tieck and Chamisso. Two years later he received a stipend to enable him to travel again, and he then visited France and Italy. This excursion was the source of what may be deemed his strongest inspiration. The luxuriant beauty of Italian scenery, and the happy, joyous life of the people, blended with the memory of his own early struggles and fancies, gave birth to the most poetical of his works, the "Improvisatore," the first chapter of which was written in Rome, and which was finished in Copenhagen, on his return. The dedication runs thus: "To the Conference-Councillor Collin, and his noble wife, in whom I found parents, whose children were brothers and sisters to me, whose house was my home, do I here offer the best of what I possess."

The novels of "O. T." and "Only a Fiddler" quickly followed. "A Poet's Bazaar" appeared in 1841. But it is unnecessary here to enumerate our author's writings. One of the prettiest and most unpretending of his little volumes is the "Picture-book without Pictures." In this, he describes the attic-chamber in Copenhagen, where he lodged whilst a student, and relates how the moon shone into his lonely room night after night, telling him about what she had seen elsewhere. As these sketches are not so well known as they deserve to be, we will give a translation of one of them. It may serve as a specimen of the rest :—

"Along the shore"—thus begins the Moon—"extends a wood, oaks and beech-trees grow there, whose fresh and fragrant shades are haunted every spring by a hundred nightingales; close by lies the sea, the ever-changing sea and between the sea and the woods runs the high-road Carriage after carriage rolls by, I do not care to follow them, my eye loves to rest upon one spot, upon the grave-mound of an old Danish warrior, where brambles and sloe-berries have grown out from among the cairn-stones. There is Nature's genuine poetry in this scene. And by how many people, think you, is this poetry felt and understood? I will repeat to thee the observations I heard there last night. First came two merchants. 'Fine trees those!' said one. 'There must be ten cart-loads of fire-wood in each,' replied the other; 'it will be a severe winter, I fancy,—how did we sell wood last year?'—and then they were gone.

"'What a miserable road!' exclaimed the next passer-by. 'And those abominable trees!' said his companion; 'no free current of air at all except from the sea,' and their carriage rattled past.

"Next drove by the diligence, all the passengers were asleep, sleeping over the very loveliest scene the whole journey could show them; the conductor was blowing his horn, thinking the while, 'Certainly I do it very well, and it sounds beautifully in this quiet place.'

"And now came two young men riding on horseback. 'Ah,' thought I, 'here is youth, and youth must have a feeling for Nature's poetry.' And in truth they both smiled as they glanced at the mossgrown barrow and dusky grove; 'I should like a walk with Christine here,' said one, and on they rode.

"And the fragrance of the wild flowers was so strong, and every breeze was at rest; the sea appeared only part of the sky which arched over the deep valley.

"Again a carriage rattled past, there were six persons in it, four were asleep; the fifth was occupied with thoughts of his tailor and his new frock-coat; the sixth put his head out of the window and asked the coachman if there was anything remarkable about that heap of stones. 'No,' was the reply, 'but the trees are remarkable.'—'How?'—'Why, you see, in the winter, when the snow lies deep, and the road is hidden under it, those trees serve me as a land-mark, and save me from driving into the sea; that is what makes them remarkable.' And this carriage passed.

"Next came an artist, his eyes sparkled, he said not a word, but kept whistling. The nightingales were singing as though each were trying to be louder than the rest; 'Be quiet!' exclaimed the artist, and he began to dot into his sketch-book the varied tints around him, 'blue, dark-brown, —it will make a splendid picture!' thought he. He took the whole landscape, just as a mirror would have done, humming the while a march of Rossini's.

"The last passer-by was a poor young girl; she sat down to rest on the warrior's grave; laying her burden by her side, her sweet, pale face was raised listening towards the grove, her eyes glistened, and as she glanced over the sea towards the sky, she clasped her hands, and I believe she repeated 'Our Father.' She, herself, comprehended not the feeling that thrilled through her; but I am persuaded that in her future years, the scene where she enjoyed that minute of repose will frequently rise before her mind, far more beautiful, nay, far more true than as it is painted in the artist's sketch-book, where the colours are so exactly copied. My beams," concludes the Moon, "followed the poor girl till daylight kissed her forehead."

It now remains to speak of the faëry-tales contained in this volume. They were written at intervals and published a few at a time. At first they were set forth as "Stories related to Children;" but as, after a while, Andersen found that they gave pleasure to children of a larger growth, he dropped the original title, and has since called every fresh series, "Nye Eventyr," or "New Tales;" the word *eventyr* literally signifying wonderful tale. And, perhaps, in no other species of composition is Andersen so much at home.

The stories respectively entitled, "The Tinder-box," "The Fellow-Travellers," "Great Claus and Little Claus," "The Wild Swans," "The Real Princess," and "The Garden of Paradise," are more or less altered from old traditionary tales told to the author in his childhood. "The Swineherd," too, is evidently a near relation to "Hacon Grizzlebeard," to whom we are introduced in MM. Asbjornsen and Moe's "Norske Folkseventyr."

The fable of "The Naughty Boy" was borrowed from Anacreon, that of "The Rose Elf" from a novel of Boccaccio's. The original story of "The Emperor's New Clothes" is to be found in "El Conde Lucanor;" a collection of moral apologues written by Don Juan Manuel.*

---

* This nobleman, born 1277, was son of a regent of Castile, and grandson to King San Fernando. He was one of the most powerful of the Spanish Ricos Hombres, and spent the greater part of his life in incessant warfare, now with the Moors, now with his own liege sovereign, Alfonso the Magnificent. It seems strange that he should have had either the taste or the leisure for inditing a book of stories, or "ensamples," as they are called. They profess to be related for the

"Holger the Dane" is the same worthy whom the writers of the old French romances celebrate as Ogier le Danois, the beloved of Morgaine la Faye; who, it is fabled, retains him to this day entranced in Avalon, in company with her brother King Arthur, and other renowned knights. According to the romance, several other fairies besides the powerful Morgaine presided at the hero's birth, each bestowing on him some "noble and virtuous" gift; and, being thus endowed, he distinguished himself in battle and council till he reached his hundredth year, when Morgaine thought fit to release him from toil and care, and to that end causes him to be shipwrecked on a rock near the castle of loadstone, the castle of Avalon. Ogier is alone, and begins to despair, when a voice bids him "not be dismayed," but so soon as night shall come, and he shall see a castle shining before him, to go towards it, making his way from bark to bark till he shall find himself upon an island; he is then to look about for a little path, and to follow it whithersoever it shall lead him.

And Ogier looks about, but can see no one. However, when night comes, and the resplendent castle of Avalon is revealed to his eyes, he commends himself to God, and contriving to make himself a bridge over the numerous vessels that lay wrecked around the rock, he arrives at the island, and passes on to the gate of the castle. Two fierce lions guard the entrance; he slays them both, and advancing into a hall finds there a horse sitting at table. The horse rises with the utmost politeness, and by signs invites Ogier to sup with him. The meal being ended, the horse prevails upon the warrior to get

---

instruction of a prince by his counsellor Patronio, each tale ending with a distich by way of moral. The story, identical with Andersen's, is to be found in Cap. 7, under the title " De un rey y de tres burladores que a el vinieron;" the imposture here is discovered, not by a child, but by a poor black man, who, having neither houses nor lands to lose, could afford to speak the truth.

upon his back, and then carries him into a bedchamber wherein to spend the night. This hospitable animal is Papillon, a great prince whom Arthur had conquered, and condemned to spend three years in silence under the form of a horse; at the end of that period he was, however, to be presented with the crown of joy which is won in Faëry land.

Next morning, while wandering in a pleasant orchard, Ogier meets a most beautiful lady clad in white and very richly adorned. She announces herself to be Morgaine la Faye, and places on the Dane's finger a ring, whereupon he, a man of a hundred years old, instantly recovers the vigour and beauty of thirty. She then leads him back to Avalon to introduce him to her brother Arthur, and as they approach the castle, a band of fay-ladies come out to meet them, singing so melodiously that the like was never heard on earth; and on entering the hall many others are seen, " toutes couronnées de couronnes tres somptueusement faictes." Morgaine la Faye sets upon Ogier's head a similar crown, and immediately he loses all memory of past pleasures and pains; the joy of battle, love for his wife, " la dame Clarice qui tant estait belle et noble," his brother Guyon, his nephew Gualthier, all are forgotten, and he is content to stay in Avalon. And such joyous pastimes did the Faëry ladies devise for him as no creature in the world could imagine, and thus time fleeted by so quickly that a year seemed no longer than a month. However, when two hundred years had expired, Morgaine, thinking the presence of her hero required to defend France and Italy from the Paynims, took the Lethean crown off his head, upon which his old ideas instantly rushed back upon him; the delights of Avalon charmed him no longer, and he panted to return to his warrior-life. The fairy gives him the horse Papillon; also a brand, which must be preserved carefully, as, so long as it remains unconsumed, so long shall his life endure. The Faëry ladies all come out to sing him a farewell, and ne and his comrade Benoist are enveloped in a cloud which raises them from the earth, and presently sets them down again by the side of a clear fountain near Montpellier. Ogier fights as he had been wont to fight, and disperses the infidels, after which Morgaine la Faye carries him back to Avalon. Since then he has never been seen by mortal eyes.

This lively French fable contrasts strikingly with the gloomy colouring of the Danish tradition, which represents the hero Holger sitting motionless in the dark vaults below Kronborg, his beard grown into the table on which he leans. It is said that a noise like the clash of arms having frequently been heard from under the fortress, great wonder and curiosity were excited; and as no one else would dare the adventure, a slave, under sentence of death, was offered his life and liberty, on condition of his penetrating into the long, dark passages beneath the fortress, and bringing back tidings of what he should see there. The adventurer discovered a large iron door, through which he advanced into a deep cavern. A lamp, nearly burnt out, hung from the roof, and just below it was seen a very large stone table, round which sate a company of steel-clad warriors, their heads all drooping upon their crossed arms. Then rose up Holger the Dane, who was seated at the farther end of the board; and as he raised his head from his arm, the stone table, into which his beard had grown, burst in twain. "Reach me hither thy hand!" quoth he to the slave; but the latter, keeping a prudent distance, presented an iron bar instead; and well it was for him that he did, for Holger grasped it so tightly as to leave the impression of his strong fingers upon the metal. At last he let it go, muttering, "It is well; I am right glad to find that there are yet men left in Denmark." And the hero settled himself to his dreams again, under the delusion that he had tested the prowess and fortitude of the knights of modern times. Another legend is told that shows the strength of this giant-champion, as displayed during his lifetime, and in rather a less dignified manner. He wanted a new suit of clothes; twelve tailors were employed, who climbed up his back by means of ladders, in order to take his measure: unfortunately, the man on the top of the right-side ladder, whilst cutting a mark in his measure, clipped his customer's ear; Holger, feeling the annoyance, unthinkingly put his hand to his ear and crushed the poor tailor between his fingers.*

Almost every country has had her own Holger, her loved and honoured champion, of whom, for several generations, the mass of the people refused to believe that he was really dead. Thus has Britain looked forward to the return of her Arthur, supposed to be lingering in Faëry land; thus do the Swiss herdsmen point to the cavern near Lake Lucerne, where " the three Tells," as the founders of the Helvetic confederacy are called, sleep peacefully till their country shall have need of them; thus, too, it has been said, the Emperor Charlemagne reposes within a mountain near Salzburg. But of all these legends, none is so closely akin to the Danish tradition as the German one of the Emperor Frederick Barbarossa slumbering within the mountain of Kyffhausen, in the Hercynian forest. He is described as sitting on his throne, his right arm resting on a stone table, which his fiery red beard, still growing during his sleep, must encircle three times before he will

* See Thiele, Danmarks Folkesagn, vol. ii. The hero's sword, too, which lay buried in a barrow near a farm-house, called Bygholm, was so heavy, that when it was dug up, twelve horses were required to convey it to the house. But it did not remain long at Bygholm, for that same night, the walls of the building began to shake so violently, that all the window panes clattered in their frames; nor was there an end to this disturbance until the sword was returned to its resting-place. When taken back, it became so much lighter that two horses were sufficient to drag it. Holger is said to have served under Charlemagne against the Saracens; his supernaturally long life is accounted for by his having in India eaten of a marvellous life-preserving fruit.

arise in his might and resume his empire. He, too, like Holger the Dane, has had his repose disturbed by curiosity. Some shepherds once visited him, and he roused himself so far as to ask, "Do the ravens still fly round the mountain?" They answered, "Yes." "Then," quoth he, "I may sleep on for another hundred years," and again his head sank down upon his hand.

We have wandered very far from Andersen and his tales. Those not already specified as borrowed are entirely his own invention; our young readers may, however, like to have a few illustrations of the national fairy mythology referred to in some of them. There is a tradition in the North that all the various spirits who once had sway over the earth have now different abodes assigned them, wherein they are condemned to remain until the end of the world. Though still retaining powers more than human, they are unhappy, and long for their release. The Dwarfs, or Mountain Trolls, are confined to the higher hills or mountains; the Elves inhabit groves and leafy trees; the Hill-people, who take an intermediate position between the Trolls and Elves, but nearest to the Elves, dwell in little hillocks or caves; the Mer-folk and Necks in the sea, in lakes, or rivers, whilst the Strömkarl, or River-man, haunts the waterfalls.

The Trolls, or Dwarfs, are misshapen, stumpy, and humpbacked; they are not generally ill-natured, but have an unfortunate propensity for thieving, especially for carrying away human infants, leaving their own deformed, weakly offspring in their place. Dwelling underground, they are very rich in gold and silver, are fond of feasting, and are skilled in supernatural lore, such as foretelling events to come. They have a great dislike to noise, especially to that of church-bells. There is a story that a farmer once saw a Troll sitting on a stone near Lake Tiis, in Zealand, and addressed him, saying, "Well, friend, whither go you?"

"Alas!" replied the Troll, in a most disconsolate tone, "I can't stay in this country any longer, there's such an eternal ringing and dinging!"

The Nisses evidently belong to the Dwarf family; they are as small as infants, but with faces like old men; they wear a grey dress and a pointed red cap. They are domestic spirits, and there is generally a Nisse in every farm-yard. He is a good, serviceable spirit sometimes, at other times exceedingly mischievous and capricious. A farmer in Jutland was once so tormented by the Nisse inhabiting his house, that he resolved to remove to another, leaving the Nisse to himself. However, the spirit was not to be got rid of so easily. The last cart-load of domestic implements, filled with tubs, barrels, &c., was just being driven away, when the farmer, happening to look back, saw, to his dismay, the Nisse sitting in one of the tubs, laughing and crying out, "Ah, we're flitting to-day, you see!" There is also said to be a Nisse attached to every church; he is called the Kirkegrim.

Of the Elves, or Ellefolk, there are many varieties; some dwell in the moors, and may be seen dancing their rounds by moonlight, leaving the grass they have trodden of a brighter and livelier green; others inhabit trees; others, again, are confined within their mounds. The sound of their voice is sweet and soft like the air; and on summer nights, those who lay their ears close to the Elve-hills, may hear their low, plaintive singing, or the murmur of the Elle-women's spinning-wheels. Sometimes, on festive occasions, they raise their mounds on red pillars, and may be seen dancing and feasting beneath. The Elle-woman is fair and golden-haired, and plays most sweetly on a stringed instrument; she is, however, hollow in the back, like a dough-trough, and it is very dangerous for a mortal youth to fall under the spell of her fascinations. Not many people are able to see the Elves. Sunday-children, *i.e.* those born on Sunday, are thus privileged. There is an Elle-woman dwelling in the elder-tree, called by some Hyldemoer, or Mother Elder; in former times a Danish peasant could never venture to break off any part of an Elder-tree without first repeating three times, " Oh Mother Elder, Mother Elder! let me take some of thy elder, and I will let thee take something of mine in return." There is a story of an Elder-tree growing in a farm-yard, that often in the twilight takes a turn up and down the yard, and peeps in through the windows at the children, when they are alone. The Elves live under a monarchical form of government, one of their Kings residing at Möen, another at Bornholm, a small island close to Zealand. The last monarch will not suffer a human prince to pass more than three nights on his isle.

It remains now only to speak of the spirits of the waters. Of those who inhabit the sea, the Merman may be more safely trusted than the Mermaid, whose seductive beauty often lures men to their destruction. She is frequently seen sitting on the surface of the waters combing her long golden hair with a golden comb, or driving her sleek, snow-white cattle to pasture on the green islets. There is a story told in Tisvilde of a Mermaid who used to drive her herd to grass in the Tibirke meadows. But some grasping, avaricious farmers, who lived on the spot, laid wait for her one evening, and, contriving to get her and her cattle shut up in a pen near the town, told her they would not let her go till she had paid them for pasturing her herd on their land. Upon her replying that she had no money, they bade her give them the belt she wore, which seemed very costly, and glittered as with precious stones. She was compelled to ransom herself by giving up the belt; but as she drove her cattle down to the shore she said to the largest bull, " Rake!" whereupon the animal began to push with his horns down into the sand, scattering it all along the shore; and as just then a north-westerly wind arose, the sand was whirled over the fields towards the town, where the church was nearly buried underneath it. Nor did the farmers gain much from the Mermaiden's belt, for, upon bringing it home, they found it to be composed, not of precious stones, but of woven rushes.

The Strömkarl, or Spirit of the Waterfall, is rarely met with save in Norway. The Neck, or Nökke, haunts the rivers; he is variously described, sometimes as appearing under the form of a horse, sometimes as an old man continually wringing the water out of his long beard; but oftenest as a beautiful, golden-haired boy, wearing a red cap. He sits on the water, playing most exquisitely on his golden harp. The following beautiful legend is told of him in Sweden. Two boys, while playing near a river, saw the Neck rise out of the water and begin to sing, and the burden of his song was still, "And I hope, and I hope that my Redeemer liveth!" And the children said, "What is the use of all your singing and playing, Neck? you will never be saved!" The spirit, at hearing this, wept bitterly, flung aside his harp, and sank below the waters. But when the children repeated what had passed to their father, he told them that they had done wrong in refusing to him all hope, and bade them go back and console him. They found the Neck sitting on the water wailing most piteously, and they said, "Neck, do not grieve so, our father says that perhaps your Redeemer liveth also;" and upon this the spirit again took up his harp and played a sweet, joyous, exulting strain. In a variation of this legend a priest says to the Neck, "Sooner shall this dry stick in my hand put forth leaves and flowers than thou shalt attain Salvation." The Neck flung away his harp and wept, and the priest rode on; but, to his amazement, he presently discovered that his cane was beginning to bud and blossom, and he went back to tell the glad tidings to the Neck, who after this played joyously the whole night through.

Who shall call a legend like this profane? is it not rather

the popular expression of the truth that "the whole creation groaneth, and travaileth together in pain until now," and that "the creature itself also shall be delivered from the bondage of corruption, into the glorious liberty of the children of God."

But here we are intruding upon ground too high and sacred. We will only add, that some antiquaries derive these legends from very early times, and look upon them as expressive of the sympathy of the first converts to Christianity with their Heathen forefathers, who died before the light of the Gospel had dawned upon their land, whose bodies rested in unhallowed ground, whose spirits had no sure hope of salvation.

With respect to the modern legends we are now about to introduce to our readers, they may be deemed by some ridiculous and puerile; there are, however, others who will remember, especially at the holy season of Christmas, that all of us, whether youths or maidens, men or women, are exhorted by Him who was once the Babe of Bethlehem, to become as little children—children in guilelessness and purity —children also in innocent gladness of heart; and surely it may safely be asserted, that Andersen's Tales chime in harmoniously, both with our Christmas hymns and our Christmas games; they are diverting enough to be the companions of our holiday; and have, for the most part, a healthful, religious feeling, which may well accord with the more serious thoughts of our holy day.

C. P

Christmas, 1851.

THE WILD SWANS.

FAR hence, in a country whither the swallows fly in our winter-time, there dwelt a King who had eleven sons, and one daughter, the beautiful Elise. The eleven brothers — they were princes — went to school with stars on their breasts and swords by their sides; they wrote on golden tablets with diamond pens, and could read either with a book or without one; in short, it was easy to perceive that they were princes. Their sister, Elise, used to sit upon a little glass stool, and had a picture-book which had cost the half of a kingdom. Oh! the children were so happy! but happy they could not be always.

Their father, the King, married a very wicked Queen, who was not at all kind to the poor children; they found this out on the first day after the marriage, when there was a grand gala at the palace; for when the children played at receiving company, instead of having as many cakes and sweetmeats as they liked, the Queen gave them only some sand in a little dish, and told them to imagine that was something nice.

The week after, she sent little Elise to be brought up by some peasants in the country, and it was not long before she told the King so many falsehoods about the poor Princes that he would have nothing more to do with them. "Away, out into the world, and take care of yourselves," said the wicked Queen; "fly away in the form of great speechless birds." But she could not make their transformation so disagreeable as she wished; the Princes were changed into eleven white Swans. Sending forth a strange cry, they flew out of the palace windows, over the park and over the wood.

It was still early in the morning when they passed by the place where Elise lay sleeping in the peasant's cottage; they flew several times round the roof, stretched their long necks, and flapped their wings, but no one either heard or saw them; they were forced to fly away, up to the clouds and into the wide world; so on they went to the wide, dark forest which extended as far as the sea-shore.

The poor little Elise stood in the peasant's cottage amusing herself with a green leaf, for she had no other plaything. She pricked a hole in the leaf and peeped through it at the sun, and then she fancied she saw her brothers' bright eyes; and whenever the warm sunbeams shone full upon her cheeks, she thought of her brothers' kisses.

One day passed exactly like the other. When the wind blew through the thick hedge of rose-trees in front of the house, she would whisper to the Roses, "Who is more beautiful than you?" but the Roses would shake their heads, and say, "Elise." And when the peasant's wife sat on Sundays at the door of her cottage reading her hymn-book, the Wind would rustle in the leaves and say to the book, "Who is more pious than thou?" "Elise," replied the Hymn-book. And what the Roses and the Hymn-book said was no more than the truth.

Elise was now fifteen years old, she was sent for home; but when the Queen saw how beautiful she was, she hated her the more, and would willingly have transformed her, like her brothers, into a wild swan, but she dared not do so, because the King wished to see his daughter.

So the next morning the Queen went into a bath made of marble, and fitted up with soft pillows and the gayest carpets;

she took three toads, kissed them, and said to one, "Settle thou upon Elise's head, that she may become dull and sleepy like thee." "Settle thou upon her forehead," said she to another, "and let her become ugly like thee, so that her father may not know her again." And "Do thou place thyself upon her bosom," whispered she to the third, "that her heart may become corrupt and evil, a torment to herself." She then put the toads into the clear water, which was immediately tinted with a green colour, and having called Elise, took off her clothes and made her get into the bath. And one toad settled among her hair, another on her forehead, and a third upon her bosom; but Elise seemed not at all aware of it; she rose up, and three poppies were seen swimming on the water. Had not the animals been poisonous and kissed by a witch, they would have been changed into roses whilst they rested on Elise's head and heart,—she was too good for magic to have any power over her. When the Queen perceived this, she rubbed walnut-juice all over the maiden's skin, so that it became quite swarthy, smeared a nasty salve over her lovely face, and entangled her long thick hair: it was impossible to recognise the beautiful Elise after this.

So when her father saw her he was shocked, and said she could not be his daughter; no one would have anything to do with her but the mastiff and the swallows; but they, poor things, could not say anything in her favour.

Poor Elise wept, and thought of her eleven brothers, not one of whom she saw at the palace. In great distress, she stole away and wandered the whole day over fields and moors, till she reached the forest. She knew not where to go, but she was so sad, and longed so much to see her brothers, who had been driven out into the world, that she determined to seek and find them.

She had not been long in the forest when night came on, and she lost her way amid the darkness. So she lay down on the soft moss, said her evening prayer, and leaned her head against the trunk of a tree. It was very still in the forest, the air was mild, and from the grass and mould around gleamed the green light of many hundred glow-worms, and when Elise lightly touched one of the branches hanging over her, bright insects fell down upon her like falling stars.

All the night long she dreamed of her brothers. They

were all children again, played together, wrote with diamond pens upon golden tablets, and looked at the pictures in the beautiful book which had cost half of a kingdom. But they did not, as formerly, make straight strokes and pothooks upon the tablets,—no, they wrote of the bold actions they had performed, and the strange adventures they had encountered, and in the picture-book everything seemed alive; the birds sang, men and women stepped from the book and talked to Elise and her brothers: however, when she turned over the leaves, they jumped back into their places, so that the pictures did not get confused together.

When Elise awoke the sun was already high in the heavens. She could not see it certainly, for the tall trees of the forest closely entwined their thickly-leaved branches, which, as the sunbeams played upon them, looked like a golden veil waving to and fro. And the air was so fragrant, and the birds perched upon Elise's shoulders. She heard the noise of water, there were several springs forming a pool with the prettiest pebbles at the bottom, bushes were growing thickly round, but the deer had trodden a broad path through them, and by this path Elise went down to the water's edge. The water was so clear that, had not the boughs and bushes around been moved to and fro by the wind, you might have fancied they were painted upon the smooth surface, so distinctly was each little leaf mirrored upon it, whether glowing in the sunlight or lying in the shade.

As soon as Elise saw her face reflected in the water she was quite startled, so brown and ugly did it look: however, when she had wetted her little hand and rubbed her brow and eyes, the white skin again appeared. So Elise took off her clothes, stepped into the fresh water, and in the whole world there was not a king's daughter more beautiful than she then appeared.

After she had again dressed herself, and had braided her long hair, she went to the bubbling spring, drank out of the hollow of her hand, and then wandered farther into the forest. She knew not where she was going, but she thought of her brothers, and of the good God, who, she felt, would never forsake her. He it was who made the wild crab-trees grow in order to feed the hungry, and who showed her a tree whose boughs bent under the weight of their fruit. She made her noonday meal under its shade, propped up the boughs, and then walked on amid the dark twilight of the forest. It was so still that she could hear her own footsteps, and the rustling of each little withered leaf that was crushed beneath her feet; not a bird was to be seen, not a single sunbeam penetrated through the thick foliage, and the tall stems of the trees stood so close together, that when she looked straight before her, she seemed enclosed by trellis-work upon trellis-work. Oh! there was a solitariness in this forest such as Elise had never known before.

And the night was so dark! not a single glow-worm sent forth its light. Sad and melancholy, she lay down to sleep, and then it seemed to her as though the boughs above her opened, and that she saw the Angel of God looking down upon her with gentle aspect, and a thousand little cherubs all around him. When she awoke in the morning she could not tell whether this was a dream, or whether she had really been so watched.

She walked on a little farther and met an old woman with a basketful of berries; the old woman gave her some of them, and Elise asked if she had not seen eleven Princes ride through the wood.

"No," said the old woman, "but I saw yesterday eleven Swans with golden crowns on their heads swim down the brook near this place."

And she led Elise on a little farther to a precipice, the base of which was washed by a brook; the trees on each side stretched their long leafy branches towards each other, and where they could not unite, the roots had disengaged themselves from the earth and hung their interlaced fibres over the water.

Elise bade the old woman farewell, and wandered by the side of the stream till she came to the place where it reached the open sea.

The great, the beautiful sea lay extended before the maiden's eyes, but not a ship, not a boat was to be seen; how was she to go on? She observed the numberless little stones on the shore, all of which the waves had washed into a round form; glass, iron, stone, everything that lay scattered there, had been moulded into shape, and yet the water which had effected this was much softer than Elise's delicate, little hand. "It rolls on unweariedly," said she, "and subdues what is so hard: I will be no less unwearied! Thank you for the lesson you have given me, ye bright rolling waves! some day, my heart tells me, you shall carry me to my dear brothers!"

There lay upon the wet sea-weed eleven white swan-feathers; Elise collected them together; drops of water hung about them, whether dew or tears she could not tell. She was quite alone on the sea-shore, but she did not care for that; the sea presented an eternal variety to her—more, indeed, in a few hours than the gentle inland waters would have offered in a whole year. When a black cloud passed over the sky, it seemed as if the sea would say, "I, too, can look dark:" and then the wind would blow and the waves fling out their white foam; but when the clouds shone with a bright red tint, and the winds were asleep, the sea also became like a rose-leaf in hue. It was now green, now white, but it ever reposed peacefully; sometimes a light breeze would be astir on the shore, causing the water to heave gently, like the bosom of a sleeping child.

At sunset Elise saw eleven Wild Swans with golden crowns on their heads fly towards the land; they flew one behind another, looking like a streaming white riband. Elise climbed the precipice, and concealed herself behind a bush: the Swans settled close to her, and flapped their long white wings.

As the sun sank beneath the water, the Swans also vanished, and in their place stood eleven handsome Princes, the brothers of Elise. She uttered a loud cry, for although they were very much altered, Elise knew that they were,— felt that they must be, her brothers; she ran into their arms, called them by their names—and how happy were *they* to see and recognise their sister, now grown so tall and so beautiful! They laughed and wept, and soon told each other how wickedly their stepmother had acted towards them.

"We," said the eldest of the brothers, "fly or swim as long as the sun is above the horizon, but when it sinks below, we appear again in our human form; we are therefore obliged to look out for a safe resting-place, for if, at sunset, we were flying among the clouds, we should fall down as soon as we resumed our own form. We do not dwell here; a land quite as beautiful as this lies on the opposite side

THE WILD SWANS.

Page 7.

of the sea, but it is far off. To reach it, we have to cross the deep waters, and there is no island midway on which we may rest at night; one little solitary rock rises from the waves, and upon it we only just find room enough to stand side by side. There we spend the night in our human form, and when the sea is rough, we are sprinkled by its foam; but we are thankful for this resting-place, for without it we should never be able to visit our dear native country. Only once in the year is this visit to the home of our fathers permitted; we require two of the longest days for our flight, and can remain here only eleven days, during which time we fly over the large forest, whence we can see the palace in which we were born, where our father dwells, and the tower of the church in which our mother was buried. Here, even the trees and bushes seem of kin to us; here the wild horses still race over the plains, as in the days of our childhood; here the charcoal-burner still sings the same old tunes to which we used to dance in our youth; hither we are still attracted; and here we have found thee, thou dear little sister! We have yet two days longer to stay here, then we must fly over the sea to a land beautiful indeed, but not our fatherland. How shall we take thee with us? we have neither ship nor boat!"

"How shall I be able to release you?" said the sister. And so they went on talking almost the whole of the night; they slumbered only a few hours.

Elise was awakened by the rustling of swans' wings, which were fluttering above her. Her brothers were again transformed, and for some time flew round in large circles; at last they flew far, far away; only one of them remained behind — it was the youngest; he laid his head in her lap, and she stroked his white wings; they remained the whole day together. Towards evening the others came back, and when the sun was set, again they stood on the firm ground in their natural form.

"To-morrow we shall fly away, and may not return for a year, but we cannot leave thee; hast thou courage to accompany us? My arm is strong enough to bear thee through the forest: shall we not have sufficient strength in our wings to transport thee over the sea?"

"Yes, take me with you," said Elise. They spent the

whole night in weaving a mat of the pliant willow bark and the tough rushes, and their mat was thick and strong. Elise lay down upon it; and when the sun had risen, and the brothers were again transformed into Wild Swans, they seized the mat with their beaks, and flew up high among the clouds with their dear sister, who was still sleeping. The sunbeams shone full upon her face, so one of the Swans flew over her head, and shaded her with his broad wings.

They were already far from land when Elise awoke: she thought she was still dreaming, so strange did it appear to her to be travelling through the air, and over the sea. By her side lay a cluster of pretty berries, and a handful of savoury roots. Her youngest brother had collected and laid them there; and she thanked him with a smile, for she knew him as the Swan who flew overhead and shaded her with his wings.

They flew so high, that the first ship they saw beneath them seemed like a white sea-gull skimming over the water. Elise saw behind her a large cloud; it looked like a mountain; and on it she saw the gigantic shadows of herself and the eleven Swans: it formed a picture more splendid than any she had ever yet seen. Soon, however, the sun rose higher, the cloud remained far behind, and then the floating, shadowy picture disappeared.

The whole day they continued flying with a whizzing noise somewhat like an arrow, but yet they went slower than usual—they had their sister to carry. A heavy tempest was gathering—the evening approached; anxiously did Elise watch the sun—it was setting; still the solitary rock could not be seen; it appeared to her that the Swans plied their wings with increasing vigour. Alas! it would be her fault if her brothers did not arrive at the place in time! they would become human beings when the sun set; and if this happened before they reached the rock, they must fall into the sea and be drowned. She prayed to God most fervently — still no rock was to be seen; the black clouds drew nearer— violent gusts of wind announced the approach of a tempest— the clouds rested perpendicularly upon a fearfully large wave which rolled quickly forwards— one flash of lightning rapidly succeeded another.

The sun was now on the rim of the sea. Elise's heart

beat violently; the Swans shot downwards so swiftly that she thought she must fall, but again they began to hover; the sun was half sunk beneath the water, and at that moment she saw the little rock below her; it looked like a seal's head when he raises it just above the water. And the sun was sinking fast—it seemed scarcely larger than a star; her foot touched the hard ground, and it vanished altogether, like the last spark on a burnt piece of paper. Arm in arm stood her brothers around her; there was only just room for her and them; the sea beat tempestuously against the rock, flinging over them a shower of foam; the sky seemed in a continual blaze with the fast-succeeding flashes of fire that lightened it, and peal after peal rolled on the thunder, but sister and brothers kept firm hold of each others' hands. They sang a psalm, and their psalm gave them comfort and courage.

By daybreak the air was pure and still, and as soon as the sun rose, the swans flew away with Elise from the rock. The waves rose higher and higher, and when they looked from the clouds down upon the blackish-green sea, covered as it was with white foam, they might have fancied that millions of swans were swimming on its surface.

As day advanced, Elise saw floating in the air before her a land of mountains intermixed with glaciers, and in the centre a palace a mile in length, with splendid colonnades rising one above another, palm-trees and gorgeous-looking flowers as large as millwheels growing beneath. She asked if this were the country to which they were flying, but the Swans shook their heads, for what she saw was the beautiful airy castle of the fairy Morgana, where no human being was admitted: and whilst Elise still bent her eyes upon it, mountains, trees, and castle, all disappeared, and in their place stood twelve churches with high towers and pointed windows. She fancied she heard the organ play, but it was only the murmur of the sea. She was now close to these churches, but behold! they have changed into a large fleet sailing under them. She looked down, and saw it was only a sea-mist passing rapidly over the water. An eternal variety floated before her eyes, till at last the actual land whither she was bound appeared in sight. Beautiful blue mountains, cedar woods, towns, and castles, rose to view. Long before sunset Elise sat down among the mountains, in front of a large cavern; delicate young creepers grew around so thickly, that it appeared covered with gay embroidered carpets.

"Now we shall see what thou wilt dream of to-night!" said her youngest brother, as he showed her the sleeping chamber destined for her.

"Oh, that I could dream how you might be released from the spell!" said she; and this thought completely occupied her; she prayed most earnestly for God's assistance; nay, even in her dreams, she continued praying; and it appeared to her that she was flying up high in the air towards the castle of the fairy Morgana. The fairy came forward to meet her, radiant and beautiful, and yet she fancied she resembled the old woman who had given her berries in the forest, and told her of the Swans with golden crowns.

"Thou *canst* release thy brothers," said she, "but hast thou courage and patience sufficient? The water is indeed softer than thy delicate hands, and yet can mould the hard stones to its will, but then it cannot feel the pain which thy tender fingers will feel; it has no heart, and cannot suffer the anxiety and grief which thou must suffer. Dost thou see these stinging-nettles which I have in my hand? there are many of the same kind growing round the cave where thou art sleeping; only those that grow there or on the graves in the churchyard are of use—remember that! Thou must pluck them, although they will sting thy hand; thou must trample on the nettles with thy feet, and get yarn from them; and with this yarn thou must weave eleven shirts with long sleeves;—throw them over the eleven Wild Swans, and the spell is broken. But, mark this! from the moment that thou beginnest thy work till it is completed, even should it occupy thee for years, thou must not speak a word; the first syllable that escapes thy lips will fall like a dagger into the hearts of thy brothers; on thy tongue depends their life. Mark well all this!"

And at the same moment the fairy touched Elise's hands with a nettle, which made them burn like fire, and Elise awoke. It was broad daylight, and close to her lay a nettle like the one she had seen in her dream. She fell upon her knees, thanked God, and then went out of the cave in order to begin her work. She plucked with her own delicate hands the disagreeable stinging-nettles: they burned large blisters

THE WILD SWANS. Page 11.

on her hands and arms, but she bore the pain willingly in the hope of releasing her dear brothers. She trampled on the nettles with her naked feet, and spun the green yarn.

At sunset came her brothers. Elise's silence quite frightened them; they thought it must be the effect of some fresh spell of their wicked stepmother; but when they saw her blistered hands, they found out what their sister was doing for their sakes. The youngest brother wept, and when his tears fell upon her hands, Elise felt no more pain— the blisters disappeared.

The whole night she spent in her work, for she could not rest till she had released her brothers. All the following day she sat in her solitude, for the Swans had flown away; but never had time passed so qiuckly. One shirt was ready; she now began the second.

Suddenly a hunting-horn resounded among the mountains. Elise was frightened. The noise came nearer; she heard the hounds barking. In great terror, she fled into the cave, bound up the nettles which she had gathered and combed into a bundle, and sat down upon it.

In the same moment a large dog sprang out from the bushes; two others immediately followed; they barked loudly, ran away, and then returned. It was not long before the hunters stood in front of the cave; the handsomest among them was the King of that country; he stepped up to Elise. Never had he seen a lovelier maiden.

"How camest thou here, thou beautiful child?" said he. Elise shook her head; she dared not speak; a word might have cost her the life of her brothers, and she hid her hands under her apron lest the King should see how she was suffering.

"Come with me," said he, "thou must not stay here! If thou art good as thou art beautiful, I will dress thee in velvet and silk; I will put a gold crown upon thy head, and thou shalt dwell in my palace!" So he lifted her upon his horse, while she wept and wrung her hands; but the King said, "I only desire thy happiness! thou shalt thank me for this some day!" and away he rode over mountains and valleys, holding her on his horse in front, whilst the other hunters followed. When the sun set, the King's magnificent capital, with its churches and cupolas, lay before them, and the

King led Elise into the palace, where, in a high marble hall, fountains were playing, and the walls and ceiling displayed the most beautiful paintings. But Elise cared not for all this splendour; she wept and mourned in silence, even whilst some female attendants dressed her in royal robes, wove costly pearls in her hair, and drew soft gloves over her blistered hands.

And now she was full dressed, and as she stood in her splendid attire, her beauty was so dazzling that the courtiers all bowed low before her, and the King chose her for his bride, although the Archbishop shook his head, and whispered that "the beautiful lady of the wood must certainly be a witch, who had blinded their eyes, and infatuated the King's heart."

But the King did not listen; he ordered music to be played, and a sumptuous banquet served up; the loveliest maidens danced round the bride, and she was led through fragrant gardens into magnificent halls, but not a smile was seen to play upon her lips or beam from her eyes. The King then opened a small room next her sleeping apartment; it was adorned with costly green tapestry, and exactly resembled the cave in which she had been found: upon the ground lay the bundle of yarn which she had spun from the nettles, and by the wall hung the shirt she had completed. One of the hunters had brought all this, thinking there must be something wonderful in it.

"Here thou mayest dream of thy former home," said the King; "here is the work which employed thee: amidst all thy present splendour it may sometimes give thee pleasure to fancy thyself there again."

When Elise saw what was so dear to her heart, she smiled, and the blood returned to her cheeks; she thought her brothers might still be released, and she kissed the King's hand; he pressed her to his heart, and ordered the bells of all the churches in the city to be rung, to announce the celebration of their wedding. The beautiful dumb maiden of the wood was to become Queen of the land.

The Archbishop whispered evil words in the King's ear, but they made no impression upon him; the marriage was solemnized, and the Archbishop himself was obliged to put the crown upon her head. In his rage he pressed the narrow rim so firmly on her forehead that it hurt her; but a heavier weight—sorrow for her brothers—lay upon her heart: she did not feel bodily pain. She was still silent—a single word would have killed her brothers; her eyes, however, beamed with heartfelt love to the King, so good and handsome, who had done so much to make her happy. She became more warmly attached to him every day. Oh! how much she wished she might confide to him all her sorrows! but she was forced to remain silent; she could not speak until her work was completed! To this end she stole away every night, and went into the little room that was fitted up in imitation of the cave; there she worked at her shirts, but by the time she had begun the seventh all her yarn was spent.

She knew that the nettles she needed grew in the churchyard, but she must gather them herself: how was she to get them?

"Oh, what is the pain in my fingers compared to the anguish my heart suffers!" thought she. "I must venture to the churchyard; the good God will not withdraw His protection from me!"

Fearful, as though she were about to do something wrong, one moonlight night she crept down to the garden, and through the long avenues got into the lonely road leading to the churchyard. She saw sitting on one of the broadest tombstones a number of ugly old witches. They took off their ragged clothes as if they were going to bathe, and digging with their long lean fingers into the fresh grass, drew up the dead bodies and devoured the flesh. Elise was obliged to pass close by them, and the witches fixed their wicked eyes upon her; but she repeated her prayer, gathered the stinging-nettles, and took them back with her into the palace. One person only had seen her—it was the Archbishop; he was awake when others slept. Now he was convinced that all was not right about the Queen; she must be a witch, who had through her enchantments infatuated the King and all the people.

In the confessional he told the King what he had seen and what he feared; and when the slanderous words came from his lips, the sculptured images of the saints shook their heads, as though they would say, "It is untrue; Elise is innocent!" But the Archbishop explained the omen quite otherwise; he thought it was a testimony against her that the holy images shook their heads at hearing of her sin.

Two large tears rolled down the King's cheeks; he returned home in doubt; he pretended to sleep at night, though sleep never visited him; and he noticed that Elise rose from her bed every night, and every time he followed her secretly and saw her enter her little room.

His countenance became darker every day; Elise perceived it, though she knew not the cause. She was much pained, and, besides, what did she not suffer in her heart for her brothers! Her bitter tears ran down on the royal velvet and purple; they looked like bright diamonds, and all who saw the magnificence that surrounded her wished themselves in her place. She had now nearly finished her work—only one shirt was wanting; unfortunately, yarn was wanting also—she had not a single nettle left. Once more, only this one time, she must go to the churchyard and gather a few handfuls. She shuddered when she thought of the solitary walk and the horrid witches, but her resolution was as firm as her trust in God.

Elise went; the King and the Archbishop followed her: they saw her disappear at the churchyard door, and when they came nearer, they saw the witches sitting on the tombstones, as Elise had seen them, and the King turned away, for he believed her whose head had rested on his bosom that very evening to be amongst them. "Let the people judge her!" said he. And the people condemned her to be burnt.

She was now dragged from the King's sumptuous apartments into a dark, damp prison, where the wind whistled through the grated window. Instead of velvet and silk, they gave her the bundle of nettles she had gathered—on that must she lay her head; the shirts she had woven must serve her as mattress and counterpane; but they could not have given her anything she valued so much: and she continued her work, at the same time praying earnestly to her God. The boys sang scandalous songs about her in front of her prison; not a soul comforted her with one word of love.

Towards evening she heard the rustling of Swans' wings at the grating. It was the youngest of her brothers, who had at last found his sister, and she sobbed aloud for joy, although she knew that the coming night would probably be the last of her life; but then her work was almost finished, and her brother was near.

The Archbishop came in order to spend the last hour with her; he had promised the King he would; but she shook her head and entreated him with her eyes and gestures to go: this night she must finish her work, or all she had suffered—her pain, her anxiety, her sleepless nights—would be in vain. The Archbishop went away with many angry words, but the unfortunate Elise knew herself to be perfectly innocent, and went on with her work.

Little mice ran busily about and dragged the nettles to her feet, wishing to help her; and the thrush perched on the iron bars of the window, and sang all night as merrily as he could, that Elise might not lose courage.

It was still twilight, just an hour before sunrise, when the eleven brothers stood before the palace-gates, requesting an audience with the King; but it could not be, they were told: it was still night, the King was asleep, and they dared not wake him. They entreated, they threatened, the guard came up, the King himself at last stepped out to ask what was the matter: at that moment the sun rose, the brothers could be seen no longer, and eleven white Swans flew away over the palace.

The people poured forth from the gates of the city, all eager to see the witch burnt. One wretched horse drew the cart in which Elise was placed, a coarse frock of sackcloth had been put on her, her beautiful long hair hung loosely over her shoulders, her cheeks were of a deadly paleness, her lips moved gently, and her fingers wove the green yarn: even on her way to her cruel death she did not give up her work; the ten shirts lay at her feet—she was now labouring to complete the eleventh. The rabble insulted her.

"Look at the witch, how she mutters! she has not a hymn-book in her hand: no, there she sits, with her accursed witchery. Tear it from her! tear it into a thousand pieces!"

And they all crowded about her, and were on the point of snatching away the shirts, when eleven white Swans came flying towards the cart; they settled all round her, and flapped their wings. The crowd gave way in terror.

"It is a sign from Heaven! she is certainly innocent!" whispered some; they dared not say so aloud.

The Sheriff now seized her by the hand—in a moment she

threw the eleven shirts over the Swans, and eleven handsome Princes appeared in their place. The youngest had, however, only one arm, and a wing instead of the other, for one sleeve was deficient in his shirt—it had not been quite finished.

"Now I may speak," said she: "I am innocent!"

And the people who had seen what had happened bowed before her as before a saint. She, however, sank lifeless in her brothers' arms; suspense, fear, and grief, had quite exhausted her.

"Yes, she is innocent," said her eldest brother, and he now related their wonderful history. Whilst he spoke a fragrance as delicious as though it proceeded from millions of roses diffused itself around, for every piece of wood in the funeral pile had taken root and sent forth branches, a hedge of blooming red roses surrounded Elise, and above all the others blossomed a flower of dazzling white colour, bright as a star; the King plucked it and laid it on Elise's bosom, whereupon she awoke from her trance with peace and joy in her heart.

And all the church-bells began to ring of their own accord, and birds flew to the spot in swarms, and there was a festive procession back to the palace, such as no King has ever seen equalled.

THE UGLY DUCKLING.

IT was beautiful in the country; it was summer-time; the wheat was yellow, the oats were green, the hay was stacked up in the green meadows, and the stork paraded about on his long red legs, discoursing in Egyptian, which language he had learned from his mother. The fields and meadows were skirted by thick woods, and a deep lake lay in the midst of the woods. Yes, it was indeed beautiful in the country! The sunshine fell warmly on an old mansion, surrounded by deep canals, and from the walls down to the water's edge there grew large burdock-leaves, so high that children could stand upright among them without being perceived. This place was as wild and unfrequented as the thickest part of the wood, and on that account a duck had chosen to make her nest there. She was sitting on her eggs; but the pleasure she had felt at first was now almost gone, because she had been there so long, and had so few visitors, for the other ducks preferred swimming on the canals to sitting among the burdock-leaves gossiping with her.

At last the eggs cracked one after another, "Tchick, tchick!" All the eggs were alive, and one little head after another peered forth. "Quack, quack!" said the Duck, and all got up as well as they could; they peeped about from under the green leaves; and as green is good for the eyes, their mother let them look as long as they pleased.

"How large the world is!" said the little ones, for they found their present situation very different to their former confined one, while yet in the egg-shells.

"Do you imagine this to be the whole of the world?" said the mother; "it extends far beyond the other side of the garden to the pastor's field; but I have never been there. Are you all here?" And then she got up. "No, not all, but the largest egg is still here. How long will this last? I am so weary of it!" And then she sat down again.

"Well, and how are you getting on?" asked an old Duck, who had come to pay her a visit.

"This one egg keeps me so long," said the mother, "it will not break; but you should see the others! they are the prettiest little ducklings I have seen in all my days; they are all like their father,—the good-for-nothing fellow, he has not been to visit me once!"

"Let me see the egg that will not break," said the old Duck; "depend upon it, it is a turkey's egg. I was cheated in the same way once myself, and I had such trouble with the young ones; for they were afraid of the water, and I could not get them there. I called and scolded, but it was all of no use. But let me see the egg—ah, yes! to be sure, that is a turkey's egg. Leave it, and teach the other little ones to swim."

"I will sit on it a little longer," said the Duck. "I have been sitting so long, that I may as well spend the harvest here."

"It is no business of mine," said the old Duck, and away she waddled.

The great egg burst at last. "Tchick! tchick!" said the little one, and out it tumbled—but, oh! how large and ugly it was! The Duck looked at it. "That is a great, strong creature," said she; "none of the others are at all like it; can it be a young turkey-cock? Well, we shall soon find out; it must go into the water, though I push it in myself."

The next day there was delightful weather, and the sun shone warmly upon all the green leaves when Mother Duck with all her family went down to the canal: plump she went into the water. "Quack! quack!" cried she, and one duckling after another jumped in. The water closed over their heads, but all came up again, and swam together in the pleasantest manner; their legs moved without effort. All were there, even the ugly, grey one.

"No! it is not a turkey," said the old Duck; "only see how prettily it moves its legs! how upright it holds itself! it is my own child: it is also really very pretty, when one looks more closely at it. Quack! quack! now come with me, I will take you into the world, introduce you in the duck-yard; but keep close to me, or some one may tread on you; and beware of the cat."

So they came into the duck-yard. There was a horrid noise; two families were quarrelling about the remains of an eel, which in the end was secured by the cat.

"See, my children, such is the way of the world," said the Mother Duck, wiping her beak, for she, too, was fond of eels. "Now use your legs," said she, "keep together, and bow to the old Duck you see yonder. She is the most distinguished of all the fowls present, and is of Spanish blood, which accounts for her dignified appearance and manners. And look, she has a red rag on her leg! that is considered extremely handsome, and is the greatest distinction a duck can have. Don't turn your feet inwards; a well-educated duckling always keeps his legs far apart, like his father and mother, just so—look! now bow your necks, and say, 'quack.'"

And they did as they were told. But the other Ducks who were in the yard looked at them, and said aloud, "Only see, now we have another brood, as if there were not enough of us already; and fie! how ugly that one is; we will not endure it;" and immediately one of the Ducks flew at him, and bit him in the neck.

"Leave him alone," said the mother, "he is doing no one any harm."

"Yes, but he is so large, and so strange-looking, and therefore he shall be teased."

"Those are fine children that our good mother has," said the old Duck with the red rag on her leg. "All are pretty except one, and that has not turned out well; I almost wish it could be hatched over again."

"That cannot be, please your highness," said the mother. "Certainly he is not handsome, but he is a very good child, and swims as well as the others, indeed rather better. I think he will grow like the others all in good time, and perhaps will look smaller. He stayed so long in the egg-shell, that is the cause of the difference;" and she scratched the Duckling's neck, and stroked his whole body. "Besides," added she, "he is a drake; I think he will be very strong, therefore it does not matter so much; he will fight his way through."

"The other ducks are very pretty," said the old Duck. "Pray make yourselves at home, and if you find an eel's head you can bring it to me."

And accordingly they made themselves at home.

But the poor little Duckling, who had come last out of its egg-shell, and who was so ugly, was bitten, pecked, and teased by both Ducks and Hens. "It is so large!" said they all. And the Turkey-cock, who had come into the world with spurs on, and therefore fancied he was an emperor, puffed himself up like a ship in full sail, and marched up to the Duckling quite red with passion. The poor little thing scarcely knew what to do; he was quite distressed, because he was so ugly, and because he was the jest of the poultry-yard.

So passed the first day, and afterwards matters grew worse and worse—the poor Duckling was scorned by all. Even his brothers and sisters behaved unkindly, and were constantly saying, "The cat fetch thee, thou nasty creature!" The mother said, "Ah, if thou wert only far away!" The Ducks bit him, the Hens pecked him, and the girl who fed the poultry kicked him. He ran over the hedge; the little birds in the bushes were terrified. "That is because I am so ugly," thought the Duckling, shutting his eyes, but he ran on. At last he came to a wide moor, where lived some Wild Ducks; here he lay the whole night, so tired and so comfortless. In the morning the Wild Ducks flew up, and perceived their new companion. "Pray who are you?" asked they; and our little Duckling turned himself in all directions, and greeted them as politely as possible.

"You are really uncommonly ugly!" said the Wild

Ducks; "however, that does not matter to us, provided you do not marry into our families." Poor thing! he had never thought of marrying; he only begged permission to lie among the reeds, and drink the water of the moor.

There he lay for two whole days—on the third day there came two Wild Geese, or rather Ganders, who had not been long out of their egg-shells, which accounts for their impertinence.

"Hark ye," said they, "you are so ugly that we like you infinitely well; will you come with us, and be a bird of passage? On another moor, not far from this, are some dear, sweet wild geese, as lovely creatures as have ever said 'hiss, hiss.' You are truly in the way to make your fortune, ugly as you are."

Bang! a gun went off all at once, and both Wild Geese were stretched dead among the reeds; the water became red with blood; bang! a gun went off again; whole flocks of wild geese flew up from among the reeds, and another report followed.

There was a grand hunting party: the hunters lay in ambush all around; some were even sitting in the trees, whose huge branches stretched far over the moor. The blue smoke rose through the thick trees like a mist, and was dispersed as it fell over the water; the hounds splashed about in the mud, the reeds and rushes bent in all directions—how frightened the poor little Duck was! he turned his head, thinking to hide it under his wings, and in a moment a most formidable-looking dog stood close to him, his tongue hanging out of his mouth, his eyes sparkling fearfully. He opened wide his jaws at the sight of our Duckling, showed him his sharp white teeth, and, splash, splash! he was gone, —gone without hurting him.

"Well! let me be thankful," sighed he; "I am so ugly, that even the dog will not eat me."

And now he lay still, though the shooting continued among the reeds, shot following shot.

The noise did not cease till late in the day, and even then the poor little thing dared not stir; he waited several hours before he looked around him, and then hastened away from the moor as fast as he could; he ran over fields and meadows, though the wind was so high that he had some difficulty in proceeding.

Towards evening he reached a wretched little hut, so wretched that it knew not on which side to fall, and therefore remained standing. The wind blew violently, so that our poor little Duckling was obliged to support himself on his tail, in order to stand against it; but it became worse and worse. He then remarked that the door had lost one of its hinges, and hung so much awry that he could creep through the crevice into the room, which he did.

In this room lived an old woman, with her Tom-cat and her Hen; and the Cat, whom she called her little son, knew how to set up his back and purr; indeed, he could even emit sparks when stroked the wrong way. The Hen had very short legs, and was therefore called "Cuckoo Short-legs;" she laid very good eggs, and the old woman loved her as her own child.

The next morning the new guest was perceived; the Cat began to mew, and the Hen to cackle.

"What is the matter?" asked the old woman, looking round; however, her eyes were not good, so she took the young Duckling to be a fat duck who had lost her way. "This is a capital catch," said she; "I shall now have ducks' eggs, if it be not a drake: we must try."

And so the Duckling was put to the proof for three weeks, but no eggs made their appearance.

Now the Cat was the master of the house, and the Hen was the mistress, and they used always to say, "We and the world," for they imagined themselves to be not only the half of the world, but also by far the better half. The Duckling thought it was possible to be of a different opinion, but that the Hen would not allow.

"Can you lay eggs?" asked she.

"No."

"Well, then, hold your tongue."

And the Cat said, "Can you set up your back? can you purr?"

"No."

"Well, then, you should have no opinion when reasonable persons are speaking."

So the Duckling sat alone in a corner, and was in a very bad humour; however, he happened to think of the fresh air and bright sunshine, and these thoughts gave him such a

THE UGLY DUCKLING.

Page 22.

strong desire to swim again, that he could not help telling it to the Hen.

"What ails you?" said the Hen. "You have nothing to do, and therefore brood over these fancies; either lay eggs or purr, then you will forget them."

"But it is so delicious to swim!" said the Duckling; "so delicious when the waters close over your head, and you plunge to the bottom!"

"Well, that is a queer sort of pleasure," said the Hen; "I think you must be crazy. Not to speak of myself, ask the Cat — he is the most sensible animal I know — whether he would like to swim, or to plunge to the bottom of the water. Ask our mistress, the old woman, — there is no one in the world wiser than she; do you think she would take pleasure in swimming, and in the waters closing over her head?"

"You do not understand me," said the Duckling.

"What, we do not understand you! So you think yourself wiser than the Cat and the old woman, not to speak of myself. Do not fancy any such thing, child, but be thankful for all the kindness that has been shown you. Are you not lodged in a warm room, and have you not the advantage of society from which you can learn something? But you are a simpleton, and it is wearisome to have anything to do with you. Believe me, I wish you well. I tell you unpleasant truths, but it is thus that real friendship is shown. Come, for once give yourself the trouble to learn to purr, or to lay eggs."

"I think I will go out into the wide world again," said the Duckling.

"Well, go," answered the Hen.

So the Duckling went. He swam on the surface of the water, he plunged beneath, but all animals passed him by, on account of his ugliness. And the autumn came, the leaves turned yellow and brown, the wind caught them and danced them about, the air was very cold, the clouds were heavy with hail or snow, and the raven sat on the hedge and croaked: — the poor Duckling was certainly not very comfortable!

One evening, just as the sun was setting with unusual brilliancy, a flock of large, beautiful birds rose from out o' the brushwood; the Duckling had never seen anything so beautiful before; their plumage was of a dazzling white, and they had long slender necks. They were swans; they uttered a singular cry, spread out their long, splendid wings, and flew away from these cold regions to warmer countries, across the open sea. They flew so high, so very high! and the little Ugly Duckling's feelings were so strange; he turned round and round in the water like a mill-wheel, strained his neck to look after them, and sent forth such a loud and strange cry, that it almost frightened himself. Ah! he could not forget them, those noble birds! those happy birds! When he could see them no longer, he plunged to the bottom of the water, and when he rose again was almost beside himself. The Duckling knew not what the birds were called, knew not whither they were flying, yet he loved them as he had never before loved anything; he envied them not, it would never have occurred to him to wish such beauty for himself; he would have been quite contented if the ducks in the duck-yard had but endured his company — the poor, ugly animal!

And the winter was so cold, so cold! The Duckling was obliged to swim round and round in the water, to keep it from freezing; but every night the opening in which he swam became smaller and smaller; it froze so that the crust of ice crackled; the Duckling was obliged to make good use of his legs to prevent the water from freezing entirely; at last, wearied out, he lay stiff and cold in the ice.

Early in the morning there passed by a peasant, who saw him, broke the ice in pieces with his wooden shoe, and brought him home to his wife.

He now revived; the children would have played with him, but our Duckling thought they wished to tease him, and in his terror jumped into the milk-pail, so that the milk was spilled about the room: the good woman screamed and clapped her hands; he flew thence into the pan where the butter was kept, and thence into the meal-barrel, and out again, and then how strange he looked!

The woman screamed, and struck at him with the tongs, the children ran races with each other trying to catch him, and laughed and screamed likewise. It was well for him that the door stood open; he jumped out among the bushes into the new-fallen snow — he lay there as in a dream.

But it would be too melancholy to relate all the trouble and misery that he was obliged to suffer during the severity of the winter : he was lying on a moor among the reeds, when the sun began to shine warmly again, the larks sang, and beautiful spring had returned.

And once more he shook his wings. They were stronger than formerly, and bore him forwards quickly, and before he was well aware of it, he was in a large garden where the apple-trees stood in full bloom, where the syringas sent forth thei fragrance, and hung their long green branches down into th winding canal. Oh! everything was so lovely, so full of the freshness of spring! And out of the thicket came three beautiful white Swans. They displayed their feathers so proudly, and swam so lightly, so lightly! The Duckling knew the glorious creatures, and was seized with a strange melancholy.

"I will fly to them, those kingly birds!" said he. "They will kill me, because I, ugly as I am, have presumed to approach them; but it matters not, better to be killed by them than to be bitten by the ducks, pecked by the hens, kicked by the girl who feeds the poultry, and to have so much to suffer during the winter!" He flew into the water, and swam towards the beautiful creatures; they saw him and shot forward to meet him. "Only kill me," said the poor animal, and he bowed his head low, expecting death; but what did he see in the water? He saw beneath him his own form, no longer that of a plump, ugly, grey bird — it was that of a Swan.

It matters not to have been born in a duck-yard, if one has been hatched from a swan's egg.

The good creature felt himself really elevated by all the troubles and adversities he had experienced. He could now rightly estimate his own happiness, and the larger Swans swam round him, and stroked him with their beaks.

Some little children were running about in the garden; they threw grain and bread into the water, and the youngest exclaimed, "There is a new one!" the others also cried out, "Yes, there is a new swan come!" and they clapped their hands, and danced around. They ran to their father and mother, bread and cake were thrown into the water, and every one said, "The new one is the best, so young and so beautiful!" and the old Swans bowed before him. The young Swan felt quite ashamed, and hid his head under his wings; he scarcely knew what to do, he was all too happy, but still not proud, for a good heart is never proud.

He remembered how he had been persecuted and derided, and he now heard every one say, he was the most beautiful of all beautiful birds. The syringas bent down their branches towards him low into the water, and the sun shone so warmly and brightly—he shook his feathers, stretched his slender neck, and in the joy of his heart said, "How little did I dream of so much happiness when I was the ugly, despised Duckling!"

THE LITTLE MERMAID.

FAR out in the wide sea, where the water is blue as the loveliest corn-flower, and clear as the purest crystal, where it is so deep that very, very many church-towers must be heaped one upon another in order to reach from the lowest depth to the surface above, dwell the Mer-people.

Now you must not imagine that there is nothing but sand below the water: no, indeed, far from it! Trees and plants of wondrous beauty grow there, whose stems and leaves are so light, that they are waved to and fro by the slightest motion of the water, almost as if they were living beings. Fishes, great and small, glide in and out among the branches, just as birds fly about among our trees.

Where the water is deepest stands the palace of the Mer-king. The walls of this palace are of coral, and the high, pointed windows are of amber; the roof, however, is composed of mussel-shells, which, as the billows pass over them, are continually opening and shutting. This looks exceedingly pretty, especially as each of these mussel-shells contains a number of bright, glittering pearls, one only of which would be the most costly ornament in the diadem of a king in the upper world.

The Mer-king, who lived in this palace, had been for many years a widower; his old mother managed the household affairs for him. She was, on the whole, a sensible sort of a lady, although extremely proud of her high birth and station, on which account she wore twelve oysters on her tail, whilst the other inhabitants of the sea, even those of distinction, were allowed only six. In every other respect she merited unlimited praise, especially for the affection she showed to the six little Princesses, her grand-daughters. These were all very beautiful children; the youngest was, however, the most lovely; her skin was as soft and delicate as a rose-leaf, her eyes were of as deep a blue as the sea, but, like all other mermaids, she had no feet; her body ended in a tail like that of a fish.

The whole day long the children used to play in the spacious apartments of the palace, where beautiful flowers grew out of the walls on all sides around them. When the great amber windows were opened, fishes would swim into these apartments as swallows fly into our rooms; but the fishes were bolder than the swallows—they swam straight up to the little Princesses, ate from their hands, and allowed themselves to be caressed.

In front of the palace there was a large garden, full of fiery red and dark blue trees; the fruit upon them glittered like gold, and the flowers resembled a bright burning sun. The sand that formed the soil of the garden was of a bright blue colour, somewhat like flames of sulphur; and a strangely beautiful blue was spread over the whole, so that one might have fancied oneself raised very high in the air, with the sky at once above and below—certainly not at the bottom of the sea. When the waters were quite still, the sun might be seen looking like a purple flower, out of whose cup streamed forth the light of the world.

Each of the little Princesses had her own plot in the garden, where she might plant and sow at her pleasure. One chose hers to be made in the shape of a whale, another preferred the figure of a mermaid, but the youngest had hers quite round like the sun, and planted in it only those flowers that were red, as the sun seemed to her. She was certainly a singular child, very quiet and thoughtful. Whilst her sisters were adorning themselves with all sorts of gay things that came out of a ship which had been wrecked, she asked for nothing but a beautiful white marble statue of a boy, which had been found in it. She put the statue in her garden, and planted a red weeping willow by its side. The tree grew up quickly, and let its long boughs fall upon the bright blue ground, where ever-moving shadows played in violet hues, as if boughs and root were embracing.

Nothing pleased the little Princess more than to hear about the world of human beings living above the sea. She made her old grandmother tell her everything she knew about ships, towns, men, and land animals, and was particularly pleased when she heard that the flowers of the upper world had a pleasant fragrance (for the flowers of the sea are scentless), and that the woods were green, and the fishes fluttering

THE LITTLE MERMAID.

Page 28.

among the branches of various gay colours, and that they could sing with a loud, clear voice. The old lady meant birds, but she called them fishes, because her grandchildren, having never seen a bird, would not otherwise have understood her.

"When you have attained your fifteenth year," added she, "you will be permitted to rise to the surface of the sea; you will then sit by moonlight in the clefts of the rocks, see the ships sail by, and learn to distinguish towns and men."

The next year the eldest of the sisters reached this happy age, but the others — alas! the second sister was a year younger than the eldest, the third a year younger than the second, and so on. The youngest had still five whole years to wait till that joyful time should come when she also might rise to the surface of the water and see what was going on in the upper world; however, the eldest promised to tell the others about everything she might see, when the first day of her being of age arrived; for the grandmother gave them but little information, and there was so much that they wished to hear.

But none of all the sisters longed so ardently for the day when she should be released from childish restraint as the youngest — she who had longest to wait, and was so quiet and thoughtful. Many a night she stood by the open window, looking up through the clear blue water, whilst the fishes were leaping and playing around her. She could see the sun and the moon; their light was pale, but they appeared larger than they do to those who live in the upper world. If a shadow passed over them, she knew it must be either a whale, or a ship sailing by full of human beings. Never could these last have imagined that, far beneath them, a little mermaiden was passionately stretching forth her white hands towards their ship's keel.

The day had now arrived when the eldest Princess had attained her fifteenth year, and was therefore allowed to rise up to the surface of the sea.

When she returned she had a thousand things to relate. Her chief pleasure had been to sit upon a sand-bank in the moonlight, looking at the large town which lay on the coast, where lights were beaming like stars, and where music was playing; she had heard the distant noise of men and carriages, she had seen the high church-towers, had listened to the ringing of the bells; and just because she could not go on shore she longed the more after all these things.

How attentively did her youngest sister listen to her words! And when she next stood, at night time, by her open window, gazing upward through the blue waters, her thoughts dwelt so eagerly upon the great city, full of life and sound, that she fancied she could hear the church-bells ringing.

Next year the second sister received permission to swim wherever she pleased. She rose to the surface of the sea, just when the sun was setting; and this sight so delighted her, that she declared it to be more beautiful than anything else she had seen above the waters.

"The whole sky seemed tinged with gold," said she; "and it is impossible for me to describe to you the beauty of the clouds. Now red, now violet, they glided over me; but still more swiftly flew over the water a flock of white swans, just where the sun was descending: I looked after them, but the sun disappeared, and the bright rosy light on the surface of the sea and on the edges of the clouds died away gradually."

It was now time for the third sister to visit the upper world. She was the boldest of the six, and ventured up a river. On its shores she saw green hills, covered with woods and vineyards, from among which arose houses and castles. She heard the birds singing, and the sun shone with so much power, that she was continually obliged to plunge below, in order to cool her burning face. In a little bay she met with a number of children, who were bathing and jumping about; she would have joined in their gambols, but the children fled back to land in great terror, and a little black animal barked at her in such a manner, that she herself was frightened at last, and swam back to the sea. But never could she forget the green woods, the verdant hills, and the pretty children, who, although they had no fins, were swimming about in the river so fearlessly.

The fourth sister was not so bold, she remained in the open sea, and said, on her return home, she thought nothing could be more beautiful. She had seen ships sailing by— so far off that they looked like sea-gulls; she had watched the merry dolphins gambolling in the water, and the enormous whales sending up into the air a thousand sparkling fountains.

The year after, the fifth sister attained her fifteenth year,—her birthday happened at a different season to that of her sisters; it was winter, the sea was of a green colour, and immense icebergs were floating on its surface. These, she said, looked like pearls, although all were much larger than the church-towers in the land of human beings. She sat down upon one of these pearls, and let the wind play with her long hair, but then all the ships hoisted their sails in terror, and escaped as quickly as possible. In the evening the sky was covered with clouds; and whilst the great mountains of ice alternately sank and rose again, and beamed with a reddish glow, flashes of lightning burst forth from the clouds, and the thunder rolled on, peal after peal. The sails of all the ships were instantly furled, and horror and affright reigned on board; but the Princess sat still on the iceberg, looking unconcernedly at the blue zig-zag of the flashes.

The first time that either of these sisters rose out of the sea, she was quite enchanted at the sight of so many new and beautiful objects; but the novelty was soon over, and it was not long ere their own home appeared far more attractive than the upper world.

Many an evening would the five sisters rise hand in hand from the depths of the ocean. Their voices were far sweeter than any human voice, and when a storm was coming on, they would swim in front of the ships and sing,—oh, how sweetly did they sing!—describing the happiness of those who lived at the bottom of the sea, and entreating the sailors not to be afraid, but to come down to them.

But the mariners did not understand their words,—they fancied the song was only the whistling of the wind,—and thus they lost the hidden glories of the sea; for if their ships were wrecked, all on board were drowned, and none but dead men ever entered the Mer-king's palace.

Whilst the sisters were swimming at evening time, the youngest would remain motionless and alone in her father's palace, looking up after them. She would have wept, but mermaids cannot weep, and therefore, when they are troubled, suffer infinitely more than human beings do.

"Oh! if I were but fifteen!" sighed she; "I know that

I should love the upper world and its inhabitants so much!"

At last the time she had so longed for arrived.

"Well, now it is your turn," said the grandmother; "come here that I may adorn you like your sisters." And winding around her hair a wreath of white lilies, whose every petal was the half of a pearl, she commanded eight large oysters to fasten themselves to the Princess's tail, in token of her high rank.

"But that is so very uncomfortable!" said the little Princess.

"One must not mind slight inconveniences when one wishes to look well," said the old lady.

How willingly would the Princess have given up all this splendour, and exchanged her heavy crown for the red flowers of her garden, which were so much more becoming to her. But she dared not do so. "Farewell!" said she; and she rose from the sea, light as a flake of foam.

When, for the first time in her life, she appeared on the surface of the water, the sun had just sunk below the horizon, the clouds were beaming with bright golden and rosy hues, the evening star was shining in the pale western sky, the air was mild and refreshing, and the sea as smooth as a looking-glass. A large ship with three masts lay on the still waters; one sail only was unfurled, for not a breath was stirring, and the sailors were quietly seated on the cordage and ladders of the vessel. Music and song resounded from the deck, and after it grew dark hundreds of lamps all on a sudden burst forth into light, whilst innumerable flags were fluttering over-head. The little Mermaid swam close up to the captain's cabin, and every now and then, when the ship was raised by the motion of the water, she could look through the clear window-panes. She saw within many richly-dressed men; the handsomest among them was a young Prince with large black eyes. He could not certainly be more than sixteen years old, and it was in honour of his birthday that a grand festival was being celebrated. The crew were dancing on the deck, and when the young Prince appeared among them, a hundred rockets were sent up into the air, turning night into day, and so terrifying the little Mermaid, that for some minutes she plunged beneath the water. However, she soon raised her little head again, and then it seemed as if all the stars were falling down upon her. Such a fiery shower she had never seen before,—never had she heard that men possessed such wonderful powers. Large suns revolved around her bright fishes floated in the air, and all these marvels were reflected on the clear surface of the sea. It was so light in the ship, that everything could be seen distinctly. Oh! how happy the young Prince was! he shook hands with the sailors, laughed and jested with them, whilst sweet notes of music mingled with the silence of the night.

It was now late, but the little Mermaid could not tear herself away from the ship and the handsome young Prince. She remained looking through the cabin-window, rocked to and fro by the waves. There was a foaming and fermentation in the depths beneath, and the ship began to move on faster,— the sails were spread, the waves rose high, thick clouds gathered over the sky, and the noise of distant thunder was heard. The sailors perceived that a storm was coming on, so they again furled the sails. The great vessel was tossed about on the tempestuous ocean like a light boat, and the waves rose to an immense height, towering over the ship, which alternately sank beneath, and rose above them. To the little Mermaid this seemed most delightful, but the ship's crew thought very differently. The vessel cracked, the stout masts bent under the violence of the billows, the water rushed in. For a minute the ship tottered to and fro, then the main-mast broke, as if it had been a reed; the ship turned over, and was filled with water. The little Mermaid now perceived that the crew was in danger, for she herself was forced to beware of the beams and splinters torn from the vessel, and floating about on the waves. But at the same time it became pitch-dark, so that she could not distinguish anything; presently, however, a dreadful flash of lightning disclosed to her the whole of the wreck. Her eyes sought the young Prince; the same instant the ship sank to the bottom. At first she was delighted, thinking that the Prince must now come to her abode, but she soon remembered that man cannot live in water, and that therefore, if the Prince ever entered her palace, it would be as a corpse.

"Die! no, he must not die!" She swam through the fragments with which the water was strewn, regardless of the

D

danger she was incurring, and at last found the Prince all but exhausted, and with great difficulty keeping his head above water. He had already closed his eyes, and must inevitably have been drowned, had not the little Mermaid come to his rescue. She seized hold of him and kept him above water, suffering the current to bear them on together.

Towards morning the storm was hushed; no trace, however, remained of the ship. The sun rose like fire out of the sea; his beams seemed to restore colour to the Prince's cheeks, but his eyes were still closed. The Mermaid kissed his high forehead and stroked his wet hair away from his face. He looked like the marble statue in her garden; she kissed him again, and wished most fervently that he might recover.

She now saw the dry land with its mountains glittering with snow. A green wood extended along the coast, and at the entrance of the wood stood a chapel or convent, she could not be sure which. Citron and melon-trees grew in the garden adjoining it, an avenue of tall palm-trees led up to the door. The sea here formed a little bay, in which the water was quite smooth, but very deep, and under the cliffs there were dry firm sands. Hither swam the little Mermaid with the seemingly dead Prince; she laid him upon the warm sand, and took care to place his head high, and to turn his face to the sun.

The bells began to ring in the large white building which stood before her, and a number of young girls came out to walk in the garden. The Mermaid went away from the shore, hid herself behind some stones, covered her head with foam, so that her little face could not be seen, and watched the Prince with unremitting attention.

It was not long before one of the young girls approached; she seemed quite frightened at finding the Prince in this state, apparently dead; soon, however, she recovered herself, and ran back to call her sisters. The little Mermaid saw that the Prince revived, and that all around smiled kindly and joyfully upon him; for her, however, he looked not; he knew not that it was she who had saved him; and when the Prince was taken into the house, she felt so sad that she immediately plunged beneath the water, and returned to her father's palace.

If she had been before quiet and thoughtful, she now

grew still more so. Her sisters asked her what she had seen in the upper world, but she made no answer.

Many an evening she rose to the place where she had left the Prince. She saw the snow on the mountains melt, the fruits in the garden ripen and gathered, but the Prince she never saw; so she always returned sorrowfully to her home under the sea. Her only pleasure was to sit in her little garden, gazing on the beautiful statue so like the Prince. She cared no longer for her flowers, they grew up in wild luxuriance, covered the steps, and entwined their long stems and tendrils among the boughs of the trees, until her whole garden became a bower.

At last, being unable to conceal her sorrow any longer, she revealed the secret to one of her sisters, who told it to the other Princesses, and they to some of their friends. Among them was a young mermaid who recollected the Prince, having been an eye-witness herself to the festivities in the ship; she knew also in what country the Prince lived, and the name of its king.

"Come, little sister!" said the Princesses, and, embracing her, they rose together arm in arm, out of the water, just in front of the Prince's palace.

This palace was built of bright yellow stones, a flight of white marble steps led from it down to the sea. A gilded cupola crowned the building, and white marble figures, which might almost have been taken for real men and women, were placed among the pillars surrounding it. Through the clear glass of the high windows one might look into magnificent apartments hung with silken curtains, the walls adorned with beautiful paintings. It was a real treat to the little royal mermaids to behold so splendid an abode; they gazed through the windows of one of the largest rooms, and in the centre saw a fountain playing, whose waters sprang up so high as to reach the glittering cupola above, through which fell the sunbeams, dancing on the water, and brightening the pretty plants which grew around it.

The little Mermaid now knew where her beloved Prince dwelt, and henceforth she went there almost every evening. She often approached nearer the land than her sisters had ventured, and even swam up the narrow channel that flowed under the marble balcony. Here, on bright moonlight nights, she would watch the young Prince, whilst he believed himself alone.

Sometimes she saw him sailing on the water in a gaily-painted boat, with many coloured flags waving above. She would then hide among the green reeds which grew on the banks, listening to his voice; and if any one in the boat noticed the rustling of her long silver veil, when it was caught now and then by the light breeze, they only fancied it was a swan flapping his wings.

Many a night, when the fishermen were casting their nets by the beacon's light, she heard them talking of the Prince, and relating the noble actions he had performed. She was then so happy, thinking how she had saved his life when struggling with the waves, and remembering how his head had rested on her bosom, and how she had kissed him when he knew nothing of it, and could never even dream of her existence.

Human beings became more and more dear to her every day; she wished that she were one of them. Their world seemed to her much larger than that of the mer-people; they could fly over the ocean in their ships, as well as climb to the summits of those high mountains that rose above the clouds; and their wooded domains extended much farther than a mermaid's eye could penetrate.

There were many things that she wished to hear explained, but her sisters could not give her any satisfactory answer; she was again obliged to have recourse to the old Queen-mother, who knew a great deal about the upper world, which she used to call "the country above the sea."

"Do men, when they are not drowned, live for ever?" she asked one day; "do they not die as we do, who live at the bottom of the sea?"

"Yes," was the grandmother's reply, "they must die like us, and their life is much shorter than ours. We live to the age of three hundred years, but, when we die, we become foam on the sea, and are not allowed even to share a grave among those that are dear to us. We have no immortal souls, we can never live again, and are like the green rushes which when once cut down are withered for ever. Human beings, on the contrary, have souls that continue to live when their bodies become dust, and as we rise out of the water to admire the abode of man, even so these souls ascend to glorious unknown dwellings in the skies, which we are not permitted to see."

"Why have not *we* immortal souls?" asked the little Mermaid. "I would willingly give up my three hundred years to be a human being for only one day, thus to become entitled to that heavenly world above."

"You must not think of that," answered her grandmother, "it is much better as it is; we live longer, and are far happier than human beings."

"So I must die, and be dashed like foam over the sea, never to rise again and hear the gentle murmur of the ocean, never again to see the beautiful flowers and the bright sun!— Tell me, dear grandmother, are there no means by which I may obtain an immortal soul?"

"No!" replied the old lady. "It is true that if thou couldest so win the affections of a human being as to become dearer to him than either father or mother; if he loved thee with all his heart, and promised, whilst the priest joined his hands with thine, to be always faithful to thee; then his soul would flow into thine, and thou wouldest become partaker of human bliss. But that can never be! for what in our eyes is the most beautiful part of our body, the tail, the inhabitants of the earth think hideous: they cannot bear it. To appear handsome to them, the body must have two clumsy props, which they call legs."

The little Mermaid sighed and looked mournfully at the scaly part of her form, otherwise so fair and delicate.

"We are happy," added the old lady, "we shall jump and swim about merrily for three hundred years; that is a long time, and afterwards we shall repose peacefully in death. This evening we have a court-ball."

The ball which the Queen-mother spoke of was far more splendid than any that earth has ever seen. The walls of the saloon were of crystal, very thick, but yet very clear; hundreds of large mussel-shells were planted in rows along them: these shells were some of rose-colour, some green as grass, but all sending forth a bright light, which not only illuminated the whole apartment, but also shone through the glassy walls so as to light up the waters around, and making the scales of the numberless fishes, great and small, crimson and purple, silver and gold-coloured, appear more brilliant than ever.

Through the centre of the saloon flowed a bright, clear stream, on the surface of which danced mermen and mermaids to the melody of their own sweet voices—voices far sweeter than those of the dwellers upon earth. The little Princess sang most sweetly of all, and they clapped their hands and applauded her. For a moment it pleased her to be thus reminded that there was neither on earth nor in the sea a more beautiful voice than hers. But her thoughts soon returned to the world above her; she could not forget the handsome Prince; she could not control her sorrow at not having an immortal soul. She stole away from her father's palace, and whilst all was joy within she sat alone, lost in thought, in her little neglected garden. On a sudden she heard the tones of horns resounding over the water far away in the distance, and she said to herself, "Now he is going out to hunt—he whom I love more than my father and my mother, with whom my thoughts are constantly occupied, and to whom I would so willingly trust the happiness of my life! All, all! will I risk to win him—and an immortal soul! Whilst my sisters are still dancing in the palace, I will go to the enchantress whom I have hitherto feared so much, but who is, nevertheless, the only person who can advise and help me."

So the little Mermaid left the garden, and went to the foaming whirlpool beyond which dwelt the enchantress. She had never been this way before; neither flowers nor seagrass bloomed along her path; she had to traverse an extent of bare, grey sand till she reached the whirlpool, whose waters were eddying and whizzing like mill-wheels, tearing everything they could seize along with them into the abyss below. She was obliged to make her way through this horrible place, in order to arrive at the territory of the enchantress. Then she had to pass through a boiling, slimy bog, which the enchantress called her turf-moor: her house stood in a wood beyond this, and a strange abode it was. All the trees and bushes around were polypi, looking like hundred-headed serpents shooting up out of the ground; their branches were long, slimy arms with fingers of worms, every member, from the root to the uttermost tip, ceaselessly moving and extending on all sides. Whatever they seized they fastened upon so that it could not loosen itself from their grasp. The little Mermaid stood still for a minute looking at this horrible wood, her heart beat with fear, and she would certainly have returned without attaining her object, had she not remembered the Prince — and immortality. The thought gave her new courage, she bound up her long waving hair, that the polypi might not catch hold of it, crossed her delicate arms over her bosom, and swifter than a fish can glide through the water, she passed these unseemly trees, who stretched their eager arms after her in vain. She could not, however, help seeing that every polypus had something in its grasp, held as firmly by a thousand little arms as if enclosed by iron bands. The whitened skulls of a number of human beings who had been drowned in the sea, and had sunk into the abyss, grinned horribly from the arms of these polypi; helms, chests, skeletons of land animals were also held in their embrace; among other things might be seen even a little mermaid whom they had seized and strangled! What a fearful sight for the unfortunate Princess!

But she got safely through this wood of horrors, and then arrived at a slimy place, where immense, fat snails were crawling about, and in the midst of this place stood a house built of the bones of unfortunate people who had been shipwrecked. Here sat the witch caressing a toad in the same manner as some persons would a pet bird. The ugly fat snails she called her chickens, and she permitted them to crawl about her.

"I know well what you would ask of me," said she to the little Princess. "Your wish is foolish enough, yet it shall be fulfilled, though its accomplishment is sure to bring misfortune on you, my fairest Princess. You wish to get rid of your tail, and to have instead two stilts, like those of human beings, in order that a young Prince may fall in love with you, and that you may obtain an immortal soul — is it not so?" Whilst the witch spoke these words, she laughed so violently that her pet toad and snails fell from her lap. "You come just at the right time," continued she; "had you come after sunset, it would not have been in my power to have helped you before another year. I will prepare for you a drink, with which you must swim to land; you must sit down upon the shore and swallow it, and then your tail will fall and shrink up to the things which men call legs. This transformation will, however, be very painful: you will feel as though a sharp knife passed through your body. All who look on you, after you have been thus changed, will say that you are the loveliest child of earth they have ever seen: you will retain your peculiar undulating movements, and no dancer will move so lightly, but every step you take will cause you pain all but unbearable; it will seem to you as though you were walking on the sharp edges of swords, and your blood will flow. Can you endure all this suffering? If so, I will grant your request.

"Yes, I will," answered the Princess, with a faltering voice; for she remembered her dear Prince, and the immortal soul which her suffering might win.

"Only consider," said the witch, "that you can never again become a mermaid, when once you have received a human form You may never return to your sisters, and your father's palace; and unless you shall win the Prince's love to such a degree, that he shall leave father and mother for you, that you shall be mixed up with all his thoughts and wishes, and unless the priest join your hands, so that you become man and wife, you will never obtain the immortality you seek. The morrow of the day on which he is united to another will see your death; your heart will break with sorrow, and you will be changed to foam on the sea."

"Still I will venture!" said the little Mermaid, pale and trembling as a dying person.

"Besides all this, I must be paid, and it is no slight thing that I require for my trouble. Thou hast the sweetest voice of all the dwellers in the sea, and thou thinkest by its means to charm the Prince; this voice, however, I demand as my recompense. The best thing thou possessest I require in exchange for my magic drink; for I shall be obliged to sacrifice my own blood, in order to give it the sharpness of a two-edged sword."

"But if you take my voice from me," said the Princess, "what have I left with which to charm the Prince?"

"Thy graceful form," replied the witch, "thy undulating motion, and speaking eyes. With such as these, it will be easy to infatuate a vain human heart. Well now! hast thou lost courage? Put out thy little tongue, that I may cut it off, and take it for myself, in return for my magic elixir."

"Be it so!" said the Princess, and the witch took up her cauldron, in order to mix her potion. "Cleanliness is a good thing," remarked she, as she began to rub the cauldron with a handful of snails. She then scratched her bosom, and let the black blood trickle down into the cauldron, every moment throwing in new ingredients, the smoke from the mixture assuming such horrible forms as were enough to fill beholders with terror, and a moaning and groaning proceeding from it which might be compared to the weeping of crocodiles. The magic drink at length became clear and transparent as pure water: it was ready.

"Here it is!" said the witch to the Princess, cutting out her tongue at the same moment. The poor little Mermaid was now dumb — she could neither sing nor speak.

"If the polypi should attempt to seize you, as you pass through my little grove," said the witch, "you have only to sprinkle some of this liquid over them, and their arms will burst into a thousand pieces." But the Princess had no need of this counsel, for the polypi drew hastily back, as soon as they perceived the bright phial, that glittered in her hand like a star: thus she passed safely through the formidable wood, over the moor, and across the foaming mill-stream.

She now looked once again at her father's palace; the lamps in the saloon were extinguished, and all the family were asleep. She would not go in, for she could not speak if she did; she was about to leave her home for ever; her heart was ready to break with sorrow at the thought. She stole into the garden, plucked a flower from the bed of each of her sisters as a remembrance, kissed her hand again and again, and then rose through the dark blue waters to the world above.

The sun had not yet risen when she arrived at the Prince's dwelling, and ascended those well-known marble steps. The moon still shone in the sky when the little Mermaid drank off the wonderful liquid contained in her phial,— she felt it run through her like a sharp knife, and she fell down in a swoon. When the sun rose she awoke, and felt a burning pain in all her limbs, but — she saw standing close to her the object of her love, the handsome young Prince, whose coal-black eyes were fixed inquiringly upon her. Full of shame, she cast down her own, and perceived, instead of the long, fish-like tail she had hitherto borne, two slender legs; but she was quite naked, and tried in vain to cover herself with her long thick hair. The Prince asked who she was, and how she had got there: and she, in reply, smiled and gazed upon him with her bright blue eyes, for, alas! she could not speak. He then led her by the hand into the palace. She found that the witch had told her true; she felt as though she were walking on the edges of sharp swords, but she bore the pain willingly: on she passed, light as a zephyr, and all who saw her wondered at her light undulating movements.

When she entered the palace, rich clothes of muslin and silk were brought to her; she was lovelier than all who dwelt there, but she could neither speak nor sing. Some female slaves, gaily dressed in silk and gold brocade, sung before the Prince and his royal parents; and one of them distinguished herself by her clear sweet voice, which the Prince applauded by clapping his hands. This made the little Mermaid very sad, for she knew that she used to sing far better than the young slave. "Alas!" thought she, "if he did but know that for his sake I have given away my voice for ever."

The slaves began to dance: our lovely little Mermaiden then arose, stretched out her delicate white arms, and hovered gracefully about the room. Every motion displayed more and more the perfect symmetry and elegance of her figure; and the expression which beamed in her speaking eyes touched the hearts of the spectators far more than the song of the slaves.

All present were enchanted, but especially the young Prince, who called her his dear little foundling. And she danced again and again, although every step cost her excessive pain. The Prince then said she should always be with him; and accordingly a sleeping place was prepared for her on velvet cushions in the ante-room of his own apartment.

The Prince caused a suit of male apparel to be made for her, in order that she might accompany him in his rides; so together they traversed the fragrant woods, where green boughs brushed against their shoulders, and the birds sang merrily among the fresh leaves. With him she climbed up steep mountains, and although her tender feet bled, so as to be remarked by the attendants, she only smiled, and followed her dear Prince to the heights, whence they could see the clouds chasing each other beneath them, like a flock of birds migrating to other countries.

During the night she would, when all in the palace were at rest, walk down the marble steps, in order to cool her burning feet in the deep waters; she would then think of those beloved ones who dwelt in the lower world.

One night, as she was thus bathing her feet, her sisters swam together to the spot, arm in arm and singing, but, alas! so mournfully! She beckoned to them, and they immediately recognised her, and told her how great was the mourning in her father's house for her loss. From this time the sisters visited her every night; and once they brought with them the old grandmother, who had not seen the upper world for a great many years; they likewise brought their father, the Mer-king, with his crown on his head; but these two old people did not venture near enough to land to be able to speak to her.

The little Mermaiden became dearer and dearer to the Prince every day; but he only looked upon her as a sweet gentle child; and the thought of making her his wife never entered his head. And yet his wife she must be, ere she could receive an immortal soul; his wife she must be, or she would change into foam, and be driven restlessly over the billows of the sea!

"Dost thou not love me above all others?" her eyes seemed to ask, as he pressed her fondly in his arms, and kissed her lovely brow.

"Yes," the Prince would say, "thou art dearer to me than any other, for no one is as good as thou art! Thou lovest me so much; and thou art so like a young maiden, whom I have seen but once, and may never see again. I was on board a ship, which was wrecked by a sudden tempest; the waves threw me on the shore, near a holy temple, where a number of young girls are occupied constantly with religious services. The youngest of them found me on the shore, and saved my life. I saw her only once, but her image is vividly impressed upon my memory, and her alone can I love. But she belongs to the holy temple; and thou, who resemblest her so much, hast been given to me for consolation; never will we be parted!"

"Alas! he does not know that it was I who saved his

life," thought the little Mermaiden, sighing deeply; "I bore him over the wild waves, into the wooded bay, where the holy temple stood; I sat behind the rocks, waiting till some one should come. I saw the pretty maiden approach, whom he loves more than me,"—and again she heaved a deep sigh, for she could not weep,—"he said that the young girl belongs to the holy temple; she never comes out into the world, so they cannot meet each other again,—and I am always with him, see him daily; I will love him, and devote my whole life to him."

"So the Prince is going to be married to the beautiful daughter of the neighbouring king," said the courtiers; "that is why he is having that splendid ship fitted out. It is announced that he wishes to travel, but in reality he goes to see the princess; a numerous retinue will accompany him." The little Mermaiden smiled at these and similar conjectures, for she knew the Prince's intentions better than any one else.

"I must go," he said to her; "I must see the beautiful princess; my parents require me to do so; but they will not compel me to marry her, and bring her home as my bride. And it is quite impossible for me to love her, for she cannot be so like the beautiful girl in the temple as thou art; and if I were obliged to choose, I should prefer thee, my little silent foundling, with the speaking eyes." And he kissed her rosy lips, played with her locks, and folded her in his arms, whereupon arose in her heart a sweet vision of human happiness and immortal bliss.

"Thou art not afraid of the sea, art thou, my sweet, silent child?" asked he, tenderly, as they stood together in the splendid ship which was to take them to the country of the neighbouring king. And then he told her of the storms that sometimes agitate the waters, of the strange fishes that inhabit the deep, and of the wonderful things seen by divers. But she smiled at his words, for she knew better than any child of earth what went on in the depths of the ocean.

At night time, when the moon shone brightly, and when all on board were fast asleep, she sat in the ship's gallery, looking down into the sea. It seemed to her, as she gazed through the foamy track made by the ship's keel, that she saw her father's palace and her grandmother's silver crown. She then saw her sisters rise out of the water, looking sorrowful and stretching out their hands towards her. She nodded to them, smiled, and would have explained that everything was going on quite according to her wishes; but just then the cabin-boy approached, upon which the sisters plunged beneath the water so suddenly that the boy thought what he had seen on the waves was nothing but foam.

The next morning the ship entered the harbour of the King's splendid capital. Bells were rung, trumpets sounded, and soldiers marched in procession through the city, with waving banners and glittering bayonets. Every day witnessed some new entertainment; balls and parties followed each other; the princess, however, was not yet in the town; she had been sent to a distant convent for education, there to be taught the practice of all royal virtues. At last she arrived at the palace.

The little Mermaid had been anxious to see this unparalleled princess; and she was now obliged to confess that she had never before seen so beautiful a creature.

The skin of the Princess was so white and delicate that the veins might be seen through it, and her dark eyes sparkled beneath a pair of finely formed eye-brows.

"It is herself!" exclaimed the Prince, when they met; "it is she who saved my life, when I lay like a corpse on the sea-shore!" and he pressed his blushing bride to his beating heart.

"Oh, I am all too happy!" said he to his dumb foundling, "what I never dared to hope for has come to pass. Thou must rejoice in my happiness, for thou lovest me more than all others who surround me."—And the little Mermaid kissed his hand in silent sorrow; it seemed to her as if her heart was breaking already, although the morrow of his marriage-day, which must inevitably see her death, had not yet dawned.

Again rung the church-bells, whilst heralds rode through the streets of the capital, to announce the approaching bridal. Odorous flames burned in silver candlesticks on all the altars; the priests swung their golden censers, and bride and bridegroom joined hands, whilst the holy words that united them were spoken. The little Mermaid, clad in silk and cloth of gold, stood behind the Princess, and held the train of the bridal dress; but her ear heard nothing of the solemn music; her eye saw not the holy ceremony: she remembered her approaching end; she remembered that she had lost both this world and the next.

That very same evening, bride and bridegroom went on board the ship; cannons were fired, flags waved with the breeze, and in the centre of the deck was raised a magnificent pavilion of purple and cloth of gold, fitted up with the richest and softest couches. Here the princely pair were to spend the night. A favourable wind swelled the sails, and the ship glided lightly over the blue waters.

As soon as it was dark, coloured lamps were hung out, and dancing began on the deck. The little Mermaid was thus involuntarily reminded of what she had seen the first time she rose to the upper world. The spectacle that now presented itself was equally splendid—and she was obliged to join in the dance, hovering lightly as a bird over the ship boards. All applauded her, for never had she danced with more enchanting grace. Her little feet suffered extremely, but she no longer felt the pain; the anguish her heart suffered was much greater. It was the last evening she might see him for whose sake she had forsaken her home and family, had given away her beautiful voice, and suffered daily the most violent pain—all without his having the least suspicion of it. It was the last evening that she might breathe the same atmosphere in which he, the beloved one, lived,—the last evening when she might behold the deep blue sea and the starry heavens—an eternal night, in which she might neither think nor dream, awaited her. And all was joy in the ship; and she, her heart filled with thoughts of death and annihilation, smiled and danced with the others till past midnight. Then the Prince kissed his lovely bride, and arm in arm they entered the magnificent tent prepared for their repose.

All was now still; the steersman alone stood at the ship's helm. The little Mermaid leaned her white arms on the gallery, and looked towards the east, watching for the dawn; she well knew that the first sunbeam would witness her dissolution. She saw her sisters rise out of the sea; deadly pale were their features; and their long hair no more fluttered over their shoulders—it had all been cut off.

"We have given it to the witch," said they, "to induce her to help thee, so that thou mayest not die. She has given to us a penknife—here it is! Before the sun rises, thou must plunge it into the Prince's heart; and when his warm blood trickles down upon thy feet, they will again be changed to a fish-like tail; thou wilt once more become a mermaid, and wilt live thy full three hundred years, ere thou changest to foam on the sea. But hasten! either he or thou must die before sunrise. Our aged mother mourns for thee so much, her grey hair has fallen off through sorrow, as ours fell before the scissors of the witch. Kill the Prince, and come down to us! Hasten! hasten! dost thou not see the red streaks on the eastern sky, announcing the near approach of the sun? A few minutes more and he rises, and then all will be over with thee." At these words they sighed deeply and vanished.

The little Mermaid drew aside the purple curtains of the pavilion, where lay the bride and bridegroom; bending over them, she kissed the Prince's forehead, and then glancing at the sky, she saw that the dawning light became every moment brighter. The Prince's lips unconsciously murmured the name of his bride—he was dreaming of her, and her only, whilst the fatal penknife trembled in the hand of the unhappy Mermaid. All at once, she threw far out into the sea that instrument of death; the waves rose like bright blazing flames around, and the water where it fell seemed tinged with blood. With eyes fast becoming dim and fixed, she looked once more at her beloved Prince, then plunged from the ship into the sea, and felt her body slowly but surely dissolving into foam.

The sun rose from his watery bed; his beams fell so softly and warmly upon her, that our little Mermaid was scarcely sensible of dying. She still saw the glorious sun; and over her head hovered a thousand beautiful, transparent forms,—so transparent were they, that through them she could distinguish the white sails of the ship, and the bright red clouds in the sky; the voices of these airy creatures had a melody so sweet and soothing, that a human ear would be as little able to catch the sound as the eye to discern their forms; they hovered around her without wings, borne by their own lightness through the air. The little Mermaid at last saw that she had a body transparent as theirs, and felt herself raised gradually from the foam of the sea to higher regions.

"Where are they taking me?" asked she, and her accents sounded just like the voices of those heavenly beings.

"Speak you to the daughters of air?" was the answer. "The mermaid has no immortal soul, and can only acquire that heavenly gift by winning the love of one of the sons of men; her immortality depends upon union with man. Neither do the daughters of air possess immortal souls, but they can acquire them by their own good deeds. We fly to hot countries, where the children of earth are wasting away under sultry pestilential breezes—our fresh, cooling breath revives them. We diffuse ourselves through the atmosphere; we perfume it with the delicious fragrance of flowers; and thus spread delight and health over the earth. By doing good in this manner, for three hundred years, we win immortality, and receive a share of the eternal bliss of human beings. And thou, poor little Mermaid! who, following the impulse of thine own heart, hast done and suffered so much, thou art now raised to the airy world of spirits, that by performing deeds of kindness for three hundred years, thou mayest acquire an immortal soul."

The little Mermaid stretched out her transparent arms to the sun, and, for the first time in her life, tears moistened her eyes.

And now again all were awake and rejoicing in the ship; she saw the Prince, with his pretty bride; they had missed her; they looked sorrowfully down on the foamy waters, as if they knew she had plunged into the sea: unseen, she kissed the bridegroom's forehead, smiled upon him, and then, with the rest of the children of air, soared high above the rosy cloud which was sailing so peacefully over the ship.

"After three hundred years we shall fly in the kingdom of heaven!"

"We may arrive there even sooner," whispered one of her sisters. "We fly invisibly through the dwellings of men, where there are children; and whenever we find a good child, who gives pleasure to his parents and deserves their love, the good God shortens our time of probation. No child is aware that we are flitting about his room; and that whenever joy draws from us a smile, a year is struck out of our three hundred. But when we see a rude, naughty child, we weep bitter tears of sorrow, and every tear we shed adds a day to our time of probation."

THE STORKS.

ON the roof of a house situated at the extremity of a small town, a Stork had built his nest. There sat the mother-stork, with her four young ones, who all stretched out their little black bills, which had not yet become red. Not far off, upon the parapet, erect and proud, stood the father-stork; he had drawn one of his legs under him, being weary of standing on two. You might have fancied him carved in wood, he stood so motionless. "It looks so grand," thought he, "for my wife to have a sentinel to keep guard over her nest; people cannot know that I am her husband; they will certainly think that I am commanded to stand here— how well it looks!" and so he remained standing on one leg.

In the street below, a number of children were playing together. When they saw the storks, one of the liveliest amongst them began to sing as much as he could remember of some old rhymes about storks, in which he was soon joined by the others:—

"Stork! stork! long-legged stork!
Into thy nest I prithee walk;
There sits thy mate,
With her four children so great.

> The first we'll hang like a cat,
> The second we'll burn,
> The third on a spit we'll turn,
> The fourth drown dead as a rat!"

"Only listen to what the boys are singing," said the little Storks; "they say we shall be hanged and burnt!"

"Never mind," said the mother, "don't listen to them; they will do you no harm."

But the boys went on singing, and pointed their fingers at the storks: only one little boy, called Peter, said, "It was a sin to mock and tease animals, and that he would have nothing to do with it."

The mother-stork again tried to comfort her little ones. "Never mind," said she; "see how composedly your father is standing there, and upon one leg only."

"But we are so frightened!" said the young ones, drawing their heads down into the nest.

The next day, when the children were again assembled to play together, and saw the storks, they again began their song:—

> "The first we'll hang like a cat,
> The second we'll burn!"—

"And are we really to be hanged and burnt?" asked the young Storks.

"No, indeed!" said the mother. "You shall learn to fly: I will teach you myself. Then we can fly over to the meadow, and pay a visit to the frogs. They will bow to us in the water, and say, 'Croak, croak!' and then we shall eat them: will not that be nice?"

"And what then?" asked the little Storks.

"Then all the storks in the country will gather together, and the autumnal exercise will begin. It is of the greatest consequence that you should fly well then; for every one who does not, the general will stab to death with his bill; so you must pay great attention when we begin to drill you, and learn very quickly."

"Then we shall really be killed after all! as the boys said. Oh, listen! they are singing it again!"

"Attend to me, and not to them!" said the mother. "After the grand exercise, we shall fly to warm countries, far, far away from here, over mountains and forests. We shall fly to Egypt, where are the three-cornered stone houses whose summits reach the clouds: they are called pyramids, and are older than it is possible for storks to imagine. There is a river, too, which overflows its banks, so as to make the whole country like a marsh, and we shall go into the marsh and eat frogs."

"Oh!" said the young ones.

"Yes, it is delightful! one does nothing but eat all the day long. And whilst we are so comfortable, in this country not a single green leaf is left on the trees, and it is so cold that the clouds are frozen, and fall down upon the earth in little white pieces." She meant snow, but she could not express herself more clearly.

"And will the naughty boys be frozen to pieces too?" asked the young Storks.

"No, they will not be frozen to pieces; but they will be nearly as badly off as if they were; they will be obliged to crowd round the fire in their little dark rooms; while you, on the contrary, will be flying about in foreign lands, where there are beautiful flowers and warm sunshine."

Well, time passed away, and the young Storks grew so tall, that when they stood upright in the nests they could see the country around to a great distance. The father-stork used to bring them every day the nicest little frogs, as well as snails, and all the other stork-tit-bits he could find. Oh! it was so droll to see him show them his tricks; he would lay his head upon his tail, make a rattling noise with his bill, and then tell them such charming stories, all about the moors.

"Now you must learn to fly!" said the mother one day; and accordingly all the four young Storks were obliged to come out upon the parapet. Oh! how they trembled! And though they balanced themselves on their wings, they were very near falling.

"Only look at me," said the mother. "This is the way you must hold your heads; and in this manner place your feet—one, two! one, two! this will help you to get on." She flew a little way, and the young ones made an awkward spring after her,—bounce! down they fell; for their bodies were heavy.

"I will not fly!" said one of the young ones, as he crept

back into the nest; "I do not want to go into the warm countries!"

"Do you want to be frozen to death during the winter? shall the boys come, and hang, burn, or roast you? Wait a little, I will call them!"

"Oh no!" said the little Stork; and again he began to hop about on the roof like the others. By the third day they could fly pretty well, and so they thought they could also sit and take their ease in the air; but bounce! down they tumbled, and found themselves obliged to make use of their wings. The boys now came into their street, singing their favourite song,—

"Stork! stork! long-legged stork!"

"Shall not we fly down and peck out their eyes?" said the young ones.

"No, leave them alone!" said the mother. "Attend to me, that is of much more importance!—one, two, three, now to the right!—one, two, three, now to the left, round the chimney-pot! That was very well; you managed your wings so neatly last time, that I will permit you to come with me to-morrow to the marsh; several first-rate stork families will be there with their children. Let it be said that mine are the prettiest and best behaved of all; and remember to stand very upright, and to throw out your chest; that looks well, and gives such an air of distinction!"

"But are we not to take revenge upon those rude boys?" asked the young ones.

"Let them screech as much as they please! You will fly among the clouds, you will go to the lands of the pyramids, when they must shiver with cold, and have not a single green leaf to look at, nor a single sweet apple to eat!"

"Yes, we shall be revenged!" whispered they, one to another. And then they were drilled again.

Of all the boys in the town, the forwardest in singing nonsensical verses was always the same one who had begun teasing the storks, a little urchin not more than six years old. The young Storks, indeed, fancied him a hundred years old, because he was bigger than either their father or mother: and what should they know about the ages of children, or grown-up human beings! All their schemes of revenge were aimed at this little boy; he had been the first to tease them, and he teased them still. The young Storks were highly excited about it, and the older they grew, the less they were inclined to endure persecution. Their mother, in order to pacify them, at last promised that they should be revenged, but not until the last day of their stay in this place.

"We must first see how you behave yourselves at the grand exercise; if then you should fly badly, and the general should thrust his beak into your breast, the boys will, in some measure, be proved in the right. Let me see how well you will behave!"

"Yes, that you shall!" said the young ones. And now they really took great pains, practised every day, and at last flew so lightly and prettily, that it was a pleasure to see them.

Well, now came the autumn. All the storks assembled, in order to fly together to warm countries for the winter. What a practising there was! Away they went over woods and fields, towns and villages, merely to see how well they could fly, for they had a long journey before them. The young Storks distinguished themselves so honourably that they were pronounced "worthy of frogs and serpents." This was the highest character they could obtain; now they were allowed to eat frogs and serpents—and eat them they did.

"Now we will have our revenge!" said they.

"Very well!" said the mother; "I have been thinking what will be best. I know where is the pool, in which all the little human children lie until the storks come and take them to their parents: the pretty little things sleep and dream so pleasantly as they will never dream again. All parents like to have a little child, and all children like to have a little brother or sister. We will fly to the pool and fetch one for each of the boys who has not sung that wicked song, nor made a jest of the storks; and the other naughty children shall have none."

"But he who first sung those naughty rhymes—that great ugly fellow! what shall we do to him?" cried the young Storks.

"In the pool there lies a little child who has dreamed away his life; we will take it for him, and he will weep because he has only a little dead brother. But as to the good boy who said it was a sin to mock and tease animals, surely you have not forgotten him? We will bring him two little ones, a brother and a sister. And as this little boy's name is Peter, you, too, shall for the future be called 'Peter!'"

And it came to pass just as the mother said; and all the storks were called "Peter," and are still so called to this very day.

THE NIGHTINGALE.

IN China, as you well know, the Emperor is Chinese, and all around him are Chinese also.—Now what I am about to relate happened many years ago, but even on that very account it is the more important that you should hear the story at once, before it is forgotten.

The Emperor's palace was the most magnificent palace in the world; it was made entirely of fine porcelain, exceeding costly; but at the same time so brittle, that it was dangerous even to touch it.

The choicest flowers were to be seen in the garden; and to the most splendid of all these little silver bells were fastened, in order that their tinkling might prevent any one from passing by without noticing them. Yes! everything in the Emperor's garden was excellently well arranged; and the garden extended so far, that even the gardener did not know the end of it; whoever walked beyond it, however, came to a beautiful wood, with very high trees; and beyond that, to a lake. The wood went down quite to the lake, which was very deep and blue; large vessels could sail close under the branches; and among the branches dwelt a Nightingale, who sang so sweetly, that even the poor fisherman, who had so much else to do, when he came out at night-time to cast his nets, would stand still and listen to her song. "Oh! how pretty that is!" he would say; but then he was obliged to mind his work, and forget the bird. Yet the following night, if again the Nightingale sang, and the fisherman came out, again he would exclaim, "Oh! how pretty that is!"

Travellers came from all parts of the world to the Emperor's city; and they admired the city, the palace, and the garden; but if they heard the Nightingale, they said, "This is best of all." And they talked about her after they went home, and learned men wrote books about the city, the palace, and the garden; nor did they forget the Nightingale: she was extolled above everything else; and poets wrote the most beautiful verses about the Nightingale of the wood near the lake.

These books went round the world, and one of them at last reached the Emperor. He was sitting in his golden arm-chair; he read and read, and nodded his head every moment; for these splendid descriptions of the city, the palace, and the garden, pleased him greatly. "But there is nothing like the Nightingale," was written in the book.

"What in the world is this?" said the Emperor. "The Nightingale! I do not know it at all! Can there be such a bird in my empire, in my garden even, without my having heard of it? Truly, one may learn something from books."

So he called his Gentleman Usher. Now this was so grand a personage, that no one of inferior rank might speak to him; and if one did venture to ask him a question, his only answer was "Pish!" which has no particular meaning.

"There is said to be a very remarkable bird here, called the Nightingale," said the Emperor; "her song, they say, is worth more than anything else in all my dominions; why has no one ever told me of her?"

"I have never before heard her mentioned," said the Gentleman Usher; "she has never been presented at court."

"I wish her to come, and sing before me this evening," said the Emperor. "The whole world knows what I have, and I do not know it myself!"

"I have never before heard her mentioned," said the Gentleman Usher; "but I will seek her—I will find her."

But where was she to be found? The Gentleman Usher ran up one flight of steps, down another, through halls, and through passages; not one of all whom he met had ever heard of the Nightingale; and the Gentleman Usher returned to the Emperor, and said, "It must certainly be an invention of the man who wrote the book. Your Imperial Majesty must not believe all that is written in books; much in them is pure invention, and there is what is called the Black Art."

"But the book in which I have read it," returned the Emperor, "was sent me by the high and mighty Emperor of Japan, and therefore it cannot be untrue. I wish to hear the Nightingale; she must be here this evening; and if she do not come, after supper the whole court shall be flogged."

"Tsing-pe!" exclaimed the Gentleman Usher; and again he ran up-stairs and down-stairs, through halls and through passages, and half the court ran with him; for not one would have relished the flogging. Many were the questions asked respecting the wonderful Nightingale, whom the whole world talked of, and about whom no one at court knew anything.

At last they met a poor little girl in the kitchen, who said, "Oh yes, the Nightingale! I know her very well. Oh! how she can sing! Every evening I carry the fragments left at table to my poor sick mother. She lives by the lake-side, and when I am coming back, and stay to rest a little in the wood, I hear the Nightingale sing; it makes the tears come into my eyes! it is just as if my mother kissed me!"

"Little Kitchen-maiden," said the Gentleman Usher, "I will procure for you a sure appointment in the kitchen, together with permission to see His Majesty the Emperor dine, if you will conduct us to the Nightingale, for she is expected at court this evening."

So they went together to the wood, where the Nightingale was accustomed to sing; and half the court went with them. Whilst on their way, a cow began to low.

"Oh!" cried the court-pages, "now we have her! It is certainly an extraordinary voice for so small an animal; surely I have heard it somewhere before."

"No, those are cows you hear lowing," said the little Kitchen-maid; "we are still far from the place."

The frogs were now croaking in the pond.

"That is famous!" said the chief court-preacher; "now I hear her; it sounds just like little church-bells."

"No, those are frogs," said the little Kitchen-maid; "but now I think we shall soon hear her."

Then began the Nightingale to sing.

"There she is!" said the little girl: "listen! listen! there she sits;" and she pointed to a little grey bird up in the branches.

"Is it possible?" said the Gentleman Usher, "I should not have thought it. How simple she looks! she must certainly have changed colour at the sight of so many distinguished personages."

"Little Nightingale!" called out the Kitchen-maid, "our gracious Emperor wishes you to sing something to him."

"With the greatest pleasure," replied the Nightingale, and she sang in such a manner that it was delightful to hear her.

"It sounds like glass bells," said the Gentleman Usher. "And look at her little throat, how it moves! It is singular that we should never have heard her before; she will have great success at court."

"Shall I sing again to the Emperor?" asked the Nightingale, for she thought the Emperor was among them.

"Most excellent Nightingale!" said the Gentleman Usher, "I have the honour to invite you to a court-festival, which is to take place this evening, when His Imperial Majesty will doubtless be enchanted with your delightful song."

"My song would sound far better among the green trees," said the Nightingale: however she followed willingly when she heard that the Emperor wished it.

There was a general cleaning and polishing at the palace; the walls and the floors, which were all of porcelain, glittered with a thousand gold lamps; the loveliest flowers, with the merriest tinkling bells, were placed in the passages; there was a running to and fro, which made all the bells to ring, so that one could not hear one's own words.

In the midst of the grand hall, where the Emperor sat, a golden perch was erected, on which the Nightingale was to sit. The whole court was present, and the little Kitchen-maid received permission to stand behind the door, for she had now actually the rank and title of "Maid of the Kitchen."

All were dressed out in their finest clothes; and all eyes were fixed upon the little grey bird, to whom the Emperor nodded, as a signal for her to begin.

And the Nightingale sang so sweetly, that tears came into the Emperor's eyes, tears rolled down his cheeks; and the Nightingale sang more sweetly still, and touched the hearts of all who heard her; and the Emperor was so delighted, that he said, " The Nightingale should have his golden slippers, and wear them round her neck." But the Nightingale thanked him, and said she was already sufficiently rewarded.

" I have seen tears in the Emperor's eyes, that is the greatest reward I can have. The tears of an Emperor have a particular value; Heaven knows I am sufficiently rewarded." And then she sang again with her sweet, lovely voice.

" It is the most amiable coquetry ever known," said the ladies present; and they put water into their mouths, and tried to move their throats as she did, when they spoke; they thought to become nightingales also. Indeed, even the footmen and chambermaids declared that they were quite contented; which was a great thing to say, for of all people they are the most difficult to satisfy. Yes, indeed! the Nightingale's success was complete. She was now to remain at court, to have her own cage; with permission to fly out twice in the day, and once in the night. Twelve attendants were allotted her, who were to hold a silken band, fastened round her foot; and they kept good hold. There was no pleasure in excursions made in this manner.

All the city was talking of the wonderful bird; and when two persons met, one would say only " night," and the other " gale," and then they sighed, and understood each other perfectly; indeed eleven of the children of the citizens were named after the Nightingale, but none of them had her tones in their throats.

One day a large parcel arrived for the Emperor, on which was written " Nightingale."

" Here we have another new book about our far-famed bird," said the Emperor. But it was not a book; it was a little piece of mechanism, lying in a box; an artificial nightingale, which was intended to look like the living one: but was covered all over with diamonds, rubies, and sapphires. When this artificial bird had been wound up, it could sing one of the tunes that the real Nightingale sang; and its tail, all glittering with silver and gold, went up and down all the time. A little band was fastened round its neck, on which was written, " The Nightingale of the Emperor of Japan is poor compared with the Nightingale of the Emperor of China."

" That is famous!" said every one; and he who had brought the bird obtained the title of " Chief Imperial Nightingale Bringer." " Now they shall sing together; we will have a duet."

And so they must sing together; but it did not succeed, for the real Nightingale sang in her own way, and the artificial bird produced its tones by wheels. " It is not his fault," said the artist; " he keeps exact time, and quite according to method."

So the artificial bird must now sing alone; he was quite as successful as the real Nightingale; and then he was so much prettier to look at; his plumage sparkled with jewels.

Three-and-thirty times he sang one and the same tune, and yet he was not weary; every one would willingly have heard him again; however, the Emperor now wished the real Nightingale to sing something—but where was she? No one had remarked that she had flown out of the open window —flown away to her own green wood.

" What is the meaning of this?" said the Emperor; and all the courtiers abused the Nightingale and called her a most ungrateful creature. " We have the best bird, at all events," said they; and for the four-and-thirtieth time they heard the same tune, but still they did not quite know it, because it was so difficult. The artist praised the bird inordinately; indeed, he declared it was superior to the real Nightingale, not only in its exterior, all sparkling with diamonds, but also intrinsically.

" For see, my noble lords, his Imperial Majesty especially, with the real Nightingale one could never reckon on what was coming; but everything is settled with the artificial bird! he will sing in this one way, and no other: this can be proved; he can be taken to pieces, and the works can be shown—where the wheels lie, how they move, and how one follows from another."

" That is just what I think," said everybody; and the artist received permission to show the bird to the people on the following Sunday. " They, too, should hear him sing," the Emperor said. So they heard him, and were as well pleased as if they had all been drinking tea; for it is tea that makes Chinese merry, and they all said, "Oh!" and raised their fore-fingers, and nodded their heads. But the fisherman, who had heard the real Nightingale, said, "It sounds very pretty, almost like the real bird: but yet there is something wanting—I know not what."

The real Nightingale was, however, banished the empire.

The artificial bird had his place on a silken cushion, close to the Emperor's bed; all the presents he received, gold and precious stones, lay around him; he had obtained the rank and title of "High Imperial Dessert Singer," and, therefore, his place was number one on the left side; for the Emperor thought that the side where the heart was situated must be the place of honour, and the heart is situated on the left side of an Emperor, as well as with other folks.

And the artist wrote five-and-twenty volumes about the artificial bird, with the longest and most difficult words that are to be found in the Chinese language. So, of course, all said they had read and understood them, otherwise they would have been stupid, and perhaps would have been flogged.

Thus it went on for a whole year. The Emperor, the court, and all the Chinese, knew every note of the artificial bird's song by heart; but that was the very reason they enjoyed it so much; they could now sing with him. The little boys in the street sang "Zizizi, cluck, cluck, cluck!" and the Emperor himself sang too—yes, indeed, that was charming!

But one evening, when the bird was in full voice, and the Emperor lay in bed and listened, there was suddenly a noise, "bang," inside the bird, then something sprang "sur-r-r--r," all the wheels were running about, and the music stopped.

The Emperor jumped quickly out of bed, and had his chief physician called; but of what use could he be? Then a clockmaker was fetched, and at last, after a great deal of discussion and consultation, the bird was in some measure put to rights again; but the clockmaker said, he must be spared much singing, for the pegs were almost worn out, and it was impossible to renew them, at least so that the music should be correct.

There was great lamentation, for now the artificial bird was allowed to sing only once a-year, and even then there were difficulties; however, the artist made a short speech full of his favourite long words, and said the bird was as good as ever: so then, of course, it was as good as ever.

When five years were passed away, a great affliction visited the whole empire, for in their hearts the people thought highly of their Emperor; and now he was ill, and it was reported that he could not live. A new Emperor had already been chosen, and the people stood in the street, outside the palace, and asked the Gentleman Usher how the Emperor was?

"Pish!" said he, and shook his head.

Cold and pale lay the Emperor in his magnificent bed; all the court believed him to be already dead, and every one had hastened away to greet the new Emperor; the men ran out for a little gossip on the subject, and the maids were having a grand coffee-party.

The floors of all the rooms and passages were covered with cloth, in order that not a step should be heard—it was everywhere so still! so very still! But the Emperor was not yet dead; stiff and pale he lay in his splendid bed, with the long velvet curtains and heavy gold tassels. A window was opened above, and the moon shone down on the Emperor and the artificial bird.

The poor Emperor could scarcely breathe; it appeared to him as though something were sitting on his chest; he opened his eyes, and saw that it was Death, who had put on the Emperor's crown, and held with one hand the golden scimetar, with the other the splendid imperial banner; whilst, from under the folds of the thick velvet hangings, the strangest-looking heads were seen peering forth; some with an expression absolutely hideous, and others with an extremely gentle and lovely aspect: they were the bad and good deeds of the Emperor, which were now all fixing their eyes upon him, whilst Death sat on his heart.

"Recollectest thou this?" whispered they one after another. "Dost thou remember that?" And thus they went on reproaching him until the sweat broke out upon his forehead.

"I have never known anything like it," said the Emperor. "Music, music, the great Chinese drum!" cried he; "let me not hear what they are saying."

But they went on; and Death, quite in Chinese fashion, nodded his head to every word.

"Music, music!" cried the Emperor. "Thou dear little artificial bird! sing, I pray thee, sing!—I have given thee gold and precious stones, I have even hung my golden slippers round thy neck—sing, I pray thee, sing!"

But the bird was silent: there was no one there to wind him up, and he could not sing without. Death continued to stare at the Emperor with his great hollow eyes! and everywhere it was still, fearfully still!

All at once the sweetest song was heard from the window, it was the little living Nightingale who was sitting on a branch outside—she had heard of her Emperor's severe illness, and was come to sing to him of comfort and hope. As she sang, the spectral forms became paler and paler, the blood flowed more and more quickly through the Emperor's feeble limbs, and even Death listened and said, "Go on, little Nightingale, go on."

"Wilt thou give me the splendid gold scimetar? Wilt thou give me the gay banner, and the Emperor's crown?"

And Death gave up all these treasures for a song; and the Nightingale sang on: she sang of the quiet churchyard, where white roses blossom, where the elder-tree sends forth its fragrance, and the fresh grass is bedewed with the tears of the sorrowing friends of the departed. Then Death was seized with a longing after his garden, and like a cold, white shadow flew out at the window.

"Thanks, thanks!" said the Emperor; "thou heavenly little bird, I know thee well! I have banished thee from my realm, and thou hast sung away those evil faces from my bed, and Death from my heart; how shall I reward thee?"

"Thou hast already rewarded me," said the Nightingale; "I have seen tears in thine eyes, as when I sang to thee for the first time: those I shall never forget; they are jewels which do so much good to a minstrel's heart! but sleep now, and wake fresh and healthy: I will sing thee to sleep."

And she sang—and the Emperor fell into a sweet sleep. Oh, how soft and kindly was that sleep!

The sun shone in at the window when he awoke, strong and healthy. Not one of his servants had returned, for they all believed him dead; but the Nightingale still sat and sang.

"Thou shalt always stay with me," said the Emperor;

"thou shalt only sing when it pleases thee, and the artificial bird I will break into a thousand pieces."

"Do not so," said the Nightingale; "truly he has done what he could; take care of him. I cannot stay in the palace; but let me come when I like: I will sit on the branches close to the window, in the evening, and sing to thee, that thou mayest become happy and thoughtful. I will sing to thee of the joyful and the sorrowing, I will sing to thee of all that is good or bad, which is concealed from thee. The little minstrel flies afar to the fisherman's hut, to the peasant's cottage, to all who are far distant from thee and thy court. I love thy heart more than thy crown, and yet the crown has an odour of something holy about it. I will come, I will sing. But thou must promise me one thing."

"Everything," said the Emperor. And now he stood in his imperial splendour which he had put on himself, and held the scimetar so heavy with gold to his heart. "One thing I beg of thee: let no one know that thou hast a little bird, who tells thee everything—then all will go on well." And the Nightingale flew away.

The attendants came in to look at their dead Emperor—lo! there they stood—and the Emperor said, "Good morning!"

LITTLE IDA'S FLOWERS.

"MY poor flowers are quite faded!" said little Ida. "Only yesterday evening they were so pretty, and now they are all drooping! What can be the reason of it?" asked she of the Student, who was sitting on the sofa, and who was a great favourite with her, because he used to tell her stories, and cut out all sorts of pretty things for her in paper; such as hearts with little ladies dancing in them, high castles with open doors, &c. "Why do these flowers look so deplorable?" asked she again, showing him a bouquet of faded flowers.

"Do you not know?" replied the Student. "Your flowers went to a ball last night, and are tired; that is why they all hang their heads."

"Surely flowers cannot dance!" exclaimed little Ida.

"Of course they can dance! When it is dark, and we are all gone to bed, they jump about as merrily as possible. They have a ball almost every night."

"May their children go to the ball, too?" asked Ida.

"Yes," said the Student; "little daisies, and lilies of the valley."

"And where do the prettiest flowers dance?"

"Have you never been in the large garden in front of the King's beautiful summer palace, the garden so full of flowers? Surely you recollect the swans which come swimming up to you, when you throw them crumbs of bread? There you may imagine they have splendid balls."

"I was there yesterday with my mother," said Ida, "but there were no leaves on the trees, neither did I see a single flower. What could have become of them? There were so many in the summer time!"

"They are now at the palace," answered the Student. "As soon as the King leaves his summer residence, and returns with all his court to the town, the flowers likewise hasten out of the garden and into the palace, where they enjoy themselves famously. Oh, if you could but see them! The two loveliest roses sit on the throne, and act King and Queen. The red cockscombs then arrange themselves in rows before them, bowing very low; they are the gentlemen of the bedchamber. After that the prettiest among the flowers come in, and open the ball. The blue violets represent midshipmen, and begin dancing with the hyacinths and crocuses, who take the part of young ladies. The tulips and the tall orange-lilies are old dowagers, whose business it is to see that everything goes on with perfect propriety."

"But," asked the astonished little Ida, "may the flowers give their ball in the King's palace?"

"No one knows anything about it," replied the Student. "Perhaps once during the night the old Castellan may come in, with his great bunch of keys, to see that all is right; but as soon as the flowers hear the clanking of the keys they are quite still, and hide themselves behind the long silk window-curtains. 'I smell flowers here,' says the old Castellan, but he is not able to find them."

"That is very funny," said Ida, clapping her little hands; "but could not I see the flowers?"

"To be sure you can see them!" returned the Student. "You have only to peep in at the window next time you go to the palace. I did so to-day, and saw a long yellow lily lying on the sofa. That was a court lady."

"Can the flowers in the Botanic Garden go there, too? Can they go so far?" asked Ida.

"Certainly, for flowers can fly if they wish it. The pretty red and yellow butterflies, that look so much like flowers, are in fact nothing else. They jump from their stalks, move their petals as if they were little wings, and fly about; as a reward for always behaving themselves well, they are allowed, instead of sitting quietly on their stalks, to flutter hither and thither all day long, till wings actually grow out of their petals. You have often seen it yourself. For the rest, it may be that the flowers in the Botanic Garden have not heard what merry-making goes on every night at the palace; but I assure you, if next time you go into the garden, you whisper to one of the flowers, that a ball is to be given at night at Fredericksberg, the news will be repeated from flower to flower, and thither they will all fly to a certainty. Then, should the Professor come into the garden, and find all his flowers gone, he will not be able to imagine what is become of them."

"Indeed!" said Ida; "and, pray, how can the flowers repeat to each other what I say to them? I am sure that flowers cannot speak."

"No, they cannot speak—you are right there," returned the Student; "but they make themselves understood by pantomime. Have you never seen them move to and fro at the least breath of air? They can understand each other this way as well as we can by talking."

"And does the Professor understand their pantomime?" asked Ida.

"Oh, certainly! One morning he came into the garden, and perceived that a tall nettle was conversing in pantomime with a pretty red carnation. 'Thou art so beautiful,' said he to the carnation, 'and I love thee so much!' But the Professor could not allow such things, so he gave a rap at the nettle's leaves, which are his fingers, and in doing so he stung himself, and since then has never dared to touch a nettle."

"Ah, ah!" laughed little Ida; "that was very droll."

"What do you mean by this?" here interrupted the tedious Counsellor, who had come on a visit; "putting such trash into the child's head!" He could not endure the Student, and always used to scold when he saw him cutting out pasteboard figures; as for instance, a man on the gallows holding a heart in his hand, which was meant for a heart-stealer; or an old witch, riding on a broomstick, and carrying her husband on the tip of her nose. He used always to say then as now: "What do you mean by putting such trash into the child's head? It is all fantastical nonsense!"

However, little Ida thought what the Student had told her about the flowers was very droll, and she could not leave off thinking of it. She was now sure that her flowers hung their heads because they were tired with dancing so much the night before. So she took them to the pretty little table, where her playthings were arranged. Her doll lay sleeping in the cradle, but Ida said to her, "You must get up, Sophy, and be content to sleep to-night in the table-drawer, for the poor flowers are ill, and must sleep in your bed: perhaps they will be well again by to-morrow." She then took the doll out of the bed; but the good lady looked vexed at having to give up her cradle to the flowers.

Ida then laid the faded flowers in her doll's bed, drew the covering over them, and told them to lie quite still, whilst she made some tea for them to drink, in order that they might be well again the next day. And she drew the curtains round the bed, that the sun might not dazzle their eyes.

All the evening she thought of nothing but the Student's words, and just before she went to bed she ran up to the window, where her mother's tulips and hyacinths stood, behind the blinds, and whispered to them, "I know very well that you are going to a ball to-night." But the flowers moved not a leaf, and seemed not to have heard her.

After she was in bed, she thought for a long time how delightful it must be to see the flowers dancing in the palace, and said to herself, "I wonder whether my flowers have been there?" but before she could determine the point, she fell asleep. During the night she awoke; she had been dreaming of the Student and the flowers, and of the Counsellor, who told her that they were making game of her. All was still in the room, the night-lamp was burning on the table, and her father and mother were both asleep.

"I wonder whether my flowers are still lying in Sophy's bed?" said she. "I should very much like to know." She raised herself a little, and looking towards the door, which stood half open, she saw that the flowers and all her playthings were just as she had left them. She listened, and it seemed to her as if some one must be playing on the harpsichord; but the tones were lower and sweeter than she had ever heard before.

"Now my flowers must certainly be dancing," said she. "Oh, how I should like to see them!" but she dared not get up, for fear of waking her father and mother. "If they would only come in here!" Still the flowers did not come, and the music sounded so sweetly. At last she could restrain herself no longer, she must see the dancing. So she crept lightly out of the bed, and stole towards the door of the room. Oh, what wonderful things she saw then!

There was no night-lamp burning here; however, it was quite light in the room, for the moon shone brightly through the windows on the floor. All the hyacinths and tulips stood there in two rows, whilst their empty pots might still be seen in front of the windows; they performed figures, and took hold of each other by the long green leaves. At the harpsichord sat a large yellow lily, which Ida fancied she must have seen before, for she remembered the Student's saying that this flower was exceedingly like Miss Laura, and how every one had laughed at his remark. Now she herself agreed that the lily did resemble this young lady, for she had exactly her way of playing, bowing her long yellow face now on one side, now on the other, and nodding her head to mark the time. A tall blue crocus now stepped forward, sprang upon the table on which lay Ida's playthings, went straight up to the bed, and drew back the curtains. There lay the sick flowers, but they rose immediately, and greeted the other flowers, who invited them to dance with them. The sick flowers appeared quite well again, and danced as merrily as the rest.

Suddenly a heavy noise, as of something falling from the table, was heard. Ida cast a glance that way, and saw that it was the rod which she had found on her bed on the morning of Shrove Tuesday, and which seemed desirous of ranking itself among the flowers. It was certainly a very pretty rod, for a wax doll was fixed on the top, wearing a hat as broad-brimmed as the Counsellor's, with a blue-and-red ribbon tied round it. It hopped upon its three red stilts in the middle of the flowers, and stamped the floor merrily with its feet. It was dancing the Mazurka, which the flowers could not dance, they were too light-footed to stamp.

All at once, the wax-doll on the rod swelled out to a giant, tall and broad, and exclaimed in a loud voice, " What do you mean by putting such trash into the child's head? It is all fantastical nonsense!" And now the doll looked as much like the Counsellor in his broad-brimmed hat, as one drop of water resembles another; her countenance looked as yellow and peevish as his: the paper flowers on the rod, however, pinched her thin legs, whereupon she shrunk up to her original size The little Ida thought this scene so droll that she could not help laughing; the ball company, however, did not notice it, and the rod continued to stamp about, till at last the doll-counsellor was obliged to dance too, whether she would or no, and make herself now thin, now thick, now tall, now short, till at last the flowers interceded for her, and the rod then left her in peace.

A loud knocking was now heard from the drawer in which lay Ida's doll. It was Sophy who made the noise. She put her head out of the drawer and asked, in great astonishment, " Is there a ball here? why has no one told me of it?"

" Will you dance with me?" asked the nutcrackers.

" Certainly you are a very fit person to dance with me!" said Sophy, turning her back upon him. She then sat down on the table, expecting that one of the flowers would come and ask her to dance, but no one came.—She coughed— " hem! hem!" still no one came. Meantime the nutcrackers danced by himself, and his steps were not at all badly made.

As no flowers came forward to ask Sophy to dance, all at once she let herself fall down upon the floor, which excited a general commotion, so that all the flowers ran up to ask her whether she had hurt herself. But she had received no injury. The flowers, however, were all very polite, especially Ida's flowers, who took the opportunity of thanking her for the comfortable bed in which they had slept so quietly, and then seized her hands to dance with her, whilst all the other flowers stood in a circle round them. Sophy was now quite happy, and begged Ida's flowers to make use of her bed again after the ball, as she did not at all mind sleeping one night in the table-drawer.

But the flowers said, " We owe you many thanks for your kindness, we shall not live long enough to need it; we shall be quite dead by to-morrow· but request the little Ida to bury us in the garden near her canary-bird, then we shall grow again next summer, and be even more beautiful than we have been this year."

"No, you must not die!" replied Sophy warmly, as she kissed the flowers. Just then the door was suddenly opened, and a number of flowers danced into the room. Ida could not conceive where these flowers came from, unless from the King's garden. First of all entered two beautiful roses wearing golden crowns, then followed stocks and pinks, bowing to the company on all sides. They had also a band of music with them; great poppies and peonies blew upon pea-shells till they were quite red in the face, whilst blue and white campanulas rang a merry peal of bells. These were followed by an immense number of different flowers, all dancing; violets, daisies, lilies of the valley, narcissuses, and others, who all moved so gracefully, that it was delightful to see them.

At last, these happy flowers wished one another "good night;" so little Ida once more crept into bed to dream of all the beautiful things she had seen.

The next morning, as soon as she was up and dressed, she went to her little table to see if her flowers were there. She drew aside the bed-curtains—yes! there lay the flowers, but they were to-day much more faded than yesterday; Sophy too was lying in the drawer, but she looked uncommonly sleepy.

"Can you not remember what you have to say to me?" asked little Ida of her; but Sophy made a most stupid face, and answered not a syllable.

"You are not at all good!" said Ida; "and yet all the flowers let you dance with them." She then chose out from her playthings a little pasteboard box with birds painted on it, and therein she placed the faded flowers. "That shall be your coffin," said she, "and when my Norwegian cousins come to see me, they shall go with me to bury you in the garden, in order that next summer you may bloom again, and be still more beautiful than you have been this year."

The two Norwegian cousins, of whom she spoke, were two lively boys, called Jonas and Adolph. Their father had given them two new cross-bows, which they brought with them to show to Ida. She told them of the poor flowers that were dead, and were to be buried in the garden. The two boys walked in front with their bows slung across their shoulders, and little Ida followed carrying the dead flowers in their pretty coffin. A grave was dug for them in the garden. Ida kissed the flowers once more, then laid the box down in the hollow, and Jonas and Adolph shot arrows over the grave with their cross-bows, for they had neither guns nor cannon

THE SWINEHERD.

THERE was once a poor Prince, who had a kingdom; his kingdom was very small, but still quite large enough to marry upon; and he wished to marry.

It was certainly rather cool of him to say to the Emperor's daughter, "Will you have me?" But so he did; for his name was renowned far and wide; and there were a hundred Princesses who would have answered "Yes!" and "Thank you kindly." We shall see what this Princess said. Listen!

It happened, that where the Prince's father lay buried there grew a rose-tree—a most beautiful rose-tree, which blossomed only once in every five years, and even then bore only one flower, but that *was* a rose! It smelt so sweet, that all cares and sorrows were forgotten by him who inhaled its fragrance.

And furthermore, the Prince had a nightingale, who could sing in such a manner that it seemed as though all sweet melodies dwelt in her little throat. So the Princess was to have the rose, and the nightingale; and they were accordingly put into large silver caskets, and sent to her.

The Emperor had them brought into a large hall, whethe Princess was playing at "Visiting," with the ladies of the court; and when she saw the caskets with the presents, she clapped her hands for joy.

"Ah, if it were but a little pussy-cat!" exclaimed she but the rose-tree, with its beautiful rose, came to view.

"Oh, how prettily it is made!" said all the court-ladies.

"It is more than pretty," said the Emperor; "it is charming!"

But the Princess touched it, and was almost ready to cry.

"Fie, papa!" said she, "it is not made at all, it is natural!"

"Fie!" cried all the courtiers, "it is natural!"

"Let us see what is in the other casket, before we get into a bad humour," proposed the Emperor. So the nightingale came forth, and sang so delightfully that at first no one could say anything ill-humoured of her.

"*Superbe! charmant!*" exclaimed the ladies; for they all used to chatter French, each one worse than her neighbour.

"How much the bird reminds me of the musical box, that belonged to our blessed Empress!" remarked an old Knight. "Oh yes! these are the same tones, the same execution."

"Yes! yes!" said the Emperor, and he wept like a child at the remembrance.

"I will still hope that it is not a real bird," said the Princess.

"Yet it is a real bird," said those who had brought it.

"Well, then let the bird fly," returned the Princess; and she positively refused to see the Prince.

However, he was not to be discouraged; he daubed his face over brown and black; pulled his cap over his ears, and knocked at the door.

"Good day to my lord the Emperor!" said he. "Can I have employment at the palace?"

"Why, yes," said the Emperor; "I want some one to take care of the pigs, for we have a great many of them."

So the Prince was appointed "Imperial Swineherd." He had a dirty little room close by the pigsty; and there he sat the whole day, and worked. By the evening, he had made a pretty little saucepan. Little bells were hung all round it; and when the pot was boiling, these bells tinkled in the most charming manner, and played the old melody:—

> Ach! du lieber Augustin,
> Alles ist weg, weg, weg!" *

But what was still more curious, whoever held his finger in the smoke of this saucepan, immediately smelt all the dishes that were cooking on every hearth in the city: this, you see, was something quite different from the rose.

Now the Princess happened to walk that way; and when she heard the tune, she stood quite still, and seemed pleased; for she could play "Lieber Augustin;" it was the only piece she knew, and she played it with one finger.

"Why, there is my piece!" said the Princess; "that swineherd must certainly have been well educated! Go in and ask him the price of the instrument."

So one of the court-ladies must run in; however, she drew on wooden slippers first.

"What will you take for the saucepan?" inquired the lady.

"I will have ten kisses from the Princess," said the swineherd.

"Yes, indeed!" said the lady.

"I cannot sell it for less," rejoined the swineherd.

"Well, what does he say?" asked the Princess.

"I cannot tell you, really," replied the lady; "it is too bad!"

"Then you can whisper it!" So the lady whispered it.

"He is an impudent fellow!" said the Princess, and she walked on; but when she had gone a little way, the bells tinkled so prettily,

> "Ach! du lieber Augustin,
> Alles ist weg, weg, weg!"

"Stay," said the Princess. "Ask him if he will have ten kisses from the ladies of my court."

"No, thank you!" answered the swineherd: "ten kisses from the Princess, or I keep the saucepan myself."

"That must not be either!" said the Princess; "but do you all stand before me, that no one may see us."

And the court-ladies placed themselves in front of her, and spread out their dresses; the swineherd got ten kisses, and the Princess—the saucepan.

That was delightful! the saucepan was kept boiling all the evening, and the whole of the following day. They knew perfectly well what was cooking at every fire throughout the

* "Ah! dear Augustine!
All is lost, lost, lost!"

city, from the chamberlain's to the cobbler's; the court-ladies danced, and clapped their hands.

"We know who has soup and who has pancakes for dinner to-day, who has cutlets, and who has eggs. How interesting!"

"Yes, but keep my secret, for I am an Emperor's daughter.'

The swineherd—that is to say the Prince, for no one knew that he was other than an ill-favoured swineherd,—let not a day pass without working at something; he at last constructed a rattle, which, when it was swung round, played all the waltzes and jig-tunes which have ever been heard since the creation of the world.

"Ah, that is *superbe!*" said the Princess when she passed by; "I have never heard prettier compositions! Go in and ask him the price of the instrument; but mind, he shall have no more kisses!"

"He will have a hundred kisses from the Princess!" said the lady who had been to ask.

"I think he is not in his right senses!" replied the Princess, and walked on: but when she had gone a little way, she stopped again. "One must encourage art," said she; "I am the Emperor's daughter. Tell him, he shall, as on yesterday, have ten kisses from me, and may take the rest from the ladies of the court."

"Oh!—but we should not like that at all!" said they. "What are you muttering?" asked the Princess; "if I can kiss him, surely you can! Remember that you owe everything to me." So the ladies were obliged to go to him again.

"A hundred kisses from the Princess!" said he, "or else let every one keep his own."

"Stand round!" said she; and all the ladies stood round her whilst the kissing was going on.

"What can be the reason for such a crowd close by the pigsty?" said the Emperor, who happened just then to step out on the balcony; he rubbed his eyes and put on his spectacles. "They are the ladies of the court; I must go down and see what they are about!" So he pulled up his slippers at the heel, for he had trodden them down.

As soon as he had got into the court-yard, he moved very softly, and the ladies were so much engrossed with counting the kisses, that all might go on fairly, that they did not perceive the Emperor. He rose on his tip-toes.

THE SWINEHERD.

Page 76.

"What is all this?" said he, when he saw what was going on, and he boxed the Princess's ears with his slipper, just as the swineherd was taking the eighty-sixth kiss.

"March out!" cried the Emperor, for he was very angry; and both Princess and swineherd were thrust out of the city.

The Princess now stood and wept, the swineherd scolded, and the rain poured down.

"Alas! unhappy creature that I am!" said the Princess. "If I had but married the handsome young Prince! Ah! how unfortunate I am!"

And the swineherd went behind a tree, washed the black-and-brown colour from his face, threw off his dirty clothes, and stepped forth in his princely robes; he looked so noble that the Princess could not help bowing before him.

"I am come to despise thee," said he. "Thou wouldst not have an honourable prince! thou couldst not prize the rose and the nightingale, but thou wast ready to kiss the swineherd for the sake of a trumpery plaything. Thou art rightly served."

He then went back to his own little kingdom, and shut the door of his palace in her face. Now she might well sing

"Ach! du lieber Augustin,
Alles ist weg, weg, weg!"

OLE LUCKÖIE; OR, THE DUSTMAN.

THERE is no one in the whole world who knows so many stories as Ole Lucköie, the Dustman — Oh! his are delightful stories.

In the evening, when children are sitting quietly at table, or on their little stools, he takes off his shoes, comes softly up-stairs, opens the door very gently, and all on a sudden throws dust into the children's eyes. He then glides behind them, and breathes lightly, very lightly, upon their necks, whereupon their heads become immediately so heavy! But it does them no harm, for the Dustman means it kindly; he only wants the children to be quiet, and they are most quiet when they are in bed. They must be quiet, in order that he may tell them his stories.

When the children are asleep, the Dustman sits down upon the bed; he is gaily dressed, his coat is of silk, but of what colour it is impossible to say, for it seems now green, now red, now blue, according to the light. Under each arm he holds an umbrella; one, which has pictures painted on it, he holds over good children, it makes them have the most delightful dreams all night long; and the other, which has nothing on it, he holds over naughty children, so that they sleep heavily, and awake in the morning without having dreamed at all.

Now let us hear what stories the Dustman told to a little boy of the name of Hialmar, to whom he came every evening for a whole week through. There are seven stories altogether, for the week has seven days.

Monday.

" Listen to me," said Ole Lucköie, as soon as he had got Hialmar into bed. " Now I will decorate your room ;" and all at once as he was speaking, the flowers in the flower-pots grew up into large trees, whose long branches extended to the ceiling, and along the walls, so that the room looked like a beautiful arbour. All these branches were full of flowers, and every flower was more beautiful even than the rose, and had so pleasant a smell. Moreover, could you have tasted them you would have found them sweeter than preserves. And fruit which shone like gold hung from the trees, also dumplings full of currants: never was the like seen before. But, at the same time, a loud lamentation was heard in the table-drawer, where Hialmar's school-books were kept.

" What is the matter ?" said the Dustman, going up to the table, and taking out the drawer. There lay the slate, on which the figures were pressing and squeezing together, because a wrong figure had got into the sum, so that it was near falling to pieces ; the pencil hopped and skipped about like a little dog—he wanted to help the sum, but he could not. And a little farther off lay Hialmar's copy-book : a complaining and moaning came thence also, it was quite unpleasant to hear it ; at the beginning of every line on each page, there stood a large letter with a little letter by its side ; this was the copy : and after them stood other letters, intended to look like the copy. Hialmar had written these ; but they seemed to have fallen over the lines, upon which they ought to have stood.

" Look, this is the way you must hold yourselves," said the copy ; " look slanting—just so, and turning round with a jerk."

" Oh ! we would do so willingly," said Hialmar's letters ; " but we cannot, we are so badly made !"

"Then you shall have some of the children's powders," said the Dustman.

"Oh no!" cried they, and stood so straight that it was a pleasure to see them.

"Well, I cannot tell you any more stories now," said the Dustman; "I must drill these letters: right, left—right, left!" So he drilled the letters till they looked as straight and perfect as only the letters in a copy can be. However, after the Dustman had gone away, and when Hialmar looked at them the next morning, they were as miserable and badly formed as before.

Tuesday.

As soon as Hialmar was in bed, the Dustman touched with his little magic wand all the pieces of furniture in the room; whereupon they all began to talk; and they all talked about themselves, excepting the spittoon, who stood quite still, and was much vexed at their being so vain, all talking about themselves without ever thinking of him who stood so modestly in the corner, and suffered himself to be spat upon.

Over the wardrobe there hung a large picture in a gilt frame, it was a landscape: there you might see tall trees, flowers blossoming in the grass, and a river that wound itself round the wood, passing many a grand old castle on its way to the sea.

The Dustman touched the picture with his magic wand; and immediately the birds began to sing, the boughs of the trees waved to and fro, and the clouds actually flew; one could see their shadows flit over the landscape.

The Dustman then lifted little Hialmar up to the frame, and Hialmar put his legs into the picture: there he stood amid the tall grass. He ran to the water's edge, and sat down in a little boat, painted red and white, with sails glittering like silver; six swans, with golden wreaths round their necks, and bright blue stars upon their heads, drew the boat along, near a green wood, where the trees were telling stories about robbers and witches, and the flowers were talking of the pretty little fairies, and of what the butterflies had said to them.

Most beautiful fishes, with scales like gold and silver, swam behind the boat, every now and then leaping up, so that the water was splashed over Hialmar's head; birds red and blue, great and small, flew after him in two long rows; the gnats danced, and the cockchafers said, "Boom, boom." They all wished to accompany Hialmar, and every one of them had a story to tell.

A pleasant voyage was that! The woods were now thick and gloomy, now like beautiful gardens beaming with flowers and sunshine. Large palaces built of glass or marble rose from among the trees; young princesses stood in the balconies—these were all little girls whom Hialmar knew well, and with whom he had often played. They stretched out their hands to him, each holding a pretty little image made of sugar, such as are seen in confectioners' shops. Hialmar seized the end of one of these little images as he sailed by, and a princess kept hold of the other, so each got half, the princess the smaller, Hialmar the larger. At every castle little princes were keeping guard; they shouldered their golden scimetars, and showered down raisins and tin-soldiers —these were real princes! Hialmar sailed sometimes through woods, sometimes through large halls, or the middle of a town. Among others, he passed through the town where his nurse lived—she who had brought him up from his infancy, and who loved him so much. She nodded and beckoned to him as he passed by, and sang the pretty verses she had herself composed and sent to him:—

"How many, many hours I think on thee,
  My own dear Hialmar, still my pride and joy!
How have I hung delighted over thee,
  Kissing thy rosy cheeks, my darling boy!

Thy first low accents it was mine to hear,
  To-day my farewell words to thee shall fly.
Oh! may the Lord thy shield be ever near,
  And fit thee for a mansion in the sky!"

And all the birds sang with her, the flowers danced upon their stalks, and the old trees nodded their heads, whilst the Dustman told stories to them also.

WEDNESDAY.

Oh, how the rain was pouring down! Hialmar could hear it even in his sleep, and when the Dustman opened the window the water came in upon the ledge; there was quite a lake in front of the house, and on it a splendid ship.

"Will you sail with me, little Hialmar?" said the Dustman; "if you will, you shall visit foreign lands to-night, and be here again by the morning."

And now Hialmar, dressed in his Sunday clothes, was in the ship: the weather immediately cleared up, and they floated down the street, cruised round the church, and were soon sailing upon the wide sea. They quickly lost sight of land, nd could see only a number of storks, who had all come from Hialmar's country, and were going to a warmer one. The storks were flying one after another, and were already very far from land. One of them, however, was so weary, that his wings could scarcely bear him up any longer; he was last in the train, and was soon far behind the others; he sank lower and lower, with his wings outspread; he still endeavoured to move them, but in vain; his wings touched the ship's cordage, he slid down the sail, and—bounce! there he stood on the deck.

So the cabin-boy put him into the place where the hens, ducks, and turkeys were kept; the poor Stork stood amongst them quite confounded.

"Only look, what a foolish fellow!" said all the Hens. And the Turkeycock made himself as big as he could, and asked him who he was; and the Ducks waddled backwards and pushed each other, crying, "Quack, quack!"

The Stork then told them about his warm Africa, about the pyramids, and about the ostrich, who races through the desert like a wild horse; but the Ducks did not understand him, and again pushed each other, saying, "Do not we all agree in thinking him very stupid?"

"Yes, indeed, he is stupid!" said the Turkeycock, and began to gobble.

So the Stork was silent, and thought of his Africa. "You have really very pretty slender legs!" said the Turkeycock. "What did they cost you per yard?"

"Quack, quack, quack!" all the Ducks began to titter; but the Stork seemed not to have heard the question.

"You might just as well have laughed with them," said the Turkeycock to him, "for it was a capital joke! But perhaps it was not high enough for you? Ah! ah! he has very grand ideas; let us go on amusing ourselves." And then he gobbled, the hens cackled, and the ducks quacked; they made a horrid noise with their amusements.

But Hialmar went to the hen-house, opened the door, and called the Stork, who immediately jumped on deck; he had now rested himself sufficiently, and bowed his head to Hialmar, as if to thank him. He then spread his wings and flew away—whilst the hens cackled, the ducks quacked, and the turkeycock turned red as fire.

"To-morrow, we will have you all made into soup!" said Hialmar; whereupon he awoke, and found himself in his own little bed. A strange journey had the Dustman taken him that night!

Thursday

"I'll tell you what!" said the Dustman, "do not be afraid, and you shall see a little mouse!" and he held out his hand, with the pretty little animal in it. "She is come to invite you to a wedding; there are two little mice here, who intend this very night to enter into matrimony. They live under the floor of the dining-room; theirs must be such a pretty house!"

"But how can I get through the little hole?" asked Hialmar. "Let me take care of that," said the Dustman. "I will make you very little!" and he touched Hialmar with his magic wand, and he became smaller and smaller, till at last he was no larger than his own fingers. "Now you can borrow the tin-soldier's clothes; I think they will just fit you; and it looks so grand to wear uniform when you are in company."

"Ah, yes!" said Hialmar, and in another moment he was dressed like the prettiest little tin-soldier.

"Will you have the goodness to sit down in your mother's thimble?" said the little Mouse. "In that case, I shall feel honoured by drawing you."

"What! will you really take so much trouble?" said Hialmar; and away they went to the Mouse's wedding.

They first came to a long passage, under the floor, which was high enough for the thimble to be drawn along through it, and was illuminated with lighted tinder throughout.

"Is there not a pleasant smell here?" said the Mouse who was drawing the thimble. "The whole passage is covered with rind of bacon; there is nothing more delightful!"

They now entered the bridal apartment; the lady Mice stood on the right hand side, whispering together, seemingly very merry; on the left side stood the gentlemen Mice, who were all stroking their whiskers with their paws. In the middle of the room the bride and bridegroom were seen, standing in the scooped-out rind of a cheese, and kissing each other incessantly, before the eyes of all present. They were already betrothed, and were to be married immediately. Strangers were arriving every moment; the Mice almost trod each other to death; and the bridal pair had placed themselves just in the centre of the door-way, so that one could neither get out nor in. The whole room was, like the passage, covered with the rind of bacon; this was all the entertainment given; for dessert, however, a pea was exhibited, in which a little Mouse belonging to the family had bitten the initials of the married couple. Was not this an exquisite idea?

All the Mice agreed that the wedding had been extremely genteel, and the conversation delightful.

So now Hialmar returned home; he had certainly been in most distinguished company; but still, he felt as though he had rather lowered himself, by becoming so small, and wearing the uniform of one of his own tin-soldiers.

Friday.

"It is incredible what a number of old people there are always wanting to have me with them," said the Dustman, "especially those who have done anything wicked. 'Dear, good Dustman,' they say to me, 'we cannot sleep a wink all night; we lie awake, and see all our bad deeds sitting on the edge of the bed, like little ugly goblins, and sprinkling scalding water over us. If you would but come and drive them away, so that we could have a little sleep,' and then they sigh so deeply, 'we will be sure to pay you well,—good night, Dustman, the money is lying at the window.' But I do not come for money," added Ole Lucköie.

"What are we to do to-night?" asked Hialmar.

"Why I do not know whether you would like to go again to a wedding? The one of which I am now speaking is quite of another kind from yesterday's. Your sister's great doll, that looks like a man, and is called Herman, is going to marry the doll Bertha; moreover, it is a birthday; so they will doubtless receive a great many presents."

"Oh, yes! I know that already," said Hialmar; "whenever the dolls want new clothes, my sister calls it either their birthday or their wedding-day. They must certainly have been married a hundred times already."

"Yes, but to-night they will be married for the hundred-and-first time; and when it has come to that number, they can never be married again. So this time the wedding will be splendid! Only look!"

And Hialmar looked upon the table, where stood the little doll's house; the windows were lighted up, and tin-soldiers presented arms at the door. The bride and bridegroom were sitting on the ground, and leaning against the leg of the table; they seemed very thoughtful,— there was, perhaps, good reason for being so. But the Dustman had, meanwhile, put on his grandmother's black gown, and married them. When the ceremony was over, all the Furniture in the room began singing the following pretty song, which had been written by the Lead-pencil:

> "Waft, gentle breeze, our kind farewell
> To the tiny house where the bridefolks dwell,
> With their skin of kid-leather fitting so well;
> They are straight and upright as a tailor's ell.
> Hurrah, hurrah for beau and belle!
> Let echo repeat our kind farewell!"

And now presents were brought to them; all eatables, however, they declined accepting: love was enough for them to live upon.

"Shall we go into the country, or make a tour in some foreign land?" asked the bridegroom. So the Swallow, who had travelled a good deal, and the old Hen, who had hatched five broods of chickens, were consulted. And the Swallow spoke of those beautiful, warm countries, where bunches of grapes, large and heavy, hang on the vines; where the air is so balmy, and the mountains are tinged with various hues, such as are never known here.

"But then they have not our green cabbages!" said the Hen. "One summer, I and all my chickens lived in the country; there was a gravel-pit, in which we might go and scrape about; besides, we had access to a garden full of green cabbages. Oh, how green they were! I cannot imagine anything more beautiful!"

"But one head of cabbage looks exactly like another,"

said the Swallow; "and then we so often have wet weather here!"

"One gets accustomed to that," said the Hen.

"But it is so cold, it freezes!"

"That is good for the cabbages," said the Hen; "besides which it can be warm sometimes. Did we not, four years ago, have a summer which lasted five weeks? It was so hot, that one could hardly breathe. Then, too, we have not all the poisonous animals which they have in foreign countries; and we are free from robbers. He is a blockhead who does not think our country the most beautiful of all! he does not deserve to live here!" and at these words tears rolled down the Hen's cheeks. "I, too, have travelled; I have been twelve miles in a coop. There is no pleasure at all in travelling."

"Yes, the Hen is a sensible animal!" said the doll Bertha. "I do not wish to travel over the mountains; one is always going up and down! No, we will go to the gravel-pit, and walk in the garden among the cabbages."

And so it was settled.

SATURDAY.

"Now may I have some stories?" asked little Hialmar as soon as the Dustman had put him to sleep

"We shall have no time for them this evening," said the Dustman, spreading his picture-umbrella over him. "Look at these Chinese!" The umbrella resembled a large Chinese plate, with blue trees and pointed bridges; little Chinese men and women stood nodding their heads among them.

"By to-morrow morning all the world must be put in order," said the Dustman; "it is a festival day — it is Sunday. I must go to the church-tower, to see whether the little Nisses are rubbing the bells, so as to make them ring merrily. I must away to the fields, to see that the winds are sweeping the dust off the grass and leaves. I must take down the stars, in order to brighten them. I put them into my apron, but first they must be numbered; and the holes in which they fit, up in the sky, must be numbered also, that every one may return to his proper place; else they would not sit firmly, and we should have too many falling stars, one coming down after another."

"Listen to me, good Mr. Ole Lucköie," said an old Portrait, which hung by the wall, near where Hialmar was sleeping. "Do you know that I am Hialmar's great-grandfather? I am much obliged to you for telling the boy stories; but you must not puzzle him. Stars cannot be taken down and brightened; they are bodies like our earth."

"Many thanks, old Great-grandfather!" said the Dustman, "many thanks! Thou art certainly very old, but I am older still! I am an old heathen; the Greeks and Romans called me the God of Dreams. I have been in families of the greatest distinction, and I go there still! I know how to deal with great and small! Now it is thy turn; say what thou pleasest!"

"So one is no longer allowed to speak one's mind!" muttered the old Portrait.

And presently Hialmar awoke.

SUNDAY.

"Good evening!" said the Dustman; and Hialmar nodded his head to him, and jumped up to turn his great-grandfather's Portrait to the wall, in order that he might not interrupt them, as yesterday.

"Now you shall tell me stories about the five green peas who all lived in one pod; and about the cock courting the hen; and about the darning-needle, who was so fine that she fancied herself a sewing-needle."

"One may have too much of a good thing!" said the Dustman. "I would rather show you something else; I will show you my brother. He never comes more than once to any one; and whomsoever he visits he takes on his horse, and tells him a story. He knows only two stories; the one unspeakably delightful, such as no one in the world can imagine; the other so dreadful, so horrible—it is not to be described." And the Dustman lifted little Hialmar up to the window, saying, "There is my brother, the other Dustman; he is also called Death! You see he is not so frightful as he is represented in picture-books, where he seems to be all bones; no, he wears clothes embroidered with silver; it is the gayest of uniforms! a mantle of black velvet flutters over his horse, behind him. See how he gallops!"

And Hialmar saw the other Dustman ride on, and take old and young with him on his horse: some he placed in front, and others behind; but he always asked first what sort of a journal they had to show.

"Good," they all replied. "Yes, but let me see it," said he; so they were obliged to show it to him; and all those who had "Very good" written in it were put in front of the horse, and heard the story that was so delightful; but those who had "Pretty good," or "Bad," inscribed in their journals, were obliged to get up behind, and listen to the horrible story. They trembled, and wept; they tried to jump down from the horse's back; but that they could not do, for they were as firmly fixed on as if they had grown there.

"Death is a most beautiful Dustman," said Hialmar: "I am not afraid of him."

"That you should not be," said the Dustman; "only take care to have a good journal to show."

"Ah, this is very instructive!" muttered the great-grandfather's Portrait. "It is always of use to give one's opinion." He was now satisfied.

These are the stories of Ole Lucköie; perhaps he may tell you more this very evening.

THE DAISY.

LISTEN to my story!
In the country, close by the road-side, there stands a summer-house — you must certainly have seen it. In front is a little garden full of flowers, enclosed by white palings; and on a bank outside the palings there grew, amidst the freshest green grass, a little Daisy. The sun shone as brightly and warmly upon the Daisy as upon the splendid large flowers within the garden, and therefore it grew hourly, so that one morning it stood fully open, with its delicate white gleaming leaves, which, like rays, surrounded the little yellow sun in their centre.

It never occurred to the little flower that no one saw her, hidden as she was among the grass; she was quite contented: she turned towards the warm sun, looked at it, and listened to the Lark who was singing in the air.

The Daisy was as happy as if it were the day of some

high festival, and yet it was only Monday. The children were at school; and whilst they sat upon their forms, and learned their lessons, the little flower upon her green stalk learned from the warm sun, and everything around her, how good God is. Meanwhile the little Lark expressed clearly and beautifully all she felt in silence! And the flower looked up with a sort of reverence to the happy bird who could fly and sing; it did not distress her that she could not do the same. "I can see and listen," thought she; "the sun shines on me, and the wind kisses me. Oh! how richly am I blessed."

There stood within the palings several grand, stiff-looking flowers; the less fragrance they had the more airs they gave themselves. The Peonies puffed themselves out, in order to make themselves larger than the Roses. The Tulips had the gayest colours of all; they were perfectly aware of it, and held themselves as straight as a candle, that they might be the better seen. They took no notice at all of the little flower outside the palings; but she looked all the more upon them, thinking, "How rich and beautiful they are! Yes, that noble bird will surely fly down and visit them. How happy am I, who live so near them, and can see their beauty!" Just at that moment, "Quirrevit!" the Lark did fly down, but he came not to the Peonies or the Tulips: no, he flew down to the poor little Daisy in the grass, who was almost frightened from pure joy, and knew not what to think, she was so surprised.

The little bird hopped about, and sang, "Oh, how soft is this grass! and what a sweet little flower blooms here, with its golden heart and silver garment!" for the yellow centre of the Daisy looked just like gold, and the little petals around gleamed silver white.

How happy the little Daisy was! no one can imagine how happy. The bird kissed her with his beak, sang to her, and then flew up again into the blue sky. It was a full quarter of an hour ere the flower recovered herself. Half ashamed, and yet completely happy, she looked at the flowers in the garden; they must certainly be aware of the honour and happiness that had been conferred upon her, they must know how delighted she was. But the Tulips held themselves twice as stiff as before, and their faces grew quite red with anger. As to the thick-headed Peonies, it was, indeed, well that they could not speak, or the little Daisy would have heard something not very pleasant. The poor little flower could see well that they were in an ill-humour, and she was much grieved at it. Soon after, a girl came into the garden with a knife sharp and bright; she went up to the Tulips and cut off one after another. "Ugh! that is horrible," sighed the Daisy; "it is now all over with them." The girl then went away with the Tulips. How glad was the Daisy that she grew in the grass outside the palings, and was a despised little flower! She felt really thankful; and when the sun set, she folded her leaves, went to sleep, and dreamed all night of the sun and the beautiful bird.

The next morning, when our little flower, fresh and cheerful, again spread out all her white leaves in the bright sunshine and clear blue air, she heard the voice of the bird; but he sung so mournfully. Alas! the poor Lark had good reason for sorrow; he had been caught, and put into a cage close by the open window. He sang of the joys of a free and unrestrained flight; he sang of the young green corn in the fields, and of the pleasure of being borne up by his wings in the open air. The poor bird was certainly very unhappy— he sat a prisoner in his narrow cage!

The little Daisy would so willingly have helped him, but how could she? Ah, that she knew not: she quite forgot how beautiful was all around her, how warmly the sun shone, how pretty and white were her leaves. Alas! she could only think of the imprisoned bird—whom it was not in her power to help.

All at once two little boys came out of the garden; one of them had a knife in his hand, as large and as sharp as that with which the girl had cut the Tulips. They went up straight to the little Daisy, who could not imagine what they wanted.

"Here we can cut a nice piece of turf for the Lark," said one of the boys; and he began to cut deep all round the Daisy, leaving her in the centre.

"Tear out the flower," said the other boy; and the little Daisy trembled all over for fear; for she knew that if she were torn out she would die, and she wished so much to live, as she was to be put into the cage with the imprisoned Lark.

"No, leave it alone!" said the first, "it looks so pretty;" and so she was let alone, and was put into the Lark's cage.

But the poor bird loudly lamented the loss of his freedom, and beat his wings against the iron bars of his cage; and the little flower could not speak—could not say a single word of comfort to him, much as she wished to do so. Thus passed the whole morning.

"There is no water here!" sang the captive Lark; "they have all gone out and forgotten me; not a drop of water to drink! my throat is dry and burning! there is fire and ice within me, and the air is so heavy! Alas! I must die; I must leave the warm sunshine, the fresh green trees, and all the beautiful things which God has created!" And then he pierced his beak into the cool grass, in order to refresh himself a little—and his eye fell upon the Daisy, and the bird bowed to her, and said, "Thou, too, wilt wither here, thou poor little flower! They have given me thee, and the piece of green around thee, instead of the whole world which I possessed before! Every little blade of grass is to be to me a green tree, thy every white petal a fragrant flower! Alas! thou only remindest me of what I have lost."

"Oh! that I could comfort him!" thought the Daisy; but she could not move a single petal; yet the fragrance which came from her delicate blossom was stronger than is usual with this flower; the bird noticed it, and although, panting with thirst, he tore the green blades in very anguish, he did not touch the flower.

It was evening, and yet no one came to bring the poor bird a drop of water; he stretched out his slender wings, and shook them convulsively; his song was a mournful wail; his little head bent towards the flower, and the bird's heart broke from thirst and desire. The flower could not now, as on the preceding evening, fold together her leaves and sleep: sad and sick, she drooped to the ground.

The boys did not come till the next morning; and when they saw the bird was dead, they wept bitterly. They dug a pretty grave, which they adorned with flower-petals; the bird's corpse was put into a pretty red box; royally was the poor bird buried! Whilst he yet lived and sang they forgot him — left him suffering in his cage — and now he was highly honoured and bitterly bewailed.

But the piece of turf with the Daisy in it was thrown out into the street: no one thought of her who had felt most for the little bird, and who had so much wished to comfort him!

THE BUCKWHEAT.

IF, after a tempest, you chance to walk through a field where Buckwheat is growing, you may observe that it is burnt as black as though a flame of fire had passed over it; and should you ask the reason, the peasant will tell you, "That the lightning has done it."

But how is it that the lightning has done it? I will tell you what the Sparrow told me; and the Sparrow heard the story from an old Willow-tree, which grew, and still grows, close to a field of Buckwheat.

This Willow-tree is tall and highly respectable; but, at the same time, old and wrinkled: its trunk has been riven asunder from top to bottom; grass and brambles grow out of the gap; the tree bends forward, and the branches hang down almost to the ground, looking like long green hair.

There were different kinds of corn growing in the fields around the Willow; rye, wheat, and oats—the beautiful oats, whose ears, when they are ripe, look like a number of little yellow canary-birds sitting upon one branch. The corn-ears were richly blessed; and the fuller they were, the lower they bowed their heads in pious humility.

But there was also a field of Buckwheat, lying just in front of the old Willow-tree; the Buckwheat bowed not like the rest of the corn; he stood stiff and proud.

"I am quite as rich as the wheat," said he; "and, besides, I am so much more handsome; my flowers are as beautiful as the blossoms of the apple-tree; it is delightful to look at me and my companions. Do you know anything more beautiful than we are, you old Willow-tree?"

And the Willow-tree bent his head, as much as to say, "Yes, indeed I do!" But the Buckwheat was puffed up with pride, and said, "The stupid tree! he is so old that grass is growing out of his body."

Now came on a dreadful storm; all the flowers of the field folded their leaves, or bent their heads, as it passed over them; the Buckwheat however, in his pride, still stood erect.

"Bow thy head as we do!" said the Flowers.

"I have no need," said the Buckwheat.

"Bow thy head as we do!" said the Corn. "The angel of storms comes flying hitherward; he has wings which reach from the clouds to the earth; he will strike thee down, before thou hast time to entreat for mercy!"

"No, I will not bow!" said the Buckwheat.

"Close thy flowers, and fold thy leaves," said the old Willow-tree; "look not into the flash, when the cloud breaks. Men even dare not do that; for the flash reveals to us God's heaven, and that sight must dazzle even human eyes; what, then, would it prove to mere vegetables like us, if we should dare to look into it,—we, who are so inferior to men?"

"So inferior, indeed!" said the Buckwheat. "Now, then, I *will* look right into God's heaven." And in his pride and haughtiness, he did gaze upon the lightning without shrinking. Such was the flash, that it seemed as if the whole world was in flames.

When the tempest was over, Flowers and Corn, greatly refreshed by the rain, once more breathed pure air; but the Buckwheat had been burnt as black as a coal by the lightning: it stood on the field a dead, useless plant.

And the old Willow-tree waved its branches to and fro in

the wind, and large drops of water fell from the green leaves, as though the tree wept. And the Sparrows asked, "Why weepest thou? it is so beautiful here! See how the sun shines; how the clouds pass over the clear sky; how sweet is the fragrance of the flowers! Why, then, weepest thou, old Willow-tree?"

And the Willow-tree told of the Buckwheat's pride and haughtiness; and of the punishment which followed. I, who relate this story, heard it from the Sparrows — they told it to me one evening when I asked them for a tale.

THE EMPEROR'S NEW CLOTHES.

MANY years ago, there was an Emperor, who was so excessively fond of new clothes that he spent all his money in dress. He did not trouble himself in the least about his soldiers; nor did he care to go either to the theatre or the chase, except for the opportunities then afforded him for displaying his new clothes. He had a different suit for each hour of the day; and as of any other king or emperor one is accustomed to say, " He is sitting in council," it was always said of him, " The Emperor is sitting in his wardrobe."

Time passed away merrily in the large town which was his capital; strangers arrived every day at the court. One day two rogues, calling themselves weavers, made their appearance. They gave out that they knew how to weave stuffs of the most beautiful colours and elaborate patterns, the clothes manufactured from which should have the wonderful property of remaining invisible to every one who was unfit for the office he held, or who was extraordinarily simple in character.

"These must, indeed, be splendid clothes!" thought the Emperor. " Had I such a suit, I might at once find out what men in my realm are unfit for their office, and also be able to distinguish the wise from the foolish! This stuff must be woven for me immediately." And he caused large sums of money to be given to both the weavers, in order that they might begin their work directly.

So the two pretended weavers set up two looms, and affected to work very busily, though in reality they did nothing at all. They asked for the most delicate silk and the purest gold thread; put both into their own knapsacks; and then continued their pretended work at the empty looms until late at night.

"I should like to know how the weavers are getting on with my cloth," said the Emperor to himself, after some little time had elapsed; he was, however, rather embarrassed when he remembered that a simpleton, or one unfit for his office, would be unable to see the manufacture. " To be sure," he thought, " he had nothing to risk in his own person; but yet he would prefer sending somebody else to bring him intelligence about the weavers, and their work, before he troubled himself in the affair." All the people throughout the city had heard of the wonderful property the cloth was to possess; and all were anxious to learn how wise, or how ignorant, their neighbours might prove to be.

" I will send my faithful old Minister to the weavers," said the Emperor at last, after some deliberation; " he will be best able to see how the cloth looks; for he is a man of sense, and no one can be more suitable for his office than he is."

So the honest old Minister went into the hall, where the knaves were working with all their might at their empty looms. "What can be the meaning of this?" thought the old man, opening his eyes very wide; "I cannot discover the least bit of thread on the looms!" However, he did not express his thoughts aloud.

The impostors requested him very courteously to be so good as to come nearer their looms; and then asked him whether the design pleased him, and whether the colours were not very beautiful; at the same time pointing to the empty frames. The poor old Minister looked and looked; he could not discover anything on the looms, for a very good reason, viz. there was nothing there. "What!" thought he again, "is it possible that I am a simpleton? I have never thought so myself; and, at any rate, if I am so, no one must know it. Can it be that I am unfit for my office? No, that must not be said either. I will never confess that I could not see the stuff."

"Well, Sir Minister!" said one of the knaves, still pretending to work, "you do not say whether the stuff pleases you."

"Oh, it is admirable!" replied the old Minister, looking at the loom through his spectacles. "This pattern, and the colours—yes, I will tell the Emperor without delay how very beautiful I think them."

"We shall be much obliged to you," said the impostors, and then they named the different colours and described the patterns of the pretended stuff. The old Minister listened attentively to their words, in order that he might repeat them to the Emperor; and then the knaves asked for more silk and gold, saying that it was necessary to complete what they had begun. However, they put all that was given them into their knapsacks, and continued to work with as much apparent diligence as before at their empty looms.

The Emperor now sent another officer of his court to see how the men were getting on, and to ascertain whether the cloth would soon be ready. It was just the same with this gentleman as with the Minister; he surveyed the looms on all sides, but could see nothing at all but the empty frames

"Does not the stuff appear as beautiful to you as it did to my Lord the Minister?" asked the impostors of the Emperor's second ambassador; at the same time making the same gestures as before, and talking of the design and colours which were not there.

"I certainly am not stupid!" thought the messenger. "It must be that I am not fit for my good, profitable office! That is very odd; however, no one shall know anything about it." And accordingly he praised the stuff he could not see, and declared that he was delighted with both colours and patterns. "Indeed, please your Imperial Majesty," said he to his sovereign, when he returned, "the cloth which the weavers are preparing is extraordinarily magnificent."

The whole city was talking of the splendid cloth which the Emperor had ordered to be woven at his own expense.

And now the Emperor himself wished to see the costly manufacture, whilst it was still on the loom. Accompanied by a select number of officers of the court, among whom were the two honest men who had already admired the cloth, he went to the crafty impostors, who, as soon as they were aware of the Emperor's approach, went on working more diligently than ever; although they still did not pass a single thread through the looms.

"Is not the work absolutely magnificent?" said the two officers of the crown already mentioned. "If your Majesty will only be pleased to look at it! what a splendid design! what glorious colours!" and at the same time they pointed to the empty frames; for they imagined that every one but themselves could see this exquisite piece of workmanship.

"How is this?" said the Emperor to himself; "I can see nothing! this is, indeed, a terrible affair! Am I a simpleton? or am I unfit to be an Emperor? that would be the worst thing that could happen. Oh, the cloth is charming!" said he aloud; "it has my entire approbation." And he smiled most graciously, and looked closely at the empty looms; for on no account would he say that he could not see what two of the officers of his court had praised so much. All his retinue now strained their eyes, hoping to discover something on the looms, but they could see no more than the others; nevertheless, they all exclaimed, "Oh! how beautiful!" and advised his Majesty to have some new clothes made from this splendid material for the approaching procession. "Magnificent! charming! excellent!" resounded on all sides; and every one was uncommonly gay. The Emperor shared in the general satisfaction, and presented the impostors with the riband of an order of knighthood to be worn in their button-holes, and the title of "Gentlemen Weavers."

The rogues sat up the whole of the night before the day on which the procession was to take place, and had sixteen lights burning, so that every one might see how anxious they were to finish the Emperor's new suit. They pretended to roll the cloth off the looms; cut the air with their scissors; and sewed with needles without any thread in them. "See!" cried they at last, "the Emperor's new clothes are ready!"

And now the Emperor, with all the grandees of his court, came to the weavers; and the rogues raised their arms, as if in the act of holding something up, saying, "Here are your Majesty's trousers! here is the scarf! here is the mantle! The whole suit is as light as a cobweb; one might fancy one has nothing at all on, when dressed in it; that, however, is the great virtue of this delicate cloth."

"Yes, indeed!" said all the courtiers, although not one of them could see anything of this exquisite manufacture.

"If your Imperial Majesty will be graciously pleased to take off your clothes, we will fit on the new suit, in front of the looking-glass."

The Emperor was accordingly undressed, and the rogues pretended to array him in his new suit; the Emperor turning round, from side to side, before the looking-glass.

"How splendid his Majesty looks in his new clothes! and how well they fit!" every one cried out. "What a design! what colours! these are, indeed, royal robes!"

"The canopy which is to be borne over your Majesty, in the procession, is waiting," announced the Chief Master of the Ceremonies.

"I am quite ready," answered the Emperor. "Do my new clothes fit well?" asked he, turning himself round again before the looking-glass, in order that he might appear to be examining his handsome suit.

The lords of the bed-chamber, who were to carry his Majesty's train, felt about on the ground, as if they were lifting up the ends of the mantle, and pretended to be carrying something; for they would by no means betray anything like simplicity, or unfitness for their office.

So now the Emperor walked under his high canopy in the midst of the procession, through the streets of his capital; and all the people standing by, and those at the windows, cried out, "Oh! how beautiful are our Emperor's new clothes! what a magnificent train there is to the mantle! and how gracefully the scarf hangs!" in short, no one would allow that he could not see these much-admired clothes, because, in doing so, he would have declared himself either a simpleton or unfit for his office. Certainly, none of the Emperor's various suits had ever excited so much admiration as this.

"But the Emperor has nothing at all on!" said a little child. "Listen to the voice of innocence!" exclaimed his father; and what the child has said was whispered from one to another.

"But he has nothing at all on!" at last cried out all the people. The Emperor was vexed, for he knew that the people were right; but he thought "the procession must go on now!" And the lords of the bed-chamber took greater pains than ever to appear holding up a train, although, in reality, there was no train to hold.

THE REAL PRINCESS.

THERE was once a Prince who wished to marry a Princess; but then she must be a real Princess. He travelled all over the world in hopes of finding such a lady; but there was always something wrong. Princesses he found in plenty; but whether they were real Princesses it was impossible for him to decide, for now one thing, now another, seemed to him not quite right about the ladies. At last he returned to his palace quite cast down, because he wished so much to have a real Princess for his wife.

One evening a fearful tempest arose, it thundered and lightened, and the rain poured down from the sky in torrents; besides, it was as dark as pitch. All at once there was heard a violent knocking at the door, and the old King, the Prince's father, went out himself to open it.

It was a Princess who was standing outside the door. What with the rain and the wind, she was in a sad condition: the water trickled down from her hair, and her clothes clung to her body. She said she was a real Princess.

"Ah! we shall soon see that!" thought the old Queen; however, she said not a word of what she was going to do, but went quietly into the bedroom, took all the bed-clothes off the bed, and put one little pea on the bedstead. She then laid twenty mattresses one upon another over the pea, and put twenty feather-beds over the mattresses.

Upon this bed the Princess was to pass the night.

The next morning, she was asked how she had slept. "Oh, very badly indeed!" she replied. "I have scarcely closed my eyes the whole night through. I do not know what was in my bed, but I had something hard under me, and am all over black and blue. It has hurt me so much!"

Now it was plain that the lady must be a real Princess, since she had been able to feel the one little pea through the twenty mattresses and twenty feather-beds. None but a real Princess could have had such a delicate sense of feeling.

The Prince accordingly made her his wife, being now convinced that he had found a real Princess. The pea, however, was put into the cabinet of curiosities, where it is still to be seen, provided it be not lost.

Was not this a lady of real delicacy?

THE TOP AND THE BALL.

A TOP and a Ball were lying close together in a drawer, among other playthings.

Thus said the Top to the Ball:

"Why should we not become bride and bridegroom, since we are thrown so much together?"

But the Ball, who was made of morocco leather, and fancied herself a very fashionable young lady, would not hear of such a proposal.

The next day, the little boy to whom the playthings belonged came to the drawer; he painted the Top red and yellow, and drove a brass-nail through the middle of it; it was glorious after that to see the Top spin round.

"Look at me now!" said he to the Ball: "what do you say to me now? Why should not we become man and wife? We suit each other so well — you can jump, and I can spin; it would be hard to find a couple happier than we should be."

"Do you think so?" said the Ball; "perhaps you do not know that my father and mother were morocco slippers, and that I have cork in my body."

"Yes, but I am made of mahogany," returned the Top; "the Burgomaster manufactured me with his own hands;

for he has a lathe of his own, and took great pleasure in turning me."

"Can I trust you in this?" asked the Ball.

"May I never be whipped again if I lie," said the Top.

"You don't talk amiss," replied the Ball; "but I am not at liberty, I am as good as betrothed to a young Swallow. Whenever I fly up in the air, he puts his head out of his nest, and says, 'Will you marry me?' I have said 'Yes' to him in my heart, and that is almost the same as a betrothal. But one thing I promise you, I will never forget you!"

"That will be of great use!" quoth the Top, and no more was then said on the subject.

Next day the Ball was taken out. The Top saw it fly like a bird into the air — so high that it could be seen no longer; it came back again, but every time it touched the ground, it sprang higher than before. Either love, or the cork she had in her body, must have been the cause of this.

The ninth time she did not return; the boy sought and sought, but she was gone.

"I know well where she is," sighed the Top; "she is in the Swallow's nest, celebrating her wedding." The more the Top thought of it, the more amiable did the Ball appear to him: that she could not be his only made his love the more vehement. Another had been been preferred to him; he could not forget that! And the Top spinned and hummed, but was always thinking of the dear Ball who, in his imagination, grew more beautiful every moment. Thus passed several years — there was constant love!

The Top was no longer young! however he was one day gilded all over; never before had he looked so handsome. He was now a gilt top, and spun most bravely, humming all the time: yes, that was famous! But all at once he sprang too high, and was gone! They sought and sought, even in the cellar; he was nowhere to be found.

Where was he?

He had jumped into a barrel full of all sorts of rubbish, cabbage-stalks, sweepings, dust, &c., which had fallen in from the gutter.

"Alas! here I lie; my gay gilding will soon be spoiled and what sort of trumpery can I have fallen in with?" And he peeped at a long cabbage-stalk which lay fearfully near him.

and at a strange round thing somewhat like an apple; but it was not an apple, it was an old Ball, which had lain several years in the gutter, and was quite soaked through with water.

"Thank goodness! at last I see an equal, with whom I may speak," said the Ball, looking fixedly at the gilt Top. "I am made of real morocco, sewed together by a young lady's hands, and I have cork in my body; but I shall never again be noticed by any one; I was on the point of marriage with the Swallow when I fell into the gutter, and there I have lain five years, and am now wet through. Only think, what a wearisome time for a young lady to be in such a situation!"

But the Top answered not a word; he thought on his long-lamented companion, and the more he heard, the more certain he felt that it was she herself.

The servant-maid now came, and was going to turn the barrel over—"Hurrah!" exclaimed she, "there is the gilt Top."

And the Top was brought back to the play-room; it was used and admired as before: but nothing more was heard of the Ball, nor did the Top ever again boast of his love for her; such a feeling must have passed away. How could it be otherwise, when he found that she had lain five years in the gutter, and that she was so much altered he scarcely knew her again when he met her in the barrel among rubbish?

THE GARDEN OF PARADISE.

THERE was once a young Prince; no one had so many and such beautiful books as he had: he could read in them the history of all the events which have ever happened in the world, and also see them represented in splendid pictures. He could gain from his books all the information he wanted about any country or people whatsoever; but there was not in them a word of what he most desired to know: viz. where the Garden of Paradise was to be found.

When the Prince was a very little boy, just beginning to go to school, his grandmother told him that every flower in the Garden of Paradise tasted like the sweetest of cakes, and the stamina like the choicest of wines; on one plant grew history, on another geography, on a third the multiplication table. Whoever ate the flower immediately knew his lesson; the more he ate, the more he learned of history, geography, or tables.

At that time, the young Prince believed all this; but afterwards, when he had grown bigger and wiser, and had learned more, he saw plainly that what constituted the beauty of the Garden of Paradise must be something quite different.

"Oh! why did Eve touch the Tree of Knowledge? Why did Adam eat of the forbidden fruit? Had I been in their place, it would never have happened. Never should sin have entered the world!"

So he said then; and when he was seventeen, he still said the same. The Garden of Paradise occupied all his thoughts.

One day he went into the wood; he went alone, for to wander thus was his chief delight.

The evening approached, the clouds gathered, the rain poured down, as if all the sky were nothing but a vast floodgate; it was as dark as we might suppose it to be at nighttime in a very deep well. The Prince now slipped among the wet grass, now stumbled over bare rocks, which projected from the stony ground. Everything was dripping with water; the poor Prince had not a dry thread on his skin. He was obliged to climb over great blocks of stone, where the water trickled down from the moss. His strength was just failing him, when he heard a strange rustling, and saw before him a large lighted cavern. A fire was burning in the centre, at which a stag might have been roasted whole; and, indeed, this was the case: a very fine stag, with branching antlers, was placed on the spit, and was slowly turned between the stems of two fir-trees. An aged woman, tall and strong, as if she were a man in disguise, sat by the fire, throwing upon it one piece of wood after another. "Come nearer," said she, "sit down by the fire, and dry your clothes."

"There is a terrible draught here," said the Prince, as he sat down on the ground.

"It will be still worse when my sons come home," answered the woman. "You are now in the Cavern of the Winds; my sons are the four Winds—do you understand me?"

"Where are your sons?" asked the Prince.

"There is no use in answering stupid questions," said the woman; "my sons do as they please—play at ball with the clouds up there!" and then she pointed to the blue sky above.

'Indeed!" said the Prince; "you speak in rather a harsh manner, and altogether do not seem so gentle as the women I am accustomed to see around me."

"Yes, they have nothing else to do! I must be harsh if I am to control my boys; however, I can control them, although they have stiff necks. Do you see those four sacks hanging by the wall? They have as much respect for them as you used to have for the rod behind the looking-glass. I puff them together, I tell you, and then they must get into the sacks; we use no ceremony; there they sit, and do not come out till it pleases me. But here comes one of them!"

It was the North Wind: he brought icy coldness with him; large hailstones danced on the ground, and flakes of snow flew around him. He was dressed in a jacket and trousers of bear's skin, a cap of seal's skin hung over his ears, long icicles hung from his beard, and one hailstone after another fell from under the collar of his jacket.

"Do not go immediately to the fire," said the Prince; "you may, perhaps, get your face and hands frost-bitten.'

"Frost-bitten!" repeated the North Wind, and he laughed aloud; "frost is my greatest delight! But what spindle-shanked boy are you? how did you get into the Cavern of the Winds?"

"He is my guest," said the old woman; "and if you are not content with this explanation, you shall go into the sack! Now you know my mind."

This was quite sufficient; and now the North Wind related whence he came, and how he had spent the last month.

"I come from the Arctic Ocean," said he, "I have been on Bear Island, along with the Russian walrus-hunters. I sat by the helm, and slept when they sailed from the North Cape; and if now and then I awoke for a short time, the stormy petrel would fly about my legs. It is a merry bird; he suddenly claps his wings, then holds them immoveably stretched out and soars aloft."

"Do not make your story so long!" said the mother. "And so you came to Bear Island?"

"That is a glorious place! the ground seems made on purpose for dancing, flat as a plate. It is composed of half-melted snow overgrown with moss; sharp stones, and the skeletons of walruses and polar bears, are strewed over it, looking like the arms and legs of giants, covered with musty green; you would fancy the sun had never shone on them. I blew a little into the clouds, in order that the people might be able to see the shed, built from a wreck, and covered with the skins of walruses, the fleshy side, all green and red, turned outwards. A living polar bear sat growling on the roof. I walked on the shore, peeped into the birds' nests, looked at the poor naked young ones, who were crying, with their beaks wide open: I blew into their thousand little throats, and they learned to be quiet. The sea-horses, with their swine-like heads, and teeth an ell long, rolled like gigantic worms beneath the waters."

"My son can relate his adventures very pleasantly," said the mother; "my mouth waters when I listen to him."

"And then the fishery began; the harpoon was thrust into the breast of the sea-horse, and a stream of blood shot up like a fountain, and streamed over the ice. Then I remembered my part of the sport; I made my ships, the rock-like ice-mountains, surround the boats. Oh! how all the crew whistled and shouted; but I whistled still louder. They were obliged to unload all the dead walruses, and to throw them, with their trunks and cordage, out upon the ice. I shook snow-flakes over them, and drove them to taste sea-water southwards. They will never come again to Bear Island!"

"Then you have done mischief!" said the mother of the Winds.

"What good I have done others may relate," replied he; "but here comes my brother of the West. I love him best of all; he smells of the sea, and has a right healthy coldness about him."

"Can that be the delicate Zephyr?" asked the Prince.

"Yes, it is Zephyr, certainly," said the old woman; "but delicate he is no longer. In days of yore he was a gallant youth; but those times have long passed away."

The West Wind looked like a wild man, but he wore a sort of padded hat to protect his head. In his hand he held a club of mahogany wood, hewn in the American forests; certainly nowhere else.

"Whence come you?" asked the mother.

"From those forest wastes," said he, "where the thorny lianas weave hedges between the trees, where the water-snake reposes in the damp grass, and men are apparently useless."

"What did you there?"

I

"I looked at the deep river, marked how it hurled itself from the rocks, and flew like dust towards the clouds, that it might give birth to the rainbow. I saw a buffalo swim down the river, the stream carried him away; a flock of wild geese were swimming also, they flew away when the water fell down the precipice; but the buffalo must have plunged with it— that pleased me, and I then raised such a storm that the primeval old trees fell to the ground with a crash, broken to splinters."

"And have you done nothing else?" inquired the old woman.

"I have cut capers in the savannahs; I have ridden wild horses, and shaken cocoa-nut trees,—ah, yes, I have such stories to tell! But we must not tell everything, that you know well, my old mother!" And he kissed his mother so roughly that she almost fell backwards. He was a wild fellow!

Now came the South Wind in his turban, and floating Bedouin mantle.

"It is very cold here," said he, as he threw wood upon the fire; "it is plain that the North Wind has arrived before me."

"It is so hot that a polar bear might be roasted here," said the North Wind.

"Thou art thyself a polar bear," returned the South Wind.

"Do you wish both of you to go into the sack?" asked the old woman. "Sit down on yonder stone, and tell me where you have been."

"In Africa, mother," answered he. "I have been hunting lions in the land of the Caffres, along with the Hottentots. Such beautiful grass grows on those plains, green as olives. The gnu danced there, and the ostrich ran races with me; but I am swifter than he. I came to the yellow sands of the desert; there one might fancy oneself at the bottom of the sea. I met with a caravan; they had just killed their last camel, in hopes of getting water to drink; but they did not find much. The sun was burning over their heads, the sands roasting beneath their feet. There seemed no end to the desert. I rolled myself up in the fine, loose sand, and threw it up into the form of an immense pillar; a famous dance it had! You should have seen how puzzled the dromedary looked, and how the merchant drew his caftan over his head.

He threw himself down before me as he was accustomed to do before Allah. Now they are all buried; a pyramid of sand stands over them: if I should one day blow it away, the sun will bleach their bones; and travellers will see that human beings have passed that way before them, otherwise they would hardly believe it."

"Then you have only done evil!" said the mother. "March into the sack!" and before he was aware of it, the South Wind was seized and confined in the sack, which rolled about on the floor until the mother sat down on it; and then he was obliged to be still.

"These are desperately wild fellows," said the Prince.

"Yes, truly," answered she; "but they must obey. Here is the fourth."

This was the East Wind, who was dressed like a Chinese.

"So you come from that corner of the world," said the mother. "I thought you had been to the Garden of Paradise?"

"I shall fly there to-morrow," said the East Wind; "it is a hundred years to-morrow since I was there. I now come from China, where I danced round the porcelain tower, so that all the bells began to ring. In the street below, the officers were being flogged till the bamboo canes broke upon their shoulders, and there were people, from the first to the ninth rank, who cried out, 'Thanks, thanks, my fatherly benefactor!' But they did not mean what they said; and I clinked the bells and sang, 'Tsing, tsang, tsu!'"

"Thou art a wild youth," said the mother; "it is well that thou goest to-morrow to the Garden of Paradise; thy visits there always contribute to thy improvement. Remember to drink plentifully from the source of wisdom, and bring me a little flask filled with it."

"I will do so," said the East Wind. "But why hast thou put my brother of the South into the sack? Let him come out; I want him to tell me all about the bird called the phœnix: the Princess in the Garden of Paradise, when I visit her once in a hundred years, always asks me about that bird. Open the sack! thou art ever my sweetest mother, and I will give thee two cups full of tea, as fresh and green as when I plucked it."

"Well, then, for the sake of the tea, and because thou art my darling, I will open the sack." She did so, and the South Wind crept forth; but he looked very much cast down because the stranger Prince had seen his disgrace.

"Here is a palm-leaf for the Princess," said the South Wind; "it was given to me by the old phœnix, the only one in the world. He has scribbled on it, with his beak, the history of his whole life; the Princess can read it herself. I saw the phœnix set fire to his own nest; I saw him as he sat within it, and was consumed like a Hindoo wife. How the dry branches crackled, and how pleasant was the odour that arose from the burning nest! At last everything was consumed by the flames,—the old phœnix was in ashes. But his egg lay glowing in the fire, it burst with a loud noise, and the young one flew out. He is now king over all the birds, and the only phœnix in the world. He has bitten a hole in the leaf I gave you; that is his greeting to the Princess."

"Well, now let us have something to eat," said the mother of the Winds, and accordingly they all sat down to partake of the roasted stag; the Prince sat next to the East Wind, and they soon became good friends.

"Only tell me this," began the Prince, "what Princess is that I heard so much about; and where is the Garden of Paradise?"

"Ho, ho!" said the East Wind, "do you want to go there? Well, then, fly with me to-morrow; but I must tell you that no human being has been there since Adam and Eve's time. You know the Scripture history, I suppose?"

"Of course," said the Prince.

"Well, when they were driven out of it, the Garden of Paradise sank under the earth; but it still retained its warm sunshine, its balmy air, and all its beauty. The queen of the fairies makes it her abode, and there also is the Island of Bliss, where death never comes, and where life is so beautiful! If you seat yourself on my back to-morrow, I will take you there; I think that may be allowed. But do not talk any longer now, for I wish to sleep."

And accordingly they all went to sleep. The Prince awaked early in the morning, and was not a little astonished to find himself already far above the clouds. He was sitting on the back of the East Wind, who kept tight hold of him, and they flew so high that woods and meadows, rivers and seas, appeared like a large coloured map.

"Good morning!" said the East Wind, "you may as well sleep a little longer, for there is not much to be seen on the flat surface beneath us, unless you can find amusement in counting churches; they stand like little bits of chalk on the green board there below." What he called the green board were fields and meadows.

"It was uncivil to depart without taking leave of your mother and brothers," said the Prince.

"That may be excused, as you were asleep," said the East Wind. And now they flew even faster than before; how fast might be seen by the tops of the trees, whose branches and leaves rustled as they passed them, and by the seas and lakes; for, as they crossed them, the waves rose higher, and large ships bowed low like swans in the water.

In the evening, when it became dark, the large towns had a most curious appearance. Lights were burning here and there; it was just like watching the sparks on a burnt piece of paper, as they vanish one after another, till at last, as children say, out goes the sexton and his family.

The Prince clapped his hands, but the East Wind begged him to be quiet and to hold fast, as otherwise he might fall, and remain suspended from the top of a church-steeple.

The eagle flew lightly over the dark woods, but the East Wind flew still more lightly; the Cossack galloped swiftly over the desert on his little horse, but the Prince rode far more swiftly.

"Now you can see the Himalaya mountains," said the East Wind; "they are the highest in Asia. We shall soon come to the Garden of Paradise." So they turned more towards the South, and inhaled the fragrance of spices and flowers. Figs and pomegranates were growing wild; red and white grapes hung from the vines. Here they descended, and stretched themselves on the soft grass, while the flowers nodded to the Wind, as if they wished to say, "Welcome, welcome!"

"Are we now in the Garden of Paradise?" asked the Prince. "No, not yet," said the East Wind, "but we shall soon be there. Do you see yonder rock, and the large cave, in front of which the vine-branches hang like large green curtains? We must go through it. Wrap your cloak around you; the sun burns here, but take a step farther, and you will find it cold as ice. The bird which is flying past the cave has one wing warm as summer, and the other as cold as winter."

"So that is the way to the Garden of Paradise," said the Prince.

They went into the cave. Oh, how freezing it was there! But this did not last long; the East Wind spread out his wings; they shone like the purest flame. Oh, what a cavern! large blocks of stone, from which water was trickling, hung in the strangest forms above them. The cave was now so narrow, that they were obliged to creep along on their hands and feet, and now again high and broad as the free air without. It looked like a subterranean chapel, with mute organ-pipes and petrified organ.

"Surely we are going through the path of Death to the Garden of Paradise," said the Prince, but the East Wind answered not a syllable, and pointed to where the loveliest blue light was beaming to meet them. The rocks above them became more and more like mists, and at last were as clear and transparent as a white cloud in the moonlight. They now breathed the softest, balmiest air,—fresh as among the mountains, fragrant as among the roses of the valley.

Here flowed a river, as clear as the atmosphere itself; gold and silver fish swam in it; purple eels, which emitted blue sparks at every motion, were playing beneath the surface, and the broad leaves of the water-lily shone with all the colours of the rainbow; the flower itself was like a glowing orange-coloured flame, receiving sustenance from the water, as a lamp from oil. A bridge of marble, shining like glassy pearl, cunningly and delicately carved, led over the water to the Island of Bliss, where bloomed the Garden of Paradise.

The East Wind took the Prince in his arms, and bore him over. The flowers and leaves sang the sweetest songs about his childhood, in soft wavy tones, such as no human voice could imitate. Whether they were palm-trees or gigantic water-plants that grew here, the Prince knew not; but he had never before seen trees so large and full of sap; and hanging about them in long wreaths were the most singular creepers, such as are seen, painted in gold or bright colours, on the margins of old missals, or winding about initial letters. There were the strangest compounds of birds, flowers, and scrolls. Close to them, in the grass, stood a flock of peacocks, with their bright tails spread out:—yes, indeed, they were peacocks!—but no, when the Prince touched them, he found they were not birds, but plants: they were large plantain-leaves, that sparkled like the splendid tails of peacocks. Lions and tigers sprang like cats over hedges, green and fragrant as the flowers of the olive; and both lions and tigers were tame. The timid wood-turtle, her plumage bright as the loveliest pearl, flapped her wings against the lion's mane; and the shy antelope stood by, and nodded his head, as if he wished to play too.

And now came the Fairy of Paradise; her garments shone like the sun, and her countenance was as gentle as that of a happy mother rejoicing over her child. She was very young and very beautiful; the fairest of maidens followed her, each having a star sparkling in her hair. The East Wind gave her the leaf of the phœnix, before described, and her eyes beamed with joy. She took the Prince by the hand, and led him into her palace, the walls of which resembled in colours those of a splendid tulip-petal held towards the sun; the dome was formed by one single bright flower, whose cup appeared the deeper the longer you looked into it. The Prince stepped to the window, and looked through one of the panes; he saw the Tree of Knowledge, with the Serpent, and Adam and Eve, standing by its side. "Were they not driven out?" asked he; and the Fairy smiled, and explained to him, that Time had stamped its image upon every pane, though not such images as we are accustomed to see; nay, rather, there was life itself; the leaves of the trees moved; men came and went, as in a mirror. He looked through another pane, and there saw Jacob's dream; the ladder rose to heaven, and angels, with their large wings, hovered up and down. Yes, everything that had happened in the world lived and moved in these panes of glass. Time only could have made such cunning pictures.

The Fairy smiled, and led the Prince into a high, spacious hall, whose walls seemed covered with transparent paintings, each countenance more lovely than the last; they were millions of blessed spirits, who smiled and sang; the uppermost of them so little,— so very little,— even more diminutive than the smallest rose-bud, marked on paper with one touch. And in the midst of the hall stood a large tree with luxuriant branches; golden apples, of different sizes, hung like oranges among the green leaves. This was the Tree of Knowledge, the fruit of which Adam and Eve had eaten; from every leaf there dropped a bright red drop of dew; it seemed as though the tree wept tears of blood.

"Let us get into the boat," said the Fairy, "we shall find it so refreshing: the boat is rocked on the swelling waves, without stirring from its place; but all the countries in the world will appear to glide past us." And it was strange to see all the coast moving: first came the high, snow-covered Alps, with their clouds and dark fir-trees; the horn's deep, melancholy tones were heard, whilst the herdsman was singing merrily in the valley below. Then the banyan-trees let their long hanging branches fall into the boat; coal-black swans glided along the water, and the strangest-looking animals and flowers were to be seen on the shore; it was New Holland, which succeeded the high, blue Alps. And now came the hymns of priests, the dance of savages, accompanied by the noise of drums, and the wooden tuba. Egypt's cloud-aspiring pyramids, overthrown pillars, and sphinxes, half buried in sand, sailed by. The northern lights beamed over the icy mountains of the north,— they were fire-works, such as no mortal could imitate. The Prince was so happy! He saw a hundred times more than we have related.

"And may I stay here always?" asked he.

"That depends upon thyself," answered the Fairy. "If thou dost not, like Adam, allow thyself to be seduced to do what is forbidden, thou mayest stay here always."

"I will not touch the apple on the Tree of Knowledge," said the Prince; "there are a thousand fruits here quite as beautiful!"

"Examine thyself. If thou art not strong enough, return with the East Wind who brought thee; he is just going to fly back, and will not return for a hundred years. The time will pass away here as if it were only a hundred hours; but it is a long time for temptation and sin. Every evening, when I leave thee, I must invite thee to 'Come with me!' I must beckon to thee, but beware of attending to my call! come not with me, for every step will but increase the temptation. Thou wilt come into the hall where the Tree of Knowledge stands, —I sleep among its fragrant hanging branches,—thou wilt bend over me, and I shall smile, but, if thou touch me, Paradise will sink beneath the earth, and be lost to thee. The sharp wind of the desert will whistle around, the cold rain will drip from thy hair, sorrow and care will be thy inheritance."

"I will stay here," said the Prince. And the East Wind kissed his forehead, and said, "Be strong, and we shall see each other again after a hundred years. Farewell! farewell!" And the East Wind spread out his great wings; they shone like lightning in harvest-time, or the northern lights in winter. "Farewell! farewell!" resounded from the trees and flowers. Storks and pelicans, like a long streaming riband, flew after him, accompanying him to the boundary of the garden.

"Now we will begin our dances," said the Fairy; "and when the sun is sinking, while I am dancing with thee, thou wilt see me beckon, thou wilt hear me say, 'Come with me:' but do not follow. For a hundred years I must repeat this call to thee every evening; every day thy strength will increase, till at last thou wilt not even think of following. This evening will be the first time,—I have warned thee!"

The Fairy then led him into a large hall of white transparent lilies; their yellow stamina formed little golden harps, sending forth clear sweet tones, resembling those of the flute. Lovely maidens, light and slender, their limbs veiled with gauze, hovered in the dance, singing how beautiful was the life that knew not death, and that the glory of Paradise must endure for ever.

And the sun was setting; the whole sky was like pure gold; and the lilies shone amid the purple gleam like the loveliest roses. The Prince saw opening before him the background of the hall where stood the Tree of Knowledge in a splendour which dazzled his eyes; a song floated over him, sweet and gentle as his mother's voice; it seemed as though she sang, "My child; my dear, dear child!"

Then the Fairy beckoned gracefully, saying, "Come with me, come with me!" and he rushed to her, forgetting his promise, even on the first evening.

The fragrance, the spicy fragrance around, became stronger;

the harps sounded more sweetly; and it seemed as though the millions of smiling heads in the hall where the Tree was growing nodded and sang, "Let us know everything! Man is lord of the earth!" And they were no longer tears of blood that dropped from the leaves of the Tree of Knowledge, they were red sparkling stars — so it appeared to him.

"Come with me, come with me!" thus spoke those trembling tones; and the Fairy bent the boughs asunder, and in another moment was concealed within them.

"I have not yet sinned," said the Prince, "neither will I," and he flung aside the boughs where she was sleeping — beautiful as only the Fairy of the Garden of Paradise could be; she smiled as she slept; he bent over her, and saw tears tremble behind her eyelashes. "Weepest thou on my account?" whispered he. "Weep not, loveliest of creatures!" and he kissed the tears from her eyes. There was a fearful clap of thunder, more loud and deep than has ever been heard on earth; all things rushed together in wild confusion; the charming Fairy vanished; the blooming Paradise sank so low! so low! The Prince saw it sink amid the darkness of night; it beamed in the distance like a little glimmering star; a deadly chill shot through his limbs; his eyes closed, and he lay for some time apparently dead.

The cold rain beat upon his face, the sharp wind blew upon his forehead, when the Prince's consciousness returned.

"What have I done?" said he. "I have sinned like Adam; I have sinned, and Paradise has sunk low, beneath the earth!" And he opened his eyes and saw the star in the distance — the star which sparkled like his lost Paradise; it was the morning-star in heaven.

He stood upright, and found himself in the wood, near the Cavern of the Winds; the mother of the Winds sat by his side; she looked very angry, and raised her hand.

"Already, on the first evening!" said she. "Truly I expected it. Well, if thou wert my son, thou shouldest go forthwith into the sack."

"He shall go there!" said Death: he was a strong old man, with a scythe in his hand, and with large black wings.

"He shall be laid in the coffin, but not now. I shall mark him, suffer him to wander yet a little while upon the earth, and repent of his sin; he may improve, he may grow good.

I shall return one day when he least expects it; I shall lay him in the black coffin. If his head and heart are still full of sin, he will sink lower than the Garden of Paradise sank; but if he have become good and holy, I shall put the coffin on my head, and fly to the star yonder. The Garden of Paradise blooms there also; he shall enter therein, and remain in the star — that bright sparkling star — for ever!"

THE FIR-TREE.

FAR away in the deep forest there once grew a pretty Fir-Tree; the situation was delightful, the sun shone full upon him, the breeze played freely around him, and in the neighbourhood grew many companion fir-trees, some older, some younger. But the little Fir-Tree was not happy: he was always longing to be tall; he thought not of the warm sun and the fresh air; he cared not for the merry, prattling peasant children who came to the forest to look for strawberries and raspberries. Except, indeed, sometimes, when after having filled their pitchers, or threaded the bright berries on a straw, they would sit down near the little Fir-Tree, and say, "What a pretty little tree this is!" and then the Fir-Tree would feel very much vexed.

Year by year he grew, a long green shoot sent he forth every year; for you may always tell how many years a fir-tree has lived by counting the number of joints in its stem.

"Oh, that I was as tall as the others are," sighed the little Tree, "then I should spread out my branches so far, and my crown should look out over the wide world around! the birds would build their nests among my branches, and when the wind blew I should bend my head so grandly, just as the others do!"

He had no pleasure in the sunshine, in the song of the birds, or in the red clouds that sailed over him every morning and evening.

In the winter-time, when the ground was covered with the white, glistening snow, there was a hare that would come continually scampering about, and jumping right over the little Tree's head—and that was most provoking! However, two winters passed away, and by the third the Tree was so tall that the hare was obliged to run round it. "Oh! to grow, to grow, to become tall and old, that is the only thing in the world worth living for;"—so thought the Tree.

The wood-cutters came in the autumn and felled some among the largest of the trees; this happened every year, and our young Fir, who was by this time a tolerable height, shuddered when he saw those grand, magnificent trees fall with a tremendous crash, crackling to the earth: their boughs were then all cut off; terribly naked, and lanky, and long did the stem look after this—they could hardly be recognised. They were laid one upon another in waggons, and horses drew them away, far, far away, from the forest. Where could they be going? What might be their fortunes?

So next spring, when the Swallows and the Storks had returned from abroad, the Tree asked them, saying, "Know you not whither they are taken? have you not met them?"

The Swallows knew nothing about the matter, but the Stork looked thoughtful for a moment, then nodded his head, and said, "Yes, I believe I have seen them! As I was flying from Egypt to this place I met several ships; those ships had splendid masts. I have little doubt that they were the trees that you speak of; they smelled like fir-wood. I may congratulate you, for they sailed gloriously, quite gloriously!"

"Oh, that I, too, were tall enough to sail upon the sea! Tell me what it is, this sea, and what it looks like."

"Thank you, it would take too long, a great deal!" said the Stork, and away he stalked.

"Rejoice in thy youth!" said the Sunbeams; "rejoice in thy luxuriant youth, in the fresh life that is within thee!"

And the Wind kissed the Tree, and the Dew wept tears over him, but the Fir-Tree understood them not.

When Christmas approached, many quite young trees were felled—trees which were some of them not so tall or of just the same height as the young restless Fir-Tree who was always longing to be away; these young trees were chosen from the most beautiful, their branches were not cut off, they were laid in a waggon, and horses drew them away, far, far away, from the forest.

"Where are they going?" asked the Fir-Tree. "They are not larger than I am; indeed, one of them was much less; why do they keep all their branches? where can they be gone?"

"We know! we know!" twittered the Sparrows. "We peeped in through the windows of the town below! we know where they are gone! Oh, you cannot think what honour and glory they receive! We looked through the window-panes and saw them planted in a warm room, and decked out with such beautiful things—gilded apples, sweetmeats, playthings, and hundreds of bright candles!"

"And then?" asked the Fir-Tree, trembling in every bough; "and then? what happened then?"

"Oh, we saw no more. That was beautiful, beautiful beyond compare!"

"Is this glorious lot destined to be mine?" cried the Fir-Tree, with delight. "This is far better than sailing over the sea. How I long for the time! Oh, that Christmas were come! I am now tall and full of branches, like the others which last year were carried away. Oh, that I were even now in the waggon! that I were in the warm room, honoured and adorned! and then—yes, then, something still better must happen, else why should they take the trouble to decorate me? it must be that something still greater, still more splendid, must happen—but what? Oh, I suffer, I suffer with longing! I know not what it is that I feel!"

"Rejoice in our love!" said the Air and the Sunshine. "Rejoice in thy youth and thy freedom!"

But rejoice he never would: he grew and grew, in winter as in summer; he stood there clothed in green, dark-green foliage; the people that saw him said, "That is a beautiful tree!" and, next Christmas, he was the first that was felled. The axe struck sharply through the wood, the tree fell to the earth with a heavy groan; he suffered an agony, a faintness that he had never expected; he quite forgot to think of his good fortune, he felt such sorrow at being compelled to leave his home, the place whence he had sprung; he knew that he should never see again those dear old comrades, or the little bushes and flowers that had flourished under his shadow, perhaps not even the birds. Neither did he find the journey by any means pleasant.

The Tree first came to himself when, in the court-yard to which he was first taken with the other trees, he heard a man say, " This is a splendid one, the very thing we want!"

Then came two smartly-dressed servants, and carried the Fir-Tree into a large and handsome saloon. Pictures hung on the walls, and on the mantel-piece stood large Chinese vases with lions on the lids; there were rocking-chairs, silken sofas, tables covered with picture-books, and toys that had cost a hundred times a hundred rix-dollars—at least so said the children. And the Fir-Tree was planted in a large cask filled with sand, but no one could know that it was a cask, for it was hung with green cloth and placed upon a carpet woven of many gay colours. Oh, how the Tree trembled! What was to happen next? A young lady, assisted by the servants, now began to adorn him.

Upon some branches they hung little nets cut out of coloured paper, every net filled with sugar-plums; from others gilded apples and walnuts were suspended, looking just as if they had grown there; and more than a hundred little wax-tapers, red, blue, and white, were placed here and there among the boughs. Dolls, that looked almost like men and women—the Tree had never seen such things before—seemed dancing to and fro among the leaves, and highest, on the summit, was fastened a large star of gold tinsel; this was, indeed, splendid, splendid beyond compare! " This evening," they said, " this evening it will be lighted up."

" Would that it were evening !" thought the Tree. " Would that the lights were kindled, for then—what will happen then? Will the trees come out of the forest to see me? Will the sparrows fly here and look in through the window-panes? Shall I stand here adorned both winter and summer?"

He thought much of it; he thought till he had bark-ache with longing, and bark-aches with trees are as bad as head-aches with us. The candles were lighted—oh, what a blaze of splendour! the Tree trembled in all his branches, so that one of them caught fire. " Oh, dear !" cried the young lady, and it was extinguished in great haste.

So the Tree dared not tremble again; he was so fearful of losing something of his splendour, he felt almost bewildered in the midst of all this glory and brightness. And now, all of a sudden, both folding-doors were flung open, and a troop of children rushed in as if they had a mind to jump over him; the older people followed more quietly; the little ones stood quite silent, but only for a moment! then their jubilee burst forth afresh; they shouted till the walls re-echoed, they danced round the Tree, one present after another was torn down.

"What are they doing?" thought the Tree; "what will happen now?" And the candles burned down to the branches, so they were extinguished,—and the children were given leave to plunder the Tree. Oh! they rushed upon him in such riot, that the boughs all crackled; had not his summit been festooned with the gold star to the ceiling he would have been overturned.

The children danced and played about with their beautiful playthings, no one thought any more of the Tree except the old nurse, who came and peeped among the boughs, but it was only to see whether perchance a fig or an apple had not been left among them.

"A story! a story!" cried the children, pulling a short thick man towards the tree. He sat down, saying, "It is pleasant to sit under the shade of green boughs; besides, the Tree may be benefited by hearing my story. But I shall only tell you one. Would you like to hear about Ivedy Avedy, or about Humpty Dumpty, who fell down-stairs, and yet came to the throne and won the Princess?"

"Ivedy Avedy!" cried some; "Humpty Dumpty!" cried others; there was a famous uproar; the Fir-Tree alone was silent, thinking to himself, "Ought I to make a noise as they do? or ought I to do nothing at all?" for he most certainly was one of the company, and had done all that had been required of him.

And the short thick man told the story of Humpty Dumpty, who fell down-stairs, and yet came to the throne and won the Princess. And the children clapped their hands and called out for another; they wanted to hear the story of Ivedy Avedy also, but they did not get it. The Fir-Tree stood meanwhile quite silent and thoughtful—the birds in the forest had never related anything like this. "Humpty

Dumpty fell down-stairs, and yet was raised to the throne and won the Princess! Yes, yes, strange things come to pass in the world!" thought the Fir-Tree, who believed it must all be true, because such a pleasant man had related it. "Ah, ah! who knows but I may fall down-stairs and win a Princess?" And he rejoiced in the expectation of being next day again decked out with candles and playthings, gold and fruit.

"To-morrow I will not tremble," thought he. "I will rejoice in my magnificence. To-morrow I shall again hear the story of Humpty Dumpty, and perhaps that about Ivedy Avedy likewise." And the Tree mused thereupon all night.

In the morning the maids came in.

"Now begins my state anew!" thought the Tree. But they dragged him out of the room, up the stairs, and into an attic-chamber, and there thrust him into a dark corner, where not a ray of light could penetrate. "What can be the meaning of this?" thought the Tree. "What am I to do here? What shall I hear in this place?" And he leant against the wall, and thought, and thought. And plenty of time he had for thinking it over, for day after day, and night after night, passed away, and yet no one ever came into the room. At last somebody did come in, but it was only to push into the corner some old trunks: the Tree was now entirely hidden from sight, and apparently entirely forgotten.

"It is now winter," thought the Tree. "The ground is hard and covered with snow; they cannot plant me now, so I am to stay here in shelter till the spring. Men are so clever and prudent! I only wish it were not so dark and so dreadfully lonely! not even a little hare! Oh, how pleasant it was in the forest, when the snow lay on the ground and the hare scampered about,—yes, even when he jumped over my head, though I did not like it then. It is so terribly lonely here."

"Squeak! squeak!" cried a little Mouse, just then gliding forward. Another followed; they snuffed about the Fir-Tree, and then slipped in and out among the branches.

"It is horribly cold!" said the little Mice. "Otherwise it is very comfortable here. Don't you think so, you old Fir-Tree?"

"I am not old," said the Fir-Tree; "there are many who are much older than I am."

"How came you here?" asked the Mice, "and what do

you know?" They were most uncommonly curious. "Tell us about the most delightful place on earth? Have you ever been there? Have you been into the store-room, where cheeses lie on the shelves, and bacon hangs from the ceiling; where one can dance over tallow-candles; where one goes in thin and comes out fat?"

"I know nothing about that," said the Tree, "but I know the forest, where the sun shines and where the birds sing!" and then he spoke of his youth and its pleasures. The little Mice had never heard anything like it before; they listened so attentively and said, "Well, to be sure! how much you have seen! how happy you have been!"

"Happy!" repeated the Fir-Tree, in surprise, and he thought a moment over all that he had been saying,—"Yes, on the whole, those were pleasant times!" He then told them about the Christmas-eve, when he had been decked out with cakes and candles.

"Oh!" cried the little Mice, "how happy you have been, you old Fir-Tree!"

"I am not old at all!" returned the Fir; "it is only this winter that I have left the forest; I am just in the prime of life!"

"How well you can talk!" said the little Mice; and the next night they came again, and brought with them four other little Mice, who wanted also to hear the Tree's history; and the more the Tree spoke of his youth in the forest, the more vividly he remembered it, and said, "Yes, those were pleasant times! but they may come again, they may come again! Humpty Dumpty fell down-stairs, and for all that he won the Princess; perhaps I, too, may win a Princess;" and then the Fir-Tree thought of a pretty little delicate Birch-tree that grew in the forest,—a real Princess, a very lovely Princess, was she to the Fir-Tree.

"Who is this Humpty Dumpty?" asked the little Mice. Whereupon he related the tale; he could remember every word of it perfectly: and the little Mice were ready to jump to the top of the Tree for joy. The night following several more Mice came, and on Sunday came also two Rats; they, however, declared that the story was not at all amusing, which much vexed the little Mice, who, after hearing their opinion, could not like it so well either.

" Do you know only that one story ? " asked the Rats.

" Only that one ! " answered the Tree; " I heard it on the happiest evening of my life, though I did not then know how happy I was."

" It is a miserable story ! Do you know none about pork and tallow ?—no store-room story ? "

" No," said the Tree.

" Well, then, we have heard enough of it ! " returned the Rats, and they went their ways.

The little Mice, too, never came again. The Tree sighed. " It was pleasant when they sat round me, those busy little Mice, listening to my words. Now that, too, is all past ! however, I shall have pleasure in remembering it, when I am taken away from this place."

But when would that be ? One morning, people came and routed out the lumber-room ; the trunks were taken away, the Tree, too, was dragged out of the corner ; they threw him carelessly on the floor, but one of the servants picked him up and carried him down-stairs. Once more he beheld the light of day.

" Now life begins again ! " thought the Tree ; he felt the fresh air, the warm sunbeams—he was out in the court. All happened so quickly that the Tree quite forgot to look at himself,—there was so much to look at all around. The court joined a garden, everything was so fresh and blooming, the roses clustered so bright and so fragrant round the trellis-work, the lime-trees were in full blossom, and the swallows flew backwards and forwards, twittering, " Quirri-virri-vit, my beloved is come ! " but it was not the Fir-Tree whom they meant.

" I shall live ! I shall live ! " He was filled with delightful hope ; he tried to spread out his branches, but, alas ! they were all dried up and yellow. He was thrown down upon a heap of weeds and nettles. The star of gold tinsel that had been left fixed on his crown now sparkled brightly in the sunshine.

Some merry children were playing in the court, the same who at Christmas-time had danced round the Tree. One of the youngest now perceived the gold star, and ran to tear it off.

" Look at it, still fastened to the ugly old Christmas-Tree ! " cried he, trampling upon the boughs till they broke under his boots.

And the Tree looked on all the flowers of the garden now blooming in the freshness of their beauty ; he looked upon himself, and he wished from his heart that he had been left to wither alone in the dark corner of the lumber-room: he called to mind his happy forest-life, the merry Christmas-eve, and the little Mice who had listened so eagerly when he related the story of Humpty Dumpty.

"Past, all past!" said the poor Tree. "Had I but been happy, as I might have been! Past, all past!"

And the servant came and broke the Tree into small pieces, heaped them up and set fire to them. And the Tree groaned deeply, and every groan sounded like a little shot; the children all ran up to the place and jumped about in front of the blaze, looking into it and crying, "Piff! piff!" But at each of those heavy groans the Fir-Tree thought of a bright summer's day, or a starry winter's night in the forest, of Christmas-eve, or of Humpty Dumpty, the only story that he knew and could relate. And at last the Tree was burned.

The boys played about in the court; on the bosom of the youngest sparkled the gold star that the Tree had worn on the happiest evening of his life; but that was past, and the Tree was past, and the story also, past! past! for all stories must come to an end, some time or other.

MOTHER ELDER.

THERE was once a little boy who had caught a cold by getting his feet wet; how he had managed it no one could conceive, for the weather was perfectly fine and dry. His mother took off his clothes, put him to bed, and brought in the teapot, intending to make him a cup of good, warm elder-tea. Just then the pleasant old man, who lodged in the uppermost floor of the house, came in — he lived quite alone, poor man! for he had neither wife nor children of his own, but he loved all his neighbours' children very fondly, and had so many charming stories and fairy tales to tell them, that it was a pleasure to see him among them.

"Now drink your tea, like a good boy," said the mother, "and who knows but you may hear a story?"

"Ah, yes, if one could only think of something new!" said the old man, smiling and nodding his head. "But where did the little one get his feet wet?" asked he.

"Where, indeed?" said the mother, "that's just what nobody can make out."

"May not I have a story?" asked the boy.

"Yes, if you can tell me exactly how deep the gutter is in the little street yonder, along which you go to school. I want to know that first."

"The water just comes up to the middle of my boot," replied the boy, "but not unless I walk through the deep hole."

"Ah, then, that's where we got our wet feet!" said the old man. "And now, I suppose, you will call upon me for a tale, but really I don't know any more."

"But you can get one ready in a moment," insisted the boy. "Mother says that everything you look at quickly becomes a fairy tale, and that everything you touch you turn into a story."

"Yes, but those stories and fairy tales are not good for much! the right sort come of their own accord; they tap at my forehead, and cry, 'Here we are!'"

"I hope they will soon come and tap!" said the little boy, and his mother laughed, put some elder-flowers into the tea-pot, and poured boiling water over them.

"Come, now for a story! tell me one, pray!"

"Yes, if the stories would but come; but they are proud, and will only visit me when it so pleases them. Hush!" cried he all of a sudden, "here we have it; keep a good look-out; now it is in the teapot."

And the little boy looked at the teapot; he saw the lid rise up, and the elder-flowers spring forth, so fresh and white they were, and they shot out long, thick branches,—even out of the spout they shot forth,—spreading on all sides, and growing larger and larger, till at last there stood by the bed-side a most charming elder-bush, a perfect tree, some of its boughs stretching over the bed and thrusting the curtains aside. Oh, how full of blossoms was this tree, and how fragrant were those blossoms! and in the midst of the tree sat a kind-looking old dame, wearing the strangest dress in the world: it was green like the elder leaves, and with a pattern of large white elder-flower clusters spreading all over it,—one could not be sure whether it were actually a gown, or real, living green leaves and flowers.

"What is her name?" inquired the little boy.

"Why, those old Greeks and Romans," replied the old man, "used to call her a Dryad, but we don't understand those outlandish names; the sailors in the New Booths* have a much better name for her, they call her Mother Elder, and that suits her very well. Now listen to me, and keep looking at the pretty elder-tree the while.

"Just such another large, blooming tree as that stands among the New Booths; it has grown up in the corner of a miserable little courtyard. Under the shade of this tree there sat one afternoon, the glorious sunshine around them, two old people, a very, very old sailor, and his very, very old wife. They were great-grandparents already, and would soon have to keep their Golden Wedding-day; but they could not exactly remember on what day it would fall, and Mother Elder sat in the tree above them, looking so pleased, just as she does now. 'Ah, I know which is the Golden Wedding-day!'† said she, but they did not hear her,—there they sat, talking over old times.

"'Can't you remember,' said the old sailor, 'the days when we were quite little ones, and used to be always running and playing about in this very same yard where we are sitting now; and how we stuck slips in the ground to make a garden?'

"'To be sure I remember it,' replied the old woman. 'We watered the slips every day, but only one of them took root, and that was an elder-slip; and it shot out its green shoots till it grew up to be this large tree that we old folks are now sitting under.'

"'So it did!' said the sailor; 'and in the corner yonder used to stand a water-pail, where I swam my boats. I carved them out with my own hand—such famous boats they were! —but I soon had to sail myself in rather larger vessels than those, though.'

"'Yes, but first we went to school to be made scholars of,' said his wife; 'and then we were confirmed: we both of us cried, I remember; and in the afternoon we went hand in

* Nyboder (New Booths) is the quarter of Copenhagen inhabited by the seamen.

† The fiftieth anniversary of a wedding-day is in Denmark called the Golden Wedding-day, and is kept as a domestic festival.

hand up to the Round Tower, and looked out upon the world; out over all Copenhagen and the sea; and then we went to Fredericksberg, where the King and Queen were sailing about the canals in their magnificent barges.'

"'But those barges were scarcely more like the great ships I sailed in than my poor little boats were,—and, oh, for how many, many years I was away on those long voyages!'

"'Yes, and how often I wept for you!" said she. 'I believed you must be dead, and gone for ever, lying low, low down beneath the deep waters. Many a night have I got up to look at the weather-cock, to see if the wind had changed; and change it did, over and over again, but still you did not return. There is one day I shall never forget; it was pouring with rain; the dustmen had come to the house where I was in service. I came down with the dust-box and remained standing at the door;—oh, what weather it was! and while I stood there, the postman came up and gave me a letter; it was from you. What a journey that letter had made! I tore it open and read it; I laughed and cried by turns, I was so happy. The letter told me you were in the warm countries, where the coffee-trees grow—what charming countries those must be!—it told me so many things, and I fancied I could see all that you had described; and the rain still kept pouring down in torrents, and there I stood at the door with the dust-box. Just then somebody came up behind me, and took hold of me——'

"'Yes, indeed, and didn't you give him a good box on the ear? didn't his ear tingle after it?'

"'But I did not know that it was you. You had arrived as soon as your letter, and you were so handsome,—but that you are still;—and you had a large yellow silk handkerchief in your pocket and a new hat on your head. Oh, what weather it was! the streets were quite flooded.'

"'And then we were married,' said the sailor; 'don't you remember that? and then we had our first little boy, and after him we had Marie, and Niels, and Peter, and Hans Christian.'

"'Ah! and how happy it was that they should all grow up to be good, and honest, and industrious, and to be loved by everybody.'

"'And their children too, they have little ones now,' added the old sailor; 'yes, they are fine healthy babies, those great-grandchildren of ours! And so it was, I fancy, just about this time of year that we had our wedding.'

"'Yes, this very day is your Golden Wedding-day!'" said Mother Elder, putting out her head between the two old people, but they fancied she was their neighbour nodding to them. They gave little heed to her, but again looked at each other, and took hold of each other's hand. Presently their children and grandchildren came out into the court; they knew well that this was the Golden Wedding-day, and had come that very morning to congratulate their parents; but the two old people had quite forgotten that, although they could remember so clearly things that had happened half a century ago. And the elder-blossoms smelled so sweetly, and the sun, which was near setting, shone full into the old couple's faces — such a red rosy light he shed over their features, and the youngest of the grandchildren danced round them, shouting with glee that this evening there should be a grand feast, for they were all to have hot potatoes for supper; and Mother Elder nodded her head to them from the tree, and shouted, 'Hurrah!' as loudly as they did."

"But I don't call that a tale at all," said the little boy in the bed.

"Don't you?" said the kind old story-teller; "well, suppose we ask Mother Elder what she thinks about it."

"No, you are right, that was not a tale," replied Mother Elder; "but now you shall have one. I will show you how the most charming fairy tales spring out of the commonest incidents of every-day life; were it not so, you know my pretty elder-bush could hardly have grown out of the teapot!" And then she took the little boy out of bed, pillowing his head upon her bosom, and the elder-boughs so richly laden with blossoms entwined around them, so that they seemed to be sitting in a thick-leaved, fragrant arbour, and the arbour flew away with them through the air — that was most delightful! Mother Elder had, all of a sudden, changed into a pretty and graceful young girl; her robe was still of the same fresh-green, white-flowered material that Mother Elder had worn; on her bosom rested a real elder-flower cluster, and a whole garland of elder-flowers was wreathed among her curling flaxen hair; her eyes were large and blue—it was a delight to behold a creature so lovely! And she and the boy embraced, and immediately they were of the same age; they loved each other, and were unspeakably happy.

Hand in hand they walked out of the arbour, and were now in the pretty flower-garden of their home. On the grass-plot they found their father's walking-stick. For the children, it seemed, there was life in this stick: as soon as they got astride it, the bright knob of the handle became a fiery, neighing head, a long black mane fluttered to and fro in the wind, four long, slender legs shot out,—a fine spirited creature was their new steed, and off he galloped with them round the grass-plot—hurrah! "Now we will ride many miles away," said the boy. "Let us ride to the dear old manor-house we went to last year." And still they rode round and round the grass-plot; the little girl, who, as we know, was no other than Mother Elder, crying out all the while, "Now we are in the country. Seest thou not yonder pretty cottage? The elder-tree lowers its branches over it, and the cock is strutting about, and scraping up the ground for the hens. See how proudly he strides! And now we are close to the church; it stands high on the hill, among the great oak-trees, one of which is quite hollow. Now we are at the smithy; the fire is blazing, and the half-naked men are banging away with their hammers, and the sparks are flying about all round. Away, away, to the old manor-house!" And all that the little maiden riding on the stick described flew past them,—the boy saw it all,—and still they only rode round and round the grass-plot. Then the children played in one of the walks, and marked out a tiny garden for themselves in the mould, and the girl took one of the elder-blossoms out of her hair, and planted it, and it grew up, just as the elder-sprig grew which was planted among the New Booths by the old sailor and his wife when they were little ones, as has been told already. And, hand in hand, the children now went on together, just as the children in the New Booths had done; but not up to the Round Tower nor to the Gardens of Fredericksberg. No, the little girl threw her arms round the little boy's waist, and then away they flew over all Denmark. And spring deepened into summer, and summer mellowed into autumn, and autumn faded away into pale, cold winter, and a thousand pictures were mirrored in the boy's eyes and heart; and still the little girl sang to him, "Never, oh never, forget thou this!" And wheresoever they flew, the sweet, strong perfume of the elder-tree floated round them; the little boy could distinguish the delicious fragrance of the roses blooming in the gardens he flew past, and the wind wafted to him the fresh odour of the beech-trees; but the elder-perfume far excelled these, he thought, for its blossoms nestled to his fairy-like maiden's heart, and over those blossoms he continually bowed his head whilst flying.

"How beautiful is spring!" exclaimed the young girl, as they stood together in the beech-wood, where the trees had newly burst into fresh vernal loveliness, where the sweet-scented woodroof grew at their feet, the pale-tinted anemones looking up so prettily amid its green. "Oh, would it were always spring in the fragrant Danish beech-wood!"

"How beautiful is summer!" said she again, as they passed an ancient baronial castle; its red, stained walls and battlements mirrored in the moat encircling them; swans swimming in the moat, and peering inquisitively up into the cool, shady avenues. A sea of green corn waved to and fro in the fields; tiny red and golden blossoms peeped out of the ditches, and the hedges were enwreathed with wild, wantoning hops and the bell-flowered white bindweed. It was evening; the moon rose large and round; the meadows were odorous with the scent of haystacks. "Never, oh never, forget thou this!"

"How beautiful is autumn!" exclaimed the little maiden; and the vault of heaven seemed to rise higher, and to grow more intensely blue, and the woods became flushed with the richest and most varied hues of crimson, green, and yellow. The hounds bounded past in full cry, whole flocks of wild fowl flew screaming over the cairn-stones, to which luxuriant brambles were clinging. In the far distance lay the deep blue sea, dotted over with white sails; old women, young maids, and children, were assembled in a barn, picking hops into a great cask; the young ones of the party were singing, and the ancient dames were telling old legends of fairies and enchantments. What could be pleasanter than this?

"How beautiful is winter!" declared our young damsel; and, behold! the trees stood around them all covered with hoar-frost—like white, branching corals they looked; the snow crisped under the children's feet with a noise as if they had creaking new boots on, and falling stars, one after another, shot across the sky. The Christmas-tree was lighted up in the parlour, everybody had had presents given him, and everybody was in good humour; the peasant's cot in the country was merry with the sound of the violin,—and the pancakes disappeared so fast! Even the poorest child might have reason to echo the words, "How beautiful is winter!"

Yes, truly, it was beautiful! and it was our faëry maiden who showed all these fair sights to the little boy, and still the elder-perfume floated round him, when a new picture rose up before his eyes,—the red flag with its white cross fluttering in the breeze,—the very same flag under which the old mariner in the New Booths had sailed. And the boy felt that he was now grown up to be a youth, and that he must go to seek his fortune in the wide world,—far away must he go to the warm countries, where grow the coffee-trees; but at their parting the young maiden took the cluster of elder-blossoms from her bosom, and gave it to him. And he kept it carefully,—he kept it between the leaves of his hymn-book, and when he was in foreign lands he never took up the book but it opened upon the place where the flower of memory lay, and the oftener he looked at it the fresher, he fancied, it became; he seemed, while he looked at it, to breathe the sweet air of the Danish beech-groves, to see peeping among the tiny elder-flowerets the pretty maiden with her bright blue eyes, and to hear her low whisper, "How beautiful is Denmark in spring, in summer, in autumn, and in winter!" And a hundred fair visions of the past flitted unbidden across his mind.

Many, very many years passed away, and he was now an old man sitting with his old wife under a flowering-tree; they held each other by the hand just as the old couple in the New Booths had done, and they talked, too, of old times, and of their Golden Wedding-day. The little maiden, with the blue eyes and the elder-blossoms in her hair, sat on the tree above, and nodded her head to them, saying, " To-day is your Golden Wedding-day !" and then she took two flower-clusters out of her hair and kissed them twice ; at the first kiss they shone like silver, after the second, like gold, and when she had set them on the two old people's heads, each cluster became a gold crown. And thus the two sat there like a crowned King and Queen, under the fragrant elder-tree ; and the old man began to tell his wife the story about Mother Elder, which had been told him when a little boy, and it seemed to them both that great part of the story was very like their own real history, and they liked that part far the best.

" Yes, so it is," said the little maiden in the tree. " Some call me Mother Elder, others call me a Dryad, but my proper name is Memory. Here I sit in the tree whilst it grows and grows ; I never forget ; I remember all things well ; I could tell such famous stories! Now let me see if you still have your flower safe ?"

And the old man opened his hymn-book; there lay the elder-flower, as fresh as though it had but just been laid between the leaves; and Memory nodded her head, and the two old people with their gold crowns sat under the tree, their faces flushed with the red evening sunlight; they closed their eyes — and then — and then — why, then, there was an end of the tale.

The little boy lay in his bed ; he did not rightly know whether he had been dreaming all this, or whether it had been told him. The teapot stood on the table, but no elder-tree was growing out of it, and his friend, the old story-teller, was just on the point of going out at the door. Whilst the boy was rubbing his eyes he was gone.

" How pleasant that was !" said the little boy. " Mother, I have been to the warm countries."

" Yes, I have no doubt of that !" replied the mother ; " after you had drunk two brimful cups of good hot elder-tea, you were likely enough to get into the warm countries !" and she covered him up well for fear he should get chilled. " You have had such a famous sound sleep while I sat disputing with him as to whether it were a faëry tale, or a real, true history."

"And where is Mother Elder?" asked the boy.

"She is in the teapot," said his mother, "and there she may stay."

ELFIN-MOUNT.

SEVERAL large Lizards were running nimbly in and out among the clefts of an old tree; they could understand each other perfectly well, for they all spoke the Lizards' language.

"Only hear what a rumbling and grumbling there is in the old Elfin-mount yonder!" observed one Lizard; "I have not been able to close my eyes for the last two nights; I might as well have had the tooth-ache, for the sleep I have had!"

"There is something in the wind, most certainly," rejoined the second Lizard. "They raise the Mount upon four red pillars till cock-crowing; there is a regular cleaning and dusting going on, and the Elfin-maidens are learning new dances—such a stamping they make in them! There is certainly something in the wind!"

"Yes; I have been talking it over with an Earth-worm of my acquaintance," said a third Lizard. "The Earth-worm has just come from the Mount; he has been grubbing in the ground there for days and nights together, and has overheard a good deal; he can't see at all, poor wretch! but no one can be quicker than he is at feeling and hearing. They are expecting strangers at the Elfin-mount — distinguished strangers; but who they are the Earth-worm would not say; most likely he did not know. All the Wills-o'-the-Wisp are engaged to form a procession of torches — so they call it; and all the silver and gold, of which there is such a store in the Elfin-mount, is being fresh rubbed up, and set out to shine in the moonlight."

"But who can these strangers be?" exclaimed all the Lizards, with one voice. "What can be in the wind? Only listen!—what buzzing and humming!"

Just then the Elfin-mount parted asunder; and an elderly Elfin-damsel came tripping out—she was the old Elfin-king's housekeeper, and distantly related to his family, on which account she wore an amber heart on her forehead, but was otherwise plainly dressed. Like all other Elves, she was hollow in the back. She was very quick and light-footed; trip, trip, trip, away she ran, straight into the marsh, to the Night-raven.

"You are invited to Elfin-mount for this very evening," said she; "but will you not first do us a very great kindness, and be the bearer of the other invitations? You do not keep house yourself, you know; so you can easily oblige us. We are expecting some very distinguished strangers, Trolds in fact; and his Elfin Majesty intends to welcome them in person."

"Who are to be invited?" inquired the Night-raven.

"Why, to the grand ball, all the world may come; even men, if they could but talk in their sleep, or do a little bit of anything in our way. But the first banquet must be very select; none but guests of the very highest rank must be present. To say the truth, I and the King have been having a little dispute; for I insist that not even ghosts may be admitted to-night. The Mer-king and his daughters must be invited first; they don't much like coming on land, but I'll promise they shall each have a wet stone, or, perhaps, something better still, to sit on; and then, I think, they cannot possibly refuse us this time. All old Trolds of the first rank we must have; also, the River-spirit and the Nisses; and, I fancy, we cannot pass over the Death-horse and Kirkegrim. True, they do not belong to our set—they are too solemn for us—but they are connected with the family, and pay us regular visits."

"Caw!" said the Night-raven; and away he flew, to bear the invitations.

The Elfin-maidens were still dancing in the Elfin-mount; they danced with long scarfs woven from mist and moonlight, and for those who like that sort of thing, it looks pretty enough. The large state-room in the Mount had been regularly cleaned and cleared out; the floor had been washed with moonshine, and the walls rubbed with witches' fat till they shone as tulips do, when held up to the light. In the kitchen, frogs were roasting on the spit; while divers other choice dishes, such as mushroom-seed salad, hemlock soup, &c., were prepared, or preparing. These were to supply the first courses; rusty nails, bits of coloured glass, and suchlike dainties, were to come in for the dessert; there were also bright saltpetre wine, and ale brewed in the brewery of the Wise Witch of the Moor.

The old Elfin-king's gold crown had been fresh rubbed with powdered slate-pencil; new curtains had been hung up in all the sleeping-rooms—yes, there was, indeed, a rare bustle and commotion!

"Now, we must have the rooms scented with cows' hairs and swine's bristles; and then, I think, I shall have done my part!" said the Elfin-king's housekeeper.

"Dear papa," said the youngest of the daughters, "won't you tell me now who these grand visitors are?"

"Well!" replied his Majesty, "I suppose there's no use in keeping it a secret. Let two of my daughters get themselves ready for their wedding-day, that's all! Two of them most certainly will be married. The Chief of the Norwegian Trolds, he who dwells in old Dofrefield, and has so many castles of freestone among those rocky fastnesses, besides a gold-mine—which is a capital thing, let me tell you—he is coming down here with his two boys, who are both to choose themselves a bride. Such an honest, straightforward, true old Norseman is this Mountain Chief! so merry and jovial! he and I are old comrades; he came down here years ago to fetch his wife; she is dead now; she was the daughter of the Rock-king at Möen. Oh, how I long to see the old Norseman again! His sons, they say, are rough, unmannerly young cubs, but perhaps report may have done them injustice and, at any rate, they are sure to improve in a year or two when they have sown their wild oats. Let me see how you will polish them up!"

"And how soon are they to be here?" inquired his youngest daughter again.

"That depends on wind and weather!" returned the Elfin-king. "They travel economically; they come at the ship's convenience. I wanted them to pass over by Sweden, but the old man would not hear of that. He does not keep pace with the times; that's the only fault I can find with him."

Just then two Wills-o'-the-Wisp were seen dancing up in a vast hurry, each trying to get before the other, and to be the first to bring the news.

"They come! they come!" cried both with one voice.

"Give me my crown, and let me stand in the moonlight!" said the Elfin-king.

And his seven daughters lifted their long scarfs and bowed low to the earth.

There stood the Trold Chief from the Dofrefield, wearing a crown composed of icicles and polished pine-cones; for the rest, he was equipped in a bear-skin cloak and sledge-boots; his sons were clad more slightly, and kept their throats uncovered, by way of showing that they cared nothing about the cold.

"Is that a mount?" asked the youngest of them, pointing to it. "Why, up in Norway we should call it a cave!"

"You foolish boy!" replied his father; "a cave you go into, a mount you go up! Where are your eyes, not to see the difference?"

The only thing that surprised them in this country, they said, was that the people should speak and understand their language.

"Behave yourselves, now!" said the old man. "Don't let your host fancy you never went into decent company before!"

And now they all entered the Elfin-mount, into the grand saloon, where a really very select party was assembled, although at such short notice that it seemed almost as though some fortunate gust of wind had blown them together. And every possible arrangement had been made for the comfort of each of the guests; the Mer-king's family, for instance, sat at table in large tubs of water, and they declared they felt quite as if they were at home. All behaved with strict good-breeding except the two young northern Trolds, who at last so far forgot themselves as to put their legs on the table.

"Take your legs away from the plates!" said their father, and they obeyed, but not so readily as they might have done. Presently they took some pine-cones out of their pockets and began pelting the lady who sat between them, and then, finding their boots incommode them, they took them off, and coolly gave them to this lady to hold. But their father, the old Mountain Chief, conducted himself very differently; he talked so delightfully about the proud Norse mountains, and the torrents, white with dancing spray, that dashed foaming down their rocky steeps with a noise loud and hoarse as thunder, yet musical as the full burst of an organ, touched by a master-hand; he told of the salmon leaping up from the wild waters while the Neck was playing on his golden harp; he told of the star-light winter nights, when the sledge-bells tinkled so merrily, and the youths ran with lighted torches over the icy crust, so glassy and transparent, that through it they could see the fishes whirling to and fro in deadly terror beneath their feet; he told of the gallant northern youths and pretty maidens singing songs of old time, and dancing the Hallinge dance—yes, so charmingly he described all this, that you could not but fancy you heard and saw it all. Oh, fie for shame! all of a sudden the Mountain Chief turned round upon the elderly Elfin-maiden, and gave her a cousinly salute —and he was not yet connected ever so remotely with the family.

The young Elfin-maidens were now called upon to dance. First they danced simple dances, then stamping dances, and they did both remarkably well. Last came the most difficult of all, the "Dance out of the dance," as it was called. Bravo! how long their legs seemed to grow, and how they whirled and spun about! You could hardly distinguish legs from arms, or arms from legs—round and round they went, such whirling and twirling, such whirring and whizzing there was, that it made the Death-horse feel quite dizzy, and at last he grew so unwell that he was obliged to leave the table.

"Hurrah!" cried the old Mountain Chief, "they know how to use their limbs with a vengeance! But can they do nothing else than dance, stretch out their feet, and spin round like a whirlwind?"

"You shall judge for yourself," replied the Elfin-king; and here he called the eldest of his daughters to him. She was transparent and fair as moonlight; she was, in fact, the most delicate of all the sisters; she put a white wand between her lips and vanished,—that was her accomplishment.

But the Mountain Chief said he should not at all like his wife to possess such an accomplishment as this, and he did not think his sons would like it either.

The second could walk by the side of herself, just as though she had a shadow, which Elves and Trolds never have.

The accomplishment of the third sister was of quite another kind: she had learned how to brew good ale from the Wise Witch of the Moor, and she also knew how to lard alder-wood with glow-worms.

"She will make a capital housewife," remarked the old Mountain Chief.

And now advanced the fourth Elfin damsel; she carried a large gold harp, and no sooner had she struck the first chord than all the company lifted their left feet—for elves are left-sided; and when she struck the second chord, they were all compelled to do whatever she wished.

"A dangerous lady, indeed!" said the old Trold Chief. Both of his sons now got up and strode out of the mount; they were heartily weary of these accomplishments.

"And what can the next daughter do?" asked the Mountain Chief.

"I have learned to love the North," replied she; "and I have resolved never to marry unless I may go to Norway."

But the youngest of the sisters whispered to the old man, "That is only because she has heard an old Norse rhyme, which says, that when the end of the world shall come, the Norwegian rocks shall stand firm amid the ruins: she is very much afraid of death, and therefore she wants to go to Norway."

"Ho, ho!" cried the Mountain Chief. "Sits the wind in that quarter? But what can the seventh and last do?"

"The sixth comes before the seventh," said the Elfin-king; for he could count better than to make such a mistake. However, the sixth seemed in no hurry to come forward.

"I can only tell people the truth," said she. "Let no one trouble himself about me; I have enough to do to sew my shroud."

And now came the seventh and last, and what could she do? Why, she could tell fairy tales, as many as any one could wish to hear.

"Here are my five fingers," said the Mountain Chief; "tell me a story for each finger."

And the Elfin-maiden took hold of his wrist, and told her stories, and he laughed till his sides ached; and when she came to the finger that wore a gold ring, as though it knew it might be wanted, the Mountain Chief suddenly exclaimed, "Hold fast what thou hast,—the hand is thine! I will have thee myself to wife."

But the Elfin-maiden said that she had still two more stories to tell, one for the ring-finger, and another for the little finger.

"Keep them for next winter, we'll hear them then," replied the Mountain Chief. "And we'll hear about the 'Loves of the Fir-Tree and the Birch,' about the Valkyria's gifts too, for we all love fairy legends in Norway, and no one there can tell them so charmingly as thou dost. And then we will sit in our rocky halls, whilst the fir-logs are blazing and crackling in the stove, and drink mead out of the golden horns of the old Norse kings; the Neck has taught me a few of his rare old ditties; besides, the Garbo will often come and pay us a visit, and he will sing thee all the sweet songs that the mountain maidens sang in days of yore,—that will be most delightful! The salmon in the torrent will spring up and beat himself against the rock walls, but in vain,—he will not be able to get in. Oh, thou canst not imagine what a happy, glorious life we lead in that dear old Norway! But where are the boys?"

Where were the boys? Why, they were racing about in

the fields, and blowing out the poor Wills-o'-the-Wisp, who were just ranging themselves in the proper order to make a procession of torches.

"What do you mean by making all this riot?" inquired the Mountain Chief. "I have been choosing you a mother, now you come and choose yourselves wives from among your aunts."

But his sons said they would rather make speeches and drink toasts,—they had not the slightest wish to marry. And accordingly they made speeches, tossed off their glasses, and turned them topsy-turvy on the table, to show that they were quite empty; after this they took off their coats, and most unceremoniously lay down on the table, and went to sleep. But the old Mountain Chief, the while, danced round the hall with his young bride, and exchanged boots with her, because that is not so vulgar as exchanging rings.

"Listen, the cock is crowing!" exclaimed the lady-housekeeper. "We must make haste and shut the window-shutters close, or the sun will scorch our complexions."

And herewith Elfin-mount closed.

But outside, in the cloven trunk, the Lizards kept running up and down, and one and all declared, "What a capital fellow that old Norwegian Trold is!"

"For my part, I prefer the boys," said the Earth-worm, but he, poor wretch! could see nothing either of them or of their father, so his opinion was not worth much.

THE SNOW QUEEN.

IN SEVEN PARTS.

Part the First,

WHICH TREATS OF THE MIRROR AND ITS FRAGMENTS.

LISTEN! We are beginning our story! When we arrive at the end of it we shall, it is to be hoped, know more than we do now.

There was once a magician! a wicked magician!! a most wicked magician!!! Great was his delight at having constructed a mirror possessing this peculiarity, viz. that everything good and beautiful, when reflected in it, shrank up almost to nothing, whilst those things that were ugly and useless were magnified, and made to appear ten times worse than before. The loveliest landscapes reflected in this mirror looked like boiled spinach, and the handsomest persons appeared odious, or as if standing upon their heads, their features being so distorted that their friends could never have recognised them. Moreover, if one of them had a freckle, he might be sure that it would seem to spread over the nose and mouth; and if a good or pious thought glanced across his mind, a wrinkle was seen in the mirror. All this the magician thought highly entertaining, and he chuckled with delight at his own clever invention. Those who frequented the school of magic where he taught spread abroad the fame of this wonderful mirror, and declared that, by its means, the world and its inhabitants might be seen now, for the first time, as they really were. They carried the mirror from place to place, till at last there was no country nor person that had not been misrepresented in it. Its admirers now must needs fly up to the sky with it, to see if they could not carry on their sport even there. But the higher they flew the more wrinkled did the mirror become,—they could scarcely hold it together. They flew on and on, higher and higher, till at last the mirror trembled so fearfully that it escaped from their hands, and fell to the earth, breaking into millions, billions, and trillions of pieces. And then it caused far greater unhappiness than before, for fragments of it, scarcely so large as a grain of sand, would be flying about in the air, and sometimes get into people's eyes, causing them to view everything the wrong way, or to have power to see only what was perverted and corrupt, each little fragment having retained the peculiar properties of the entire mirror. Some people were so unfortunate as to receive a little splinter into their hearts,—that was terrible! the heart became cold and hard, like a lump of ice. Some pieces were large enough to be used as window-panes, but it was of no use to look at one's friends through such panes as those. Other fragments were made into spectacles, and then what trouble people had with setting and resetting them! The wicked magician was greatly amused with all this, and he laughed till his sides ached.

There are still some little splinters of this mischievous mirror flying about in the air; we shall hear more about them very soon.

Part the Second.

A LITTLE BOY AND A LITTLE GIRL.

In a large town, where there are so many houses and inhabitants that there is not room enough for all the people to possess a little garden of their own, and therefore many are obliged to content themselves with keeping a few plants in pots, there dwelt two poor children whose garden was somewhat larger than a flower-pot. They were not brother and sister, but they loved each other as much as if they had been, and their parents lived in two attics exactly opposite. The roof of one neighbour's house nearly joined the other, the gutter ran along between, and there was in each roof a little window, so that you could stride across the gutter from one window to the other.

The parents of each child had a large wooden box in which grew herbs for kitchen use, and they had placed these boxes upon the gutter, so near that they almost touched each other. A beautiful little rose-tree grew in each box, scarlet-runners entwined their long shoots over the windows, and, uniting with the branches of the rose-trees, formed a flowery arch across the street. The boxes were very high, and the children knew that they might not climb over them, but they often obtained leave to sit on their little stools under the rose-trees, and thus they passed many a delightful hour.

But when winter came there was an end to these pleasures. The windows were often quite frozen over, and then they heated half-pence on the stove, held the warm copper against the frozen pane, and thus made a little round peep-hole, behind which would sparkle a bright gentle eye, one from each window.

The little boy was called Kay, the little girl's name was Gerda. In summer time they could get out of window and jump over to each other; but in winter there were stairs to run down, and stairs to run up, and sometimes the wind roared, and the snow fell without doors.

"Those are the white bees swarming there!" said the old grandmother.

"Have they a queen bee?" asked the little boy, for he knew that the real bees have one.

"They have," said the grandmother. "She flies yonder where they swarm so thickly: she is the largest of them, and never remains upon the earth, but flies up again into the black cloud. Sometimes, on a winter's night, she flies through the streets of the town, and breathes with her frosty breath upon the windows, and then they are covered with strange and beautiful forms, like trees and flowers."

"Yes, I have seen them!" said both the children—they knew that this was true.

"Can the Snow Queen come in here?" asked the little girl.

"If she do come in," said the boy, "I will put her on the warm stove, and then she will melt."

And the grandmother stroked his hair and told him some stories.

That same evening, after little Kay had gone home, and was half-undressed, he crept upon the chair by the window and peeped through the little round hole. Just then a few snow-flakes fell outside, and one, the largest of them, remained lying on the edge of one of the flower-pots. The snow-flake appeared larger and larger, and at last took the form of a lady dressed in the finest white crape, her attire being composed of millions of star-like particles. She was exquisitely fair and delicate, but entirely of ice,—glittering, dazzling ice; her eyes gleamed like two bright stars, but there was no rest nor repose in them. She nodded at the window, and beckoned with her hand. The little boy was frightened and jumped down from the chair; he then fancied he saw a large bird fly past the window.

There was a clear frost next day, and soon afterwards came spring,—the trees and flowers budded, the swallows built their nests, the windows were opened, and the little children sat once more in their little garden upon the gutter that ran along the roofs of the houses.

The roses blossomed beautifully that summer, and the little girl had learned a hymn in which there was something about roses: it reminded her of her own. So she sang it to the little boy, and he sang it with her:—

> "Our roses bloom and fade away,
> Our Infant Lord abides alway.
> May we be blessed His face to see,
> And ever little children be!"

And the little ones held each other by the hand, kissed the roses, and looked up into the blue sky, talking away all the time. What glorious summer days were those! how delightful it was to sit under those lovely rose-trees, which seemed as if they never intended to leave off blossoming! One day Kay and Gerda were sitting looking at their picture-book, full of birds and animals, when suddenly—the clock on the old church tower was just striking five—Kay exclaimed, "Oh, dear! what was that shooting pain in my heart! and now again, something has certainly got into my eye!"

The little girl turned and looked at him; he winked his eyes—no, there was nothing to be seen.

"I believe it is gone," said he; but gone it was not. It was one of those glass splinters from the Magic Mirror,—the wicked glass which made everything great and good reflected in it to appear little and hateful, and which magnified everything ugly and mean. Poor Kay had also received a splinter in his heart,—it would now become hard and cold, like a lump of ice. He felt the pain no longer, but the splinter was there.

"Why do you cry?" asked he; "you look so ugly when you cry! there is nothing the matter with me. Fie!" exclaimed he again, "this rose has an insect in it, and just look at this! after all they are ugly roses! and it is an ugly box they grow in!" Then he kicked the box and tore off the roses.

"Oh, Kay, what are you doing?" cried the little girl? but when he saw how it grieved her, he tore off another rose, and jumped down through his own window, away from his once dear little Gerda.

Ever afterwards, when she brought forward the picture-book, he called it a baby's book; and when her grandmother told stories, he interrupted her with a but, and sometimes, whenever he could manage it, he would get behind her, put on her spectacles, and speak just as she did; he did this in a very droll manner, and so people laughed at him. Very soon he could mimic everybody in the street. All that was singular and awkward about them could Kay imitate, and his neighbours said, "What a remarkable head that boy has!" But no, it was the glass splinter which had fallen into his eye, the glass splinter which had pierced into his heart—it was these which made him regardless whose feelings he wounded, and even made him tease the little Gerda who loved him so fondly.

His games were now quite different from what they used to be—they were so rational! One winter's day, when it was snowing, he came out with a large burning glass in his hand, and holding up the skirts of his blue coat, let the snow-flakes fall upon them.

"Now, look through the glass, Gerda!" said he, returning to the house. Every snow-flake seemed much larger, and resembled a splendid flower, or a star with ten points; they were quite beautiful. "See, how curious!" said Kay; "these are far more interesting than real flowers; there is not a single blemish in them; they would be quite perfect, if only they did not melt."

Soon after this, Kay came in again, with thick gloves on his hands, and his sledge slung across his back; he called out to Gerda, "I have got leave to drive on the great square where the other boys play!" and away he went.

The boldest boys in the square used to fasten their sledges firmly to the waggons of the country people, and thus drive a good way along with them; this they thought particularly pleasant. Whilst they were in the midst of their play, a large sledge, painted white, passed by; in it sat a person wrapped in a rough white fur, and wearing a rough white cap. When the sledge had driven twice round the square, Kay bound to it his little sledge, and was carried on with it. On they went, faster and faster, into the next street; the person who drove the large sledge turned round and nodded kindly to Kay, just as if they had been old acquaintances, and every time Kay was going to loose his little sledge, turned and nodded again, as if to signify that he must stay. So Kay sat still, and they passed through the gates of the town. Then the snow began to fall so thickly that the little boy could not see his own hand, but he was still carried on; he tried hastily to unloose the cords and free himself from the large sledge, but it was of no use,—his little carriage could not be unfastened, and glided on as swift as the wind. Then he cried out as loud as he could, but no one heard him — the snow fell and the sledge flew; every now and then it made a spring, as if driving over hedges and ditches. He was very much frightened, he would have repeated "Our Father," but he could remember nothing but the multiplication table.

The snow-flakes seemed larger and larger; at last they looked like great white fowls. All at once they fell aside, the large sledge stopped, and the person who drove it arose from the seat; he saw that the cap and coat were entirely of snow, that it was a lady, tall and slender, and dazzlingly white — it was the Snow Queen!

"We have driven fast!" said she, "but no one likes to be frozen — creep under my bear-skin." And she seated him in the sledge by her side, and spread her cloak around him: he felt as if he were sinking into a drift of snow.

"Are you still cold?" asked she, and then she kissed his brow. Oh! her kiss was colder than ice, it went to his heart, although that was half frozen already; he thought he should die,— it was, however, only for a moment,— directly afterwards he was quite well, and no longer felt the intense cold around.

"My sledge! do not forget my sledge!"—he thought first of that—it was fastened to one of the white fowls which flew behind with it on his back. The Snow Queen kissed Kay again, and he entirely forgot little Gerda, her grandmother, and all at home.

"Now you must have no more kisses!" said she, "else I should kiss thee to death."

Kay looked at her, she was so beautiful; a more intelligent, more lovely countenance, he could not imagine; she ne longer appeared to him ice, cold ice, as at the time when she sat outside the window and beckoned to him; in his eyes she was perfect, he felt no fear, he told her how well he could reckon in his head, even fractions; that he knew the number of square miles of every country, and the number of the inhabitants contained in different towns. She smiled, and then it occurred to him that, after all, he did not yet know so very much; he looked up into the wide, wide space, and she flew with him high up into the black cloud while the storm was raging; it seemed now to Kay as though singing songs of olden time.

They flew over woods and over lakes, over sea and over land; beneath them the cold wind whistled, the wolves howled, the snow glittered, and the black crow flew cawing over the plain, whilst above them shone the moon, so clear and tranquil.

Thus did Kay spend the long, long winter night; all day he slept at the feet of the Snow Queen.

Part the Third.

THE ENCHANTED FLOWER-GARDEN.

But how fared it with little Gerda, when Kay never returned? Where could he be? No one knew, no one could give any account of him. The boys said that they had seen him fasten his sledge to another larger and very handsome one, which had driven into the street, and thence through the gates of the town. No one knew where he was, and many were the tears that were shed; little Gerda wept much and long, for the boys said he must be dead; he must have been drowned in the river that flowed not far from the town. Oh, how long and dismal the winter days were now!

At last came the spring, with its warm sunshine.

"Alas, Kay is dead and gone!" said little Gerda.

"That I do not believe," said the Sunshine.

"He is dead and gone," said she to the Swallows.

"That we do not believe," returned they, and at last little Gerda herself did not believe it.

"I will put on my new red shoes," said she, one morning, "those which Kay has never seen, and then I will go down to the river and ask after him."

It was quite early; she kissed her old grandmother, who was still sleeping, put on her red shoes, and went alone through the gates of the town towards the river.

"Is it true," said she, "that thou hast taken my little playfellow away? I will give thee my red shoes, if thou wilt restore him to me!"

And the wavelets of the river flowed towards her in a manner which she fancied was unusual; she fancied that they intended to accept her offer, so she took off her red shoes, though she prized them more than anything else she possessed, and threw them into the stream; but they fell near the shore, and the little waves bore them back to her, as though they would not take from her what she most prized, as they had not got little Kay. However, she thought she had not thrown the shoes far enough, so she stepped into a little boat which lay among the reeds by the shore, and, standing at the farthest end of it, threw them from thence into the water. The boat was not fastened, and her movements in it caused it to glide away from the shore; she saw this, and hastened to get out, but, by the time she reached the other end of the boat, it was more than a yard distant from the land; she could not escape, and the boat glided on.

Little Gerda was much frightened and began to cry, but no one besides the sparrows heard her, and they could not carry her back to the land; however, they flew along the banks, and sang as if to comfort her, " Here we are, here we are!" The boat followed the stream, little Gerda sat in it quite still; her red shoes floated behind her, but they could not overtake the boat, which glided along faster than they did.

Beautiful were the shores of that river,—lovely flowers, stately old trees, and bright green hills dotted with sheep and cows, were seen in abundance, but not a single human being.

" Perhaps the river may bear me to my dear Kay," thought Gerda, and then she became more cheerful, and amused herself for hours with looking at the lovely country around her. At last she glided past a large cherry-garden, wherein stood a little cottage, with thatched roof and curious red and blue windows; two wooden soldiers stood at the door, who presented arms when they saw the little vessel approach.

Gerda called to them, thinking that they were alive, but they, naturally enough, made no answer. She came close up to them, for the stream drifted the boat to the land.

Gerda called still louder, whereupon an old lady came out of the house, supporting herself on a crutch; she wore a large hat, with most beautiful flowers painted on it.

" Thou poor little child!" said the old woman, " the mighty flowing river has indeed borne thee a long, long way." And she walked right into the water, seized the boat with her crutch, drew it to land, and took out the little girl.

Gerda was glad to be on dry land again, although she was a little afraid of the strange old lady.

" Come and tell me who thou art, and how thou camest hither," said she.

And Gerda told her all, and the old lady shook her head, and said, " Hem! hem!" And when Gerda asked if she had seen little Kay, the lady said that he had not arrived there yet, but that he would be sure to come soon, and that in the meantime Gerda must not be sad; that she might stay with her, might eat her cherries, and look at her flowers, which were prettier than any picture-book, and could each tell her a story.

She then took Gerda by the hand; they went together into the cottage, and the old lady shut the door. The windows were very high, and their panes of different coloured glass, red, blue, and yellow, so that when the bright daylight streamed through them, various and beautiful were the hues reflected upon the room. Upon a table in the centre was placed a plate of very fine cherries, and of these Gerda was allowed to eat as many as she liked; and whilst she was eating them, the old dame combed her hair with a golden comb, and the bright flaxen ringlets fell on each side of her pretty, gentle face, which looked as round and as fresh as a rose.

"I have long wished for such a dear little girl," said the old lady. "We shall see if we cannot live very happily together." And, as she combed little Gerda's hair, the child thought less and less of her foster-brother Kay, for the old lady was an enchantress. She did not, however, practise magic for the sake of mischief, but merely for her own amusement. And now she wished very much to keep little Gerda to live with her; so, fearing that if Gerda saw her roses, she would be reminded of her own flowers and of little Kay, and that then she might run away, she went out into the garden, and extended her crutch over all her rose-bushes, upon which, although they were full of leaves and blossoms, they immediately sank into the black earth, and no one would have guessed that such plants had ever grown there.

Then she led Gerda into this flower-garden. Oh, how beautiful and how fragrant it was! Flowers of all seasons and all climes grew there in fulness of beauty; certainly no picture-book could be compared with it. Gerda bounded with delight, and played among the flowers, till the sun set behind the tall cherry-trees; after which a pretty little bed, with crimson silk cushions, stuffed with blue violet leaves, was prepared for her, and here she slept so sweetly, and had such dreams as a queen might have on her bridal eve.

The next day she again played among the flowers in the warm sunshine, and many more days were spent in the same manner. Gerda knew every flower in the garden, but numerous as they were, it seemed to her that one was wanting— she could not tell which. She was sitting one day looking at her hostess's hat, which had flowers painted on it, and behold, the loveliest among them was a rose! The old lady had entirely forgotten the painted rose on her hat, when she made the real roses to disappear from her garden and sink into the ground. This is often the case when things are done hastily.

"What!" cried Gerda, "are there no roses in the garden?" And she ran from one bed to another: sought and sought again, but no rose was to be found. She sat down and wept, and it so chanced that her tears fell on a spot where a rose-tree had formerly stood, and as soon as her warm tears had moistened the earth, the bush shot up anew, as fresh and as blooming as it was before it had sunk into the ground; and Gerda threw her arms around it, kissed the blossoms, and immediately recalled to memory the beautiful roses at home, and her little playfellow Kay.

"Oh, how could I stay here so long?" exclaimed the little maiden; "I left my home to seek for Kay. Do you not know where he is?" she asked of the Roses; "think you that he is dead?"

"Dead he is not," said the Roses; "we have been down in the earth; the dead are there, but not Kay."

"I thank you," said little Gerda; and she went to the other flowers, bent low over their cups, and asked, "Know you not where little Kay is?"

But every flower stood in the sunshine dreaming its own little tale; they related their stories to Gerda, but none of them knew anything of Kay.

"And what think you?" said the Tiger-lily.

"Listen to the drums beating, boom! boom! they have but two notes, always boom! boom! Listen to the dirge the women are singing! listen to the chorus of the priests! Enveloped in her long red robes stands the Hindoo wife on the funeral pile, the flames blaze around her and her dead husband, but the Hindoo wife thinks not of the dead. She thinks only of the living, and the anguish which consumes her spirit is keener than the fire which will soon reduce her body to ashes. Can the flame of the heart expire amid the flames of the funeral pile?"

"I do not understand that at all!" said little Gerda.

"That is my tale!" said the Tiger-lily.

"What says the Convolvulus?"

"Hanging over a narrow mountain causeway behold an ancient baronial castle, thick evergreens grow amongst the time-stained walls, their leafy branches entwine about the balcony, and there stands a beautiful maiden; she bends over the balustrades and fixes her eyes with eager expectation on the road winding beneath. The rose hangs not fresher and lovelier on its stem than she; the apple-blossom which the wind threatens every moment to tear from its branch is not more fragile and trembling. Listen to the rustling of her rich silken robe! Listen to her half-whispered words, ' He comes not yet!'"

"Is it Kay you mean?" asked little Gerda.

"I do but tell you my tale—my dream," replied the Convolvulus.

"What says the little Snowdrop?"

"Between two trees hangs a swing; two pretty little maidens, their dress as white as snow, and long green ribands fluttering from their hats, sit and swing themselves in it; their brother stands up in the swing,—he has thrown his arms round the ropes to keep himself steady, for in one hand he holds a little cup, in the other a pipe made of clay—he is blowing soap-bubbles. The swing moves, and the bubbles fly upwards with bright, ever-changing colours; the last hovers on the edge of the pipe, and moves with the wind. The swing is still in motion, and a little black dog, almost as light as the soap-bubbles, rises on his hind feet, and tries to get into the swing also; away goes the swing, the dog falls, is out of temper, and barks; he is laughed at, and the bubbles burst. A swinging-board, a frothy, fleeting image, is my song."

"What you describe may be all very pretty, but you speak so mournfully, and there is nothing about Kay."

"What say the Hyacinths?"

"There were three fair sisters—transparent and delicate they were; the kirtle of the one was red, that of the second blue, of the third pure white. Hand in hand they danced in the moonlight, beside the quiet lake; they were not fairies, but daughters of men. Sweet was the fragrance when the maidens vanished into the wood; the fragrance grew stronger; three biers, whereon lay the fair sisters, glided out from the depths of the wood and floated upon the lake, the glow-worms flew shining around like little hovering lamps. Sleep the dancing maidens, or are they dead? The odour from the flowers tells us they are corpses. The evening bells peal out their dirge."

"You make me quite sad," said little Gerda. "Your fragrance is so strong I cannot help thinking of the dead maidens; alas! and is little Kay dead? The Roses have been under the earth, and they say 'No.'"

"Ding dong! ding dong!" rang the Hyacinth bells. "We toll not for little Kay—we know him not. We do but sing our own song—the only one we know."

And Gerda went to the Buttercup, which shone so brightly from among her smooth green leaves.

"Thou art like a little bright sun," said Gerda; "tell me, if thou canst, where I may find my playfellow."

And the Buttercup glittered so brightly, and looked at Gerda. What song could the Buttercup sing? Neither was hers about Kay.

"One bright spring morning the sun shone warmly upon a little court-yard, the bright beams streamed down the white walls of a neighbouring house, and close by grew the first yellow flower of spring, glittering like gold in the warm sunshine. An old grandmother sat without in her arm-chair, her granddaughter, a pretty, lowly maiden, had just returned home from a short visit; she kissed her grandmother,—there was gold, pure gold, in that loving kiss:

'Gold was the flower!
Gold the fresh, bright, morning hour!'

"That is my litle story," said the Buttercup.

"My poor old grandmother!" sighed Gerda. "Yes, she must be wishing for me, just as she wished for little Kay. But I shall soon go home again, and take Kay with me. It is of no use to ask the flowers about him, they only know their own song, they can give me no information." And she folded her little frock round her, that she might run the faster; but, in jumping over the Narcissus, it caught her foot, as if wishing to stop her. So she turned and looked at the tall yellow flower, saying, "Have you any news to give me?" She bent over the Narcissus, waiting for an answer. And what said the Narcissus?

"I can look at myself, I can see myself! Oh, how sweet is my fragrance! Up in the little attic-chamber stands a little dancer. She rests sometimes on one leg, sometimes on two. She has trampled the whole world under her feet: she is nothing but an illusion. She pours water from a teapot upon a piece of cloth she holds in her hand—it is her bodice; cleanliness is a fine thing!—her white dress hangs on the hook; that has also been washed by the water from the teapot, and dried on the roof of the house; she puts it on, and wraps a saffron-coloured handkerchief round her neck; it makes the dress look all the whiter. With one leg extended, there she stands, as though on a stalk. I can look at myself—I see myself!"

"I don't care if you do," said Gerda. "You need not have told me that;" and away she ran to the end of the garden.

The gate was closed, but she pressed upon the rusty lock till it broke; the gate sprang open, and little Gerda, with bare feet, ran out into the wide world. Three times she looked back; there was no one following her; she ran till she could run no longer, and then sat down to rest upon a large stone. Casting a glance around, she saw that the summer was past, that it was now late in the autumn. Of course, she had not remarked this in the enchanted garden, where there were sunshine and flowers all the year round.

"How long I must have stayed there!" said little Gerda. "So, it is now autumn! Well, then, there is no time to lose;" and she rose to pursue her way.

Oh, how sore and weary were her little feet! and all around looked so cold and barren; the long willow-leaves had already turned yellow, and the dew trickled down from them in large drops. The leaves fell off the trees, one by one; the sloe alone bore fruit, and its berries were so sharp and bitter! Cold, and grey, and sad, seemed the world to her that day.

Part the Fourth.

THE PRINCE AND THE PRINCESS.

Gerda was again obliged to stop and take rest. Suddenly a large Raven hopped upon the snow in front of her, saying, "Caw! Caw! Good-day! Good-day!" He had sat for some time on the withered branch of a tree just opposite, eyeing the little maiden, and wagging his head; and he now came forward to make acquaintance, and to ask her whither she was going all alone. That word "alone" Gerda understood right well—she felt how sad a meaning it has. She told the Raven the history of her life and fortunes, and asked if he had seen Kay.

And the Raven nodded his head, half doubtfully, and said, "That is possible!—possible!"

"Do you think so?" exclaimed the little girl, and she kissed the Raven so vehemently, that it is a wonder she did not squeeze him to death.

"More moderately!—moderately!" said the Raven. "I think I know; I think it may be little Kay; but he has certainly forsaken thee for the Princess."

"Dwells he with a Princess?" asked Gerda.

"Listen to me," said the Raven; "but it is so difficult to speak your language! Do you understand Ravenish? if so, I can tell you much better."

"No I have never learned Ravenish," said Gerda, "but

my grandmother knew it, and Pye-language also. Oh, how I wish I had learned it!"

"Never mind," said the Raven, "I will relate my story in the best manner I can, though bad will be the best;" and he told all he knew.

"In the kingdom wherein we are now sitting there dwells a Princess, a most uncommonly clever Princess. All the newspapers in the world has she read, and forgotten them again, so clever is she. It is not long since she ascended the throne, which I have heard is not quite so agreeable a situation as one would fancy; and immediately after she began to sing a new song, the burden of which was this, 'Why should I not marry me?' 'There is some sense in this song!' said she, and she determined she would marry; but at the same time declared that the man whom she would choose must be able to answer sensibly whenever people spoke to him, and must be good for something else besides merely looking grand and stately. The ladies of the court were then all drummed together, in order to be informed of her intentions, whereupon they were highly delighted; and one exclaimed, 'That is just what I wish;' and another, that she had lately been thinking of the very same thing. Believe me," continued the Raven, "every word I say is true, for I have a tame beloved who hops at pleasure about the palace, and she has told me all this."

Of course, the "beloved" was also a raven, for birds of a feather flock together.

"Proclamations, adorned with borders of hearts, were immediately issued, wherein, after enumerating the style and titles of the Princess, it was set forth that every well-favoured youth was free to go to the palace and converse with the Princess; and that whoever should speak in such wise as showed that he felt himself at home, there would be the one the Princess would choose for her husband.

"Yes, indeed," continued the Raven, "you may believe me; all this is as true as that I sit here. The people all crowded to the palace; there was famous pressing and squeezing; but it was all of no use, either the first or the second day; the young men could speak well enough while they were outside the palace-gates, but when they entered, and saw the royal guard in silver uniform, and the lackeys on the staircase in gold, and the spacious saloon all lighted up, they were quite confounded. They stood before the throne where the Princess sat; and when she spoke to them, they could only repeat the last word she had uttered, which, you know, it was not particularly interesting for her to hear over again. It was just as though they had been struck dumb the moment they entered the palace; for as soon as they got out, they could talk fast enough. There was a regular procession constantly moving from the gates of the town to the gates of the palace. I was there, and saw it with my own eyes," said the Raven. "They grew both hungry and thirsty whilst waiting at the palace, but no one could get even so much as a glass of water; to be sure, some of them, wiser than the rest, had brought with them slices of bread and butter; but none would give any to his neighbour, for he thought to himself, 'Let him look hungry, and then the Princess will be sure not to choose him.'"

"But Kay, little Kay, when did he come?" asked Gerda; "was he among the crowd?"

"Presently, presently! we have just come to him. On the third day arrived a youth with neither horse nor carriage; gaily he marched up to the palace; his eyes sparkled like yours: he had long beautiful hair, but was very meanly clad."

"That was Kay!" exclaimed Gerda. "Oh, then I have found him!" and she clapped her hands with delight.

"He carried a knapsack on his back," said the Raven.

"No, not a knapsack," said Gerda, "a sledge, for he had a sledge with him when he left home."

"It is possible," rejoined the Raven; "I did not look very closely; but this I heard from my beloved, that when he entered the palace-gates and saw the royal guard in silver and the lackeys in gold upon the staircase, he did not seem in the least confused, but nodded pleasantly, and said to them, 'It must be very tedious standing out here; I prefer going in.' The halls glistened with light; Cabinet Councillors and Excellencies were walking about barefooted, and carrying golden keys. It was just the place to make a man solemn and silent; and the youth's boots creaked horribly, yet he was not at all afraid."

"That most certainly was Kay!" said Gerda; "I know he had new boots; I have heard them creak in my grandmother's room."

"Indeed they did creak!" said the Raven; "but merrily went he up to the Princess, who was sitting upon a pearl as large as a spinning-wheel, whilst all the ladies of the court, with the maids of honour and their handmaidens ranged in order, stood on one side, and all the gentlemen in waiting, with their gentlemen, and their gentlemen's gentlemen, who also kept pages, stood ranged in order on the other side, and the nearer they were to the door the prouder they looked. The gentlemen's gentlemen's page, who always wears slippers, one dare hardly look at, so proudly he stands at the door."

"That must be dreadful!" said little Gerda. "And has Kay really won the Princess?"

"Had I not been a Raven I should have won her myself, notwithstanding my being betrothed. The young man spoke as well as I speak when I converse in Ravenish; that I have heard from my tame beloved. He was handsome and lively. 'He did not come to woo her,' he said; 'he had only come to hear the wisdom of the Princess;' and he liked her much, and she liked him in return."

"Yes, to be sure, that was Kay," said Gerda; "he was so clever, he could reckon in his head even fractions! Oh, will you not take me into the palace?"

"Ah! that is easily said," replied the Raven; "but how is it to be done? I will talk it over with my tame beloved; she will advise us what to do, for I must tell you that such a little girl as you are will never gain permission to enter publicly."

"Yes, I shall!" cried Gerda. "When Kay knows that I am here, he will immediately come out and fetch me."

"Wait for me at the trellis yonder," said the Raven. He wagged his head, and away he flew.

The Raven did not return till late in the evening. "Caw, caw!" said he. "My tame beloved greets you kindly, and sends you a piece of bread which she took from the kitchen; there is plenty of bread there, and you must certainly be hungry. It is not possible for you to enter the palace, for you have bare feet; the royal guard in silver uniform, and the lackeys in gold, would never permit it; but do not weep, thou shalt go there. My beloved knows a little back-staircase leading to the sleeping apartments, and she knows also where to find the key."

And they went into the garden, down the grand avenue, where the leaves dropped upon them as they passed along, and, when the lights in the palace one by one had all been extinguished, the Raven took Gerda to a back-door, which stood half open. Oh, how Gerda's heart beat with fear and expectation! it was just as though she was about to do something wrong, although she only wanted to know whether Kay was really there. Yes, it must be he! she remembered so well his bright eyes and long hair. She would see if his smile were the same it used to be when they sat together under the rose-trees. He would be so glad to see her; to hear how far she had come for his sake; how all at home mourned his absence. Her heart trembled with fear and joy.

They went up the staircase; a small lamp, placed on a cabinet, gave a glimmering light; on the floor stood the tame Raven, who first turned her head on all sides, and then looked at Gerda, who made her curtsey, as her grandmother had taught her.

"My betrothed has told me much about you, my good young maiden," said the tame Raven; "your adventures, too, are extremely interesting! If you will take the lamp, I will show you the way. We are going straight on — we shall not meet any one now."

"It seems to me as if some one were behind us," said Gerda; and, in fact, there was a rushing sound as of something passing; strange-looking shadows flitted rapidly along the wall; horses with long, slender legs and fluttering manes; huntsmen, knights, and ladies.

"These are only Dreams!" said the Raven; "they come to amuse the great personages here at night; you will have a better opportunity of looking at them when you are in bed. I hope that when you arrive at honours and dignities, you will show a grateful heart."

"Do not talk of that!" said the Wood-Raven.

They now entered the first saloon; its walls were covered with rose-coloured satin, embroidered with gold flowers. The Dreams rustled past them, but with such rapidity that Gerda could not see them. The apartments through which they passed vied with each other in splendour, and at last they reached the sleeping-hall. In the centre of this room stood a pillar of gold, resembling the stem of a large palm-tree, whose leaves of glass—costly glass—formed the ceiling, and depending from the tree, hung near the floor, on thick golden stalks, two beds in the form of lilies. The one was white, wherein reposed the Princess; the other was red, and here must Gerda seek her playfellow Kay. She bent aside one of the red leaves, and saw a brown neck. Oh, it must be Kay! She called him by his name aloud—held the lamp close to him; the Dreams again rushed by; he awoke, turned his head, and, behold! it was not Kay.

The Prince resembled him only about the throat; he was, however, young and handsome. And the Princess looked out from the white lily-petals, and asked what was the matter. Then little Gerda wept and told her whole story, and what the Ravens had done for her.

"Poor child!" said the Prince and Princess; and they praised the Ravens, and said they were not at all angry with them. Such liberties must never be taken again in their palace, but this time they should be rewarded.

"Would you like to fly away free to the woods?" asked the Princess, addressing the Ravens; "or to have the appointment secured to you as Court-Ravens, with the perquisites belonging to the kitchen, such as crumbs and leavings?"

And both the Ravens bowed low and chose the appointment at court, for they thought of old age, and said it would be so comfortable to be well provided for in their declining years.

Then the Prince arose, and made Gerda sleep in his bed; and she folded her little hands, thinking, "How kind both men and animals are to me!" She closed her eyes and slept soundly and sweetly, and all the Dreams flitted about her; they looked like angels from heaven, and seemed to be drawing a sledge, whereon Kay sat and nodded to her; but this was only fancy, for as soon as she awoke all the beautiful visions had vanished.

The next day she was dressed from head to foot in silk and velvet. She was invited to stay at the palace and enjoy all sorts of diversions; but she begged only for a little carriage and a horse, and a pair of little boots. All she desired was to go again into the wide world to seek Kay.

And they gave her the boots, and a muff besides. She was dressed so prettily; and as soon as she was ready, there drove up to the door a new carriage of pure gold, with the arms of the Prince and Princess glittering upon it like a star, the coachman, footman, and outriders all wearing gold crowns. The Prince and Princess themselves helped her into the carriage and wished her success. The Wood-Raven, who was now married, accompanied her the first three miles; he sat by her side, for riding backwards was a thing he could not bear. The other Raven stood at the door flapping her wings; she did not go with them on account of a headache she had felt ever since she had received her appointment, in consequence of eating too much. The carriage was well provided with sugar-plums, fruit, and gingerbread nuts.

"Farewell! farewell!" cried the Prince and Princess; little Gerda wept, and the Raven wept out of sympathy. But his farewell was a far sorer trial; he flew up to the branch of a tree, and flapped his black wings at the carriage till it was out of sight.

Part the Fifth

THE LITTLE ROBBER-MAIDEN.

They drove through the dark, dark forest, the carriage shone like a torch; unfortunately, its brightness attracted the eyes of the robbers who dwelt in the forest-shades: they could not bear it.

"That is gold! gold!" cried they; forward they rushed, seized the horses, stabbed the outriders, coachman, and footmen to death, and dragged little Gerda out of the carriage.

"She is plump, she is pretty, she has been fed on nut-kernels!" said the old Robber-wife, who had a long bristly beard, and eyebrows hanging like bushes over her eyes. "She is like a little fat lamb! and how smartly she is dressed!" and she drew out her bright dagger, glittering most terribly.

"Oh, oh!" cried the woman; for at the very moment she had lifted her dagger to stab Gerda, her own wild and wilful daughter jumped upon her back and bit her ear violently. "You naughty child!" said the mother.

"She shall play with me," said the little Robber-maiden. "She shall give me her muff and her pretty frock, and sleep with me in my bed!" And then she bit her mother again, till the Robber-wife sprang up and shrieked with pain, whilst the robbers all laughed, saying, "Look at her playing with her young one!"

"I will get into the carriage!" and so spoiled and wayward was the little Robber-maiden, that she always had her own way, and she and Gerda sat together in the carriage, and drove over stock and stone, farther and farther into the wood. The little Robber-maiden was about as tall as Gerda, but much stronger; she had broad shoulders, and a very dark skin; her eyes were quite black, and had an expression almost melancholy. She put her arm round Gerda's waist, and said, "She shall not kill thee so long as I love thee! Art thou not a princess?"

"No," said Gerda; and then she told her all that had happened to her, and how much she loved little Kay.

The Robber-maiden looked earnestly in her face, shook her head, and said, "She shall not kill thee, even if I do quarrel with thee; then, indeed, I would rather do it myself!" And she dried Gerda's tears, and put both her hands into the pretty muff that was so soft and warm.

The carriage at last stopped in the middle of the courtyard of the Robbers' castle. This castle was half-ruined; crows and ravens flew out of the openings, and some fearfully large bull-dogs, looking as if they could devour a man in a moment, jumped round the carriage; they did not bark, for that was forbidden.

The maidens entered a large smoky hall, where a tremendous fire was blazing on the stone floor; the smoke rose up to the ceiling, seeking a way of escape, for there was no chimney; a large cauldron, full of soup, was boiling over the fire, whilst hares and rabbits were roasting on the spit.

"Thou shalt sleep with me and my little pets to-night!" said the Robber-maiden. Then they had some food, and afterwards went to a corner, wherein lay straw and a piece of carpet. Nearly a hundred pigeons were perched on staves and laths around them; they seemed to be asleep, but were startled when the little maidens approached.

"These all belong to me!" said Gerda's companion; and seizing hold of one of the nearest, she held the poor bird by the feet, and swung it. "Kiss it," said she, flapping it into Gerda's face. "The rabble from the wood sit up there," continued she, pointing to a number of laths fastened across a hole in the wall. "Those are wood-pigeons; they would fly away, if I did not keep them shut up. And here is my old favourite!" She pulled forward by the horn a Reindeer, who wore a bright copper ring round his neck, by which he was fastened to a large stone. "We are obliged to chain him up, or he would run away from us; every evening I tickle his neck with my sharp dagger, it makes him fear me so much!" and the Robber-maiden drew out a long dagger from a gap in the wall, and passed it over the Reindeer's throat; the poor animal struggled and kicked, but the girl laughed, and then she pulled Gerda into bed with her.

"Will you keep the dagger in your hand whilst you sleep?" asked Gerda, looking timidly at the dangerous plaything.

"I always sleep with my dagger by my side," replied the little Robber-maiden. "One never knows what may happen. But now tell me all over again what you told me before about Kay, and the reason of your coming into the wide world all by yourself." And Gerda again related her history, and the Wood-pigeons imprisoned above listened, but the others were fast asleep. The little Robber-maiden threw one arm round Gerda's neck, and holding the dagger with the other, was also soon asleep. One could hear her heavy breathing, but Gerda could not close her eyes throughout the night; she knew not what would become of her, whether she would even be suffered to live. The robbers sat round the fire drinking and singing. Oh, it was a dreadful night for the poor little girl!

Then spoke the Wood-pigeons, "Coo, coo, coo! We have seen little Kay. A white fowl carried his sledge; he himself was in the Snow Queen's chariot, which passed through the wood whilst we sat in our nest. She breathed upon us young ones as she passed, and all died of her breath excepting us two,—coo, coo, coo!"

"What are you saying?" cried Gerda; "where was the Snow Queen going? do you know anything about it?"

"She travels most likely to Lapland, where ice and snow abide all the year round. Ask the Reindeer bound to the rope there."

"Yes, ice and snow are there all through the year. It is a glorious land!" said the Reindeer; "there, free and happy, one can roam through the wide, sparkling valleys! there the Snow Queen has her summer-tent; her strong castle is very far off, near the North Pole, on the island called Spitzbergen."

"Oh, Kay, dear Kay!" sighed Gerda.

"You must lie still," said the Robber-maiden, "or I will thrust my dagger into your side."

When morning came Gerda repeated to her what the Wood-pigeons had said, and the little Robber-maiden looked grave for a moment, then nodded her head, saying, "No matter! no matter! Do you know where Lapland is?" asked she of the Reindeer.

"Who should know but I?" returned the animal, his eyes kindling. "There was I born and bred, there how often have I bounded over the wild icy plains!"

"Listen to me!" said the Robber-maiden to Gerda; "you see all our men are gone; my mother is still here, and will remain; but towards noon she will drink a little out of the great flask, and after that she will sleep; then I will do something for you!" And so saying she jumped out of bed, sprung upon her mother, pulled her by the beard, and said, "My own dear mam, good morning!" and the mother caressed her so roughly, that she was red and blue all over; however, it was from pure love.

When her mother was fast asleep, the Robber-maiden

went up to the Reindeer and said, "I should have great pleasure in stroking you a few more times with my sharp dagger, for then you look so droll; but never mind, I will unloose your chain and help you to escape, on condition that you run as fast as you can to Lapland, and take this little girl to the castle of the Snow Queen, where her playfellow is. You must have heard her story, for she speaks loud enough, and you know well how to listen."

The Reindeer bounded with joy, and the Robber-maiden lifted Gerda on his back, taking the precaution to bind her on firmly, as well as to give her a little cushion to sit on. "And here," said she, "are your fur boots, you will need them in that cold country: the muff I must keep myself, it is too pretty to part with; but you shall not be frozen; here are my mother's huge gloves—they reach up to the elbow—put them on. Now your hands look as clumsy as my old mother's!"

And Gerda shed tears of joy.

"I cannot bear to see you crying!" said the little Robber-maiden; "you ought to look glad. See, here are two loaves and a piece of bacon for you, that you may not be hungry on the way." She fastened this provender also on the Reindeer's back, opened the door, called away the great dogs, and then cutting asunder with her dagger the rope which bound the Reindeer, shouted to him, "Now, then, run! but take good care of the little girl."

And Gerda stretched out her hands to the Robber-maiden, and bade her farewell, and the Reindeer fleeted through the forest,—over stock and stone, over desert and heath, over meadow and moor. The wolves howled and the ravens shrieked. "Isch! isch!" a red light flashed; one might have fancied the sky was sneezing.

"Those are my dear old Northern Lights!" said the Reindeer; "look at them, how beautiful they are!" And he ran faster than ever; night and day he ran. The loaves were eaten, so was the bacon; at last they were in Lapland

Part the Sixth.

THE LAPLAND WOMAN, AND THE FINMARK WOMAN.

They stopped at a little hut—a wretched hut it was; the roof very nearly touched the ground, and the door was so low, that whoever wished to go either in or out was obliged to crawl upon hands and knees. No one was at home except an old Lapland woman, who was busy boiling fish over a lamp filled with train oil. The Reindeer related to her Gerda's whole history, not, however, till after he had made her acquainted with his own, which appeared to him of much more importance. Poor Gerda, meanwhile, was so overpowered by the cold that she could not speak.

"Ah, poor things!" said the Lapland woman, "you have still a long way before you! you have a hundred miles to run before you can arrive in Finmark. The Snow Queen dwells there, and burns blue lights every evening. I will write for you a few words on a piece of dried stock-fish—paper I have none—and you may take it with you to the wise Finmark woman who lives there; she will advise you better than I can."

So when Gerda had well warmed herself and taken some

food, the Lapland woman wrote a few words on a dried stockfish, bade Gerda take care of it, and bound her once more firmly on the Reindeer's back. Onwards they sped; the wondrous Northern Lights, now of the loveliest, brightest blue colour, shone all through the night; and amidst these splendid illuminations they arrived in Finmark, and knocked at the chimney of the Wise-woman, for door to her house she had none.

Hot, very hot was it within, so much so that the Wise-woman wore scarcely any clothing; she was low in stature, and very dirty. She immediately loosened little Gerda's dress, took off her fur boots and thick gloves, laid a piece of ice on the Reindeer's head, and then read what was written on the stock-fish. She read it three times; after the third reading she knew it by heart, and threw the fish into the porridge-pot, for it might make a very excellent supper, and she never wasted anything.

The Reindeer then repeated his own story, and when that was finished he told of little Gerda's adventures, and the Wise-woman twinkled her wise eyes, but spoke not a word.

"Thou art so powerful," continued the Reindeer, "that I know thou canst twist all the winds of the world into a rope, of which if the pilot loosen one knot, he will have a favourable wind; if he loosen the second, it will blow sharp; and if he loosen the third, so tremendous a storm will arise that the trees of the forest will be uprooted, and the ship wrecked. Wilt thou not mix for this little maiden that wonderful draught which will give her the strength of twelve men, and thus enable her to overcome the Snow Queen?"

"The strength of twelve men!" repeated the Wise-woman; "that would be of much use, to be sure!" and she walked away, drew forth a large parchment roll from a shelf, and began to read. What strange characters were seen inscribed on the scroll, as the Wise-woman slowly unrolled it! She read so intently, that the perspiration ran down her forehead.

But the Reindeer pleaded so earnestly for little Gerda, and Gerda's eyes were raised so entreatingly and tearfully, that at last the Wise-woman's eyes began to twinkle again out of sympathy, and she drew the Reindeer into a corner, and putting a fresh piece of ice upon his head, whispered thus:—

"Little Kay is still with the Snow Queen, in whose abode everything is according to his taste, and, therefore, he believes it to be the best place in the world. But that is because he has a glass splinter in his heart, and a glass splinter in his eye; until he has got rid of them he will never feel like a human being, and the Snow Queen will always maintain her influence over him."

"But canst thou not give something to little Gerda whereby she may overcome all these evil influences?"

"I can give her no power so great as that which she already possesses. Seest thou not how strong she is? Seest thou not that both men and animals must serve her—a poor little girl, wandering barefoot through the world? Her power is greater than ours; it proceeds from her heart—from her being a loving and innocent child. If this power, which she already possesses, cannot give her access to the Snow Queen's palace, and enable her to free Kay's eye and heart from the glass fragment, we can do nothing for her! Two miles hence is the Snow Queen's garden, thither thou canst carry the little maiden; put her down close by the bush bearing red berries and half covered with snow: lose no time, and hasten back to this place!"

And the Wise-woman lifted Gerda on the Reindeer's back, and away they went.

"Oh, I have left my boots behind! I have left my gloves behind!" cried little Gerda, when it was too late. The cold was piercing, but the Reindeer dared not stop; on he ran until he reached the bush with the red berries. Here he set Gerda down, kissed her, the tears rolling down his cheeks the while, and ran fast back again, which was the best thing he could do. And there stood poor Gerda, without shoes, without gloves, alone in that barren region—that terrible icy-cold Finmark.

She ran on as fast as she could—a whole regiment of snow-flakes came to meet her; they did not fall from the sky, which was cloudless and bright with the Northern Lights, they ran straight along the ground, and the farther Gerda advanced the larger they grew. Gerda then remembered how large and curious the snow-flakes had appeared to her when one day she had looked at them through a burning-glass; these, however, were very much larger—they were living forms; they were, in fact, the Snow Queen's guards. Their shapes were the strangest that could be imagined; some looked like great ugly porcupines, others like snakes rolled into knots with their heads peering forth, and others like little fat bears with bristling hair,—all, however, were alike dazzlingly white, —all were living snow-flakes.

Little Gerda began to repeat "Our Father." Meanwhile the cold was so intense that she could see her own breath, which, as it escaped her mouth, ascended into the air like vapour; more dense grew this vapour, and at length shaped itself into the forms of little bright angels, which, as they touched the earth, became larger and more distinct. They wore helmets on their heads, and carried shields and spears in their hands; their number increased so rapidly that, by the time Gerda had finished her prayer, a whole legion stood around her. They thrust with their spears against the horrible snow-flakes, which fell into thousands of pieces, and little Gerda walked on, unhurt and undaunted. The angels touched her hands and feet, and then she scarcely felt the cold, and boldly approached the Snow Queen's palace.

But before we accompany her there, let us see what Kay is doing. He is certainly not thinking of little Gerda, least of all can he imagine that she is now standing at the palace-gate.

Part the Seventh,

WHICH TREATS OF THE SNOW QUEEN'S PALACE, AND OF WHAT CAME TO PASS THEREIN.

The walls of the palace were formed of the driven snow, its doors and windows of the cutting winds; there were above a hundred halls, the largest of them many miles in extent, all illuminated by the Northern Lights; all alike vast, empty, icily cold, and dazzlingly white. No sounds of mirth ever resounded through these dreary spaces; no cheerful scene refreshed the sight — not even so much as a bear's ball, such as one might imagine sometimes takes place; the tempest forming a band of musicians, and the polar bears standing on their hind-paws and exhibiting themselves in the oddest positions. Nor was there ever a card-assembly, wherein the cards might be held in the mouth, and dealt out by the paws; nor even a small select coffee-party for the white young lady foxes. Vast, empty, and cold were the Snow Queen's chambers, and the Northern Lights flashed now high, now low, in regular gradations. In the midst of the empty, interminable snow-saloon lay a frozen lake; it was broken into a thousand pieces; but these pieces so exactly resembled each other, that the breaking of them might well be deemed a work of more than human skill. The Snow Queen, when at home, always sat in the centre of this lake; she used to say that she was then sitting on the Mirror of Reason, and that hers was the best—indeed, the only one—in the world.

Little Kay was quite blue, nay, almost black with cold: but he did not observe it, for the Snow Queen had kissed away the shrinking feeling he used to experience, and his heart was like a lump of ice. He was busied among the sharp icy fragments, laying and joining them together in every possible way, just as people do with what are called Chinese Puzzles. Kay could form the most curious and complete figures,—this was the ice-puzzle of reason,—and in his eyes these figures were of the utmost importance. He often formed whole words; but there was one word he could never succeed in forming—it was Eternity. The Snow Queen had said to him, "When thou canst put that figure together, thou shalt become thine own master, and I will give thee the whole world, and a new pair of skates besides." But he could never do it.

"Now I am going to the warm countries," said the Snow Queen; "I shall flit through the air, and look into the black cauldrons"—she meant the burning mountains, Etna and Vesuvius. "I shall whiten them a little; that will be good for the citrons and vineyards." So away flew the Snow Queen, leaving Kay sitting all alone in the large, empty hall of ice. He looked at the fragments, and thought and thought till his head ached: he sat so still and so still that one might have fancied that he, too, was frozen.

Cold and cutting blew the winds when little Gerda passed through the palace-gates, but she repeated her evening prayer, and they immediately sank to rest. She entered the large, cold, empty hall. She saw Kay, she recognised him, she flew upon his neck, she held him fast, and cried, "Kay! dear, dear Kay! I have found thee at last!"

But he sat still as before—cold, silent, motionless. His unkindness wounded poor Gerda deeply, hot and bitter were the tears she shed, they fell upon his breast, they reached his heart, they thawed the ice, and dissolved the tiny splinter of glass within it; he looked at her whilst she sang her hymn,—

> "Our roses bloom and fade away,
> Our Infant Lord abides alway!
> May we be blessed His face to see,
> And ever little children be!"

Then Kay burst into tears; he wept till the glass splinter floated in his eye and fell with his tears; he knew his old companion immediately, and exclaimed with joy, "Gerda, my dear little Gerda, where hast thou been all this time?—And where have I been?"

He looked around him, "How cold it is here!—how wide and empty!" and he embraced Gerda whilst she laughed and wept by turns. Even the pieces of ice took part in their joy; they danced about merrily, and when they were wearied and lay down, they formed of their own accord the mystical letters of which the Snow Queen had said, that when Kay could put them together, he should be his own master, and that she would give him the whole world, with a new pair of skates besides.

And Gerda kissed his cheeks, whereupon they became fresh and glowing as ever; she kissed his eyes, and they sparkled like her own; she kissed his hands and feet, and he was once more healthy and merry. The Snow Queen might now come home as soon as she liked—it mattered not; Kay's charter of freedom stood written on the mirror in bright icy characters.

They took each other by the hand, and wandered forth out of the palace—talking, meanwhile, about the aged grandmother, and the rose-trees on the roof of their houses; and as they walked on, the winds were hushed into a calm, and the sun burst forth in splendour from among the dark storm-clouds. When they arrived at the bush with the red berries, they found the Reindeer standing by, awaiting their arrival; he had brought with him another and younger Reindeer, whose udders were full, and who gladly gave her warm milk to refresh the young travellers.

The old Reindeer and the young Hind now carried Kay and Gerda on their backs, first to the little hot room of the Wise-woman of Finmark, where they warmed themselves, and received advice how to proceed in their journey home,—and afterwards to the abode of the Lapland woman, who made them some new clothes, and provided them with a sledge.

The whole party now ran on together till they came to

the boundary of the country; but just where the green leaves began to sprout, the Lapland woman and the two Reindeers took their leave. " Farewell!—farewell!" said they all. And the first little birds they had seen for many a long day began to chirp and warble their pretty songs; and the trees of the forest burst upon them full of rich and variously-tinted foliage. Suddenly, the green boughs parted asunder, and a spirited horse galloped up. Gerda knew it well, for it was the one which had been harnessed to her gold coach; and on it sat a young girl wearing a bright scarlet cap, and with pistols on the holster before her. It was, indeed, no other than the Robber-maiden, who, weary of her home in the forest, was going on her travels, first to the North, and afterwards to other parts of the world. She at once recognised Gerda, and Gerda had not forgotten her. Most joyful was their greeting!

"A fine gentleman you are, to be sure, you graceless young truant!" said she to Kay; "I should like to know if you deserved that any one should be running to the end of the world on your account!"

But Gerda stroked her cheeks, and asked after the Prince and Princess.

"They are gone travelling into foreign countries," replied the Robber-maiden.

"And the Raven?" asked Gerda.

"Ah! the Raven is dead," returned she. "The tame beloved has become a widow; so she hops about with a piece of black worsted wound round her leg; she moans most piteously, and chatters more than ever! But tell me now all that has happened to you, and how you managed to pick up your old play-fellow."

And Gerda and Kay told their story.

"Snip-snap-snurre-basselurre!" said the Robber-maiden; she pressed the hands of both;—promised that if ever she passed through their town she would pay them a visit, and then bade them farewell, and rode away out into the wide world.

Kay and Gerda walked on hand in hand, and wherever they went it was spring, beautiful spring, with its bright flowers and green leaves.

They arrived at a large town, the church bells were ringing merrily, and they immediately recognised the high towers rising into the sky—it was the town wherein they had lived. Joyfully they passed through the streets, joyfully they stopped at the door of Gerda's grandmother. They walked up the stairs and entered the well-known room. The clock said "Tick, tick!" and the hands moved as before; only one alteration could they find, and that was in themselves, for they saw that they were now full-grown persons. The rose-trees on the roof blossomed in front of the open window, and there beneath them stood the children's stools. Kay and Gerda went and sat down upon them, still holding each other by the hands; the cold, hollow splendour of the Snow Queen's palace they had forgotten, it seemed to them only an unpleasant dream. The grandmother, meanwhile, sat amid God's bright sunshine, and read from the Bible these words: "Unless ye become as little children, ye shall not enter into the kingdom of heaven."

And Kay and Gerda gazed on each other; they now understood the words of their hymn,—

"Our roses bloom and fade away,
Our Infant Lord abides alway!
May we be blessed His face to see,
And ever little children be!"

There they sat, those two happy ones, grown up and yet children — children in heart, while all around them glowed bright summer — warm, glorious summer.

HOLGER THE DANE.

"THERE is in Denmark an old castle called Kronborg; it stands close by the Sound of Elsinore, where every day large ships, English, Russian, and Prussian, may be seen sailing along. And as they pass the old castle, they salute it with their cannons, 'Boom!'—and the castle answers with its cannons, 'Boom!' This is the same as saying, 'Good day!' and 'Thank you!' No ships sail past during the winter, for then the Sound is covered with ice, and becomes a very broad highway leading from Denmark to Sweden; the Danish and Swedish flags flutter overhead, and Danes and Swedes walk and drive to and fro—meet and say to each other 'Good day!' 'Thank you!'—not with the report of cannons, but with a hearty, friendly shake of the hands; and they buy wheaten bread and biscuits of each other, because every one fancies foreign bread the best. But the glory of the scene is still the old Kronborg, and beneath, in those dark, tremendous caverns, where no man can approach, sits

Holger the Dane. He is clothed in iron and steel, he rests his head on his sinewy arms, his long beard hangs over the marble table, into which it seems to have grown fast. There he sleeps and dreams, and in his dreams he sees all that is going on up in Denmark. Every Christmas-eve an angel of God comes to him, and tells him that he has dreamt truly, and that he may sleep on, for Denmark is in no danger. But whenever danger shall threaten her, then will Holger the Dane arise in his might, and as he disengages his beard, the marble table will burst in twain!—then will he come forth and fight in such wise that all the countries of the world shall ring with the fame thereof!"

All this about Holger the Dane was told one evening by an old grandfather to his little grandson, and the boy was sure that all that his grandfather said must be true. Now this old man was a carver, one of those whose employment is to carve the beaks of ships, and as he sat talking to the little boy, he cut out of wood a large figure intended to represent Holger the Dane; there he was with his long beard, standing so proudly erect, holding in one hand his broad battle-sword, and leaning the other on his Danish coat-of-arms.

And the old grandfather told so many anecdotes about different men and women famed in Danish history, that at last the little boy began to imagine he must know quite as much as Holger the Dane, for he could only dream about these things; and after the child had gone to bed, he still thought over what he had heard, and pressed his chin down into the mattress, fancying that he, too, had a long beard, and that it had grown into the bed.

But the old grandfather still sat at his work, carving the Danish coat-of-arms, and when he had finished it, he looked at the whole figure, and thought over all that he had heard, and read, and told that evening to the little boy; and he nodded his head, and wiped his spectacles, and then put them on again, saying, "Ah, yes, Holger the Dane will certainly not come in my time, but the boy in the bed yonder, he, perchance, may see him and stand beside him in the hour of need." And again the old grandfather nodded his head, and the more he looked at his Holger the Dane, the more he felt persuaded that this was a very good figure that he had just made; he could almost fancy it had colour, and that the armour shone like real iron and steel; the hearts on the Danish arms grew redder and redder, and the lions, with their gold crowns, sprang forward fiercely—so it seemed—while he looked at them.

"Surely this is the prettiest coat-of-arms in the world!" said the old man. "The lions denote strength, and the hearts symbolize mildness and love." He looked on the uppermost lion, and thought of King Canute, who subjected proud England to Denmark's throne; he looked at the second lion, and then remembered Waldemar, who gathered the Danish states into one, and vanquished the Vends; he looked at the third lion, and thought of Margaret, who united the crowns of Denmark, Sweden, and Norway. He looked at the red hearts, and they seemed to shine brighter than ever; they were changed into moving flames, and his thoughts followed each flame.

The first flame led him into a dark, narrow dungeon, wherein sat a captive, a beautiful woman. It was Eleanora Ulfeld, the daughter of Christian the Fourth; the flame settled upon her bosom, and bloomed like a rose above the heart of that noblest and best of all Danish women.

"Yes, that is one heart in Denmark's standard!" quoth the old grandfather.

And his thoughts followed the second flame, and it led him to the sea, where the cannons roared and the ships lay wrapped in smoke; and the flame rested, like the badge of an order of knighthood, upon Hvitfeldt's breast, just when, to save the fleet, he blew up himself and his ship.

And the third flame led him into Greenland's wretched huts, where stood the priest, Hans Egede, with love in his words and deeds, and the flame shone like a star upon his breast, pointing to the third heart in the Danish standard.

And the old grandfather's thoughts preceded the fourth flame, for he knew well whither that hovering torch-light would lead. In the peasant woman's lonely chamber stood Frederick the Sixth, writing his name with chalk on the rafters; the flame flickered about his bosom, flickered in his heart,—it was in that peasant's cot that his heart became a heart for Denmark's arms. And the old grandfather wiped his eyes, for he had known and served King Frederick of the silver-white hair and kind blue eyes, and he folded his hands and gazed before him in silence. Just then the old man's daughter-in-law came up and reminded him that it was late, and time for him to rest, and that the board was spread for supper.

"But what a beautiful figure you have made, grandfather!" said she. "Holger the Dane, and our old coat-of-arms complete! I fancy I have seen this face before."

"No, that you have not," replied the old man, "but I have seen it, and I have tried to cut it in wood, just as I remember it. It was on the 2d of April when the English fleet lay off the coast, when we showed ourselves to be Danes of the true old breed! I was of Steen Billes' squadron; I stood on deck of the 'Denmark;' there was a man by my side — it really seemed that the cannon-balls feared and shunned him! So merrily he sang the fine old battle-songs, and fired and fought as if he were more than mortal. I can recall his face even now; but whence he came or whither he went, I knew not; indeed, no one knew. I have often thought it must have been Holger the Dane himself, and that he had swam down from Kronborg to help us in the hour of danger; that was only my fancy, perhaps — at any rate, here stands his likeness."

And the figure cast its huge shadow up the wall, even to the ceiling, and the shadow seemed to move too, just as though the real living Holger the Dane were actually present in the room; but this might be because the flame of the candle flickered so unsteadily. And his son's wife kissed the old grandfather, and led him to the large arm-chair at the table, where she and her husband, who of course was son to the old grandfather, and father to the little boy in bed, sat down to eat their evening meal. And the old grandfather talked the while about the Danish lions and the Danish hearts, and about the strength and gentleness they were meant to typify. And he showed how that there was another kind of strength, quite different from that which lies in the sword, pointing, as he spoke, to the shelf where a few old, well-read, well-worn books were lying, among them Holberg's comedies,—those comedies which people take up and read again and again, because they are so charmingly written that all the characters described in them seem as well known to you as persons you have lived with all your life.

"You see he, too, knew how to carve," remarked the old man; "he could carve out people's humours and caprices." And then the old grandfather nodded at the looking-glass, over which the almanack, with the "Round Tower "* on its cover, was stuck, saying, "Tycho Brahe, he again—he was one of those who used the sword—not to cut into human flesh and bone, but to make clear a plain highway among all the stars of heaven! And then he, whose father was of my own craft, the old carver's son, he with the white hair and broad shoulders, whom we ourselves have seen, he whose fame is in all countries of the earth! he, to be sure, could sculpture in stone,—I can only carve wood. Ah, yes, Holger the Dane comes to us in many different ways, that all the world may hear of Denmark's strength! Now, shall we drink Bertel Thorwaldsen's health?"

But the little boy in bed, all this while, saw distinctly before him the ancient castle of Kronborg, standing alone above the Sound of Elsinore, and the real Holger the Dane sitting in the caverns underground, with his beard grown fast into the marble table, and dreaming of all that happens in the world above him. And Holger the Dane, among other things, dreamt of the narrow, meanly-furnished chamber wherein sat the wood-carver; he heard all that was said there, and bowed his head in his dream, saying,

"Yes, remember me still, good Danish people! Bear me in mind! I will not fail to come in your hour of need!"

And the sun shone brightly on Kronborg's towers, and the wind wafted the notes of the hunter's horn across from the neighbour country, the ships sailed past and saluted the castle—"Boom, boom!" and Kronborg returned in answer —"Boom, boom!" But, loud as their cannons roared, Holger

---

* The astronomical tower in Copenhagen, so called from its cylindrical form.

the Dane awaked not yet, for they did but mean, "Good day!" and "Thank you!"

The cannons must mean something very different from that before he will awake; yet awake he will, when there is need, for worth and strength dwell in Holger the Dane.

TOMMELISE.

ONCE upon a time there lived a young wife who longed exceedingly to possess a little child of her own, so she went to an old witch-woman and said to her, " I wish so very much to have a child—a little tiny child—won't you give me one, old mother?"

"Oh, with all my heart!" replied the witch. "Here is a barley-corn for you; it is not exactly of the same sort as those that grow on the farmer's fields, or that are given to the fowls in the poultry-yard, but do you sow it in a flower-pot, and then you shall see what you shall see!"

"Thank you, thank you!" cried the woman, and she gave the witch a silver sixpence, and then, having returned home, sowed the barley-corn, as she had been directed, whereupon a large and beautiful flower immediately shot forth from the flower-pot. It looked like a tulip, but the petals were tightly folded up,—it was still in bud.

"What a lovely flower!" exclaimed the peasant-woman, and she kissed the pretty red and yellow leaves, and as she kissed them the flower gave a loud report and opened. It was indeed a tulip, but on the small green pointal in the centre of the flower there sat a little tiny girl, so pretty and delicate, but her whole body scarcely bigger than the young peasant's thumb. So she called her Tommelise.

A pretty varnished walnut-shell was given her as a cradle, blue violet leaves served as her mattresses, and a rose-leaf was her coverlet. Here she slept at night; but in the day-time she played on the table. The peasant-wife had filled a plate with water, and laid flowers in it, their blossoms bordering the edge of the plate while the stalks lay in the water; on the surface floated a large tulip-leaf, and on it Tommelise might sit and sail from one side of the plate to the other, two white horse-hairs having been given her for oars. That looked quite charming! And Tommelise could sing too, and she sang in such low, sweet tones as never were heard before.

One night, while she was lying in her pretty bed, a great ugly toad came hopping in through the broken window-pane. The toad was such a great creature, old and withered-looking, and wet too; she hopped at once down upon the table where Tommelise lay sleeping under the red rose-petal.

"That is just the wife for my son," said the Toad; and she seized hold of the walnut-shell, with Tommelise in it, and hopped away with her through the broken pane down into the garden.

Here flowed a broad stream, its banks were muddy and swampy, and it was amongst this mud that the old Toad and her son dwelt.

Ugh, how hideous and deformed he was! just like his mother. "Coax, coax, brekke-ke-kex!" was all he could find to say on seeing the pretty little maiden in the walnut-shell.

"Don't make such a riot, or you'll wake her," said old Mother Toad. "She may easily run away from us, for she is as light as a swan-down feather. I'll tell you what we'll do; we'll take her out into the brook, and set her down on one of the large water-lily leaves, it will be like an island to her, who is so light and small. Then she cannot run away from us, and we can go and get ready the state-rooms down under the mud, where you and she are to dwell together."

Out in the brook there grew many water-lilies, with their broad green leaves, each of which seemed to be floating over the water. The leaf which was the farthest from the shore was also the largest; to it swam old Mother Toad, and on it she set the walnut-shell, with Tommelise.

The poor little tiny creature awoke quite early next morning, and, when she saw where she was, she began to weep most bitterly, for there was nothing but water on all sides of the large green leaf, and she could in no way reach the land.

Old Mother Toad was down in the mud, decorating her apartment with bulrushes and yellow buttercups, so as to make it quite gay and tidy to receive her new daughter-in-law. At last she and her frightful son swam together to the leaf where she had left Tommelise; they wanted to fetch her pretty cradle, and place it for her in the bridal chamber, before she herself was conducted into it. Old Mother Toad bowed low in the water, and said to her, "Here is my son; he is to be thy husband; and you will dwell together so comfortably down in the mud!"

"Coax, coax, brekke-ke-kex!" was all that her son could say.

Then they took the neat little bed and swam away with it, whilst Tommelise sat alone on the green leaf, weeping, for she did not like the thought of living with the withered old Toad, and having her ugly son for a husband. The little fishes that were swimming to and fro in the water beneath had heard what Mother Toad had said, so they now put up their heads,—they wanted to see the little maid. And when they saw her, they were charmed with her delicate beauty, and it vexed them very much that the hideous old Toad should carry her off. No, that should never be! They surrounded the green stalk in the water, whereon rested the water-lily leaf, and gnawed it asunder with their teeth, and then the leaf floated away down the brook, with Tommelise on it,—away, far away, where the old Toad could not follow.

Tommelise sailed past so many places, and the wild birds among the bushes saw her and sang, "Oh, what a sweet little maiden!" On and on, farther and farther, floated the leaf: Tommelise was on her travels.

A pretty little white butterfly kept fluttering round and round her, and at last settled down on the leaf, for he loved Tommelise very much, and she was so pleased. There was nothing to trouble her, now that she had no fear of the old Toad pursuing her, and wherever she sailed everything was so beautiful, for the sun shone down on the water, making it bright as liquid gold. And now she took off her sash, and tied one end of it round the butterfly, fastening the other end firmly into the leaf. On floated the leaf, faster and faster, and Tommelise with it.

Presently a great Cock-chafer came buzzing past; he caught sight of her, and immediately fastening his claw round her slender waist, flew up into a tree with her. But the green leaf still floated down the brook, and the butterfly with it; he was bound to the leaf, and could not get loose.

Oh, how terrified was poor Tommelise when the Cock-chafer carried her up into the tree! and how sorry she felt, too, for the darling white butterfly which she had left tied fast to the leaf! she feared that, if he could not get away, he would perish of hunger. But the Cock-chafer cared nothing for that. He settled with her upon the largest leaf in the tree, gave her some honey from the flowers to eat, and hummed her praises, telling her she was very pretty, although she was not at all like a Hen-chafer. And by-and-by all the Chafers who lived in that tree came to pay her a visit; they looked at Tommelise, and one Miss Hen-chafer drew in her feelers, saying, "She has only two legs; how miserable that looks!" "She has no feelers!" cried another. "And see how thin and lean her waist is; why, she is just like a human being!" observed a third. "How very, very ugly she is!" at last cried all the Lady-chafers in chorus. The Chafer who had carried off Tommelise still could not persuade himself that she was otherwise than pretty, but, as all the rest kept repeating and insisting that she was ugly, he at last began to think they must be in the right, and determined to have nothing more to do with her; she might go wherever she would, for aught he cared, he said. And so the whole swarm flew down from the tree with her, and set her on a daisy: then she wept because she was so ugly that the Lady-chafers would not keep company with her; and yet Tommelise was the prettiest little creature that could be imagined, soft, and delicate, and transparent as the loveliest rose-leaf.

All the summer long poor Tommelise lived alone in the wide wood. She wove herself a bed of grass-straw, and hung it under a large burdock-leaf, which sheltered her from the rain; she dined off the honey from the flowers, and drank

TOMMELISE. *Page* 194

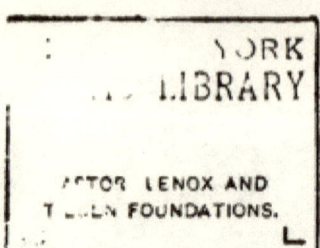

from the dew that every morning spangled the leaves and herblets around her. Thus passed the summer and autumn; but then came winter—the cold, long winter. All the birds who had sung so sweetly to her flew away, trees and flowers withered, the large burdock-leaf, under which Tommelise had lived, rolled itself up, and became a dry, yellow stalk, and Tommelise was fearfully cold, for her clothes were wearing out, and she herself was so slight and frail; poor little thing! she was nearly frozen to death. It began to snow, and every light flake that fell upon her made her feel as we should if a whole shovelful of snow were thrown upon us; for we are giants in comparison with a little creature only an inch long. She wrapped herself up in a withered leaf, but it gave her no warmth—she shuddered with cold.

Close outside the wood, on the skirt of which Tommelise had been living, lay a large corn-field; but the corn had been carried away long ago, leaving only the dry, naked stubble standing up from the hard frozen earth. It was like another wood to Tommelise, and oh, how she shivered with cold as she made her way through! At last she came past the Field-Mouse's door; for the Field-Mouse had made herself a little hole under the stubble, and there she dwelt snugly and comfortably, having a room full of corn, and a neat kitchen and store-chamber besides. And poor Tommelise must now play the beggar-girl; she stood at the door and begged for a little piece of a barley-corn, for she had had nothing to eat during two whole days.

"Thou poor little thing!" said the Field-Mouse, who was indeed a thoroughly good-natured old creature, "come into my warm room and dine with me."

And as she soon took a great liking to Tommelise, she proposed to her to stay. "You may dwell with me all the winter if you will, but keep my room clean and neat, and tell me stories, for I love stories dearly." And Tommelise did all that the kind old Field-Mouse required of her, and was made very comfortable in her new abode.

"We shall have a visitor presently," observed the Field-Mouse; "my next-door neighbour comes to see me once every week. He is better off than I am, has large rooms in his house, and wears a coat of such beautiful black velvet. It would be a capital thing for you if you could secure him for your husband; but unfortunately he is blind, he cannot see you. You must tell him the prettiest stories you know."

But Tommelise did not care at all about pleasing their neighbour, Mr. Mole, nor did she wish to marry him. He came and paid a visit in his black-velvet suit; he was so rich and so learned! and the Field-Mouse declared his domestic offices were twenty times larger than hers; but the sun and the pretty flowers he could not endure; he was always abusing them, though he had never seen either. Tommelise was called upon to sing for his amusement, and by the time she had sung " Lady-bird, lady-bird, fly away home!" and " The Friar of Orders Gray," the Mole had quite fallen in love with her through the charm of her sweet voice; however, he said nothing, he was such a prudent, cautious animal.

He had just been digging a long passage through the earth from their house to his, and he now gave permission to the Field-Mouse and Tommelise to walk in it as often as they liked; however, he bade them not be afraid of the dead bird that lay in the passage; it was a whole bird, with beak and feathers entire, and therefore he supposed it must have died quite lately, at the beginning of the winter, and had been buried just in the place where he had dug his passage.

The Mole took a piece of tinder, which shines like fire in the dark, in his mouth, and went on first to light his friends through the long, dark passage, and when they came to the place where the dead bird lay, he thrust his broad nose up against the ceiling and pushed up the earth, so as to make a great hole for the light to come through. In the midst of the floor lay a swallow, his wings clinging firmly to his sides, his head and legs drawn under the feathers; the poor bird had evidently died of cold. Tommelise felt so very sorry, for she loved all the little birds who had sung and chirped so merrily to her the whole summer long; but the Mole kicked it with his short legs, saying, " Here's a fine end to all its whistling! a miserable thing it must be to be born a bird! None of my children will be birds, that's a comfort! Such creatures have nothing but their ' quivit,' and must be starved to death in the winter."

" Yes, indeed, a sensible animal like you may well say so," returned the Field-Mouse; " what has the bird got by all his chirping and chirruping? when winter comes it must starve and freeze; and it is such a great creature too!"

Tommelise said nothing, but when the two others had turned their backs upon the bird, she bent over it, smoothed down the feathers that covered its head, and kissed the closed eyes. "Perhaps it was this one that sang so delightfully to me in the summer time," thought she; "how much pleasure it has given me, the dear, dear bird!"

The Mole now stopped up the hole through which the daylight had pierced, and then followed the ladies home. But Tommelise could not sleep that night, so she got out of her bed and wove a carpet out of hay, and then went out and spread it round the dead bird; she also fetched some soft cotton from the Field-Mouse's room, which she laid over the bird, that it might be warm amid the cold earth.

"Farewell, thou dear bird!" said she, "farewell! and thanks for thy beautiful song in the summer time, when all the trees were green and the sun shone so warmly upon us!" And she pressed her head against the bird's breast, but was terrified to feel something beating within it. It was the bird's heart—the bird was not dead; it had lain in a swoon, and now that it was warmer, its life returned.

Every autumn all the swallows fly away to warm countries; but if one of them linger behind, it freezes and falls down as though dead, and the cold snow covers it.

Tommelise trembled with fright, for the bird was very large compared with her, who was only an inch in length. However, she took courage, laid the cotton more closely round the poor swallow, and fetching a leaf which had served herself as a coverlet, spread it over the bird's head.

The next night she stole out again, and found that the bird's life had quite returned, though it was so feeble that only for one short moment could it open its eyes to look at Tommelise, who stood by with a piece of tinder in her hand—she had no other lantern. "Thanks to thee, thou sweet little child!" said the sick Swallow. "I feel delightfully warm now, soon I shall recover my strength, and be able to fly again, out in the warm sunshine."

"Oh no," she replied, "it is too cold without; it snows and freezes! thou must stay in thy warm bed; I will take care of thee."

She brought the Swallow water in a flower-petal, and he drank, and then told her how he had torn one of his wings in a thorn-bush, and therefore could not fly fast enough to keep up with the other swallows, who were all migrating to the warm countries. He had at last fallen to the earth, and more than that he could not remember; he did not at all know how he had got underground.

However, underground he remained all the winter long, and Tommelise was kind to him, and loved him dearly, but she never said a word about him either to the Mole or the Field-Mouse, for she knew they could not endure the poor Swallow.

As soon as the spring came, and the sun's warmth had penetrated the earth, the Swallow said farewell to Tommelise, and she opened for him the covering of earth which the Mole had thrown back before. The sun shone in upon them so deliciously, and the Swallow asked whether she would not go with him; she might sit upon his back, and then they would fly together far out into the greenwood. But Tommelise knew it would vex the old Field-Mouse, if she were to leave her.

"No, I cannot; I must not go," said Tommelise.

"Fare thee well, then, thou good and pretty maiden!" said the Swallow, and away he flew into the sunshine. Tommelise looked after him, and the tears came into her eyes, for she loved the poor Swallow so much.

"Quivit, quivit," sang the bird, as he flew into the greenwood.

And Tommelise was now sad indeed. She was not allowed to go out into the warm sunshine; the wheat that had been sown in the field above the Field-Mouse's house grew up so high that it seemed a perfect forest to the poor little damsel, who was only an inch in stature.

"This summer you must work at getting your wedding-clothes ready," said the Field-Mouse; for their neighbour, the blind, dull Mole, in the black-velvet suit, had now made his proposals in form to Tommelise. "You shall have worsted and linen in plenty; you shall be well provided with all manner of clothes and furniture, before you become the Mole's wife."

So Tommelise was obliged to work hard at the distaff, and the Field-Mouse hired four spiders to spin and weave night and day. Every evening came the Mole, and always began to talk about the summer soon coming to an end, and that then —when the sun would no longer shine so warmly, scorching the earth till it was as dry as a stone—yes, then, his nuptials with Tommelise should take place. But this sort of conversation did not please her at all; she was thoroughly wearied of his dulness and his prating. Every morning, when the sun rose, and every evening when it set, she used to steal out at the door; and when the wind blew the tops of the corn aside, so that she could see the blue sky through the opening, she thought how bright and beautiful it was out here, and wished most fervently to see the dear Swallow once more; but he never came, he must have been flying far away in the beautiful greenwood.

Autumn came, and Tommelise's wedding-clothes were ready.

" Four weeks more, and you shall be married !" said the Field-Mouse. But Tommelise wept, and said she would not marry the dull Mole.

" Fiddlestick !" exclaimed the Field-Mouse ; "don't be obstinate, child, or I shall bite thee with my white teeth ! Is he not handsome, pray ? Why, the Queen has not got such a black-velvet dress as he wears ! And isn't he rich — rich both in kitchens and cellars? Be thankful to get such a husband !"

So Tommelise must be married. The day fixed had arrived, the Mole had already come to fetch his bride, and she must dwell with him, deep under the earth, never again to come out into the warm sunshine, which she loved so much, and which he could not endure. The poor child was in despair at the thought that she must now bid a last farewell to the beautiful sun, of which she had at least been allowed to catch a glimpse every now and then while she lived with the Field-Mouse.

" Farewell, thou glorious sun !" she cried, throwing her arms up into the air, and she walked on a little way beyond the Field-Mouse's door ; the corn was already reaped, and only the dry stubble surrounded her. " Farewell, farewell !" repeated she, as she clasped her tiny arms round a little red flower that grew there. " Greet the dear Swallow from me, if thou shouldest see him."

" Quivit ! quivit !"— there was a fluttering of wings just

over her head: she looked up, and behold! the little Swallow was flying past. And how pleased he was when he perceived Tommelise! She told how that she had been obliged to accept the disagreeable Mole as a husband, and that she would have to dwell deep underground, where the sun never pierced. And she could not help weeping as she spoke.

"The cold winter will soon be here," said the Swallow; "I shall fly far away to the warm countries. Wilt thou go with me? Thou canst sit on my back, and tie thyself firmly to me with thy sash, and thus we shall fly away from the stupid Mole and his dark room, far away over the mountains, to those countries where the sun shines so brightly, where it is always summer, and flowers blossom all the year round. Come and fly with me, thou sweet little Tommelise, who didst save my life when I lay frozen in the dark cellars of the earth!"

"Yes, I will go with thee!" said Tommelise. And she seated herself on the bird's back, her feet resting on the outspread wings, and tied her girdle firmly round one of the strongest feathers, and then the Swallow soared high into the air, and flew away over forest and over lake — over mountains whose crests are covered with snow all the year round. How Tommelise shivered as she breathed the keen frosty air! However, she soon crept down under the bird's warm feathers, her head still peering forth, eager to behold all the glory and beauty beneath her.

At last they reached the warm countries. There the sun shone far more brightly than in her native clime. The heavens seemed twice as high, and twice as blue; and ranged along the sloping hills grew, in rich luxuriance, the loveliest green and purple grapes. Citrons and melons were seen in the groves, the fragrance of myrtles and balsams filled the air; and by the wayside gambolled groups of pretty merry children chasing large bright-winged butterflies.

But the Swallow did not rest here; still he flew on; and still the scene seemed to grow more and more beautiful. Near a calm blue lake, overhung by lofty trees, stood a half-ruined palace of white marble, built in times long past; vine-wreaths trailed up the long slender pillars, and on the capitals, among the green leaves and waving tendrils, many a swallow had built his nest, and one of these nests belonged to the Swallow on whose back Tommelise was riding.

"This is my house," said the Swallow; "but if thou wouldest rather choose for thyself one of the splendid flowers growing beneath us, I will take thee there, and thou shalt make thy home in the loveliest of them all."

"That will be charming!" exclaimed she, clapping her tiny hands.

On the green turf beneath, there lay the fragments of a white marble column which had fallen to the ground, and around these fragments twined some beautiful large white flowers. The Swallow flew down with Tommelise, and set her on one of the broad petals. But what was her surprise when she saw sitting in the very heart of the flower a little mannikin, fair and transparent as though he were made of glass, wearing the prettiest gold crown on his head, and the brightest, most delicate wings on his shoulders, yet scarcely one whit larger than Tommelise herself. He was the Spirit of the flower. In every blossom there dwelt one such fairy youth or maiden, but this one was the king of all these Flower-spirits.

"Oh, how handsome he is, this King!" whispered Tommelise to the Swallow. The fairy prince was quite startled at the sudden descent of the Swallow, who was a sort of giant compared with him; but when he saw Tommelise he was delighted, for she was the very loveliest maiden he had ever seen. So he took his gold crown off his own head and set it upon hers, asked her name, and whether she would be his bride and reign as queen over all the Flower-spirits. This, you see, was quite a different bridegroom from the son of the ugly old Toad, or the blind Mole with his black velvet coat. So Tommelise replied "Yes" to the beautiful prince; and then the lady and gentlemen fairies came out, each from a separate flower, to pay their homage to Tommelise; so gracefully and courteously they paid their homage! and every one of them brought her a present. But the best of all the presents was a pair of transparent wings; they were fastened on Tommelise's shoulders, and enabled her to fly from flower to flower. That was the greatest of pleasures! and the little Swallow sat in his nest above and sang to her his sweetest song; in his heart, however, he was very sad, for he loved Tommelise, and would have wished never to part from her.

"Thou shalt no longer be called Tommelise," said the

King of the Flowers to her, "for it is not a pretty name, and thou art so lovely! We will call thee Maia."

"Farewell! farewell!" sang the Swallow, and away he flew from the warm countries far away back to Denmark. There he had a little nest just over the window of the man who writes stories for children. "Quivit! quivit! quivit!" he sang to him, and from him we have learned this history.

GREAT CLAUS AND LITTLE CLAUS.*

ONCE upon a time there lived in the same village two men bearing the very same name; one of them chanced to possess four horses, the other had only one horse; so, by way of distinguishing them from each other, the proprietor of four horses was called "Great Claus," and he who owned but one horse was known as "Little Claus." And now we shall relate their true and veritable history.

All the week long Little Claus had to plough for Great Claus, and to lend him his one horse, and in return Great Claus lent him his four horses, but only for one day in the week, and that day was Sunday. Hurrah! a proud man then was Little Claus; and how he brandished his whip over his five horses! for all five were his, he thought, for this one day at least. And the sun shone so brightly, and all the bells in the church-tower were ringing, the people were dressed in their best and walking to church, and as they passed they looked at Little Claus, who was driving his five horses, and he was so pleased that he kept cracking his whip again and again, crying out the while "Hip, hip, hurrah! five fine horses, and all of them mine!"

"You must not say that," observed Great Claus; "only one of the horses is yours; you know that well enough."

* "Claus" is a contraction of Nicholas.

But when another party of church-goers passed close by him, Little Claus quite forgot that he had been told he must not say so, and cried out again, "Hip, hip, hurrah! five fine horses, all mine!"

"Did not I tell you to hold your tongue?" exclaimed Great Claus, very angrily. "If you say that again, I'll give your one horse such a blow on the forehead as shall strike him dead on the spot, and then there'll soon be an end to your boasting about your five fine horses."

"Oh, but I'll never say it again, indeed I won't!" said Little Claus, and he quite intended to keep his word. But presently some more people came by, and when they nodded a friendly "good morning" to him he was so delighted, and it seemed to him such a grand thing to have five horses to plough his bit of a field, that he really could not contain himself; he flourished his whip aloft and shouted out, "Hip, hip, hurrah! five fine horses, every one of them mine!"

"I'll soon cure you of that!" cried Great Claus, in a fury, and, taking up a large stone, he flung it at the head of Little Claus' horse—so heavy was the stone that the poor creature fell down dead.

"Alas, now I have no horses at all!" cried Little Claus, and he began to weep. As soon as he had recovered himself a little, he set to work to flay the skin off his dead horse, dried the skin thoroughly in the air, and then putting it into a sack, he slung the sack across his shoulders, and set out on his way to the nearest town, intending to sell the skin.

He had a long way to go, and the road led him through a large and thickly-grown wood. And here a violent tempest burst forth; the clouds, the rain, and the dark firs, bowed to and fro by the wind, so bewildered poor Claus that he lost his path, and before he could recover it evening had darkened into night; he could neither return homewards nor get on to the town.

However, not far off stood a large farm-house; the window-shutters were closed, but Little Claus could see lights shining out through the creaks. "Perhaps I may get shelter there," thought he, so he went up to the house, and knocked at the door.

The farmer's wife came and opened it to him, but when she heard what he wanted, she very obligingly told him he must go and ask elsewhere; he shouldn't come into her house; her good man was from home, and she couldn't be receiving strangers in his absence.

"Well, then, I must sleep outside, under this stormy sky," replied Little Claus, and the farmer's wife shut the door in his face.

Close by stood a hay-stack, and between it and the house there was a little pent-house with a flat straw roof.

"I'll get up there," said Little Claus to himself, on perceiving this; "it will make me a capital bed. Only I do hope the stork yonder may not take it into his head to fly down and bite my legs." For a stork had made his nest on the roof, and had mounted guard beside the nest, as wide awake as could be, although it was night.

So Little Claus crept up on the pent-house, and there he turned and twisted about till he had made himself a right comfortable couch. The window-shutters did not close properly at the top, so that from his high and airy position he could see all that went on in the room.

There he saw a large table spread with bread and wine, roast meat and fried fish; the farmer's wife and the sexton sat at table—no one else was there: the farmer's wife was pouring out a glass of wine for the sexton, who meantime was eagerly helping himself to a large slice of the fish—he happened to be particularly fond of fish.

"Too bad, really, to keep it all to themselves!" sighed Little Claus. "If they would but give me a little, wee morsel!" and he stretched out his head as near to the window as he could. Oh, what a magnificent cake he could see now! Why, this was quite a banquet!

Presently he heard the sound of hoof-tramps approaching from the road. It was the farmer riding home.

A regularly good-hearted fellow was this farmer, but he had one peculiar weakness, namely, that he never could endure to see a sexton—the sight made him half mad. Now, the sexton of the neighbouring town happened to be first cousin to his wife, and they were old playmates and good friends; so, this evening, knowing that the farmer would be from home, he had come to pay his cousin a visit, and the good woman, being very pleased to see him, had brought out all the choice things in her larder wherewith to regale him. But now, as, while they were sitting together so comfortably, they heard the tramp of the farmer's horse, they both started up, and the woman bade the sexton creep into a large empty chest that stood in a corner of the room. He did so, for he knew that the poor farmer would be almost driven wild if he came in and saw a sexton standing unexpectedly before him. And the farmer's wife then made a great bustle to hide all the wine and the dishes inside her baking-oven, for fear her husband, if he saw the table spread with them, should ask for whom she had been preparing such a grand entertainment.

"Oh dear! oh dear!" sighed Little Claus from his couch on the pent-house, when he saw the feast all put on one side.

"Anybody up there?" inquired the farmer, on hearing the voice; and he looked up and perceived Little Claus. "Why are you lying there? Come down into the house with me."

And Little Claus explained that he had lost his way, and asked the farmer if he would not give him shelter for the night.

"To be sure I will," replied the good-natured man. "Come in quickly, and let's have something to eat."

The woman received them both with a great show of welcome, covered one end of the long table, and brought out a large dish of oatmeal. The farmer set to with a capital appetite, but Little Claus could not eat for thinking of the good roast meat, the fish, the wine, and the delicious cake which he had seen stowed away inside the oven.

He had put his sack containing the horse's skin under the table, and now, as he could not relish the oatmeal porridge, he began trampling the sack under his feet till the dry skin creaked aloud.

"Hush!" muttered Little Claus, as if speaking to his sack, but at the same moment he trod upon it again, so as to make it creak louder than before.

"What have you got in your sack?" asked the farmer.

"Oh! I've got a little conjuror there," replied Little Claus, "and he says we are not to be eating oatmeal porridge any longer, for he has conjured a feast of beef-steak, fried fish, and cake into the oven on purpose for us."

"A conjuror, did you say?" exclaimed the farmer, and up he got in a vast hurry to look into the oven and see whether the conjuror had spoken truly And there, to be sure! were fish, and steak, and cake; the conjuror had been as good as his word. The farmer's wife durst not utter a syllable of explanation; almost as much bewildered as her husband, she set the viands on the table, and the farmer and his guest began with a hearty appetite to eat of the good cheer before them.

Presently Little Claus trampled on his sack again, and again made the skin creak.

"What does your conjuror say now?" asked the farmer.

"He says," replied Little Claus, "that he has also conjured three bottles of wine here for us; you will find them standing just in the corner of the oven." So the woman was now obliged to bring out the wine that she had concealed, and the farmer poured himself out a glass and began to think it would be a fine thing to have such a capital conjuror as this.

"A right proper sort of conjuror, this of yours!" observed he, at last. "I should rather like to see him: will he let me, do you think?"

"Oh, of course," returned Little Claus; "my conjuror will do anything I ask him. That you will, won't you?" asked he, again treading on his sack. "Didn't you hear him say 'Yes?' But I warn you, he will look somewhat dark and unpleasing;—after all, it is scarcely worth while to see him!"

"Oh, I shall not be afraid,—what will he look like?"

"Why, he will appear for all the world just like a sexton."

"A sexton!" repeated the farmer, "that is a pity! You must know that I cannot endure the sight of a sexton; but no matter, since I shall know that it is not a real sexton, but only your conjuror, I shall not care about it. Oh, I've plenty of courage — only don't let him come too near me!"

"Well, I'll speak to my conjuror about it again," said Little Claus, and he trod on his skin till it went "creak, creak, creak," and bent his ear down, as though to listen.

"What does he say now?"

"He says he will transport himself into yonder chest in the corner; you have only to lift up the lid, and there you will see him; but you must mind and shut the lid close down again."

"Will you help me to hold up the lid? it is very heavy," said the farmer, and he went up to the chest wherein his wife had concealed the real sexton, who sat with his limbs huddled up, trembling, and holding his breath, lest he should be discovered—certainly in no very comfortable state.

The farmer gently raised the lid of the chest and peeped under it. "Ugh!" cried he, and immediately started back in affright. "Oh dear! oh dear! I saw him, he looked exactly like our sexton in the town—oh, how horrible!"

However, he sat down at table again, and began to drink glass after glass of wine, by way of recovering from the shock. The wine soon revived his fallen courage. Neither he nor his guest ever thought of going to bed; there they sat, talking and feasting till late in the night.

"Did you ever see your conjuror before?" inquired the farmer of Claus.

"Not I," replied Little Claus, "I should never have thought of asking him to show himself, if you had not proposed it. He knows he is not handsome; he does not wish to obtrude himself into any company; he talks to me, and I to him, and isn't that enough?"

"Oh, indeed, it is!" rejoined the farmer, quickly. Then, after a minute's hesitation, he went on, "Do you know, I should like very much to have your conjuror; would you mind selling him to me? Name your own price; I don't care if I give you a whole bushelful of silver on the spot."

"Oh, how can you ask such a thing?" exclaimed Little Claus, "such a useful, such a faithful servant as he is to me—how could I think of parting with him? Why, he's worth his weight in gold ten times over."

"I can't offer you gold," replied the farmer, "but I should like so very much to have him!—that is, provided he would never show his ugly self to me again."

"Oh, no fear of that," said Little Claus; "and really, since you have been so kind as to give me shelter to-night, I do not think I can refuse you any request. I will let you have my conjuror for a bushel of silver,—only the bushel must be crammed full, you know."

"Certainly it shall," answered the farmer; "and the chest yonder too, you shall have that into the bargain; I don't want it to remain an hour longer in the house; it will always be reminding me of the odious sexton-face I saw inside it."

So the bargain was struck, and Little Claus gave the farmer his sack, with the dry skin in it, and received instead

GREAT CLAUS AND LITTLE CLAUS.

Page 208.

a whole bushelful of silver. The farmer also gave him a large wheel-barrow, wherewith to convey home his money and his chest.

"Farewell!" said Little Claus, and away he drove the wheel-barrow, the unfortunate sexton still lying concealed in the chest.

On the opposite side of the wood flowed a broad, deep river; the current was so strong that no one could swim against it, so a bridge had lately been built over it. Little Claus took his way over the bridge, but stopped short in the middle of it, saying, very loud, on purpose that the man in the chest might hear him, "Now, what on earth can be the use of this great tumble-down chest to me? and it's as heavy, too, as if it were filled with stones; it quite tires me out. I'll fling it out into the river; if it chooses to float homewards to me, well and good; if not, it may let it alone; all the same to me."

And he lifted the chest as though intending to throw it into the water.

"Oh, pray, don't do that!" cried the sexton in the chest. "Let me get out first, pray."

"Holloa!" exclaimed Little Claus; "is the chest bewitched? If so, the sooner it's off my hands the better."

"Oh, no, no!" cried the sexton. "Let me out, and I'll give you another whole bushelful of money."

"Ah, that's quite another matter," said Little Claus; and he immediately set down the chest, and lifted the lid. Out crept the sexton, greatly to his own satisfaction. He kicked the empty chest into the water, and then took Little Claus to his house with him, where he gave him the bushelful of money, as agreed. Little Claus had now a wheel-barrow full of money.

"Certainly, I must own I have been well paid for my horse's skin," said he to himself, as he entered his own little room, and overturned all his money in a great heap on the floor. "It will vex Great Claus, I'm afraid, when he finds out how rich my horse's skin has made me."

And now he sent a little boy to Great Claus to borrow a measure of him.

"What can he want with a measure, I wonder?" thought Great Claus, and he cunningly smeared the bottom of the measure with clay, hoping that some part of whatever was measured might cleave to the clay. And accordingly, when

P

the measure was returned to him, he discovered three silver coins sticking at the bottom.

"Fine doings, upon my word!" exclaimed Great Claus, in amazement; and off he set forthwith to the house of his namesake. "Where did you get all that money?" thundered he.

"Oh, I got it by my horse's skin, which I sold yesterday," was the reply.

"Really?" exclaimed Great Claus. "What, are horses' skins so dear as that? Who would have thought it?" And he ran quickly home, took an axe, and struck all his four horses on the head with it, then flayed off the skins, and drove into the town.

"Skins, skins! who will buy skins?" cried he, as he passed through the streets.

All the shoemakers and tanners in the town came running up to him, and asked his price.

"I will have a bushelful of money for each," replied Great Claus.

"Are you mad?" cried they. "Do you think we reckon our money by bushels?"

"Skins, fresh skins! who will buy skins?" shouted he again; and still, to all who asked how much he wanted for them, he replied, "A bushelful of money."

"The rude boor! he is trying to make fools of us," declared one of his customers at last, in very great wrath.

"Skins, fresh skins, fine fresh skins!" cried they all, mimicking him. "Out of the town with him, the great ass! or he shall have no skin left on his own shoulders." And Great Claus was ignominiously thrust out of the town, and returned home in no very good humour.

"Little Claus shall pay for this," muttered he. "Sleep soundly this night, Little Claus, for thou shalt hardly wake again."

It so chanced that Little Claus' grandmother died that same evening; she had always been very cross and ill-natured to him in her lifetime, but now, on finding her dead, he felt really sorry for her. He laid the dead woman in his own warm bed, in hopes that the warmth might bring her to life again; for his own part, he thought he could spend the night in a chair in a corner of the room — he had often done so before.

About midnight the door opened, and Great Claus, his axe in his hand, came in. He knew well where Little Claus' bed was wont to stand; he went straight up to it, and struck the dead grandmother a violent blow on the forehead.

"There's for you," cried he; "now you'll never make a fool of me again." And herewith he went out of the room and returned home.

"What a very wicked man he is!" sighed Little Claus. "So he wanted to kill me. It was a good thing that old grandmother was dead already, or that blow would have hurt her very much."

The next day, in the evening, he met Great Claus in a lane near the village. Great Claus started back, and stared at him. "What, aren't you dead? I thought I killed you last night."

"Yes, you wicked man!" replied Little Claus, "I know you came into my room intending to kill me, but my grandmother, not I, was lying in the bed; it was she that you struck with your pick-axe, and you deserve to be hanged for it."

"And are you going to tell people about it?" said Great Claus. "That you never shall!" He was carrying a very large sack; he seized Little Claus by the waist and thrust him into the sack, crying out, "I will drown thee at once, and that will be the end of thy tale-telling."

But he had a long way to walk before he reached the river, and Little Claus was by no means a light burden. The road led past the church, the organ was playing, for the service had just begun. Among the congregation Great Claus saw a man he wanted to speak to. "Little Claus cannot get out of the sack by himself," thought he, "and no one can help him, for all the people are in church. I can just go in and call that man back into the porch for a minute." So he set down the heavy sack and ran into church.

"Oh dear! oh dear!" sighed Little Claus inside the sack; he turned and twisted in vain, it was not possible for him to get the string loose. Just then a very, very old cattle-driver passed by, his hair white as snow, and with a stout staff in his hand; he was driving a large herd of cows and bullocks before him, many more than he, feeble as he was, could manage. One of them rushed up against the sack and turned it over and over.

"Oh, help me, pray!" cried Little Claus. "I am so young to die; help me out of the sack."

"What, is there a man in the sack?" and the ancient cattle-driver bent down, though with some difficulty, and untied the string. "The bullock has not hurt you, I hope?" But Little Claus sprang out so briskly as showed he was not hurt, and set himself immediately to rooting up the withered stump of a tree which stood by the roadside, and which he rolled into the sack, then, tying the string, he placed the sack exactly as Great Claus had left it. The cattle had, meantime, passed on.

"Will you not drive these cattle home to the village for me?" asked the old man. "I am so weary, and I want to go into church so much."

"Right gladly will I help you since you have helped me," replied Little Claus, and he took the cattle-driver's goad from his hand, and followed the herd in his stead.

Presently Great Claus came running back again; he took up the sack, and again flung it across his shoulders, thinking, "How much lighter the burden seems now; it always does one good to rest for ever so short a time." So on he trudged to the river, flung the sack out into the water, and shouted after it, "There now, Little Claus, you shall never cheat me any more!"

He then turned homewards, but, on passing a spot where several roads crossed, whom should he meet but Little Claus himself, with his herd of cattle!

"How comes this?" exclaimed Great Claus. "Is it really you? Did not I drown you, then, after all?"

"I believe you meant to drown me," said Little Claus; "you threw me into the river just half an hour ago, did you not?"

"But how did you come by all these beautiful cattle?" asked Great Claus, in utter amazement, his eyes wandering admiringly from one to another of the herd.

"These are sea-cattle," said Little Claus. "Ah, I'll tell you the whole story! I am really much obliged to you for drowning me; it has made me richer than ever, as you may see. I was so frightened when I lay in the sack, and the wind whistled so uncomfortably into my ears, when you threw me down from the bridge into the cold water. I sank to the bottom at once, but I was not hurt, for I was received by the softest, freshest grass. Immediately the sack was opened, and the most beautiful young girl you can imagine, clad in snow-white robes, and with a green wreath in her wet hair, took me by the hand, saying, 'Art thou Little Claus? Here are some cattle of thine, and a mile farther up the road, another and larger herd is grazing, and I will give thee that herd also.' And then I understood that the river was a sort of high-road for the people of the sea, and that on it they walked and drove to and fro, from the sea far up into the land, where the river rises, and thence back to the sea again. And no place can be more beautiful than it is at the bottom of the water; the prettiest flowers and the freshest grass grow there; and the fishes swimming in the water slipped to and fro about my ears, just as birds flutter about us up here, in the air. And such gaily-dressed people I saw there, and such a multitude of cattle grazing in pastures inclosed with hedges and ditches!"

"Then, why were you in such a hurry to come up again?" inquired Great Claus. "I shouldn't have done so, not I, when I found it so pleasant there."

"Ah!" rejoined Little Claus; "that was so cleverly done on my part! Did not I tell you that the sea-lady told me that a mile up the road—and by the road she could only mean the river, she can't come into our land-roads—there was another and larger herd of cattle for me? But I knew that the river makes a great many turns and windings, and therefore I thought I'd just spare myself half a mile of the way by taking the short cut across the land. So here I am, you see, and I shall soon get to my sea-cattle!"

"Oh, what a lucky fellow you are!" exclaimed Great Claus. "Don't you think that I might have some cattle given to me too, if I went down to the bottom of the river?"

"How can I tell?" asked Little Claus, in reply.

"You envious scoundrel! you want to keep all the beautiful sea-cattle for yourself, I warrant!" cried Great Claus. "Either you will carry me to the water's edge, and throw me over, or I will take out my great knife and kill you. Make your choice!"

"Oh no! please don't be so angry," entreated Little Claus. "I cannot carry you in the sack to the river; you are too heavy for me; but if you will walk there yourself, and then creep into the sack, I will throw you over with all the pleasure in the world."

"But if, when I get to the bottom, I find no sea-cattle for me, I shall kill you all the same when I come back — remember that!" said Great Claus; and to this arrangement Little Claus made no objection. They walked together to the river. As soon as the thirsty cattle saw the water, they ran on as fast as they could, eagerly crowding against each other, and all wanting to drink first.

"Only look at my sea-cattle!" said Little Claus. "See how they are longing to be at the bottom of the river."

"That's all very well," said Great Claus, "but you must help me first." And he quickly crept into the great sack, which had lain stretched across the shoulders of one of the oxen. "Put a heavy stone in with me," said Great Claus, "else, perhaps, I shall not sink to the bottom."

"No fear of that," replied Little Claus. However, he put a large stone into the sack, tied the strings, and pushed the sack into the water — plump! — there it fell, straight to the bottom.

"I am much afraid he will not find his sea-cattle," observed Little Claus, and he drove his own herd quietly home to the village.

THE CONSTANT TIN-SOLDIER.

THERE were once five-and-twenty Tin-soldiers, all brothers, for they had all been made out of one old tin-spoon. They carried muskets in their arms, and held themselves very upright, and their uniforms were red and blue — very gay indeed. The first word that they heard in this world, when the lid was taken off the box wherein they lay, was, "Tin-soldiers!" It was a little boy who made this exclamation, clapping his hands at the same time. They had been given to him because it was his birth-day, and he now set them out on the table. The soldiers resembled each other to a hair; one only was rather different from the rest; he had but one leg, for he had been made last, when there was not quite tin enough left; however, he stood as firmly upon his one leg as the others did upon their two. And this identical Tin-soldier it is whose fortunes seem to us worthy of record.

On the table where the Tin-soldiers were set out were several other playthings, but the most charming of them all was a pretty pasteboard castle. Through its little windows one could look into the rooms. In front of the castle stood some tiny trees, clustering round a little mirror intended to represent a lake, and waxen swans swam in the lake, and were reflected on its surface. All this was very pretty; but prettiest of all was a little damsel standing in the open doorway of the castle. She, too, was cut out of pasteboard; but she had on a frock of the clearest muslin, a little sky-blue riband was flung across her shoulders like a scarf, and in the midst of this scarf was set a bright gold wing. The little lady stretched out both her arms, for she was a dancer, and raised one of her legs so high in the air that the Tin-soldier could not find it, and fancied that she had, like him, only one leg.

"That would be just the wife for me," thought he; "but, then, she is of rather too high rank, she lives in a castle. I have only a box; besides, there are all our five-and-twenty men in it, it is no place for her! However, there will be no harm in my making acquaintance with her." And so he stationed himself behind a snuff box that stood on the table; from this place he had a full view of the delicate little lady, who still remained standing on one leg, yet without losing her balance.

When evening came, all the other Tin-soldiers were put away into the box, and the people of the house went to bed. The playthings now began to play in their turn; they pretended to visit, to fight battles, and give balls. The Tin-soldiers rattled in the box, for they wanted to play too, but the lid would not come off. The nut-crackers cut capers, and the slate-pencil played at commerce on the slate; there was such a racket that the canary-bird waked up, and began to talk too; but he always talked in verse. The only two who did not move from their places were the Tin-soldier and the little dancer; she constantly remained in her graceful position, standing on the point of her foot, with outstretched arms; and as for him, he stood just as firmly on his one leg, never for one moment turning his eyes away from her.

Twelve o'clock struck—crash! open sprang the lid of the snuff-box; but there was no snuff inside it; no, out jumped a little black Conjuror; in fact, it was a Jack-in-the-box.

"Tin-soldier!" said the Conjuror, "wilt thou keep thine eyes to thyself?"

But the Tin-soldier pretended not to hear.

"Well, only wait till to-morrow!" quoth the Conjuror.

When the morrow had come, and the children were out of bed, the Tin-soldier was placed on the window-ledge, and, whether the Conjuror or the wind occasioned it, all at once the window flew open, and out fell the Tin-soldier, head foremost, from the third story to the ground. A dreadful fall was that! his one leg turned over and over in the air, and at last he rested, poised on his soldier's cap, with his bayonet between the paving-stones.

The maid-servant and the little boy immediately came down to look for him; but although they very nearly trod on him, they could not see him. If the Tin-soldier had but called out, "Here I am!" they might easily have found him; but he thought it would not be becoming for him to cry out, as he was in uniform.

It now began to rain; every drop fell heavier than the last; there was a regular shower. When it was over, two boys came by.

"Look," said one, "here is a Tin-soldier! he shall have a sail for once in his life."

So they made a boat out of an old newspaper, put the Tin-soldier into it, and away he sailed down the gutter, both the boys running along by the side and clapping their hands. The paper-boat rocked to and fro, and every now and then veered round so quickly that the Tin-soldier became quite giddy; still he moved not a muscle, looked straight before him, and held his bayonet tightly clasped.

All at once the boat sailed under a long gutter-board; he found it as dark here as at home in his own box.

"Where shall I get to next?" thought he; "yes, to be sure, it is all that Conjuror's doing! Ah, if the little maiden were but sailing with me in the boat, I would not care for its being twice as dark!"

Just then a great Water-Rat, that lived under the gutter-board, darted out.

"Have you a passport?" asked the Rat. "Where is your passport?"

But the Tin-soldier was silent, and held his weapon with a still firmer grasp. The boat sailed on, and the Rat followed. Oh! how furiously he showed his teeth, and cried out to sticks and straws, "Stop him, stop him! he has not paid the toll! he has not shown his passport!" But the stream grew stronger and stronger. The Tin-Soldier could already catch a glimpse of the bright day-light before the boat came from under the tunnel, but at the same time he heard a roaring noise, at which the boldest heart might well have trembled. Only fancy! where the tunnel ended, the water of the gutter fell perpendicularly into a great canal; this was as dangerous for the Tin-soldier as sailing down a mighty waterfall would be for us.

He was now so close that he could no longer stand upright; the boat darted forwards, the poor Tin-soldier held himself as stiff and immoveable as possible, no one could accuse him of having even blinked. The boat spun round and round, three, nay, four times, and was filled with water to the brim; it must sink. The Tin-soldier stood up to his neck in water, deeper and deeper sank the boat, softer and softer grew the paper; the water went over the soldier's head, he thought of the pretty little dancer, whom he should never see again, and these words rang in his ears:—

> "Wild adventure, mortal danger
> Be thy portion, valiant stranger!"

The paper now tore asunder, the Tin-soldier fell through the rent; but in the same moment he was swallowed up by a large fish.

Oh, how dark it was! worse even than under the gutter-board, and so narrow too!—but the Tin-soldier's resolution was as constant as ever; there he lay, at full length, shouldering his arms.

The fish turned and twisted about, and made the strangest movements! at last he became quite still; a flash of lightning, as it were, darted through him. The daylight shone brightly, and some one exclaimed, "Tin-soldier!" The fish had been caught, taken to the market, sold, and brought home into the kitchen, where the servant-girl was cutting him up with a large knife. She seized the Tin-soldier by the middle with two of her fingers, and took him into the parlour, where every one was eager to see the wonderful man who had travelled in the maw of a fish;—however, our little warrior was by no means proud. They set him on the table, and there—no, how could anything so extraordinary happen in this world!—the Tin-soldier was in the very same room in which he had been before; he saw the same children, the same playthings stood on the table, among them the beautiful castle with the pretty little dancing maiden, who was still standing upon one leg, whilst she held the other high in the air; she, too, was constant. It quite affected the Tin-soldier; he could have found it in his heart to weep tin-tears, but such weakness would have been unbecoming in a soldier. He looked at her, and she looked at him, but neither spoke a word.

And now one of the little boys took the Soldier and threw him without ceremony into the stove. He did not give any reason for so doing, but, no doubt, the Conjuror in the snuff-box must have had a hand in it.

The Tin-soldier now stood in a blaze of red light; he felt extremely hot; whether this heat was the result of the actual fire, or of the flames of love within him, he knew not. He had entirely lost his colour; whether this change had happened during his travels, or were the effect of strong emotion, I know not. He looked upon the little damsel, she looked upon him, and he felt that he was melting; but, constant as ever, he still stood shouldering his arms. A door opened, the wind seized the Dancer, and, like a sylph, she flew straightway into the stove, to the Tin-soldier; they both flamed up into a blaze—and were gone! The Soldier was melted to a hard lump, and when the maid took the ashes out the next day, she found his remains in the shape of a little tin-heart: of the Dancer there remained only the gold wing, and that was burnt black as a coal.

THE NAUGHTY BOY.

THERE was once an old poet, such a good, honest old poet! He was sitting alone in his own little room on a very stormy evening; the wind was roaring without, and the rain poured down in torrents. But the old man sat cosily by his warm stove, the fire was blazing brightly, and some apples were roasting in front of it.

"Those poor people who have no roof to shelter them to-night will, most assuredly, not have a dry thread left on their skin," said the kind-hearted old man.

"Oh, open the door! open the door! I am so cold, and quite wet through besides—open the door!" cried a voice from without. The voice was like a child's, and seemed half choked with sobs. "Rap, rap, rap!" it went on knocking at the door, whilst the rain still kept streaming down from the clouds, and the wind rattled among the window-panes.

"Poor thing!" said the old Poet; and he arose and opened the door. There stood a little boy, almost naked; the water trickled down from his long flaxen hair; he was shivering with cold, and, had he been left much longer out in the street, he must certainly have perished in the storm.

"Poor boy!" said the old Poet again, taking him by the hand, and leading him into his room. "Come to me, and we'll soon make thee warm again, and I will give thee some wine, and some roasted apples for thy supper, my pretty child!"

And, of a truth, the boy was exceedingly pretty. His eyes shone as bright as stars, and his hair, although dripping with water, curled in beautiful ringlets. He looked quite like a little cherub, but he was very pale, and trembled in every limb with cold. In his hand he held a pretty little cross-bow, but it seemed entirely spoilt by the rain, and the colours painted on the arrows all ran one into another.

The old Poet sat down again beside the stove, and took the little boy in his lap; he wrung the water out of his streaming hair, warmed the child's hands within his own, and gave him sweet mulled wine to drink. The boy soon became himself again, the rosy colour returned to his cheeks, he jumped down from the old man's lap, and danced around him on the floor.

"Thou art a merry fellow!" said the Poet. "Thou must tell me thy name."

"They call me Cupid," replied the boy. "Don't you know me? There lies my bow—ah, you can't think how capitally I can shoot! See, the weather is fine again now; the moon is shining bright."

"But thy bow is spoilt," said the old man.

"That would be a sad disaster, indeed," remarked the boy, as he took the bow in his hand and examined it closely. "Oh, it is quite dry by this time, and it is not a bit damaged, the string, too, is quite strong enough, I think. However, I may as well try it." He then drew his bow, placed an arrow before the string, took his aim, and shot direct into the old Poet's heart. "Now you may be sure that my cross-bow is not spoilt!" cried he, as, with a loud laugh, he ran away.

The naughty boy! This was, indeed, ungrateful of him, to shoot to the heart the good old man who had so kindly taken him in, warmed him, and dried his clothes, giving him sweet wine and nice roasted apples for supper!

The poor Poet lay groaning on the ground, for the arrow had wounded him sorely. "Fie, for shame, Cupid!" cried he, 'thou art a wicked boy! I will tell all good children how thou hast treated me, and bid them take heed, and never play with thee, for thou wilt assuredly do them a mischief, as thou hast done to me."

All the good boys and girls to whom he related this story were on their guard against the wicked boy Cupid; but, notwithstanding, he made fools of them again and again—he is so terribly cunning! When the students are returning home from lecture he walks by their side, dressed in a black gown, and with a book under his arm. They take him to be a fellow-student, and so they suffer him to walk arm-in-arm with them, just as if he were one of their intimate friends. But whilst they are thus familiar with him, all of a sudden he thrusts his arrows into their bosoms. Even when young girls are going to church, he will follow and watch for his opportunity: he is always waylaying people. In the theatre, he sits in the great chandelier, and kindles such a bright, hot flame, men fancy it a lamp, but they are soon undeceived. He wanders about in the Royal Gardens and all the public walks, making mischief everywhere; nay, once he even shot thy father and mother to the heart! Only ask them, dear child, and they will certainly tell thee all about it. In fine, this fellow, this Cupid, is a very wicked boy! Do not play with him! He waylays everybody, boys and girls, youths and maidens. men and women, rich and poor, old and young. Only think of this, he once shot an arrow into thy good old grandmother's heart! It happened a long time ago, and she has recovered from the wound, but she will never forget him, depend upon it. Fie, for shame! wicked Cupid! Is he not a mischievous boy? Beware of him, beware of him, dear child!

THE ANGEL.

'WHENEVER a good child dies, an Angel of God comes down to earth, takes the dead child in his arms, and, spreading out his large white wings, flies with him over all the places that were dear to him. And the Angel gathers a handful of flowers, and takes them to the good God, that they may bloom yet more beautifully in heaven than they did upon earth. And the flower which most pleases its Creator receives a voice, and, supremely happy, joins in the chorus of the blessed Angels."

Thus spoke an Angel of God while carrying a dead child to heaven, and the child listened as though in a dream, and together they flew over all those places where the child had formerly played, and they passed over gardens full of lovely flowers. "Which flower shall we take with us and plant in heaven?" asked the Angel.

And there stood a fair delicate rose-tree, but an evil hand had broken the stem, so that all the branches, with their large half-opened buds, hung faded down to the ground. "Poor tree!" said the child, "let us take it, that it may bloom again with the good God in heaven."

And the Angel took it, and kissed the child, and the little one half opened his eyes. They plucked many a splendid garden flower, but they also took the meek little daisy and the wild hearts-ease.

"Now we have flowers enough!" said the child, and the Angel seemed to assent, but he did not yet fly up to heaven.

It was night, it was very still; they stayed near a town, they hovered over one of its narrowest streets, where straw, ashes, and rubbish of all kinds, were scattered; there had been a removal that day, lying on the ground were broken plates, bits of plaster, rags, fragments of old hats; in short, nothing but things unseemly.

Amidst this confusion the Angel pointed to the broken pieces of an old flower-pot, and a lump of earth fallen out of it; they were only held together by the roots of a large faded field-flower, which was no longer worth looking at, and had, therefore, been thrown out into the street.

"We will take this flower with us," said the Angel. "I will tell thee about it as we are flying."

And they flew away, and the Angel spake as follows:

"There once lived in a low cellar down in that little narrow street a poor, sick boy; he had been confined to his bed from his earliest years; perhaps now and then he was able to take a few turns up and down his little room on his crutches, but that was all he could do. Sometimes, during the summer, the sunbeams would stream through his little cellar-window, and then, if the child sat up and felt the warm sun shining upon him, and could see the crimson blood in his slight, wasted, transparent fingers, as he held them up to the light, he would say, 'To-day I have been out!' He only knew the pleasant woods and their bright vernal green by the neighbour's son bringing him the first fresh boughs of the beech-tree, which he would hold over his head, and then fancy he was under the shade of the beech-trees, with the birds warbling, and the sun shining around him.

"One day, in spring, the neighbour's son brought him some field-flowers, and among them was one with a root, so it was put into a flower-pot and placed at the window, close by the bed. And, being carefully planted, it flourished, and put forth fresh shoots, and bore flowers every year; it was like a beautiful garden to the poor boy—his little treasure upon earth; he watered it, and tended it, taking care that every sunbeam, from the first to the last which penetrated his little low window, should fall upon the plant. And its flowers, with their soft colours and fragrance, mingled with his dreams, and towards them he turned when he was dying, when our Lord called him to Himself. The child has now been a year with the blessed—for a year the plant has stood by the window faded and forgotten, and to-day it was thrown out among the rubbish into the street. And this is the flower which we have just now taken, for this poor, faded field-flower has given more pleasure than the most splendid blossoms in the garden of a queen."

"But how do you know all this?" asked the child whom the Angel was bearing to heaven.

"How do I know it?" said the Angel, "I was myself that little sick boy who went upon crutches. Ought I not to know my own flower?" And the child opened wide its eyes, and looked into the Angel's fair, bright countenance—and in the same moment they were in heaven.

And the dead child received wings like the Angel's, and flew with him hand in hand; and a voice was given to the poor, faded field-flower, and it sang with the Angels surrounding the great God, some very near Him, and others forming larger circles, farther and farther away, extending into infinity, but all equally blessed.

And they all sang together, the Angels, the good child, and the poor, faded field-flower, which had lain among the rubbish of that dark and narrow street.

THE CLOGS OF FORTUNE.

Chapter I.

A Beginning.

EVERY author has something peculiar in his style of writing, and those who are unfriendly to him quickly fasten upon this peculiarity, shrug up their shoulders and exclaim, "There he is again!" Now I well know how to provoke this exclamation; I have only to begin my story as I had intended, thus:

"Rome has its Corso, Naples its Toledo,"—"Ah, there's that Andersen again!" say they—however, it matters not, I shall continue. "Copenhagen has its East Street,"—well, we will leave it so.

In one of the houses near the New Market a party was assembled, a great number of people had been invited, probably only for the sake of receiving invitations in return. About half the guests were seated at card-tables, the rest patiently awaited the result of a challenge to conversation just given by the hostess. "Come, let us see how we can amuse ourselves!"

Amongst other subjects the Middle Ages was started, and some persons present asserted that this period was far more interesting than our own times, Councillor Knap defending the opinion with so much zeal, that the lady of the house immediately came over to his side. And then they both declaimed eagerly against Oersted's Treatise on "Old Times and New Times," wherein the preference is given to the latter, the Councillor declaring the times of King Hans, viz. the close of the fifteenth century, to be decidedly the best and happiest.

Leaving this discussion, which was only interrupted for a moment by the arrival of a newspaper containing nothing worth the trouble of reading, we will now quit the guest-chamber, and betake ourselves to the ante-room, where cloaks, sticks, and clogs are left. Here are sitting two females, the one young, the other old, and at first sight we might imagine them to be maid-servants, come to accompany their ladies home, but on a nearer view it is seen that their figures are noble, their hands and complexion delicate, their bearing majestic and queenly. In fact, they are fairies; the younger is certainly not Dame Fortune herself, but she is the handmaid of one of her ladies of the bedchamber, and allowed to distribute her lesser gifts; the other, who looks somewhat gloomy, is Care! one who always attends to her affairs personally, because she is then sure no mistakes will happen.

They were telling each other where they had been that day; the handmaid of Fortune had as yet only related a few insignificant actions, such as having saved a new hat from a shower of rain, or having procured for an honest, plain man a greeting from some distinguished nobody, &c. &c.; she had, however, reserved for her last communication one of a most unusual nature.

"I have also to tell you," said she, "that this is my birthday, in honour of which there has been intrusted to me a pair of Clogs, which I am to have the privilege of bestowing upon mortals. These Clogs have the power of instantly transporting every one who puts them on to the place where he desires to be; his every wish with regard to time, place, or circumstance will at once be fulfilled, and the favoured mortal thus rendered completely happy."

"Mark me!" said Care, "he will, on the contrary, be very unhappy, and will bless the moment which frees him from thy Clogs."

"That is your opinion!" returned the other. "Nevertheless, I now place them by the door; presently some one will put them on, and become the fortunate man!"

Such was their dialogue.

Chapter II.

WHAT BEFELL THE COUNCILLOR.

It grew late, Councillor Knap, still deep in the times of King Hans, was about to return home, and as fate would have it, he got hold of the Clogs of Fortune instead of his own, and, putting them on, stepped out into East Street. But the magic power of the Clogs having, according to his wish, carried him back to the fifteenth century, his feet sank into a mass of filth and mud, the streets of that period not having the advantage of a stone pavement.

"How disgustingly dirty it is here!" said the Councillor; "why, the footpath is gone, and all the lamps are out!"

The moon had not yet risen high enough to give much light, besides which the atmosphere was rather thick, so that every object around him was enveloped in mist, and seemed indistinct. One solitary lamp burned before an image of the Virgin in a corner of the street; its light, however, was but faint; in fact, the Councillor did not remark it till he stood just underneath, and then his eyes fell upon the painted figure.

"That must be some exhibition," thought he, "and they have forgotten to take in the sign."

Two men in the costume of the middle ages passed by him.

"How odd those people look! I suppose they are coming from a masquerade."

Suddenly was heard the noise of drums and fifes, torches flashed brightly,—the Councillor started at seeing a most unusual procession pass by. First came a whole troop of drummers, who handled their instrument very cleverly, and then followed yeomen with bows and arrows. The chief person amid the throng was a priest in very solemn garb. Greatly astonished, the Councillor asked what all this meant, and who the priest was.

"That is the Bishop of Zealand," was the reply. "What, in the name of common sense, can have possessed the Bishop?" said the Councillor, and he sighed, and shook his head; "it could not possibly be the Bishop." Still ruminating on this subject, he walked on through East Street, and over Bridge Place, without looking either to the right or left. The bridge leading to Palace Square was not to be found; instead of it he approached the edge of the water, and at last came up to two men seated in a boat.

"May we ferry your honour over to Holm?" asked they.

"Over to Holm!" repeated the Councillor, who was by no means aware of having been transported into the happy period he so much admired, "I want to go to Christianshaven, and thence to Little Market Street."

The men looked at him without answering.

"Only tell me where the bridge is!" said he; "it is shameful that the lamps are not lighted! and it is so dirty that one might as well walk through a bog."

The longer he talked to the boatmen, the less he could understand them. At last he exclaimed, "I cannot make out your Bornholmish dialect!" and, very much provoked, he turned his back upon them. The bridge was not to be found, neither were there any railings. "It is scandalous how things are suffered to go on here!" cried he. Never had he found so much cause to complain of the times as on this evening. "I think I had better take a coach." Thus he determined, but what had become of the coaches? not one was to be seen. "I must go back to the New Market; there are always coaches there, and without one I shall never find my way to Christianshaven."

So back he went through East Street, and had almost reached the end of it, when the moon burst forth from behind the clouds.

"What can that scaffolding be up there?" cried he, on seeing the East Gate, which stood formerly at the end of East Street.

He found an outlet, and through it he went in the expectation of arriving at the New Market, when, lo! he beheld a vast green plain; a few bushes grew here and there, and right through the middle flowed a broad canal or river, one could not say which. A few miserable wooden hovels, inhabited by the Dutch skippers, which occasioned the place to be called the Dutch Meadow, stood on the opposite shore.

"Either I see a *fata morgana*, or else I have lost my wits," grumbled the Councillor, quite in consternation. "What can be the matter? what can be the matter?"

He turned back with the settled conviction that he was ill. On re-entering the street he looked more closely at the houses, and perceived that they were mostly built of wood, and that many had only thatched roofs.

"No, it must be that I am very unwell!" sighed he; "and yet I did but drink one glass of punch; however, it seems that was one too many. It was so absurd of them to give us punch and hot salmon! I shall take the liberty of telling my lady hostess so; I have a good mind to turn back now and let her know how ill I feel; but no, that would seem so ridiculous; besides, it is a question whether every one is not gone to bed."

He looked for the house, but it was not to be found.

"It is horrible! I do not even know East Street! Why, there are no shops to be seen; I can see nothing but old, wretched, tumble-down houses, just as though I were at Roeskilde or Ringsted! Alas, I must be very ill! it is of no use to deceive myself. But where in the world is the agent's house gone to? this is not it, surely! However, I see there are some persons up still. Ah, I am indeed very ill!"

He pushed against a half-open door whence the light came. It was a tavern of those times, a sort of beer-house; the room looked not unlike one of the old-fashioned clay-floored halls of Holstein. A number of people,— seamen, citizens of Copenhagen, and a few students, sat within in deep converse, and took little heed of the new-comer.

"Pardon my intrusion," said the Councillor to the landlady, who advanced to meet him, " I have just been taken ill! will you be so kind as to send for a coach to convey me to Christianshaven?"

The woman started, and shook her head. She then addressed him in German; whereupon the Councillor, presuming that she did not understand Danish, expressed his wish in German. This, together with his dress, confirmed the woman in her idea that he was a foreigner; one thing, at all events, she comprehended, viz. that he was ill, so she brought him a pitcher of water; it had somewhat of a brackish taste, although just drawn from the well.

The Councillor supported his head on his hand, drew a deep breath, and grumbled to himself about the strange things he saw around him.

"Is that the 'News' of this evening?" asked he, on seeing the woman remove a large sheet of paper.

She did not understand his meaning; however, she gave him the paper, which proved to be a coarse wood-engraving, representing a meteor which had been seen not long ago in the town of Cologne.

"This is very ancient!" exclaimed the Councillor, much excited by the sight of such a choice relic; "how did you come by this rare print? it is highly interesting, although the subject is fabulous. These meteors are now explained to be the reflections of the northern lights; they are probably occasioned by electricity?"

Those who sat near him and heard his speech looked on him with astonishment, and one of them rose respectfully from his seat, took off his hat, and said, with a face of wondrous gravity, " You must be a very learned man, monsieur!"

"Oh, no, indeed!" returned the Councillor; "I can but

take my part in conversation when it turns upon subjects which everybody understands."

"*Modestia* is a fine virtue!" said the man, "otherwise I would say, *Mihi secus videtur;* however, for the present, I suspend my *judicium.*"

"May I ask to whom I have the pleasure of speaking?" inquired the Councillor.

"I am *Baccalaureus Scripturæ Sacræ,*" replied the man.

This answer satisfied the Councillor, the name corresponded with the dress. "He must be some old-fashioned country schoolmaster," he thought; "an original, such as one meets with sometimes in Jutland."

"This is, of a truth, no *locus docendi,*" resumed the stranger; "yet, I pray you, disdain not to converse with me! you are, doubtless, well read in the works of the ancients?"

"Oh, yes!" answered the Councillor; "I am fond of reading all ancient writings that are profitable; and, indeed, I like modern books pretty well, excepting those 'Tales of Everyday Life,' of which, I think, we have enough in reality."

"Tales of Everyday Life?" repeated our Baccalaureus.

"Oh, I mean those new novels, of which people talk so much."

"As to that," said the man, with a smile, "they certainly contain a great deal of wit, and are read at court. The King particularly likes the Romance of Sir Iwain and Sir Gawain, which, you know, treats of King Arthur and his Knights of the Round Table; he and his great lords once jested merrily over it."*

"It is strange that I have never read it!" said the Councillor. "It must be one of Heiberg's newest."

"No," said the man, "it is not published by Heiberg, but by Godfrey von Gehmen."

"Is he the author?" cried the Councillor; "that is a very old name! Was he not the first man who printed books in Denmark?"

* Holberg relates, in his "History of the Kingdom of Denmark," that King Hans, after reading the romance of King Arthur, said, laughingly, to his favourite Otto Rud, "Sir Iwain and Sir Gawain, of whom I read in this book, were indeed gallant knights; such knights are not to be found now!" Whereupon Otto Rud replied, "If there were still such warriors as King Arthur, there would also be found many such knights as Sir Iwain and Sir Gawain."

"Yes, he is certainly our first printer," returned the stranger.

So far, so good; and now one of the honest burghers began to speak of the severe pestilence which had raged a few years before, meaning that of 1484. The Councillor thought that they were talking of the cholera; so that also passed off well enough. The era of the war of the Pirates (1490) was so near that it was naturally alluded to; the English pirates, they said, had taken their ships on their very shores; and the Councillor, who had lived through the events of 1801, joined with them heart and soul in abusing the English. But after this, conversation did not go on smoothly; every moment it became more and more discordant; the honest Baccalaureus was so ignorant that the simplest, most matter-of-fact assertions of the Councillor sounded to him far too positive and fantastic. They looked at each other quite angrily; Baccalaureus at last spoke Latin, in the hope of being better understood, but it was all of no use.

"How are you now?" asked the hostess, pulling the Councillor by the sleeve. In the heat of debate he had entirely forgotten all that had happened, but he now recollected himself.

"Where am I?" said he, his head feeling dizzy again.

"We will have claret, mead, and Bremer-beer!" cried one of the guests, "and you shall drink with us!"

Two girls came in; one of them wore a parti-coloured hood. They poured out the liquor, and bowed to the company. The Councillor shivered from head to foot.

"What is all this? what is all this?" cried he; but he was obliged to drink with them; they quite overpowered the good man; he was in despair; and when one of them said he was drunk, he never for a moment doubted the fact; he begged them to fetch him a coach, and then they thought he was speaking Muscovitish.

Never had he been before in such low company. "One might suppose the country had become heathen again," thought he: "this is the most horrible hour of my life!" The idea occurred to him to stoop under the table and creep out of the room. He did so; but before he had reached the door, the others, perceiving his intention, seized hold of his feet; by good luck the Clogs fell off, and with them the whole scene of enchantment vanished.

The Councillor saw a lamp burning brightly before him,

and behind the lamp a large house. Every object was familar to him, he was once more in East Street, such as we know it; he was lying on the pavement, his legs kicking against the door of a house, and exactly opposite sat the watchman, enjoying a sound sleep.

"To think that I have lain here dreaming in the street!" said he. "Yes, to be sure, this is East Street, so gay and handsome, and so well lighted! It is terrible that one glass of punch should have had such an effect upon me."

Two minutes afterwards he was comfortably seated in a coach, which soon brought him to Christianshaven; he remembered all the trouble he had experienced, and prized the more that happy reality, our own time, which, with all its faults, he now found so far pleasanter than the period of which he had lately made trial.

Chapter III.

THE WATCHMAN'S ADVENTURES.

"There's a pair of Clogs!" said the Watchman; "they must belong to the Lieutenant who lodges up there; they lie just by the door."

The honest man would have rung the bell and restored

them to their supposed owner, for there were still lights burning in the Lieutenant's room, but he was afraid of disturbing the slumbers of the other people in the house.

"It must be right warm and comfortable to have such things on one's feet!" said he; "they are made of such soft leather." He slipped his feet into them. "How strangely everything goes on in this world! that Lieutenant might now, if he chose, get into his own warm bed; but only see! he does no such thing; there he walks up and down on the floor. He is a happy man; he has neither wife nor children to provide for, and he goes to parties every evening. Oh, if I were he, I should indeed be a happy man!"

No sooner said than done; the Clogs had their effect; the soul of the watchman passed into the Lieutenant's. There he stood in his chamber, holding between his finger and thumb a tiny sheet of rose-coloured note-paper, on which a poem was written, a poem composed by the Lieutenant's own accomplished self. For where is the man who at some time or other of his life has not had lyrical moments? and if he then write down his thoughts, behold! there is poetry. Here is the Lieutenant's poem:

"WOULD I WERE RICH!"

"Would I were rich!"—when but a thoughtless child
I oft exclaimed, among my playmates wild,
"Would I were rich! an officer I'd be,
With sword and feather'd plume so gay to see!"
And time passed on; one wish was granted me,
An officer I was; yet, poor as ever;—
Thou know'st it, Lord, whose help forsook me never!

One eve I sat, my spirits fresh and young,
A little girl about me fondly clung;
For fairy-tales she craved—a countless store
Had I of these, though otherwise so poor.
That pretty child! how well she loved my lore!
How oft she promised ne'er from me to sever!
Thou know'st it, Lord, be thou her guardian ever!

Would I were rich!" I lift to heaven my prayer;
The child has ripened to a maiden fair.
She is so gentle, graceful, good, and kind—
Had she my heart's sad secret but divined,
Could I, as erst, in her eyes favour find?—
No, I am poor, and must be silent ever,—
So wills our Lord, whose wisdom erreth never.

> Would I were rich in patience, as in love!
> Then might my prayer meet answer from above,
> Thou, my beloved, love me in return,
> From these weak lines my youth's sad history learn—
> But, no! the truth thou must not yet discern—
> For I am poor, my future dark as ever,—
> Bless her, good Lord, and leave her friendless never!

Such verses as these people write when they are in love, but no sensible man will allow them to be printed. Here was expressed one of the sharpest sorrows of life, viz. the animal necessity of struggling after, if not the fruit, at least one of the stray leaves from the bread-fruit tree. The higher the station, the more bitter is the pang. Poverty is the stagnant pool of life; no picture of beauty can be reflected therein. Look at the poor summer bird, whose wing is broken beyond hope of recovery, whose soaring flight is checked for ever, and you see one whose energies, both of body and mind, are pressed to the earth by the heavy hand of poverty. The words Lieutenant, Love, and Lack of gold, form a triangle, or, if you will, the half of Fortune's shattered die. The Lieutenant felt his misery acutely; he leaned his head against the window-frame, and sighed deeply.

"The poor Watchman out in the street is far happier than I! He knows not what I call want;—he has a home, a wife, and children, who weep with him in his sorrow, and rejoice with him in his joy. Oh, how much happier should I be, could I exchange my situation for his, and wander through life with no other hopes than he has! Yes, he is certainly happier than I am!"

In that same moment, the Watchman became once more a Watchman. The Clogs of Fortune had caused his soul to pass into the Lieutenant's; but there, as we have just seen, he felt less satisfied, and preferred the life he had a few minutes before despised. Thus the Watchman became a Watchman again.

"That was a stupid dream!" said he; "but it was droll enough, certainly. I thought I was the Lieutenant up there, and yet that I was not comfortable. I wanted my old woman, and the babies, to smother me with kisses."

He sat still thinking over his dream—it would not go out of his head. The Clogs of Fortune were still on his feet. Suddenly, a falling star shot down from the sky.

"There it goes!" said he. "How many stars are up there! I should like very much to be able to look at those bright things closer, especially the moon. The Student for whom my wife washes says, 'that when we die, we shall fly about from one star to another.' That cannot be true, but it would be extremely pleasant. Now, if I could but just make a little jump up to the moon, I should not mind leaving my body behind lying here on the steps!"

There are certain thoughts and wishes to which we should beware of giving utterance, but doubly cautious should he be who has on his feet the Clogs of Fortune. Mark, now, what happened to the Watchman.

Few amongst us are not acquainted with the rapidity of steam-travelling, for we have proved it, either in railway carriages over the land, or in steamboats over the sea. But the velocity of steam, compared to that of light, is as the progress of the sloth, or the pace of the snail; for light travels nineteen millions of times faster than the fleetest race-horse. Electricity is, however, far swifter even than light; and on the wings of electricity flies the soul when freed from its earthly encumbrance. The rays of the sun require only eight minutes and a few seconds for a journey of twenty millions of Danish miles, but the soul performs the same distance in an infinitely shorter period. To her the space between the heavenly bodies is no more than would be to us the distance between the houses of friends living in the same town, even when those houses stand tolerably near each other. Such an electric shock in the heart deprives us, however, of all use of our bodies; unless, indeed, like the Watchman, we happen to have the Clogs of Fortune on our feet.

In the course of a few seconds the Watchman had traversed two hundred and forty thousand miles, and had arrived at the moon, which, as every one knows, is composed of much finer materials than the earth, and is what we should call light as new-fallen snow. He found himself upon one of the numerous mountains which may be seen in Dr. Mädler's large map of the Moon, the interior of which might be described as a cauldron about half a Danish mile in depth. At the foot of the mountain lay a town, of whose appearance an idea might be formed by putting the white of an egg into a glass of water, for the substance of which it was composed was just as soft;

and similar towers, with cupolas and hanging balconies, all perfectly transparent, hovered to and fro in the thin, clear atmosphere. Our earth was seen above, looking like a great, dark-red ball.

He saw a number of creatures around him, who must certainly have been what we call human beings, but they looked very different from us; they seemed quite of another species, and it would require a far more luxuriant fancy than that possessed by astronomers to imagine anything like them. They had a language of their own; I suppose no one would expect the soul of the Watchman to understand it; nevertheless, understand it he did, for our spirits have far greater capabilities than we are inclined to believe.

Thus the Watchman's soul understood perfectly the language of the dwellers in the moon. They were disputing about our earth, and doubting whether it could be inhabited; the air, they thought, must be too thick for any reasonable moon-dweller to breathe; and, indeed, most were of opinion that of all the heavenly bodies the moon alone was inhabited.

However, we will not listen to what was said, but rather betake ourselves to East Street, and see what has become of the Watchman's body.

Lifeless on the steps it lay; the Morning Star (a club armed with iron spikes) had fallen out of its hand; its eyes were fixed with an upward gaze upon the moon, whither its right-honourable companion, the soul, had wandered.

"What is the hour, Watchman?" asked a passer-by. As no answer came, the inquirer gently tapped the apparently sleeping figure on the nose, whereupon down it fell at full length upon the ground. The Watchman was dead! All his companions were greatly shocked when they heard of the accident; the story was repeated from one to another; a great deal was said about it; and at daybreak the body was carried to the hospital.

Now suppose the soul were to return to seek the body in East Street, and find it gone! perhaps she might then apply to the Police to make inquiries, next to the Directory Office, in order to advertise it among other things lost, stolen, or strayed; and, last of all, she might perchance seek her companion in the hospital. But never fear, believe me the soul is always wise when left to herself, it is only the body that renders her stupid.

As was said before, the Watchman's body was taken to the hospital, where, naturally enough, the first thing done was to take off the Clogs. The soul must now return: she flew straight to the body, and in a few seconds there was once more life in the man. And he declared that this had been the most dreadful night of his life, that not for two gold pieces would he experience such sensations again. However, all was over now.

That same day he left the hospital, but the Clogs were left behind.

CHAPTER IV.

A CRITICAL MOMENT — AN EVENING'S DRAMATIC READINGS — A MOST UNUSUAL JOURNEY.

Every inhabitant of Copenhagen knows the situation of Frederick's Hospital; nevertheless, it may be well to give a short description of it, as it is just possible that others besides inhabitants of Copenhagen may read this story.

This hospital is separated from the street by a tolerably high railing, the iron staves composing which stand so far apart from each other that—so it is said—some very thin students have at times found it possible to squeeze themselves through, and thus make delightfully frequent visits to their friends in the town. The part of the body which they had most difficulty in squeezing through was the head; consequently, in this case, as indeed in many another, the smallest heads were most convenient. So much by way of introduction.

One of the young men, of whom it could be said only physically that he had a thick head, happened to be on watch that evening: the rain poured down in torrents, yet, despite these two hindrances, the weather and the size of his head, he must go out just for a quarter of an hour. It was not worth while, he thought, to trouble the porter about such a trifle, when he could by an effort slip through the iron rails, and, while pondering over the subject, he stumbled upon the Clogs which the Watchman had left behind him. That these were the Clogs of Fortune of course never occurred to him; it was plain, however, that they might be serviceable in such weather as this, and so he put them on. The only question with him was whether he would be able to squeeze himself through, or not; he had never tried the experiment before.

"How I wish I had my head through!" said he. No sooner said than done; the head, though very large and thick, at once glided through as easily as possible—such was the power of the Clogs. But the body must needs follow.

"Ugh, I am too stout!" said he. "I thought the difficulty was the head! I shall never get through."

He tried to draw his head back again, but that was impossible. He could move his neck to and fro at pleasure, and that was all he could do. His first impulse was to be in a pet, the very next moment his spirits had sunk below zero. The Clogs of Fortune had brought him into this most distressing situation, and unfortunately the thought never entered his head that he might wish himself free; instead of wishing, he strove, and consequently could not stir from the spot. The rain poured down—not a person was to be seen in the street. The entrance-bell he could not reach—how in the world was he to get loose? It was probable that there he must stand until morning; that then a smith must be sent for to file away one of the staves; that all this would not be the work of a moment; that, in the meantime, all the boys belonging to the large school just opposite would be let loose; that the whole district of Nyboder would hasten to the spot, for the pleasure of seeing him in the pillory: a famous running and funning there will be! "Ugh!" cried he, "the blood is rushing to my head! it will drive me mad! I am half crazy already! Oh, if I could but get loose!"

Now this was just what he should have said before; no sooner had he expressed the wish than it was fulfilled — his head was free. Into the house he rushed, nearly distracted by the fright which the Clogs of Fortune had occasioned him.

But we must not suppose that his adventures were ended. No, indeed, the worst were yet to come.

The night passed away quietly enough, as did also the day following. Meantime, the Clogs had not been taken away. In the evening there were dramatic readings at the little theatre in Kannike Street. The house was crammed. Among other pieces recited was a new poem, called "My Aunt's Spectacles," by H. C. Andersen, the substance of which was as follows. The poet's aunt, who in the good old times would certainly have been entitled to the honour of being burnt as a witch, had an extraordinary skill in fortune-telling. She seemed to know beforehand all the chances and changes of this changing world; and though not yet in "the sunset of life," her wondrous "mystical lore" made —

"Coming events cast their shadows before."

Every one coveted her secret, but in vain. She would never reveal it; at last, however, her youngest and favourite nephew entreated her so earnestly to confide it to him — only just to him — that the good lady's resolution gave way; and putting on a face of solemn importance, she took off her spectacles and presented them to him, declaring that the marvellous power of second sight was vested in them, and them only. "Try them yourself, my boy," she said, seeing him look incredulous. "Go to any place of public resort, secure a position whence you can overlook the crowd, put on my spectacles, and forthwith all the people you survey through them will be to your eyes like a pack of cards spread out on a table; their most secret thoughts and wishes will be laid bare; and you will, moreover, be enabled without difficulty to foresee their future lot." The youth could scarcely wait an instant to thank the good lady for her kindness, he was in such haste to run off and test his new acquisition. He remembered that there would be dramatic readings at the theatre that very evening—nothing could be more convenient, for nowhere could he overlook a great throng of people so easily as from the stage; accordingly, thither he repaired. Then, presenting himself to the audience, he puts on his spectacles, and begs permission to tell the fortunes of the individuals composing the crowd. And now he begins by expressing astonishment at the curious sight opened to his view; he drops mysterious hints about the Queen of Hearts, "whose dark thrilling eyes," he declares, "are fixed with intensity upon the Knave of Diamonds; he would give worlds to have such glances directed towards himself." The Knave of Clubs he next notices as "the richest man in that assembly, although unfortunately——" but here he stops short, as unwilling to reveal family secrets. He then proposes finding out the happiest person present—the one who should live longest—the future fortunes of the nation—the success which should attend forthcoming representations at the theatre. Still he evades giving direct, intelligible information, declaring himself quite bewildered; he is resolved not to hurt the feelings of the audience by his communications; and yet he fears that they must distrust his vaunted powers. Thus he can only, with the deepest respect, leave them to their own conclusions and bid farewell to the assembly.

The poem, absurd as it was, being well recited, was received with great applause. Amongst the audience was our friend from the hospital, who seemed to have entirely forgotten his adventure of the preceding evening; the Clogs of Fortune were again on his feet; for, as no one had claimed them, and the streets were dirty, he thought he might as well make use of them.

The first part of the poem pleased him exceedingly, and, although his attention was soon distracted, the idea still haunted him. He fancied he should much like to have such a pair of spectacles himself; perhaps, he thought, they might enable the wearer to look straight into people's hearts, and this would be far more interesting than the knowledge of future events, for whatever was to happen must be clear enough to every one when the time came, whereas the heart —who could ever boast of having read that? " Say it were only the hearts of the row of gentlemen and ladies sitting on the front benches,—could I look into them, what a revelation there would be!—a sort of shop would open before me. Ah, how my eyes would search into every corner! For instance, in that of the lady sitting just opposite, I should certainly find an extensive assortment of fashionable millinery, caps, ribands, and silk; the shop of the lady next her would probably be found perfectly empty,—it would, however, be all the better for cleansing. But are there no shops of substantial wares? Ah, yes," sighed he, " I know one in which everything is solid and good, but unfortunately a shopman is there—more's the pity!—and he is perpetually crying out, ' Be so kind as to walk in, gentlemen; here you will find everything you want.' I wish I really could step in, like a pleasant thought, and glide on from heart to heart!"

These last words sufficed to awaken the dormant power of the Clogs; the whole man immediately shrank up, and commenced a most unusual journey, for it travelled through the hearts of the front row of spectators. The first heart he entered was that of a lady, and for a moment he fancied himself in the Orthopœdic Institute or Hospital for the Deformed, in the chamber whose walls are hung with plaster casts of diseased limbs. There was, however, this difference— in the Institute the casts are taken at the period of the patients' entry, here they had been taken after the originals had departed. They were, in fact, casts of very dear and particular friends, whose deformities, whether of body or mind, were thus carefully preserved.

Suddenly he passed thence into another female heart; but this appeared to him like a solemn, glorious church. The white dove of innocence brooded over the altar; he could most gladly have fallen on his knees before it, but that he must away—away into the next heart. Still, however, he heard the deep tones of the organ, and it seemed as though he had become another and a better man, not altogether unworthy to enter the neighbouring sanctuary. And here was revealed to him a miserable garret, wherein reposed a sick mother. Poor and miserable was that chamber in appearance, yet God's warm sunshine streamed through the open window; beautiful roses bloomed in the little wooden box on the roof; and two sky-blue birds warbled from their branches a glorious song of joy, peace, and love, whilst the sick mother implored a blessing upon her daughter.

He now crept upon hands and feet through an over-filled butcher's shop; there was flesh, and flesh, and nothing but flesh, all round him. This was the heart of a rich, respectable man, whose name may doubtless be found in the Directory.

He next entered the heart of the last person's wife. This was an old ruined dove-cot; the husband's portrait was made use of as a weather-cock, and seemed connected in some manner with the doors, which accordingly opened and shut as the man moved.

Thence he glided into a cabinet formed of mirrors, like the room shown in Castle Rosenborg. These mirrors, however, possessed the power of magnifying to an almost incredible degree. In the centre, on the floor, sat, like the Dalai Lama of Thibet, the individual's own insignificant self, apparently wholly occupied with the contemplation of his own astounding greatness.

After this he believed himself transported into a needle-case filled with sharp-pointed needles. "Surely," thought he, "this must be the heart of an old maid!" But no, it was the heart of a young officer, who had been honoured with several orders of knighthood, and who was said to be a man of superior understanding and refinement.

The unfortunate youth crept out of the last heart in the row quite bewildered; he could not arrange his thoughts, he could only believe that all he had seen and felt was the work of his too active imagination.

"Alas!" sighed he, "am I going mad? I feel insufferably hot,—the blood is rushing to my head!" All at once he remembered the singular incident of the preceding evening, how that his head had remained fixed between the iron railings of the Hospital. "That is it," said he; "I must attend to it before it is too late; perhaps a Russian bath would be serviceable. How I wish I were extended on the upper board!"

Accordingly he found himself forthwith lying on the highest shelf of a vapour-bath; yes, there he lay with all his clothes on, boots, clogs, everything; hot drops of water trickled down from the ceiling on his face.

"Ugh!" shrieked he, starting up with astonishment. The attendant shrieked also, when he saw a man standing full dressed in the bath. Our hero had just sufficient presence of mind to whisper in explanation, "'Tis for a wager;" but the first thing he did when he reached home was to lay a large blistering plaster over his chest, and another across his back, in order to draw out his madness.

Next morning his back was covered with blood, and this was all that he had gained from the Clogs of Fortune.

Chapter V.

THE METAMORPHOSES OF THE COPYING CLERK.

We have not forgotten the Watchman all this time, neither had he forgotten the Clogs which he had found in the street, and which had been carried with himself to the Hospital. He now came and fetched them away; but as neither the Lieutenant nor any one else in his street would own them, the Clogs were at last taken to the Police Office.

"They look exactly like mine," said one of the Copying Clerks, placing them by the side of his own. "No eye but a shoemaker's could see any difference between them."

"Mr. Clerk," said a man who just then entered with some papers.

The Clerk turned round to answer the summons. When the man's business was despatched, and he again looked at the Clogs, he could not make up his mind whether the pair on the right or on the left hand side were his own. "It must be those that are wet!" thought he, and a most unfortunate thought it was, for they were the Clogs of Fortune. But, after all, why should not mistakes happen sometimes in the Police Office, as well as everywhere else? So he drew on the Clogs, put his papers into his pocket, and tucked under his arm some manuscripts which he had to copy at home. It was now Sunday morning, the weather was fine—"A walk to Fredericksberg," thought he, "will do me good," so out he went.

Nowhere could there be found a more quiet, sober-minded person than this young man; right glad are we that he should enjoy the simple pleasure this walk will afford him; it is just the very thing for him after sitting still so long. And he walked on for some time in such a straightforward, matter-of-fact fashion that the Clogs had no opportunity of displaying their magical powers.

In the avenue he met an acquaintance of his, one of our younger poets, who told him that he was going next day to set out on his summer excursion.

"What, roaming again?" said the Clerk. "Happy man that you are, free to go wherever you please! we common mortals are condemned to wear a chain."

"But the chain is fastened to the bread-fruit tree!" replied the Poet. "You need have no care for the morrow, and when you grow old, a pension is given you."

"For all that, your lot is the happier," returned the Clerk; "it must be so pleasant to sit under a tree all day writing verses, and then to have flattering speeches made you by all the world—besides, you are your own master. Ah! you should only try for once how wearisome it is to spend all your time in an office, writing about some trival matter or other!"

The Poet shook his head, the Clerk likewise shook his head, each kept his own opinion, and they parted.

"Strange people are those poets!" said the Clerk. "I should like very much to understand them and their ways, to become a poet myself; I am sure I should not write such whining, pining nonsense as some do!—What a lovely spring day this is! just the day for a poet! The air is so unusually clear! the clouds are so beautiful! and such a delicious fragrance comes from the trees and flowers, I have not felt as I do at this moment for many years!"

It will be seen from the latter part of this speech that he has now in truth become a poet. Not that any great alteration was apparent in him; it is, indeed, an absurdity to imagine that a poet must needs be totally different from other men; on the contrary, there may frequently be found natures more poetical than many of our acknowledged poets — the principal difference being that the poet has a better mental memory, and can thus hold fast his ideas and feelings till they are clearly embodied in words, which others cannot do. However this may be, the transformation of a common-place nature into one capable of appreciating all that is beautiful and good is indeed a change, and as such the Clerk's metamorphosis is striking enough.

"This delightful fragrance!" said he, "how it reminds me of my Aunt Magdalen's violets! Ah, that was when I was a little boy! What a long time it is since I thought of her, the good old aunt! She used to live behind the Exchange yonder. Let the winter be ever so severe, she always kept a bough or a few green shoots in water. How sweet the violets were! And then I used to lay a heated penny on the frozen window-pane to make a little peep-hole: what a pretty view I had through it! There was the canal, with the ships lying so still amid the frozen water, and forsaken by all the mariners; one noisy, screaming crow forming their whole garrison. And when at last the fresh spring breezes returned, then every-thing received new life; with song and merriment the ice was broken up, the ships were rigged and tackled, and away they sailed to foreign lands. But I have always stayed behind; I must always stay behind, and sit in the office and see others come to fetch their passports, that they may travel abroad! Such is my lot! Alas!" sighed he; then suddenly checking himself, "Why, what can ail me? I have never thought or felt in this manner before; it must be the effect of the spring air; it gives me almost as much pain as pleasure!" He felt in his pockets for his papers. "These will make me think of something else," said he, as his eye wandered over the first sheet — "'Madame Sigbrith, an original tragedy, in five acts,'" read he aloud. "What is this? why, it is in my own hand-writing; did I write this tragedy? 'The Cabal on the Ram-parts, vaudeville.' How came all these papers in my pocket? somebody must have put them in. And here is a letter!" Exactly so; the letter came from the manager of a theatre; both the pieces whose titles he had read were rejected, and the manager's opinion of them was expressed in terms any-thing but courteous. "Hem! hem!" said the Clerk, and he sat down on a bench — his thoughts seemed so fresh, his spirits so elastic. Involuntarily he plucked one of the flowers near him; it was but a common little daisy, yet what botanists could only teach us after several long lectures this simple floweret explained in a minute. She related the myth of her birth, told of the power of the sunshine which had unfolded her delicate leaves and drawn forth her fragrance, and thus called forth thoughts of those human struggles which in a similar manner awaken the slumbering feelings of men. Light and Air are the faithful lovers of the flower; Light is the favoured one, and to him she turns continually; but when Light disappears, she folds her petals together, and sleeps in the safe guardianship of Air. "It is Light which makes me so beautiful!" said the flower. "But it is Air that preserves thy life!" whispered the Poet's voice.

A boy, standing a few paces distant, just then threw his stick into a ditch, the water splashed up among the green branches waving above, and the Clerk thought of the millions of little insects in those drops of water which must have been hurled upwards, and to whom such an evolution must have been as fearful as it would be for us to be suddenly whirled high into the region of the clouds. The Clerk smiled as he mused over this, and over the great change he felt to have stirred up such new fancies. "I know," he said, "that I am only dreaming; but how strange it is that I should dream, and yet be aware all the while that I am dreaming! I wonder whether I shall remember this to-morrow when I awake. I feel happier than I ever was before; I seem thoroughly awake — have a clear perception of everything — and yet I am sure that if I have any recollection of my present thoughts and feelings to-morrow, they will all appear to me stupid nonsense. So it is; all those clever and beautiful things one says and hears in one's dreams are just like faëry gold — rich and precious at night, but, when daylight returns, found to be nothing but stones and withered leaves. Alas!" said he, sighing quite sadly, and looking up at the merry little singing birds as they hopped from bough to bough, "their lot is far happier than mine; they can fly — that is a glorious art! — happy he who is born to soar! Ah, yes, if I could change myself into anything, it should be into such a little lark as that!"

In the same moment, the sleeves and flaps of his coat

were united together and formed wings, his clothes became feathers, and the Clogs claws; he was aware of the change, and laughed inwardly. "Well," said he, "now I may be sure that I am dreaming, though, certainly, I never dreamed anything so ridiculous as this before!" He flew up into the green branches and sang; but there was no poetry in the song, for the poetic nature was gone. The Clogs, like every one else who does anything worth the doing, could only do one thing at a time. The Clerk wished to be a poet; and, accordingly, he became a poet. He then wished to be a little bird, and a bird he became; but a poet he could be no longer.

"This is pleasant enough," said he. "All day I sit in the office attending to business, and at night I can dream of flying about in the form of a lark in Fredericksberg Gardens. What a capital farce this would make!"

He then flew down from the bench, turned his head on all sides, and struck with his beak the tender blades of grass, which, compared with his present size, appeared as large as the palm-branches of North Africa.

It was but for a moment; suddenly he seemed enveloped in darkness, something to him monstrous and heavy was thrown over him. It was a large school-boy's cap; the hand of one of the juveniles of Nyboder passed underneath it, and seized the Clerk by the back and wings. In the first impulse of surprise he cried out, "You impudent young rascal! I am Clerk at the Police Office!" But this sounded to the boy like "Pipipi!" He struck the bird on the beak and walked away with it.

In the Avenue he met two schoolboys of the higher class — in rank, at least; in learning they were amongst the lowest in the school,—they bought the bird for fourpence. And thus the Copying Clerk was taken back to Copenhagen, and became a member of a family in Gother Street.

"It is well that I am only dreaming," said the Clerk, "else I should really be angry. First I was a poet, and now I am a lark! I suppose it was the poetic nature which changed me into a little insignificant bird! It is a miserable condition enough, especially when one falls into the hands of boys. I wonder what will become of me next!"

The boys brought him into an elegantly furnished apartment, where they were received by a stout, good-humoured-looking lady, who was by no means pleased at their bringing in with them a common field-bird, as she called the lark; however, for once she said she would excuse it, and they might put their little prisoner into the empty cage that hung by the window. "Perhaps that may please my pretty Poll," added she, smiling tenderly on a large green parroquet who was swinging himself in his splendid cage. "It is Poll's birthday, so the little field-bird must come and congratulate him."

Poll answered not a word, but continued to swing himself backwards and forwards with a very stately air, whilst a pretty little Canary-bird, who had been only the preceding summer brought from the warm, spicy land of his birth, at once began a loud song of welcome.

"Be quiet, you noisy thing!" said the lady, throwing a white pocket-handkerchief over his cage.

"Pipi," sighed he; "that is a horrible snow-storm!" and he immediately ceased singing.

The Clerk, or, as the lady called him, the field-bird, was put into a little cage close to the Canary-bird's, and not far off that of the Parrot. The only human phrase which Poll knew was, "Come, let us be men!" and comical enough it sounded sometimes. Everything else that he said or shrieked was as unintelligible as the twittering of the Canary-bird, except to the Clerk, who, being now a bird himself, could understand both his companions perfectly well.

"Once," sang the Canary-bird, "I was free, flying about among green palms and flowering almond-trees; I flew with my brothers and sisters over the beautiful flowers and the clear, mirror-like lake bordered with so many fragrant shrubs. There, too, were parrots with glorious plumage; they used to tell such merry stories, so long and so many!"

"Those were wild, uneducated birds," returned the Parrot. "Come, let us be men! Why don't you laugh? If the lady and all the strangers that come here can laugh at it, surely you can do so too. Not to be able to enjoy a good joke shows a great defect in the understanding. Come, let us be men!"

"Oh, dost thou not remember those lovely maidens who danced under the shade of their wide-spreading tents, and under trees so tall and so full of blossom? Dost thou not remember the delicious fruit on the trees, and the fresh, cool juice in the wild herbs which grew so luxuriantly at their feet!"

"Oh yes!" said the Parrot, "but I am much more comfortable here. I am well fed and treated with consideration. I know I am a clever fellow, and that is enough for me. Let us be men! You, indeed, have what they call a poetic soul, but I have solid acquirements and plenty of wit; you have genius, but no prudence; thus you are always bursting out with those wild piercing notes of yours, and thus you are continually silenced. No one ever presumes to cover up my cage — no, indeed, for I cost a good deal more than you did; besides, I can defend myself with my beak, and confound them with my wit. Come, let us be men!"

"Oh, my beloved, my beautiful fatherland!" sang the Canary-bird, "ever will I sing of thy dark-leaved trees and thy peaceful bays, where the long, drooping branches fondly kiss the dancing waters; ever will I sing of the gladsome movements of my bright-hued brothers and sisters, as they sported and sang among those splendid cactuses!"

"Pray give up this melancholy strain!" said the Parrot. "Say something which may make us laugh. Laughter is a sign of the highest intellect. Do you think that a dog or a horse could laugh? no, but they can cry: only men can laugh. Ha! ha! ha!" screamed Poll, and ended with the repetition of his single piece of wit—"Come, let us be men!"

"Thou little, grey Danish bird," said the Canary, "thou, too, art become a prisoner! It may be cold in thy native woods, but there at least thou hast freedom. Oh, fly away! they have forgotten to shut the door of thy cage; the window is open — fly quickly, fly away!"

Instinctively the Clerk hopped out of his cage; in that same moment the half-opened door was heard to creak, and stealthily, stealthily, with eyes green and glistening, crept into the room—the cat. The Canary fluttered about in his cage, the Parrot flapped his wings and screamed, "Come, let us be men!" the Clerk was seized with mortal terror and flew out of the window. For a long while he flew over houses and streets, at last he felt the want of rest. The house exactly opposite seemed familiar to him — one window was open—in he flew, into his own room. He perched upon the table.

Almost unconsciously he repeated the Parrot's witticism, "Come, let us be men!" and the next moment the Lark had become the Copying Clerk, comfortably seated upon his own table.

Chapter VI.

THE BEST AND LAST GIFT THE CLOGS COULD BESTOW.

Next day, early in the morning, while the Clerk was yet in bed, a knocking was heard at his door; it was his neighbour, the young Divinity Student, who lived on the same floor. He came in.

"Lend me your Clogs," said he; "it is damp in the garden, although the sun is shining gloriously. I shall go out and smoke."

He drew on the Clogs, and was presently walking in the garden, an enclosure which could boast of possessing both an apple and a plum-tree. Even so small a garden as this is highly prized in Copenhagen.

The Student walked up and down,—it was just six o'clock; a post-horn sounded from the street.

"Oh, to travel! to travel!" exclaimed he, "that is the greatest happiness this world can give! that is my chief, my highest wish! Then would my restless longings be stilled. But far, far away must it be. I would see that glorious Switzerland, I would visit Italy, I would —— "

It was well both for himself and for us that the Clogs fulfilled his wish without delay, else he would have gone roaming nobody knows where. He travelled. He was travelling in Switzerland, pent up with eight other passengers inside a diligence; he had a bad pain in his head, a worse in his back, and his feet were miserably swollen by their long confinement in tight boots. He was in a state between sleeping and waking. Within his right-! and pocket were his letters of credit, in his left pocket the passport, and in the little leathern purse, sewn inside his waistcoat, a few louis d'ors. Every dream foretold the loss of one or other of these treasures; thus he was continually starting up with feverish impatience, his hand describing a triangular movement from the right pocket to the left, and thence to his bosom, to feel whether all was safe. Umbrellas, sticks, and hats, were suspended from the roof of the vehicle, shaking together over his head, and impeding the magnificent view opening before him.

Dark, sombre, and grand, was the landscape now spread around. The vast fir-woods looked no larger than little tufts of heather, shading those tremendous mountains whose summits were lost in the clouds. It began to snow,—the wind blew cold.

"Ah!" sighed he, "if we were but on the other side of the Alps, then it would be summer, and I should be able to get my letters of credit cashed. The anxiety I feel about my money prevents me from enjoying Switzerland. Oh, that I were on the other side!"

And immediately he was on the other side, travelling in Italy, between Florence and Rome. Before him, amid the dark, blue-tinted mountains, lay the lake of Thrasymene, looking like flaming gold as it reflected the glorious evening sky. Here, on the spot where Hannibal defeated Flaminius, peaceful vines now lovingly entwine their bright, graceful tendrils, and pretty, half-naked children are guarding a herd of coal-black swine, crowded under the group of fragrant laurel-trees growing by the way-side. Could we paint this picture so as to do it justice, every one would exclaim with delight, "Beautiful Italy!" But the Divinity Student and his fellow-travellers said nothing.

Poisonous flies and musquitoes swarmed around them by thousands; vainly did the unfortunate travellers strike at their tormentors with a myrtle bough—they cared little for that; on the contrary, they stung the more. There was not a person in the carriage whose face was not swelled and disfigured by their bites. As for the poor horses, the flies settled upon them in such swarms that they looked like carrion; and, if the driver alighted from his seat to chase them away, in another moment they were there again. The sun set; a sudden chill thrilled through the entire landscape; it was like breathing the cold, damp air of a sepulchre, after a day's enjoyment of the warmth of summer. The clouds and surrounding mountains now assumed that peculiar green hue which is sometimes observed in old paintings, and which to the untravelled eye might seem unnatural. It was, indeed, a beautiful scene—but the stomach was empty, the body wearied; all the ardent longings of the heart were centred upon a comfortable lodging for the night—a blessing scarcely to be expected.

Their road led through an olive forest, just as at home they might have had to wind their way through clumps of crooked willow-trees. And here stood a solitary hostel. Some half-score of begging cripples lay encamped in front of it; the most robust of them looking, to borrow an expression of Marryat's, like "Famine's eldest son, just come of age;" while, of the rest, some were blind, some crawled about with withered limbs, and some displayed shrunken arms and fingerless hands. Here was wretchedness indeed. "Eccellenza, miserabili!" moaned they in full chorus, all eagerly stretching out their diseased members. The hostess received her newly-arrived guests, attired in a dirty blouse, with bare feet and dishevelled hair. The doors were kept together by packthread; the floor of the room was composed of bricks half broken up; bats flew backwards and forwards under the low ceiling; and as to the odour . . . .

"It would be as well if we had our supper served up in the stable," said one of the travellers; "there, at least, one knows the atmosphere one breathes."

The windows were opened to let in a little fresh air, when

forthwith arose the withered arms, and again was heard the eternal "Miserabili, Eccellenza!" Various inscriptions might be seen adorning the walls, more than half of them about " La bella Italia," although anything but complimentary.

Supper was brought in; first came a soup composed of water seasoned with pepper and rancid oil. The latter ingredient also played chief part in the salad; stale eggs and roasted cocks'-combs formed the most savoury dishes, and even the wine had a culinary taste—it was, in fact, a genuine mixture. At night, the travellers' boxes were piled up against the door; one of the party was to guard them while the others slept. The lot fell upon our Divinity Student. Oh, how close was that room! The heat was most oppressive; the musquitoes buzzed and stung without mercy; the "Miserabili" outside groaned and moaned, even in their dreams.

"Yes, travelling would be very pleasant!" sighed the Student, "if only one had not a body! or if it could rest while the spirit roamed at large, free and unfettered! Wherever I go, I am still tormented with an unaccountable craving which consumes my very soul. I long after something better than I can find; something enduring—yes, something perfect; but where, and what is it? And yet I do know what it is I desire; it is Happiness—complete, lasting Happiness!"

No sooner had he spoken these words than he was once again at home; long white curtains hung before the windows, and on the floor, in the centre of the room, was a black coffin. There he lay, sleeping the quiet sleep of death: his wish was fulfilled, his body rested while his spirit wandered free and unencumbered by its earthly tabernacle. "Call no man happy till he is in his grave:" such were the words of Solon, and here was a fresh confirmation of the sage's wisdom.

Every corpse is, as it were, a sphinx, still propounding the same unalterable, unanswerable question. Thus did the mysterious Sphinx, now lying in the black coffin before us, recall the ever-painful doubt expressed in the following verses, which the Student had written two days previously:—

> " Oh mighty Death, thy silence wakens dread,
>   Fain would we raise the veil that hides thy brow;
> ' Whither,' we ask, ' is the loved spirit fled?
>   Our brother and our friend, where dwells he now ! '

"We ask in vain, the thought which strove to scale,
  Boldly aspiring, the cloud-hidden skies,
Recoils in terror— Faith and Knowledge fail,
  And awe and darkness blind our straining eyes.

"Yet, dark-brow'd Angel, welcome to our door!
  Poor struggling human spirit, hail thy guest!
Thy griefs, the world's unkindness vex no more
  When Death's cold arms are clasped around thy breast."

Two figures are seen moving in the room: we recognise them both; they are the ambassador of Fortune, and the fairy Care. They are bending over the dead man.

"Seest thou now," said Care, "what sort of happiness thy Clogs have conferred on humanity?"

"Surely," replied Pleasure, "they bestowed a real blessing upon him who slumbers here, if on no other."

"Nay," rejoined Care, "his departure was his own choice,—he did not wait for his summons. The eyes of his spirit had not yet been opened to discern those hidden treasures with which this world abounds; he had not accomplished his destined task. I will confer on him a true benefit."

And she took the Clogs off his feet. Immediately the sleep of death was ended—the dead man arose with renewed life and vigour. Care vanished, and with her vanished the Clogs; doubtless she considered they had been proved to be her rightful property.

THE SHEPHERDESS AND THE CHIMNEY-SWEEPER.

HAVE you never seen an old-fashioned, oaken-wood cabinet, quite black with age, and covered with varnish and carving-work? Just such a piece of furniture, an old heir-loom that had been the property of its present mistress's great-grandmother, once stood in a parlour; it was carved from top to bottom, roses, tulips, and little stags' heads with long branching antlers, peering forth from amid the curious scrolls and foliage surrounding them. Moreover, in the centre panel of the cabinet was carved the full-length figure of a man, who seemed to be perpetually grinning, perhaps at himself, for in truth he was a most ridiculous figure; he had crooked legs, small horns on his forehead, and a long beard. The children of the house used to call him " the crooked-legged Field-marshal-Major-General-Corporal-Sergeant," for this was a long, hard name, and not many figures, whether carved in wood or in stone, could boast of such a title. There he stood, his eyes always fixed upon the table under the pier-glass, for on this table stood a pretty little porcelain Shepherdess, her mantle gathered gracefully round her, and fastened with a red rose; her shoes and hat were gilt, her hand held a crook—oh, she was charming! Close by her stood a little Chimney-sweeper, likewise of porcelain; he was as clean and neat as any of the other figures; indeed, the manufacturer might just as well have made a prince as a chimney-sweeper of him, for, though elsewhere black as a coal, his face was as fresh and rosy as a girl's, which was certainly a mistake —it ought to have been black. His ladder in his hand, there he kept his station, close by the little Shepherdess; they had been placed together from the first, had always remained on the same spot, and had thus plighted their troth to each other. They suited each other so well, they were both young people, both of the same kind of porcelain, both alike fragile and delicate.

Not far off stood a figure three times as large as the others; it was an old Chinese Mandarin, who could nod his head. He, too, was of porcelain, and declared that he was grandfather to the little Shepherdess. He could not prove his assertion; however, he insisted that he had authority over her; and so, when "the crooked-legged Field-marshal-Major-General-Corporal-Sergeant" made proposals to the little Shepherdess, he nodded his head in token of his consent.

"Now you will have a husband," said the old Mandarin to her,—"a husband who, I verily believe, is of mahogany-wood; you will be the wife of a Field-marshal-Major-General-Corporal-Sergeant, of a man who has a whole cabinet full of silver-plate, besides a store of no one knows what in the secret drawers!"

"I will not go into that dismal cabinet!" declared the little Shepherdess. "I have heard say that eleven porcelain ladies are already imprisoned there."

"Then you shall be the twelfth, and you will be in good company!" rejoined the Mandarin. "This very night, when the old cabinet creaks, your nuptials shall be celebrated, as sure as I am a Chinese Mandarin!" Whereupon he nodded his head and fell asleep.

But the little Shepherdess wept, and turned to the beloved of her heart, the porcelain Chimney-sweep.

"I believe I must ask you," said she, "to go out with me into the wide world, for here we cannot stay."

"I will do everything you wish," replied the little Chimney-sweeper; "let us go at once; I think I can support you by my profession."

"If we could but get off the table!" sighed she. "I shall never be happy till we are away, out in the wide world."

And he comforted her, and showed her how to set her little foot on the carved edges and gilded foliage twining round the leg of the table, till at last they reached the floor. But turning to look at the old cabinet, they saw everything in a grand commotion, all the carved stags putting their little heads farther out, raising their antlers, and moving their throats, whilst "the crooked-legged Field-marshal-Major-General-Corporal-Sergeant" sprang up, and shouted out to the old Chinese Mandarin, "Look, they are eloping! they are eloping!"

They were not a little frightened, and quickly jumped into an open drawer for protection.

In this drawer there were three or four incomplete packs of cards, and also a little puppet-theatre; a play was being performed, and all the Queens, whether of Diamonds, Hearts, Clubs, or Spades, sat in the front row fanning themselves with the flowers they held in their hands; behind them stood the Knaves, showing that they had each two heads, one above and one below, as most cards have. The play was about two persons who were crossed in love, and the Shepherdess wept over it, for it was just like her own history.

"I cannot bear this!" said she. "Let us leave the drawer." But when they had again reached the floor, on looking up at the table, they saw that the old Chinese Mandarin had awakened, and was rocking his whole body to and fro with rage.

"Oh, the old Mandarin is coming!" cried the little Shepherdess, and down she fell on her porcelain knees in the greatest distress.

"A sudden thought has struck me," said the Chimney-sweeper; "suppose we creep into the large Pot-pourri Vase that stands in the corner; there we can rest upon roses and lavender, and throw salt in his eyes if he come near us."

"That will not do at all," said she; "besides, I know that the old Mandarin was once betrothed to the Pot-pourri Vase, and, no doubt, there is still some slight friendship existing between them. No, there is no help for it, we must wander forth together into the wide world."

"Hast thou, indeed, the courage to go with me into the wide world?" asked the Chimney-sweeper. "Hast thou considered how large it is, and that we may never return home again?"

"I have," replied she.

And the Chimney-sweeper looked keenly at her, and then said, "My path leads through the chimney! hast thou, indeed, the courage to creep with me through the stove, through the flues and the tunnel? Well do I know the way! we shall mount up so high that they cannot come near us, and at the top there is a cavern that leads into the wide world."

And he led her to the door of the stove.

"Oh, how black it looks!" sighed she. However, she went on with him, through the flues and through the tunnel, where it was dark, pitch dark.

"Now we are in the chimney," said he; "and look what a lovely star shines above us!"

And there was actually a star in the sky, shining right down upon them, as if to show them the way. And they crawled and crept—a fearful path was theirs—so high, so very high! but he guided and supported her, and showed her the best places whereon to plant her tiny porcelain feet, till they reached the edge of the chimney, where they sat down to rest, for they were very tired, and indeed not without reason. Heaven with all its stars was above them, and the town with all its roofs lay beneath them; the wide, wide world surrounded them. The poor Shepherdess had never imagined all this; she leant her little head on her Chimney-sweeper's arm, and wept so vehemently that the gilding broke off from her waistband.

"This is too much!" exclaimed she. "This can I not endure! The world is all too large! Oh, that I were once more upon the little table under the pier-glass! I shall never be happy till I am there again. I have followed thee out into the wide world, surely thou canst follow me home again, if thou lovest me!"

And the Chimney-sweeper talked very sensibly to her, reminding her of the old Chinese Mandarin and "the crooked-legged Field-marshal-Major-General-Corporal-Sergeant;" but she wept so bitterly, and kissed her little Chimney-sweep so fondly, that at last he could not but yield to her request, unreasonable as it was. So with great difficulty they crawled down the chimney, crept through the flues and the tunnel, and at length found themselves once more in the dark stove; but they still lurked behind the door, listening, before they would venture to return into the room. Everything was quite still; they peeped out,—alas! on the ground lay the old Chinese Mandarin; in attempting to follow the run-aways, he had fallen down off the table, and had broken into three pieces —his head lay shaking in a corner; "the crooked-legged Field-marshal-Major-General-Corporal-Sergeant" stood where he had always stood, thinking over what had happened.

"Oh, how shocking!" exclaimed the little Shepherdess; "old grandfather is broken in pieces, and we are the cause! I shall never survive it!" and she wrung her delicate hands.

"He can be put together again," replied the Chimney-sweeper. "He can very easily be put together; only be not so impatient! If they glue his back together, and put a strong rivet in his neck, then he will be as good as new again, and will be able to say plenty of unpleasant things to us."

"Do you really think so?" asked she. And then they climbed up the table to the place where they had stood before.

"See how far we have been!" observed the Chimney-sweeper; "we might have spared ourselves all the trouble."

"If we could but have old grandfather put together!" said the Shepherdess. "Will it cost very much?"

And he was put together; the family had his back glued and his neck riveted; he was as good as new, but could no longer nod his head.

"You have certainly grown very proud since you broke in pieces!" remarked "the crooked-legged Field-marshal-Major-General-Corporal-Sergeant;" "but I must say, for my part, I do not see that there is anything to be proud of. Am I to have her, or am I not? Just answer me that!"

And the Chimney-sweeper and the little Shepherdess looked imploringly at the old Mandarin, they were so afraid lest he should nod his head; but nod he could not, and it was disagreeable to him to tell a stranger that he had a rivet in his neck, so the young porcelain people always remained together, they blessed the grandfather's rivet, and loved each other till they broke in pieces.

THE TINDER-BOX.

A SOLDIER was marching along the high-road — right, left! right, left! He had his knapsack on his back and a sword by his side, for he had been to the wars, and was now returning home. And on the road he met an old Witch — a horrid-looking creature she was, her lower lip hung down almost to her neck.

"Good evening, Soldier!" said she. "What a bright sword, and what a large knapsack, you have, my fine fellow! I'll tell you what, you shall have as much money for your own as you can wish!"

"Thanks, old Witch!" cried the Soldier.

"Do you see yonder large tree?" said the Witch, pointing to a tree that stood close by the wayside. "It is quite hollow within. Climb up to the top, and you will find a hole large enough for you to creep through, and thus you will get down into the tree. I will tie a rope round your waist, so that I can pull you up again when you call me."

"But what am I to do down in the tree?" asked the Soldier.

"What are you to do?" repeated the Witch; "why, fetch money, to be sure! As soon as you get to the bottom, you will find yourself in a wide passage; it is quite light, more than a hundred lamps are burning there. Then you will see three doors; you can open them, the keys are in the locks. On opening the first door you will enter a room; in the midst of it, on the floor, lies a large chest; a dog is seated on it, his eyes are as large as tea-cups; but never you mind, don't trouble yourself about him! I will lend you my blue apron; you must spread it out on the floor, then go briskly up to the dog, seize him, and set him down on it; and after that is done, you can open the chest, and take as much money out of it as you please. That chest contains none but copper coins; but if you like silver better, you have only to go into the next room; there you will find a dog with eyes as large as mill-wheels, but don't be afraid of him; you have only to set him down on my apron, and then rifle the chest at your leisure. But if you would rather have gold than either silver or copper, that is to be had too, and as much of it as you can carry, if you pass on into the third chamber. The dog that sits on this third money-chest has two eyes, each as large as the Round Tower. A famous creature he is, as you may fancy; but don't be alarmed, just set him down on my apron, and then he will do you no harm, and you can take as much golden treasure from the chest as you like."

"Not a bad plan that, upon my word!" said the Soldier. "But how much of the money am I to give you, old woman? For you'll want your full share of the plunder, I've a notion!"

"Not a penny will I have," returned the Witch. "The only thing I want you to bring me is an old tinder-box, which my grandmother left there by mistake last time she was down in the tree."

"Well, then, give me the rope to tie round my waist, and I'll be gone," said the Soldier.

"Here it is," said the Witch, "and here is my blue apron."

So the Soldier climbed the tree, let himself down through the hole in the trunk, and suddenly found himself in the wide passage, lighted up by many hundred lamps, as the Witch had described.

He opened the first door. Bravo! There sat the dog with eyes as large as tea-cups, staring at him as though in utter amazement.

"There's a good creature!" quoth the Soldier, as he spread the Witch's apron on the floor, and lifted the dog upon it. He then filled his pockets with the copper coins in the chest, shut the lid, put the dog back into his place, and passed on into the second apartment.

Huzza! there sat the dog, with eyes as large as mill-wheels.

"You had really better not stare at me so," remarked the Soldier, "it will make your eyes weak!" and herewith he set the dog down on the Witch's apron. But when, on raising the lid of the chest, he beheld the vast quantity of silver money it contained, he threw all his pence away in disgust, and hastened to fill his pockets and his knapsack with the pure silver.

And he passed on into the third chamber. Now, indeed, that was terrifying! The dog in this chamber actually had a pair of eyes each as large as the Round Tower, and they kept rolling round and round in his head like wheels.

"Good evening!" said the Soldier, and he lifted his cap respectfully, for such a monster of a dog as this he had never in his life before seen or heard of. He stood still for a minute or two, looking at him, then thinking, "the sooner it's done the better!" he took hold of the immense creature, removed him from the chest to the floor, and raised the lid of the chest.

Oh, what a sight of gold was there! enough to buy not only all Copenhagen, but all the cakes and sugar-plums, all the tin-soldiers, whips, and rocking-horses in the world! Yes, he must be satisfied now. Hastily the Soldier threw out all the silver money he had stuffed into his pockets and knapsack, and took gold instead; not only his pockets and knapsack, but his soldier's cap and boots, he crammed full of gold—bright gold!—heavy gold!—he could hardly walk for the weight he carried. He lifted the dog on the chest again, banged the door of the room behind him, and called out through the tree,—

"Halloo, you old Witch! pull me up again!"

"Have you got the tinder-box?" asked the Witch.

"Upon my honour, I'd quite forgotten it!" shouted the Soldier, and back he went to fetch it. The Witch then drew him up through the tree, and now he again stood in the highroad, his pockets, boots, knapsack, and cap stuffed with gold pieces.

"Just tell me now, what are you going to do with the tinder-box?" inquired the Soldier.

"That's no concern of yours," returned the Witch. "You've got your money, give me my tinder-box this instant!"

"Well, take your choice," said the Soldier; "either tell me at once what you want with the tinder-box, or I draw my sword, and cut off your head."

"I won't tell you!" screamed the Witch.

So the Soldier drew his sword and cut off her head. There she lay! but he did not waste time in looking at what he had done, he made haste to knot all his money securely in the Witch's blue apron, made a bundle of it and slung it across his back, put the tinder-box into his pocket, and went straight to the nearest town.

It was a large, handsome town; a city, in fact. He walked into the first hotel in the place, called for the best rooms, and ordered the choicest and most expensive dishes for his supper, for he was now a rich man, with plenty of gold to spend.

The servant who cleaned his boots could not help thinking they were disgracefully shabby and worn to belong to such a grand gentleman. However, next day he provided himself with new boots and very gay clothes besides. Our Soldier was now a great man, and the people of the hotel were called in to give him information about all the places of amusement in the city, and about their King, and the beautiful Princess, his daughter.

"I should rather like to see her!" observed the Soldier, "just tell me when I can?"

"No one can see her at all," was the reply; "she dwells in a great copper palace, with ever so many walls and towers round it. No one but the King may go and visit her there, because it has been foretold that she will marry a common soldier, and our King would not like that at all."

"Shouldn't I like to see her though, just for once!"

thought the Soldier, but it was of no use for him to wish it.

And now he lived such a merry life, went continually to the theatre, drove out in the Royal Gardens, and gave so much money in alms to the poor! to all, in fact, who asked him. And this was well done in him; to be sure, he knew by past experience how miserable it was not to have a shilling in one's pocket. He was always gaily dressed, and had such a crowd of friends, who one and all declared he was a most capital fellow — a real gentleman! And that pleased our Soldier uncommonly. But as he was now giving and spending every day, and never received anything in return, his money began to fail him, and at last he had only twopence left, and was forced to remove from the splendid apartments where he had lodged hitherto, and take refuge in a little bit of an attic-chamber, where he had to brush his boots and darn his clothes himself, and where none of his friends ever came to see him, because there were so many stairs to go up, it was quite fatiguing.

It was a very dark evening, and he could not afford to buy himself so much as a rushlight. However, he remembered all at once that there were a few matches lying in the tinder-box that the old Witch had bade him fetch out of the hollow tree. So he brought out this tinder-box and began to strike a light, but no sooner had he rubbed the flint-stone and made the sparks fly out than the door burst suddenly open, and the Dog with eyes as large as tea-cups, and which he had seen in the cavern beneath the tree, stood before him and said, "What commands has my master for his slave?"

"Upon my honour, this is a pretty joke!" cried the Soldier; "a fine sort of tinder-box this is, if it will really provide me with whatever I want. Fetch me some money this instant!" said he to the Dog; whereupon the creature vanished, and lo! in half a minute he was back again, holding in his mouth a large bag full of pence. So now the Soldier understood the rare virtue of this charming tinder-box. If he struck the flint only once, the dog that sat on the chest full of copper came to him; if he struck it twice, the dog that watched over the silver answered the summons; and if he struck it three times, he was forthwith attended by the monstrous guardian of the golden treasure.

The Soldier could now remove back to his princely apartments, he bought himself an entirely new suit of clothes, and all his friends remembered him again and loved him as much as ever.

But one evening the thought occurred to him, "How truly ridiculous it is that no one should be allowed to see this Princess! they all say she is so very beautiful—what a shame it is that she should be mewed up in that great copper palace with the towers guarding it round! And I do want so to see her—where's my tinder-box, by-the-bye?" He struck the flint, and lo! before him stood the Dog with eyes as large as tea-cups.

"It is rather late, I must own," began the Soldier; "but I do want to see the Princess so much—only for one minute, you know!"

And the Dog was out of the door, and before the Soldier had time to think of what he should say or do, he was back again with the Princess sitting asleep on his back. A real Princess was this! so beautiful, so enchantingly beautiful! the Soldier could not help himself, he knelt down and kissed her hand.

The Dog ran back to the palace with the Princess that very minute; however, next morning, while she was at breakfast with the King and Queen, the Princess said that she had had such a strange dream during the past night. She had dreamt that she was riding on a dog, an enormously large dog, and that a soldier had knelt down to her and kissed her hand.

"A pretty sort of a dream, indeed!" exclaimed the Queen.

And she insisted that one of the old ladies of the court should watch by the Princess's bedside on the following night, in case she should again be disturbed by dreams.

The Soldier longed so exceedingly to see the fair Princess of the copper palace again; accordingly, next evening, the Dog was summoned to fetch her. So he did, and ran as fast as he could; however, not so fast but that the ancient dame watching at the Princess's couch found time to put on a pair of waterproof boots before running after them. She saw the Dog vanish in a large house; then, thinking to herself, "Now I know what to do," she took out a piece of chalk and made a great white cross on the door. She then went home and betook herself to rest, and the Princess was home almost as soon. But on his way the Dog chanced to observe the white cross on the door of the hotel where the Soldier lived; so he immediately took another piece of chalk and set crosses on every door throughout the town. And this was wisely done on his part.

Early in the morning came out the King, the Queen, the old court-dame, and all the officers of the royal household, every one of them curious to see where the Princess had been.

"Here it is!" exclaimed the King, as soon as he saw the first street-door with a cross chalked on it.

"My dear, where are your eyes?—this is the house," cried the Queen, seeing the second door bear a cross.

"No, this is it, surely—why, here's a cross too!" cried all of them together, on discovering that there were crosses on all the doors. It was evident that their search would be in vain, and they were obliged to give it up.

But the Queen was an exceedingly wise and prudent woman; she was good for something besides sitting in a state-carriage, and looking very grand and condescending. She now took her gold scissors, cut a large piece of silk stuff into strips, and sewed these strips together, to make a pretty neat little bag. This bag she filled with the finest, whitest flour, and with her own hands tied it to the Princess's waist, and when this was done, again took up her golden scissors, and cut a little hole in the bag, just large enough to let the flour drop out gradually all the time the Princess was moving.

That evening the Dog came again, took the Princess on his back, and ran away with her to the Soldier. Oh, how the Soldier loved her, and how he wished he were a prince, that he might have this beautiful Princess for his wife!

The Dog never perceived how the flour went drip, dripping, all the way from the palace to the Soldier's room, and from the Soldier's room back to the palace. So next morning the King and Queen could easily discover where their daughter had been carried, and they took the Soldier, and cast him into prison.

And now he sat in the prison. Oh! how dark it was, and how wearisome! and the turnkey kept coming in to remind him that to-morrow he was to be hanged. This piece of news was by no means agreeable, and the tinder-box had been left in his lodgings at the hotel.

When morning came, he could, through his narrow iron grating, watch the people all hurrying out of the town to see him hanged; he could hear the drums beating, and presently, too, he saw the soldiers marching to the place of execution. What a crowd there was rushing by! among the rest was a shoemaker's apprentice in his leathern apron and slippers; he bustled on with such speed that one of his slippers flew off and bounded against the iron staves of the Soldier's prison-window.

"Stop, stop, little 'prentice!" cried the Soldier; "it's of no use for you to be in such a hurry, for none of the fun will begin till I come; but if you'll oblige me by running to my lodgings and fetching me my tinder-box, I'll give you twopence. But you must run for your life!" The shoemaker's boy liked the idea of earning twopence, so away he raced after the tinder-box, returned, and gave it to the Soldier, and then—ah, yes, now we shall hear what happened then!

Outside the city a gibbet had been erected; round it were marshalled the soldiers, with many hundred thousand people, men, women, and children; the King and Queen were seated on magnificent thrones, exactly opposite the judges and the whole assembled council.

Already had the Soldier mounted the topmost step of the ladder, already was the executioner on the point of fitting the rope round his neck, when, turning to their Majesties, he began to entreat most earnestly that they would suffer a poor criminal's innocent fancy to be gratified before he underwent his punishment. He wished so much, he said, to smoke a pipe of tobacco, and as it was the last pleasure he could enjoy in this world, he hoped it would not be denied him.

The King could not refuse this harmless request; accordingly the Soldier took out his tinder-box and struck the flint—once he struck it, twice he struck it, three times he struck it!—and lo! all the three wizard Dogs stood before him, the Dog with eyes as large as tea-cups, the Dog with eyes as large as mill-wheels, and the Dog with eyes each as large as the Round Tower!

"Now help me, don't let me be hanged!" cried the

Soldier. And forthwith the three terrible Dogs fell upon the judges and councillors, tossing them high into the air — so high, that on falling down to the ground again they were broken in pieces.

"We will not ——" began the King, but the monster Dog, with eyes as large as the Round Tower, did not wait to hear what his Majesty would not; he seized both him and the Queen, and flung them up into the air after the councillors. And the soldiers were all desperately frightened, and the people shouted out with one voice, "Good Soldier, you shall be our King, and the beautiful Princess shall be your wife, and our Queen!"

So the Soldier was conducted into the royal carriage, and all the three Dogs bounded to and fro in front, little boys whistled upon their fingers, and the guards presented arms. The Princess was forthwith sent for and made Queen, which she liked much better than living a prisoner in the copper palace. The bridal festivities lasted for eight whole days, and the three wizard Dogs sat at the banquet-table, staring about them with their great eyes.

THE RED SHOES.

THERE was once a little girl, very pretty and delicate, but so poor that in summer-time she went barefoot, and in winter wore large wooden shoes, so that her little ankles grew quite red and sore.

In the village dwelt the shoemaker's mother; she sat down one day, and made out of some old pieces of red cloth a pair of little shoes; they were clumsy enough certainly, but they fitted the little girl tolerably well, and she gave them to her. The little girl's name was Karen.

It was the day of her mother's funeral when the red shoes were given to Karen; they were not at all suitable for mourning, but she had no others, and in them she walked with bare legs behind the miserable straw-bier.

Just then a large old carriage rolled by; in it sat a large old lady; she looked at the little girl and pitied her, and she said to the priest, "Give me the little girl, and I will take care of her."

And Karen thought it was all for the sake of the red shoes that the old lady had taken this fancy to her; but the old lady said they were frightful, and they were burnt. And Karen was dressed very neatly; she was taught to read and to work; and people told her she was pretty, but the Mirror said, "Thou art more than pretty, thou art beautiful!"

It happened one day that the Queen travelled through that part of the country, with her little daughter, the Princess; and all the people, Karen amongst them, crowded in front of the palace, whilst the little Princess stood, dressed in white, at a window, for every one to see her. She wore neither train nor gold crown; but on her feet were pretty red morocco shoes, much prettier ones, indeed, than those the shoemaker's mother had made for little Karen. Nothing in the world could be compared to these red shoes!

Karen was now old enough to be confirmed; she was to have both new frock and new shoes. The rich shoemaker in the town took the measure of her little foot. Large glass cases, full of neat shoes and shining boots, were fixed round the room; however, the old lady's sight was not very good, and, naturally enough, she had not so much pleasure in looking at them as Karen had. Amongst the shoes was a pair of red ones, just like those worn by the Princess. How gay they were! and the shoemaker said, they had been made for a count's daughter, but had not quite fitted her.

"They are of polished leather," said the old lady; "see how they shine!"

"Yes, they shine beautifully!" exclaimed Karen. And as the shoes fitted her, they were bought, but the old lady did not know that they were red, for she would never have suffered Karen to go to confirmation in red shoes. But Karen did so.

Everybody looked at her feet, and as she walked up the nave to the chancel, it seemed to her that even the antique sculptured figures on the monuments, with their stiff ruffs and long black robes, fixed their eyes on her red shoes; of them only she thought when the Bishop laid his hand on her head, when he spoke of Holy Baptism, of her covenant with God, and how that she must now be a full-grown Christian. The organ sent forth its deep, solemn tones; the children's sweet voices mingled with those of the choristers, but Karen still thought only of her red shoes.

That afternoon, when the old lady was told that Karen

had worn red shoes at her confirmation, she was much vexed, and told Karen that they were quite unsuitable, and that henceforward, whenever she went to church, she must wear black shoes, were they ever so old.

Next Sunday was the Communion-day; Karen looked first at the red shoes, then at the black ones, then at the red again, and—put them on.

It was beautiful, sunshiny weather; Karen and the old lady walked to church through the corn-fields; the path was very dusty.

At the church-door stood an old soldier; he was leaning on crutches, and had a marvellously long beard, not white, but reddish-hued, and he bowed almost to the earth, and asked the old lady if he might wipe the dust off her shoes. And Karen put out her little foot also. "Oh, what pretty dancing shoes!" quoth the old soldier; "take care, and mind you do not let them slip off when you dance;" and he passed his hands over them.

The old lady gave the soldier a halfpenny, and then went with Karen into church.

And every one looked at Karen's red shoes; and all the carved figures, too, bent their gaze upon them; and when Karen knelt before the altar, the red shoes still floated before her eyes; she thought of them, and of them only, and she forgot to join in the hymn of praise,—she forgot to repeat "Our Father."

At last all the people came out of church, and the old lady got into her carriage. Karen was just lifting her foot to follow her, when the old soldier standing in the porch exclaimed, "Only look, what pretty dancing-shoes!" And Karen could not help it, she felt she must make a few of her dancing-steps; and after she had once begun, her feet continued to move, just as though the shoes had received power over them; she danced round the churchyard—she could not stop—the coachman was obliged to run after her—he took hold of her and lifted her into the carriage, but the feet still continued to dance, so as to kick the good old lady most cruelly. At last the shoes were taken off, and the feet had rest.

And now the shoes were put away in a press, but Karen could not help going to look at them every now and then.

T

The old lady lay ill in bed; the doctor said she could not live much longer; she certainly needed careful nursing, and who should be her nurse and constant attendant but Karen? But there was to be a grand ball in the town; Karen was invited; she looked at the old lady, who was almost dying, she looked at the red shoes—she put them on; there could be no harm in doing that, at least; she went to the ball, and began to dance.

But when she wanted to move to the right, the shoes bore her to the left; and when she would dance up the room, the shoes danced down the room, danced down the stairs, through the streets, and through the gates of the town. Dance she did, and dance she must, straight out into the dark wood.

Something all at once shone through the trees! she thought at first it must be the moon's bright face, shining blood red through the night mists; but no, it was the old soldier with the red beard—he sat there, nodding at her, and repeating, "Only look, what pretty dancing-shoes!"

She was very much frightened, and tried to throw off her red shoes, but could not unclasp them. She hastily tore off her stockings; but the shoes she could not get rid of—they had, it seemed, grown on to her feet. Dance she did, and dance she must, over field and meadow, in rain and in sunshine, by night and by day—by night! that was most horrible! She danced into the lonely churchyard, but the dead there danced not—they were at rest: she would fain have sat down on the poor man's grave, where the bitter tansy grew, but for her there was neither rest nor respite. She danced past the open church-door; there she saw an Angel, clad in long white robes, and with wings that reached from his shoulders to the earth; his countenance was grave and stern, and in his hand he held a broad glittering sword.

"Dance shalt thou," said he; "dance on, in thy red shoes, till thou art pale and cold, and thy skin shrinks and crumples up like a skeleton's! Dance shalt thou still, from door to door; and wherever proud, vain children live, thou shalt knock, so that they may hear thee and fear! Dance shalt thou, dance on——"

"Mercy!" cried Karen; but she heard not the Angel's answer, for the shoes carried her through the gate, into the fields, along highways and by-ways, and still she must dance.

One morning she danced past a door she knew well; she heard psalm-singing from within, and presently a coffin, strewn with flowers, was borne out. Then Karen knew that the good old lady was dead, and she felt herself a thing forsaken by all mankind, and accursed by the Angel of God.

Dance she did, and dance she must, even through the dark night; the shoes bore her continually over thorns and briers, till her limbs were torn and bleeding. Away she danced over the heath to a little solitary house; she knew that the headsman dwelt there, and she tapped with her fingers against the panes, crying,—

"Come out! come out!—I cannot come in to you, I am dancing."

And the headsman replied, "Surely thou knowest not who I am. I cut off the heads of wicked men, and my axe is very sharp and keen."

"Cut not off my head!" said Karen; "for then I could not live to repent of my sin; but cut off my feet with the red shoes."

And then she confessed to him all her sin, and the headsman cut off her feet with the red shoes on them; but even after this the shoes still danced away with those little feet over the fields, and into the deep forests.

And the headsman made her a pair of wooden feet, and hewed down some boughs to serve her as crutches, and he taught her the psalm which is always repeated by criminals, and she kissed the hand that had guided the axe, and went her way over the heath.

"Now I have certainly suffered quite enough through the red shoes," thought Karen; "I will go to church and let people see me once more!" and she went as fast as she could to the church-porch; but as she approached it, the red shoes danced before her, and she was frightened and turned back.

All that week through she endured the keenest anguish and shed many bitter tears; however, when Sunday came, she said to herself, "Well, I must have suffered and striven enough by this time; I dare say I am quite as good as many of those who are holding their heads so high in church."

So she took courage and went there, but she had not passed the churchyard-gate before she saw the red shoes again dancing before her, and in great terror she again turned back, and more deeply than ever bewailed her sin.

She then went to the pastor's house, and begged that some employment might be given her, promising to work diligently and do all she could; she did not wish for any wages, she said, she only wanted a roof to shelter her, and to dwell with good people. And the pastor's wife had pity on her, and took her into her service. And Karen was grateful and industrious. Every evening she sat silently listening to the pastor, while he read the Holy Scriptures aloud. All the children loved her, but when she heard them talk about dress and finery, and about being as beautiful as a queen, she would sorrowfully shake her head.

Again Sunday came, all the pastor's household went to church, and they asked her if she would not go too, but she sighed and looked with tears in her eyes upon her crutches.

When they were all gone, she went into her own little lowly chamber—it was but just large enough to contain a bed and a chair—and there she sat down with her psalm-book in her hand; and whilst she was meekly and devoutly reading in it, the wind wafted the tones of the organ from the church into her room, and she lifted up her face to heaven and prayed, with tears, "Oh, God, help me!"

Then the sun shone brightly, so brightly!—and behold! close before her stood the white-robed Angel of God, the same whom she had seen on that night of horror at the church-porch, but his hand wielded not now, as then, a sharp, threatening sword,—he held a lovely green bough, full of roses. With this he touched the ceiling, which immediately rose to a great height, a bright gold star sparkling in the spot where the Angel's green bough had touched it. And he touched the walls, whereupon the room widened, and Karen saw the organ, the old monuments, and the congregation all sitting in their richly-carved seats and singing from their psalm-books.—

For the church had come home to the poor girl in her little narrow chamber, or rather the chamber had grown, as it were, into the church; she sat with the rest of the pastor's household, and when the psalm was ended, they looked up and nodded to her, saying, "Thou didst well to come, Karen!"

"This is mercy!" said she.

And the organ played again, and the children's voices in the choir mingled so sweetly and plaintively with it!—The bright sunbeams streamed warmly through the windows upon Karen's seat; her heart was so full of sunshine, of peace and gladness, that it broke; her soul flew upon a sunbeam to her Father in heaven, where not a look of reproach awaited her—not a word was breathed of the Red Shoes.

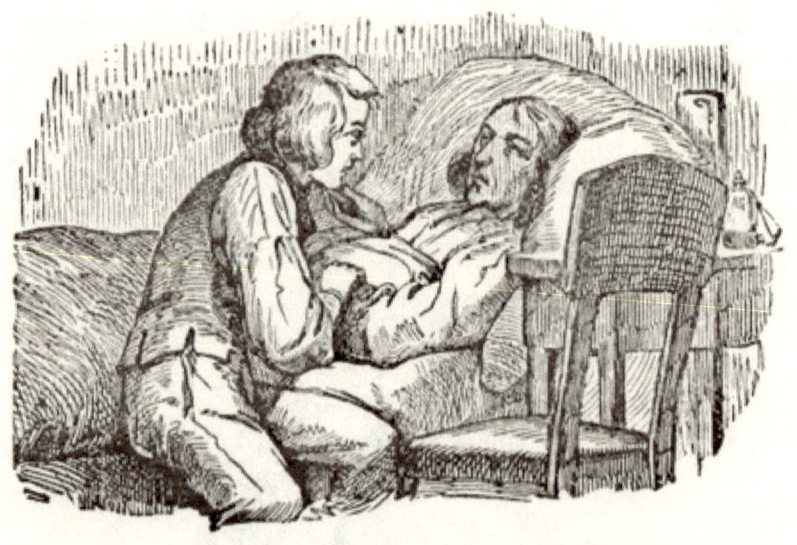

THE FELLOW-TRAVELLERS.

POOR Hans was so unhappy! for his father was very ill, and at the point of death. There was no one but himself to tend the sick man in his little, low-roofed chamber, the lamp on the table burned with a faint, expiring light, and it was already quite late in the evening.

"Thou hast always been a good and dutiful son to me, Hans," said the dying father; "fear not, our Lord will be with thee, and help thee through the world." As he spoke, he looked so fondly at the boy, with his grave, loving eyes; then, fetching a deep breath, he died—as calmly as though he had but fallen asleep. But Hans wept bitterly, for now he had no friend nor relative in all the wide world, neither father nor mother, neither sister nor brother. Poor Hans! He knelt down beside the bed, and kissed his dead father's hand, weeping such bitter, salt tears, all the while; till, at last, his eyes closed through utter weariness, and he fell asleep, his head resting against the hard corner of the bedstead.

He dreamed a strange dream; he saw sun and moon bowing before him, and he saw his father fresh and healthy again; and he heard him laugh as he had been wont to laugh when he was right happy and merry. A beautiful girl, wearing a gold crown upon her long dark hair, smilingly extended her hand to Hans, and his father said, " Seest thou what a rare bride thou hast won? She is the very loveliest maiden in the world." Then he awoke; all the glory and beauty of his dream was gone, his father lay cold and dead in his bed, and there was no one with him.— Poor Hans!

The next week the funeral took place. Hans followed close behind the coffin, he watched it till only one corner was left uncovered—one more shovelful of earth, and that too was seen no longer; he felt as though his heart must burst with sorrow. The congregation around him were singing a psalm,—words and music melted into each other so sweetly, that they brought the tears into his eyes,— he wept, and weeping relieved the violence of his grief. The sun was shining gloriously on the green trees, as though he would say, " Thou must not be so unhappy, Hans! See how beautiful and blue is yonder sky; far beyond it dwells thy father now, and there he prays the Almighty that He will be thy guardian and shield, and that all may go well with thee."

" I will always be good," thought Hans, "and then I shall some day join my father in heaven; and oh, what joy it will be when we see each other again! I shall have so many things to tell him, and he, too, will tell me so many things— will teach me about heavenly bliss and glory, as he taught me here on earth. Oh, what joy it will be!"

Hans thought over this fancy so long, and the picture became so vivid in his mind, that he smiled with pleasure even whilst the tears were still undried on his face. The little birds in the chestnut-trees above his head kept twittering, " Quivit, quirri-quirri-vit; " they were so joyous, although they, too, had been present at the funeral. But they surely knew that the dead man was now at rest, perhaps in bliss; that he had, or soon would have wings, far larger and lovelier than theirs, because he had been a good man whilst he lived on earth, and therefore they rejoiced. Hans watched them flying away from the green trees, far out into the world, and he felt the most ardent longing to fly with them.

His first care was now to carve a large wooden cross to plant upon his father's grave; he brought it to the spot that same evening, and found that the grave was already strewn with sand and flowers. Stranger hands had done this, for all loved the good father who was dead.

Early next morning, Hans packed up his little travelling bundle, and carefully secured in his belt his whole inheritance, consisting of fifty rix-dollars and a few silver pennies, wherewith he intended to start on his wanderings through the wide world. First, however, he went to the churchyard, to his father's grave, repeated the Lord's Prayer over it, and then said, "Farewell, dear father! I will always be good, that thou mayest still pray the Almighty to be my guide and shield."

By the side of the footpath which Hans now trod grew many wild flowers—so fresh and so bright they looked in the warm sunshine; and whenever the wind passed that way, they nodded to Hans, as if they would say, "Welcome to the green meadow-lands! Is it not pleasant here?" But Hans turned round once more, to cast a last glance at the old church where he had been baptized when an infant, and whither he had gone every Sunday with his father to worship God and sing His praises. And on looking back he saw standing in one of the holes of the church-tower the little Nisse, with his pointed red cap, and shading his face with his bent arm from the sun, which shone straight into his eyes. Hans nodded farewell to him, and the little Nisse swung his red cap aloft, pressed his hand to his heart, and kissed his fingers repeatedly, to show that he wished the young traveller well, and hoped he might have a right pleasant journey.

Hans now began to think of the vast number of beautiful sights that he would see in the great, glorious world, and he walked on faster and faster, farther and farther, by roads that he had never traversed before; he knew not the villages he passed through, nor the people that he met, he was now quite in a strange land, and surrounded by strangers.

The first night he was forced to lay himself down to rest in a hay-stack under the open sky—other couch he had none. But he was perfectly satisfied, and thought that not even the King could be lodged more magnificently than he was. The wide meadow, with the brooklet flowing through it, and with the blue heavens spread above, formed a beautiful state-bedchamber. The green turf, with its tiny red and white flowerets, was his carpet; the elder bushes and wild roses were vases of flowers; and the brooklet, with the reeds growing on its banks, and nodding to him a friendly " good morning " and " good evening," served as his water-ewer. The moon was a gloriously large night-lamp, hung high up amid the blue canopy of heaven, yet without any danger of setting fire to the curtains; Hans could sleep in perfect security. And he slept well and soundly, and did not wake till the sun had risen, and all the little birds around him sang loudly, " Good morning! good morning! Have you not yet got up?"

On continuing his wanderings, and reaching the next village, he heard the church-bells ringing; it was Sunday, and all the people were going to church. And Hans went with them, sang hymns, and listened reverently to the Word of God, and felt as though he were once again in his own parish church, where he had been baptized, and had, Sunday after Sunday, knelt by his father's side.

In the churchyard outside there were so many graves, and on some of them high grass was growing. " Perhaps my father's grave will soon look like these," thought Hans, " now that I am away, and there is no one to pluck out the grass and strew flowers over it." So he began to busy himself with clearing the graves here and there from weeds, set upright those wooden crosses that had fallen down, and restored the wreaths, which the wind had carried away, to their places. " Who knows but that some one may do the same by my father's grave, since I cannot do it?" thought he.

At the churchyard-gate stood an old beggar-man, leaning on his crutch; Hans gave him his few silver pennies, and then went on his way, cheerful and contented, farther out into the world.

Towards evening a violent tempest arose; Hans made great haste to get under shelter, but dark night had gathered round him before he had caught sight of a house where he might take refuge. At last he discovered himself to be close beside a little church, which stood alone on the summit of a hill; the door was ajar, and he crept in; here he would stay till the storm was allayed.

" I will sit down in this corner," said he; " I am quite tired out, and it will do me good to rest a little while." And after first folding his hands and repeating his evening prayer, he leaned his head back against the wall, and quickly fell into a sound sleep, whilst it lightened and thundered outside.

When he awoke it was midnight, the storm had passed by, and the moon shone in through the high church-windows, its light falling full upon an open coffin that lay on the floor in the midst of the church. A dead man lay in the coffin, and it had been taken into the church to be left there till the grave was dug for it next morning, because the dead man had been a stranger, with no house of his own and no relatives to take charge of his remains. Hans did not feel terrified at this sight, for he had a good conscience, and he knew that the dead can do no harm to any one, only the living, the wicked it is that work us ill. And two wicked living men were those dark figures that stood by the coffin; they were come with the evil intent of taking the poor helpless corpse out of the coffin, and throwing it out at the church-door.

"Why do you want to do that?" asked Hans, when he discovered their intention; "it is very wicked of you. In God's name, let the dead rest in peace."

"Rest, indeed!" cried one of the men; "when he has made fools of us both, when he has borrowed money from us which he could not repay—and now he is dead, and we shall never get a farthing of our due. But we'll have our revenge, that we will, and he shall lie like a dog outside the church-door!"

"I have only fifty rix-dollars," said Hans; "it is the whole of my portion, but I will gladly give them to you, if you will promise me, upon your honour, to leave this poor dead man in peace. I shall be able to get on without the money, no doubt: I have strong, healthy limbs of my own, and our Lord will help me."

"Of course," replied the two wicked men, "if you will pay his debts we shall do him no harm, you may depend upon that!" And so they took the money that Hans offered them, laughed loud and scornfully at his simplicity, and went their way. Hans then laid the corpse straight again in the coffin, folded the cold, stiff hands, and bade the dead man farewell. He then left the church, and walked with a light heart through the wood.

The moonbeams pierced in here and there through the trees surrounding him, and wherever their clear light fell were revealed the figures of the pretty, tiny elves, gambolling so merrily, and they were not in the least startled by his approach; they knew that he must be good and innocent, since none but those who are free from evil thoughts and wishes have power to see the elves. Some of them were no larger than one of Hans' fingers, and had their long flaxen hair fastened up with golden combs; by two and two they seesawed upon the heavy drops of dew that spangled the leaves and grass. Every now and then a dew-drop trickled down, and both little sprites were flung down with it into the long grass, and then what laughter there was among the rest of the merry, mocking elves! It was quite droll to see their play. They sang too, and Hans recollected all their pretty songs and glees,—he had heard them often when he was a little boy. And great brown spiders, with silver crowns on their heads, were made to spin long suspension-bridges and palaces from one tree to another for them, and the dew fell upon these delicate structures, and they glistened like glass in the clear moonlight. And thus their gambols went on till sunrise. Then the tiny elves crept into the flower-cups to sleep, and the wind took hold of their aëry castles and suspension-bridges, and carried them by fragments through the air.

Hans had just stepped out from the wood, when a deep, manly voice shouted from behind him, "Halloo, comrade! whither go you?"

"Out into the wide world," replied Hans; "I have neither father nor mother, I am a poor unfriended lad; but I trust the angels will help me and be with me."

"I, too, am going into the world," rejoined the stranger. "Suppose we join company?"

"Why should we not?" answered Hans, and thus they were soon agreed. They went on together, talked, and became good friends. But Hans quickly discovered his stranger comrade was much cleverer and more experienced than he was; he seemed to have travelled in every country on the earth, and to have learnt everything.

It was almost noon, and the sun stood high above their heads, when they sat down under a wide-spreading tree to eat their breakfast. While they were thus engaged, it so chanced that an old woman, very much wrinkled and almost crooked-backed, came hobbling by on her crutch. Over her shoulders she carried a bundle of fagots, which she had collected in the wood; she had gathered up her apron, and out of one corner of it projected three bundles of ferns and willow-boughs. Just as she was passing them her foot slipped, she fell, and gave vent to a shrill cry of pain; for she had broken her leg, poor old woman!

Hans instantly sprang up to help her, and proposed that they should carry her home. But his companion coolly began to unpack his knapsack, took out of it a little box, and said that he had there a healing ointment which would at once heal her leg and restore its strength, so that she would be able to get home without any assistance, and that as easily as if she had not fallen down at all. But if he did so much good to her, he should require her to do something for him, namely, to give him the three bundles of ferns and willow-boughs which she carried in her apron.

"So you will be well paid, will you, master Doctor?" quoth the old crone, with a strange, uncomfortable smile distorting her features. She did not like to part with her willow-twigs, she said, for she had some trouble in procuring them. However, it was not exactly pleasant either to lie in the high-road with her leg broken; accordingly she gave up the contents of her apron to the stranger, and he, in return, bent over her and anointed her leg with his precious ointment; whereupon the old woman rose up and hobbled onward with considerable less difficulty than before she had fallen down. A famous ointment was this! but it is not to be had at the apothecary's.

"What can you want with those bundles of dry wood?" inquired Hans of his fellow-traveller.

"A fancy of mine!" was the reply. "They are in my eyes prettier and more fragrant than bouquets of roses. We can none of us account for our fancies, you know."

"Surely we shall have a storm presently," observed Hans, after a pause, pointing to some dark, threatening forms that rose up into the sky over the horizon. "What terribly black, thick clouds!"

"What a mistake," said his companion; "they are not clouds at all, they are mountains! You cannot imagine how fresh and keen is the air on their crests, where clouds are around as well as above you, and such a wide prospect is spread beneath! We are getting on bravely!"

But though these cloud-like mountains seemed so near, the wanderers wended on the whole day without getting close up to them. Black fir-woods clothed the mountain-sides, and stones as large as whole towns lay scattered here and there. It would cost them hard labour, the stranger said, to cross the mountains. So he and Hans agreed to turn into an inn and rest, that they might start fresh and strong on the morrow upon their mountain-rambles.

The guest-room in the inn they found crowded with people, for a man with a puppet-show had just arrived and prepared his little theatre, and the people had been gathering together in this apartment to see the pretty sight. So they sat round, ranged in chairs, but the best and foremost place of all had been secured by a stout old butcher, his mastiff — such a grim-looking animal! — standing by his side, and staring with all his might, just like any other spectator.

And now the show began. A King and Queen were discovered sitting on magnificent thrones, and wearing gold crowns on their heads, and long trains to their robes. The prettiest little wooden dolls, with glass eyes and thick mustachios, were stationed at the doors and windows, which they kept opening and shutting, so that their Majesties might enjoy a free current of air. It was such a pretty show, and all was going on so smoothly and pleasantly, no tears, no bloodshed, nothing sad and tragic, it was a perfect comedy, when unfortunately — just as the Queen rose up from her throne and walked across the floor — the great mastiff, whom the sturdy master, in his eagerness to watch the show, had quite forgotten to hold in, the great mastiff, I say, — it is quite impossible to guess what he could be thinking of — sprung up, and with one bound clearing the stage, seized the pretty Queen by her slender waist, so roughly that she was nearly broken in two; it was really quite terrible to see her!

The poor show-man was so much grieved by this mischance that he was very near shedding tears; the Queen was his very best doll, and the mastiff had actually bitten her head off before he could be forced to give up his victim. However, the spectators having all gone their ways, Hans' fellow-traveller went up to the poor man and comforted him, assuring him he would find a remedy. And taking out of his knapsack the little jar which he had used to heal the old woman's leg, he rubbed some of the ointment over the wounded doll, after which not only was it perfectly healed, but it received the power of moving all its limbs by itself without there being any need of pulling the wires; it had, indeed, become almost like a living human being, except that it could not speak. The show-man was delighted beyond measure to see his Queen-doll dance and walk of herself; it was what none of his other dolls could do.

Late in the night, when all the people in the inn were in bed, there was heard a heavy groaning and sighing, and it went on so long, that at last everybody got up to see what could be the matter. The puppet show-man rushed in a great hurry to his little theatre, for it seemed to him that the sighing came from thence. And a strange sight met his eyes. The King and the soldiers were lying heaped one upon another, keeping up a perpetual groaning, and trying to make their great glassy eyes expressive of sorrowful entreaty, for they were all wanting to be anointed, as their Queen had been, so that they, too, might be able to move of themselves. The Queen, meantime, knelt on one knee, and lifted her pretty gold crown on high, as though imploring, "Take my crown, if you will, only anoint my consort and my courtiers!" and the show-man was so much affected by this scene, that he immediately offered to give the stranger all the money he might receive for his entertainment on the following evening, if he would but anoint four or five of his best dolls with his wonder-working ointment. But the stranger said he did not want any money; he wished nothing of him except the large sabre which the show-man wore by his side; and on that being given him, he readily anointed six of the dolls, which forthwith danced so prettily and gracefully that all the young girls in the inn, who were present, felt an irresistible inclination to begin dancing too. And dance they did; and coachman and kitchen-maid, waiter and chamber-maid, danced also, and all the guests joined them; nay, even the fire-tongs advanced and led out the shovel to perform the mazurka; but no sooner had these two made the first stamp than they both fell down, one over the other. Oh, a merry night was that!

Next morning Hans and his fellow-traveller started early to climb up the high mountains, through the vast pine-woods. They had clambered up so high that the church-towers far beneath them showed like little red berries scattered among the green of the landscape, and they could see over so many, many miles of country! So much of the beauty of this fair world Hans had never before seen, and the sun shone warmly amid the blue vault of heaven, and the wind bore to him the notes of hunters' bugle-horns from various quarters—so sweet and wild were those notes!—and the tears stood in his eyes with transport and gratitude.

His comrade, meantime, stood by with folded hands, as though in a deep reverie, yet nothing above or beneath, in sky or mountain-cleft, in wood or town, escaped his keen glance. Presently a strain of deep, unearthly music seemed floating over their heads; Hans looked up, and, behold! a large white swan hovering in the air above, singing as Hans had never before heard any bird sing, but it was its death-song. Ever fainter and weaker grew the notes, its graceful throat was bowed forward, and slowly it sank downwards, till at last it fell dead at their feet—the beautiful bird!

"See what magnificent wings the creature has!" observed the stranger; "so large, and purely white! they are well worth having; I will take them with me. Now, you see, Hans," added he, as with one stroke he severed the wings from the dead swan, "that this sabre is of some use to me."

They continued their wanderings over the mountains for many, many leagues; till at last they saw lying beneath them a large city, with more than a hundred towers and cupolas, glistening like silver in the sunshine. In the very heart of this city rose a stately marble palace, its roofs overlaid with red gold; here dwelt the King of the country.

Our two travellers did not choose to go straight into the city, they turned into a little wayside inn to shake the dust off their clothes, for they wished to make themselves look somewhat more decent and respectable before they appeared in the streets of the city. And here the innkeeper began to talk to them about the King, how that he was such a kind, good-hearted old man, and had never done an ill turn to any one all his life; but that his daughter, the Princess, alas! she was a very wicked lady. She had no lack of beauty, if beauty could recommend her, for scarcely in all the world could a fairer maiden be found; but then she was a sorceress, and through her malignant arts many a young and comely prince had lost his life. She had given free leave to all men, of whatever condition of life, to come and be her suitors; any one might come,—be he a prince, or be he a tailor, it was all the same to her; she made him play with her at "What are my thoughts like?" and if he could guess her thoughts three times, then she engaged to give him her hand, and he would be king over the whole country when her father died. But if he could not guess right the three times, and no one yet ever had done so, she always caused him to be immediately put to a cruel death; one he was hanged, another beheaded, so wantonly wicked and bloodthirsty was this Princess. Her father, the good old King, was cut to the heart by her cruelty and perversity, but still he could not interfere, for he had once declared that he would have nothing to do with her love affairs,—that she might do exactly as she pleased. So every time that there came a young prince to play at this fatal game with her and failed, he was either hanged or beheaded; neither was it of any use to warn him beforehand, the Princess could so infatuate people when she chose. The old King, the innkeeper went on to say, was so much afflicted by all the misery thus brought upon the land, that he and all his soldiers spent one day every year in fasting and prayer, kneeling all day on the hard stones, praying that the Princess's cruel heart might relent; but relent she never would. All the old women who were given to brandy-drinking, on that day were wont to colour their potation black, before they drank it, in token of their sympathy with the universal mourning—and what could they do more than that?

"The hateful Princess!" exclaimed Hans, when the innkeeper had finished his relation. "To think of her bewitching people's hearts in this manner! I should never be such a fool, however charming she might be; I should hate her, rather than love her!"

Just as he spoke thus a loud "hurrah!" from the people in the road made him hurry to the window. The Princess herself was riding past, and so enchantingly beautiful was she that people invariably forgot all her cruelty in their admiration, and always burst into a loud cry of joy whenever she appeared among them. Twelve fair young girls, all clad in white silk robes, and each bearing a golden tulip in her hand, rode on coal-black steeds before or beside her; the Princess herself had a snow-white palfrey, very richly caparisoned. Her riding-habit was of cloth of gold, sown, as it were, with rubies and diamonds; the whip which she held in her hand glittered like a sunbeam; the gold crown that pressed her rich dark tresses seemed composed of stars, and the light gauze-like mantle that robed her shoulders was composed of many thousand various-hued butterflies' wings. Magnificent, indeed, was her attire; but all this splendour was as nothing compared with the sunshine of her smile, the piercing light that flashed from her dark eyes, and the majesty enthroned on her high white forehead.

As soon as Hans beheld her the blood rushed to his face, and he could not utter a single word. The Princess looked, in truth, the very same as the fair maiden wearing the gold crown whom he had seen in his dream on the night of his father's death. So beautiful he could not have imagined any mortal maiden to be, and he could not help loving her with all his heart. It could not be true, he said to himself, the tale he had heard of her being a hard, cruel sorceress, who would have people hanged or beheaded when they could not guess her thoughts. "Every one has free leave to become her suitor, even the poorest,—I will go up to the palace and woo her, for I feel I cannot live without her."

They all tried to persuade him to give up this idea, assuring him that he would fare no better than the suitors who had been before him. His fellow-traveller, especially, entreated him on no account to go up to the palace, but Hans would not listen to these friendly warnings; he carefully cleansed his dress, brushed his shoes till they were quite bright, washed his hands and face, combed his long fair hair, and then started on his way alone through the city, straight up to the marble palace.

"Come in!" said the King's voice, when Hans knocked at the door. Hans entered, and the good old King came forward to meet him, wearing his dressing-gown and embroidered slippers, yet with his gold crown on his head, and holding in one hand the sceptre, in the other the orb, the symbols of kingly power. "Wait a bit," said he, and he put the golden

U

orb under his arm, that he might extend his hand to Hans, and bid him heartily welcome. But as soon as ever he heard that Hans came as a suitor to his daughter he began to weep most bitterly, so that sceptre and orb rolled down on the floor, and he was obliged to dry his eyes on his dressing-gown. The poor old King!

"Do not think of it!" implored he; "it will be with you as with all the rest. Come and look here."

And he led Hans out into the Princess's pleasure-garden; a ghastly sight greeted him here! To many of the trees hung the wasted skeletons of three or four kings' sons who had wooed the Princess, but had not succeeded in guessing her thoughts. Every time the wind rustled the foliage of the trees, the dry skeletons rattled and clattered together; so horrible was the sight and sound, that the birds had all been scared away, and now never durst rest their wings in this grove of death; the flowers were tied up to human bones instead of sticks, and grisly skulls grinned from behind every flower-pot, or every plant that required shade from the winds. A pleasant garden, in truth, was this for a Princess!

"Here thou mayest see," said the old King to Hans, "what thy fate will be. Give up the mad thought, I beseech thee! Think, too, how unhappy it will make me; have pity on me if not on thyself!"

Hans kissed the hand of the kind old King, and tried to comfort him with the assurance that he felt quite sure that he should succeed in winning the Princess, and that he could not possibly live without her.

And now the Princess herself, returning from her excursion, came riding into the court of the palace with all her ladies. The King and Hans went up to her and wished her good-day. She was so gracious and friendly, she offered her hand to Hans, and he loved her more passionately than ever, and could less than ever persuade himself that she was really the wicked sorceress that people took her to be.

They returned to the saloon, and a troop of prettily dressed little pages came in, and handed round sweetmeats and gingerbread nuts to every one,— the King, the Princess, her ladies, and Hans. But the old King was so sad and downcast that he could enjoy nothing, and the gingerbread-nuts were too hard for his teeth.

THE FELLOW-TRAVELLERS.

It was settled that Hans should come up to the palace again next morning, and that the judges and the whole assembled council were to be present as witnesses to the Princess's game of "What are my thoughts like?" If he guessed rightly this first time, he was to come again in like manner on the two following days; but, hitherto, not one of the suitors to the Princess's hand had survived the first day of trial.

Hans did not lose his confidence in the least; on the contrary, his spirits rose more and more; he thought only of the beautiful Princess, and would not believe but that he should succeed—how he knew not, and would not trouble himself with thinking about it. Almost dancing with joy, he made his way back out of the town to the roadside inn, where his fellow-traveller was awaiting him.

And here he could never weary of telling how kind and gracious the Princess had been towards him, and of extolling her surpassing loveliness. Already he longed most ardently for the morrow, when he might again go to the palace, and must guess the thought of his beloved.

But his fellow-traveller sadly shook his head. "I love thee so much!" he said, "and we might yet have stayed a long while together, and now I must lose thee already! My poor dear Hans! But I will not disturb thy happiness on the last evening, perhaps, that we may spend together. We will be merry, right merry; to-morrow, when thou art gone, I shall have time enough to weep."

All the people in the city had heard by this time of the arrival of a new suitor to the Princess, and there was general mourning in consequence. The theatres were shut up, the gardens and promenades were deserted, the King and the priests spent the day kneeling in the churches, and the cake-women tied black-crape sashes round their pretty sugar figures, for it was thought impossible that Hans could fare better than the suitors that had come before him.

That evening the stranger ordered a large bowl of punch to be brought in, and told Hans that he must drink to the Princess's health. But no sooner had Hans emptied his first glass than he felt his eyelids grow so heavy that he could no longer hold them up—he sank back in his chair and fell into a sound sleep. His fellow-traveller lifted him gently into bed, and it being now quite night and dark, he took out the large wings which he had cut off from the dead swan, and fastened them upon his shoulders. Then, taking the bundle of ferns the old woman had given him, he opened the window and flew out of the city straight to the marble palace, where he concealed himself in the corner of a bow-window belonging to the Princess's sleeping-room.

Perfect stillness reigned throughout the city; at last the clock struck a quarter to twelve, whereupon the Princess's window opened, and the Princess herself, clad in a loose white mantle, and borne up by long black wings, flew out. Over the town she flew, and towards a high mountain in the distance, but Hans' fellow-traveller instantly made himself invisible, and followed the Princess through the air close behind her. A pleasant excursion was that! but the stranger waved his bundle of ferns three times in the air, muttering, "Blow, winds! blow, north, south, east, and west!" whereupon the four winds arose and struggled in the air, beat in the Princess's face, and took hold of her white over-wrapper, and kept it fluttering to and fro, till it spread out like a wide ship-sail on either side of her, the moon shining through it.

"How cold it is!—how dreadfully cold!—and how windy!" sighed the Princess. At last she reached the mountain, and tapped it with her hand, whereupon a deep hollow rumbling, like thunder, was heard from within, and the mountain yawned asunder and opened. The Princess entered, Hans' fellow-traveller still following; no one could see him, however, he was invisible.

They passed through a long wide passage, whose walls glistened strangely, for more than a thousand red-hot spiders were running up and down them. The passage led into a large hall built of silver and gold; flowers, some red, some blue, and as large as sunflowers, glistened from the walls; but if any one had been so far deluded as to approach near to pluck them, he would soon have discovered that their green twisted stalks were in reality poisonous snakes, and that the false flowers themselves were formed by the blue and red fire that issued from the venomous mouths of these snakes. The ceiling was sown with glow-worms and bats, which kept flapping their thin bluish wings to and fro incessantly. In the centre of the hall stood a throne, supported upon four horse-skeletons, harnessed with the web of the fiery-red spiders; the throne itself was of milk-white glass, and the cushions inside it were supplied by little black mice, who were continually snapping and biting at one another's tails. Above it was a canopy of crimson spiders' webs, studded with the prettiest little green flies, all glittering like precious stones. On the throne sat an aged Troll, wearing a crown on his great ugly head, and holding a sceptre in his hand. He kissed the Princess on the forehead, and bade her sit down on the throne beside him. And now the band struck up. Great black grasshoppers played on the Jew's harp, and the owl came out with his "Tu-whit, tu-whoo!" as chief vocalist. It was, in sooth, a ridiculous concert. Little black Nisses, with Wills-o'-the-wisp on their caps, danced round and round the hall. The other personages of the Troll's court certainly entered the saloon with a very grand air, and did their best to keep up the dignity befitting their gay attire; but it did not need the keen-sightedness of our stranger traveller, who, having stationed himself close behind the throne, saw and heard everything, though no one could see him, to perceive what shams they were; for, in reality, they were nothing else than broomsticks with cabbage heads, which the Troll had bewitched into some sort of life, and to which he had given gaily-embroidered dresses. They just served to keep up his state, and what did he want more?

After the dancing had gone on for some time, the Princess told the Trold that she had a new suitor, and asked what she should think of next morning when he came up to the palace to guess her thoughts.

"Listen! I will tell thee," replied the Troll. "Choose something very easy and simple, and he will be the less likely to think of it. Think on thine own shoe—that he will never guess. Then you can have his head cut off. But, mind! don't forget to bring me his eyes to-morrow night—I will have them, or I will have thine own. Remember our compact!"

The Princess bowed very low, and promised not to forget. Presently the Troll repeated some magic words, which made the mountain groan and yawn asunder, and the Princess flew out again. But Hans' fellow-traveller followed her, swift as thought, and with his wizard ferns conjured up the four winds to blow more strongly than before; and the Princess sighed heavily over the cold and windy weather, and made all possible haste to get back to the bow-window of her sleeping-room. And the stranger, who was right weary of his night-exercise, flew quickly back to the room where Hans was asleep, took off his wings, and laid himself down to rest.

It was quite early in the morning when Hans awoke. He left his bed, and his fellow-traveller arose also; he would not tell Hans of his flying adventure during the night, but, without making any mention of the mountain Troll, he begged Hans, when he went up to the palace, to ask the Princess if she had not thought of her own shoe.

"I may as well guess that as anything else," was Hans' reply; "and truly I believe the angels may have whispered it to thee during the night, my friend, for I hope and trust they are on my side. But now let us bid each other farewell, for, if I do not guess right, I shall hardly see thee again."

So Hans went on his way to the palace. The wide festal saloon was crowded with people. The councillors were seated in large easy-chairs, with cushions of eider-down to lean their heads upon, because they all had the head-ache through having so many hard questions to think about. The old King rose up when Hans came in, and began drying his eyes with a white pocket-handkerchief. Presently the Princess entered. She looked lovelier even than yesterday, and greeted the whole assembly with such a winning smile,—such enchanting grace! But to Hans she held out her hand, saying, "Good morning, my friend."

And now the game began:—"What are my thoughts like?" asked the Princess; and she looked at Hans so archly, so merrily, as she spoke! But no sooner did she hear him bring out in answer the single word, "Shoe!" than she turned pale, and all her limbs began to tremble. This availed her nothing—she could not deny that he had guessed right.

Hurrah! how glad the good old King was! he jumped up and kicked his slippers into the air for joy; and the spectators all clapped their hands, some to applaud the King, some to show how pleased they were at Hans' victory—for victory it was for this one day, at least.

His comrade, too, was well satisfied when he heard of his success; but as for Hans himself, he folded his hands in quiet thankfulness that he had been saved from peril of death. The very next day he must undergo his second trial.

The evening passed just like the foregoing evening. As soon as Hans was asleep, his fellow-traveller flew out, and followed the Princess to the weird mountain; this time, however, he took with him not only the old woman's fern bundle, but one of the willow-boughs, and called up therewith a storm, not only of wind but of rain; in torrents it poured upon the poor Princess, and right glad was she to reach the shelter of the mountain. Within it, no one perceived the stranger, but he was there, nevertheless, and heard and saw everything that went on. This time it was settled that the Princess should think of her glove; Hans received his instructions accordingly, and could not but guess aright: and such joy as there was at the palace!

The whole court cut capers just as they had seen the King do on the former occasion; but as for the Princess, she threw herself down upon a sofa, and would not speak a single word.

And now Hans had but to guess once more. If he succeeded on the third day also, the beautiful Princess, whom he loved so passionately, would become his bride, and he should be king over the whole country after her old father's death; but if he guessed wrong, then, alas! he must lose his life, and his bright blue eyes would be carried as a tribute to the wicked mountain Troll.

Hans went to rest earlier than usual that evening, and soon fell into a sound and peaceful slumber. His fellow-traveller then fastened the swan-wings on his shoulders, buckled the sabre to his girdle, took all the three wizard wands in his hand, and, thus equipped, flew off to the marble palace.

The night was pitch-dark, and the wind had risen already; but when the traveller had waved aloft each of his wands three times, thus stirring up the threefold powers of wind, rain, and hail, a most tremendous storm burst forth. The trees in the garden of skeletons bowed like reeds to the blast; it lightened every moment, and the thunder rolled on continuously, as though it would never cease the whole night long. The bow-window opened, and the Princess fluttered out into the wild atmosphere. She was pale as death; not that she was afraid of tempests, for she was wont to delight in them; but this night, when her white mantle spread out around her like a sail unfurled by the wind, when the rain streamed pitilessly on her face, and the hailstones pelted her on all sides, she hovered on slowly and with pain, and her wings could scarcely bear her up; she expected to sink to the ground every instant. At last she won the weird mountain.

"There's such a hailstorm without!" said she, on entering; "I never knew such weather as it is."

"One may have too much even of a good thing," replied the Troll.

And now she told him, shivering with fear and dread all the while she spoke, that Hans had most unaccountably guessed right the second time; if he should win on the third trial also, the game would be his, indeed, and she might never again come to the weird mountain, never again pay her tribute to the Troll, as she had sworn to do—her life would be forfeit; or, even if the Troll would free her from her engagement, she could not live, since she should be forbidden to practise the magic arts it had cost her so much to learn. And she wept most bitterly.

"Never fear! he shall not guess this time, depend upon it!" replied the Troll; "I will find something he has never thought of in his life, unless, indeed, he be a greater wizard than myself. But now let us be right merry!" And he took the Princess by the hand, and danced with her all round the hall, the Nisses and Wills-o'-the-Wisp all doing the like, and the red spiders springing merrily up and down the glistening walls. The owl tu-whooed and tu-whitted with all his might; the crickets chirped, and the black grasshoppers blew on the Jew's harps. A regular wizard ball was that.

After they had danced themselves weary, the Princess said she must hasten home, for she feared she might be missed at the palace. The Troll, who seemed unwilling to let her go, then declared he would escort her, so that they might have the more time together.

So away they flew through the storm, the traveller waving his three wands close behind them; never had the Troll been out in such a hurricane. When they arrived at the palace he bade the Princess farewell, and at the same moment whispered to her, "Think of my head!" But Hans' fellow-traveller overheard it, and while the Princess was slipping into her room through the window and just as the Troll was about

THE NEW YORK
PUBLIC LIBRARY

ASTOR, LENOX AND
TILDEN FOUNDATIONS.
C　　　　　　L

THE FELLOW-TRAVELLERS.

Page 297.

to turn round and fly back to his mountain, he seized him by the long black beard, and, drawing his sabre, cut off his huge demon-head from his shoulders. The trunk he threw into the sea, to be food for the fishes; but the head he merely dipped into the water, and then wrapped it up in his silk handkerchief, took it home with him to the inn, and lay down to rest.

Next morning he gave the bundle to Hans, charging him not to untie it until the Princess called upon him to declare what she was thinking of.

There was such a crowd in the King's hall that day, that the people all pressed one against the other, like radishes tied up in a bunch, and every man trod on his neighbour's toes. The judges and councillors all sat in their easy-chairs, with the soft eider-down cushions to lean their heads on, and the old King had on an entirely new suit of clothes; his gold crown, and his sceptre, too, had been fresh polished, and glittered marvellously. But the Princess was very pale, and was clad in black robes, as though she were going to a funeral.

"What are my thoughts like?" asked she of Hans, for the third time, and immediately he untied the handkerchief; but he started back with horror and amazement on beholding the hideous head of the mountain Troll. And a shudder thrilled through all the by-standers, and the Princess sat mute and motionless as a statue, and could not utter a syllable. At last she rose from her seat, and held out her snow-white hand to Hans, in token that he had guessed rightly this third time also, and thus had won the game. Looking neither at him nor at any one present, her eyes still riveted on the misshapen head in the handkerchief, and drawing in her breath heavily, she sighed rather than said, "Now art thou my lord and master! this evening must our bridals be solemnized."

"Oh! with all my heart!" cried the old King; "yes, this very evening; how glad I am!" And the whole assembly burst into a loud "hurrah!"

The band was called out to play in the streets, the church-bells were all set ringing, and the cake-women were in a great hurry to take the black crape off their sugar figures, for mourning was now changed into joy. Three oxen were roasted whole in the market-place, besides fowls and ducks without end; so that every one who wanted might come and have dinner. The fountains flowed with wine instead of water; and if you went into the baker's shop to buy a penny roll, he would give you six buns into the bargain—buns with currants in them too.

In the evening the whole city was illuminated, the soldiers fired their guns, the little boys ran about letting off crackers; there was eating and drinking, dancing and singing, in the palace, among all the fair ladies and gallant cavaliers of the court—no end to the rejoicings!

But amid all this gaiety the Princess remained pale and sad; she had no love for Hans in return for the love he bore her, and she still mourned for being debarred the practice of her secret arts. Hans at last went in despair to his fellow-traveller to ask his counsel how to win his fair bride's love, and to lure forth a smile from her face. And his fellow-traveller gave him a little phial, filled with a colourless liquid, like water, together with three feathers from the swan-wings, bidding him steep each of the three feathers in the liquid, and then sprinkle the Princess's forehead with the drops clinging to the feathers—three times must he sprinkle her with each of the three feathers, and thus she would become free from her enchantment.

Hans did exactly as his fellow-traveller had counselled him. He sprinkled the Princess's brow three times with the first feather, and she uttered a loud shriek, and was transformed into a coal-black swan, with fiery-red eyes. He sprinkled the black swan with the second feather, whereupon it became pure white, excepting one black ring encircling its slender throat. He steeped the third feather, and shook the drops three times over the white swan's head, and forthwith the swan was gone, and his own beloved and lovely Princess, —nay, a thousand times lovelier than ever, stood in its place, her cheeks glowing, her eyes sparkling so brightly, so meekly, and shedding tears of joy and thankfulness.

She now told him, that wandering alone a few years back near the weird mountain, the evening hour, when evil spirits hold their sway, came on. She was surprised by the mountain Troll within his domain, and in his own hour. He cast his wicked spells upon her, to make her serve his cruel purposes, and so potent were those spells that not even the death of the Troll himself could entirely release her from them. Again and again she thanked Hans for having freed her from their hateful enchantments.

The good old King and all his court rejoiced yet more after this change. Presently Hans' fellow-traveller, his wandering-staff in his hand, and his knapsack on his back, came to the place to ask for Hans. Hans embraced him very eagerly, entreating him to stay always with him, and share in his great happiness. But his fellow-traveller shook his head, saying, very kindly and mildly, "No, that cannot be; my time is up. I have now paid my debt. Rememberest thou not the dead man whom his evil-minded creditors would not have suffered to rest in his coffin? Thou didst give all thy substance to secure him peace and rest. I am that same dead man!"

And in the same moment he was gone.

The bridal festivities lasted for a whole month. Hans and his fair Princess loved each other dearly, and the good old King lived through many happy days, and delighted in nothing so much as in his tiny grand-children, who used to play with his bright sceptre, and "ride-a-cock-horse to Banbury cross" on his knees. But Hans, in the course of time, ruled over the whole country, and became a great and powerful monarch.

THE LEAPING-MATCH.

THE Flea, the Grasshopper, and the Frog, once wanted to try which of them could jump highest; so they invited the whole world, and anybody else who liked to come and see the grand sight. Three famous jumpers were they, as was seen by every one when they met together in the room.

"I will give my daughter to him who shall jump highest," said the King; "it would be too bad for you to have the trouble of jumping, and for us to offer you no prize."

The Flea was the first to introduce himself; he had such polite manners, and bowed to the company on every side, for he was of noble blood; besides, he was accustomed to the society of man, which had been a great advantage to him.

Next came the Grasshopper; he was not quite so slightly and elegantly formed as the Flea; however, he knew perfectly well how to conduct himself, and wore a green uniform, which belonged to him by right of birth. Moreover, he declared himself to have sprung from a very ancient and honourable Egyptian family, and that in his present home he was very highly esteemed; so much so, indeed, that he had been taken out of the field and put into a card-house three stories high, built on purpose for him, and all of court-cards, the coloured sides being turned inwards. As for the doors and windows in his house, they were cut out of the body of the Queen of Hearts. " And I can sing so well," added he, " that sixteen parlour-bred crickets, who have chirped and chirped ever since they were born, and yet could never get anybody to build them a card-house, after hearing me have fretted themselves ten times thinner than ever, out of sheer envy and vexation!"

Both the Flea and the Grasshopper knew excellently well how to make the most of themselves, and each considered himself quite an equal match for a Princess.

The Frog said not a word; however, it might be that he thought the more, and the house-dog, after going snuffing about him, confessed that the Frog must be of a good family. And the old councillor, who in vain received three orders to hold his tongue, declared that the Frog must be gifted with the spirit of prophecy, for that one could read on his back whether there was to be a severe or a mild winter, which, to be sure, is more than can be read on the back of the man who writes the weather-almanack.

" Ah, I say nothing for the present!" remarked the old King; " but I observe everything, and form my own private opinion thereupon."

And now the match began. The Flea jumped so high that no one could see what had become of him, and so they insisted that he had not jumped at all, " which was disgraceful, after he had made such a fuss!"

The Grasshopper jumped only half as high, but he jumped right into the King's face, and the King declared he was quite disgusted by his rudeness.

The Frog stood still as if lost in thought; at last people fancied he did not intend to jump at all.

" I'm afraid he is ill!" said the Dog; and he went snuffing at him again, when lo! all at once he made a little sidelong jump into the lap of the Princess, who was sitting on a low stool close by.

Then spoke the King—" There is nothing higher than my daughter, therefore he who jumps up to her jumps highest; but only a person of good understanding would ever have thought of that; and thus the Frog has shown us that he has understanding. He has brains in his head, that he has!"

And thus the Frog won the Princess.

"I jumped highest for all that!" exclaimed the Flea. "But it's all the same to me; let her have the stiff-legged, slimy creature, if she like him! I jumped highest, but I am too light and airy for this stupid world; the people can neither see me nor catch me; dulness and heaviness win the day with them!"

And so the Flea went into foreign service, where, it is said, he was killed.

And the Grasshopper sat on a green bank, meditating on the world and its goings on, and at length he repeated the Flea's last words,—"Yes, dulness and heaviness win the day!—dulness and heaviness win the day!" And then he again began singing his own peculiar, melancholy song,—and it is from him that we have learnt this history; and yet, my friend, though you read it here in a printed book, it may not be perfectly true.

THE ROSE-ELF.

IN the centre of a large garden there grew a rose-tree, full of lovely roses, and in one of these, the loveliest of all, dwelt a little Elf; he was so very, very little, that no human eye could see him. He had a bower behind each rose-petal; he was fair and slender as only a child can be, and had wings that reached from his shoulders down to his feet.

Oh, how fragrant were his chambers! and how bright and transparent their walls! they were formed by delicate, pale-coloured rose-leaves.

He spent the whole day in basking in the warm sunshine, flying from flower to flower, dancing on the butterfly's wings, and reckoning how many steps it took him to run over all the roads and foot-paths of a single lime-leaf; for what we call the veins of the leaf were to him roads and foot-paths, and the journey seemed almost endless. The sun set before he had ended his task; he had set off too late.

It now grew very cold, the dew fell fast, the wind blew, the best thing he could do was to make haste home; but though he did make all possible haste, the roses were all closed before he could reach them, and he could not get in—

not a single rose was open. The poor little Elf was greatly terrified; he had never before been out in the night air, he had always slumbered so sweetly behind the warm rose-leaves. Oh, it would certainly be the death of him!

At the other end of the garden he knew that there was an arbour of honey-suckles, whose flowers looked like great painted horns,—he resolved to get into one of these, and sleep there till morning. Accordingly, he flew to the spot. But hush! there were two persons in the arbour; a young, handsome man, and a most beautiful girl: they sat close together, wishing that they might never part again all their lives long; they loved each other so much,—more than the best child in the world can love his father and mother.

"And yet we must part!" said the young man. "Thy brother does not care about our happiness, and therefore he sends me far, far away, over the mountains, and across the wide ocean. Farewell, my sweet bride, for surely thou art my bride!"

And they embraced each other: and the young girl wept and gave him a rose: but before giving it to him, she impressed upon it a kiss so warm that the flower opened, whereupon the little Elf immediately flew in and leant his head against the delicate, fragrant walls. He could hear distinctly the words, "Farewell! farewell!" and he felt that the rose was placed in the young man's bosom; oh, how violently the heart throbbed within! the little Elf could not sleep at all for hearing the throbbing.

The rose was not suffered to remain long in its warm resting-place, the man soon took it out, and whilst he was walking alone through the dark wood, he kissed the flower so often and so vehemently, that our tiny Elf was well-nigh squeezed to death. He could feel through the rose-leaves how the man's lips were burning, and the rose opened more and more, just as though the hot mid-day sun were shining upon it.

But there came another man through the wood, looking gloomy and wrathful; it was the beautiful young girl's wicked brother; he drew out a sharp knife, and while the young lover was kissing the rose, he stabbed him to death, cut off his head, and buried both head and body in the moist earth under a lime-tree.

"Now he is dead, and we are rid of him!" thought the wicked brother: "he will never come back again. He was to have taken a long journey over the mountains, and beyond the sea; men often lose their lives in travelling, as he has done! He will never come back again, and my sister dares not question me about him."

So he shoved with his foot some withered leaves over the upturned earth, and then walked home amid the shades of night. But he did not go alone, as he imagined; the tiny Elf went with him, sitting rolled up in a withered lime-leaf which had fallen into the wicked man's hair while he was digging the grave. The man put on his hat, and then it was so dark for our little Elf, who was underneath, trembling with horror and indignation at the shameful deed he had witnessed.

By the morning the wicked man had reached his home; he took off his hat, and went into his sister's sleeping-room; the bright and beautiful girl lay dreaming of him whom she loved so well, and who, she imagined, was now wandering far away across mountain and forest. Her wicked brother bent over her with a hideous, devilish smile, the withered leaf fell out of his hair upon the counterpane, but he did not notice it, and went away, intending to sleep a little while himself. The Elf now glided out of the withered leaf, crept into the ear of the sleeping girl, and told her, as though in a dream, all about the horrible murder of her lover; he described to her the spot where her brother had buried the corpse, close under the lime-tree, and added, "In token that all I have told thee is not a mere dream, thou shalt find a withered leaf upon thy bed, when thou awakest!"

Oh, what bitter tears she shed when she awoke and actually found the withered lime-leaf on her bed! but she dared not speak to any one of her great affliction. The window was left open all day, so the little Elf could easily have flown out to the roses and other flowers in the garden; however, he could not find it in his heart to leave one who was so unhappy. A monthly rose-tree stood at the window, he got into one of its flowers, and sat looking at the poor girl. Her brother often came into the room, and seemed very merry, but she dared not speak a word to him of her heart's sorrow.

As soon as it was night, she stole out of the house and

going to the wood, to the place where the lime-tree grew, she swept away the dry leaves, and dug in the earth till she found the corpse of the murdered man. Oh, how she wept and prayed our Lord that she, too, might die!

Gladly would she have taken the corpse home with her, but that she could not do, so she took up the head, kissed the pale cold lips and closed eyes, and shook the earth out of the beautiful hair. "This I will keep!" said she; and then, after covering the dead body afresh with earth, she returned home, taking with her the head of the murdered young man, and also a little bough from a jasmine-tree that blossomed near the grave.

When she reached home she fetched the largest flower-pot she could find, put into it the head, covered it over with mould, and planted the slip of jasmine above it.

"Farewell, farewell!" whispered the little Elf; he could no longer bear to witness so much misery, and he flew into the garden to his own rose. But he found it was faded by this time,—only a few pale leaves were still clinging to the green calyx.

"Alas, how quickly does everything good and beautiful pass away!" sighed the Elf. At last he found a rose that would suit for his home, and laid himself down among its fragrant petals.

And from henceforth he flew every morning to the window of the poor girl's room, and every morning he found her standing over the flower-pot weeping. Her salt tears fell upon the jasmine; and day by day, as she grew paler and paler, the plant grew fresher and greener, one little shoot after another pushed forth, and the delicate white buds unfolded into flowers. And she kissed the flowers; but her wicked brother mocked her, and asked her if she had lost her wits,—he could not conceive why she was incessantly weeping over that jasmine.

One day she leaned her head against the flower-pot and fell asleep. And while she was sleeping thus, the little Rose-elf flew into the room; he crept into her ear, and repeated to her the conversation he had heard in the arbour on that sad evening, described to her the sweet-smelling rose, and told of the love that the Flower-spirits bore her. She dreamed very sweetly, and while she was dreaming her life departed,—she died a quiet, peaceful death; she was now at perfect rest with him whom she had loved so dearly.

And the blossoms of the jasmine opened their delicate white bells, and sent forth a fragrance wondrously sweet and strong. This was the only way in which they could bewail the dead.

But the wicked brother noticed the beautiful blooming shrub and its delicious odour, and, considering it now his property, he took it away into his sleeping-room, and placed it near the bed. The little Rose-elf followed it, flew from flower to flower, for in each flower there dwelt a little spirit, and to each he told of the murdered young man whose glossy hair lay in the mould under their roots,—told them of the wicked brother and the heart-broken sister.

"We know it," replied all the spirits of the flowers, "we know it. Have not we sprung forth from the rich dark tresses of the dead? We know it! we know it!" and they all nodded their heads in the strangest manner.

The Rose-elf could not conceive how they could take it so quietly, and he flew away to the Bees, who were gathering honey in the garden, and told the story to them. And the Bees told their Queen, and she gave orders that next morning they should all go and kill the murderer.

That very same night, however,— it was the first night after his sister's death —whilst the brother was asleep in the bed near which the jasmine-tree was placed, each little flower-cup opened, and out flew the Flower-spirits, invisible, but armed each with a poisoned arrow. They first crept into his ear, and made him dream of his sinful deed, and then flew through his parted lips, and stabbed him in the tongue with their poisonous shafts.

"Now we have avenged the dead," said they; and they flew back into the white jasmine-cups.

After day had dawned, the bed-room window being suddenly flung open, the Rose-elf flew in, followed by the Queen-bee and her whole swarm; they had come to sting the murderer to death.

But he was already dead. Some persons were standing round the bed, declaring, "The strong scent of the jasmines has killed him!"

The Rose-elf then understood that the Flower-spirits had taken vengeance on the murderer; he explained it to the

Queen-bee, and she, with her whole swarm, buzzed round the flower-pot in token of approval. In vain did people try to drive them off. At last a man took up the flower-pot, intending to carry it away, whereupon one of the Bees stung him in the hand, so that the pot fell to the ground and broke in pieces.

All who were present then saw the ghastly head of the murdered youth, and guessed that the dead man in the bed must be a murderer.

And the Queen-bee flew buzzing about in the garden, singing of the vengeance of the Flowers—of the Rose-elf—and how that behind the tiniest leaf there lurks a spirit who knows when crime is committed, and can punish the evil-doer.

THE FLYING TRUNK.

THERE was once a merchant, so rich that he might have paved the whole street where he lived, and an alley besides, with pieces of silver; but this he did not do—he knew another way of using his money, and whenever he laid out a shilling, he gained a crown in return. A merchant he lived, and a merchant he died.

All his money then went to his son. But the son lived merrily, and spent all his time in pleasures; went to masquerades every evening, made bank-notes into paper-kites, and played at ducks and drakes in the pond with gold pieces instead of stones. In this manner his money soon vanished, until at last he had only a few pennies left, and his wardrobe was reduced to a pair of slippers and an old dressing-gown. His friends cared no more about him, now that they could no longer walk abroad with him. One of them, however, more good-natured than the rest, sent him an old trunk, with this advice, " Pack up, and be off!"

This was all very fine, but he had nothing that he could pack up; so he put himself into the trunk.

It was a droll trunk. When the lock was pressed close it could fly. The merchant's son did press the lock, and lo, up flew the trunk with him through the chimney, high into the clouds, on and on, higher and higher. The lower part cracked, which rather frightened him, for, if it had broken in two, a pretty fall he would have had!

However, it descended safely, and he found himself in Turkey. He hid the trunk under a heap of dry leaves in a wood, and walked into the next town; he could do so very well, for, among the Turks, everybody goes about clad as he was, in dressing-gown and slippers. He met a nurse, carrying a little child in her arms. "Harkye, Turkish nurse," quoth he. "What palace is that with the high windows close by the town?"

"The King's daughter dwells there," replied the nurse. "It has been prophesied of her that she shall be made very unhappy by a lover, and therefore no one may visit her except when the King and Queen are with her."

"Thank you," said the merchant's son; and he immediately went back into the wood, sat down in his trunk, flew up to the roof of the palace, and crept through the window into the Princess's apartment.

She was lying asleep on the sofa. She was so beautiful that the merchant's son could not help kneeling down to kiss her hand, whereupon she awoke, and was not a little frightened at the sight of this unexpected visitor; but he told her that he was the Turkish Prophet, and had come down from the sky on purpose to woo her; and on hearing this she was well pleased.

So they sat down side by side, and he talked to her about her eyes, how that they were beautiful dark-blue seas, and that thoughts and feelings floated like mermaidens therein; and he spoke of her brow, how that it was a fair, snowy mountain, with splendid halls and pictures, and many other suchlike things he told her.

Oh, these were charming stories! and thus he wooed the Princess, and she immediately said "Yes!"

"But you must come here on Saturday," said she; "the King and Queen have promised to drink tea with me that evening; they will be so proud and so pleased when they hear that I am to marry the Turkish Prophet! And mind you tell them a very pretty story, for they are exceedingly fond of stories; my mother likes them to be very moral and aristocratic, and my father likes them to be merry, so as to make him laugh."

"Yes, I shall bring no other bridal present than a tale," replied the merchant's son; and here they parted, but not before the Princess had given her lover a sabre all covered with gold. He knew excellently well what use to make of this present.

So he flew away, bought a new dressing-gown, and then sat down in the wood to compose the tale which was to be ready by Saturday, and, certainly, he found composition not the easiest thing in the world.

At last he was ready, and, at last, Saturday came.

The King, the Queen, and the whole court, were waiting tea for him at the Princess's palace. The suitor was received with much ceremony.

"Will you not tell us a story?" asked the Queen; "a story that is instructive and full of deep meaning."

"But let it make us laugh," said the King.

"With pleasure," replied the merchant's son; and now you must hear his story.

"There was once a bundle of Matches, who were all extremely proud of their high descent, for their genealogical tree,— that is to say, the tall fir-tree, from which each of them was a splinter,— had been a tree of great antiquity, and distinguished by its height from all the other trees of the forest. The Matches were now lying on the mantel-piece, between a Tinder-box and an old iron Saucepan, and to these two they often talked about their youth. 'Ah, when we were upon the green branches,' said they; 'when we really lived upon green branches — that was a happy time! Every morning and evening we had diamond-tea, that is dew; the whole day long we had sunshine, at least whenever the sun shone, and all the little birds used to tell stories to us. It might easily be seen, too, that we were rich, for other trees were clothed with leaves only during the summer; whereas, our family could afford to wear green clothes both summer and winter. But at last came the wood-cutters, then was the great revolution, and our family was dispersed; the paternal trunk obtained a situation as mainmast to a magnificent ship, which could sail round the world if it chose, the boughs were transported to various places, and our vocation was henceforth to kindle lights for low, common people. Now you will understand how it comes to pass that persons of such high descent as we are should be living in a kitchen.'

"'To be sure, mine is a very different history,' remarked the iron Saucepan, near which the Matches were lying. 'From the moment I came into the world, until now, I have been rubbed and scrubbed, and boiled over and over again—oh, how many times! I love to have to do with what is solidly good, and am really of the first importance in this house. My only recreation is to stand clean and bright upon this mantel-piece after dinner, and hold some rational conversation with my companions. However, excepting the Water-pail, who now and then goes out into the court, we all of us lead a very quiet, domestic life here. Our only news-monger is the Turf-basket, but he talks in such a democratic way about 'government' and 'the people'—why, I assure you, not long ago, there was an old Jar standing here, who was so much shocked by what he heard said, that he fell down from the mantel-piece, and broke into a thousand pieces!—that Turf-basket is a Liberal, that's the fact—'

"'Now you talk too much,' interrupted the Tinder-box, and the steel struck the flint, so that the sparks flew out. 'Why should we not spend a pleasant evening?'

"'Yes, let us settle who is of highest rank among us!' proposed the Matches.

"'Oh no, for my part, I would rather not speak of myself,' objected the Earthenware Pitcher. 'Suppose we have an intellectual entertainment? I will begin, I will relate something of every-day life, such as we have all experienced; one can easily transport oneself into it, and that is so interesting! Near the Baltic, among the Danish beech-groves—'

"'That is a capital beginning!' cried all the Plates at once; 'it will certainly be just the sort of story for me!'

"'Yes, there I spent my youth in a very quiet family; the furniture was rubbed, the floors were washed, clean curtains were hung up every fortnight.'

"'How very interesting! what a charming way you have of describing things!' said the Hair-broom. 'Any one might guess immediately that it is a lady who is speaking; the tale breathes such a spirit of cleanliness!'

"'Very true; so it does!' exclaimed the Water-pail, and

in the excess of his delight he gave a little jump, so that some of the water splashed upon the floor.

"And the Pitcher went on with her tale, and the end proved as good as the beginning.

"All the Plates clattered applause, and the Hair-broom took some green parsley out of the sand-hole and crowned the Pitcher, for he knew that this would vex the others, and thought he, 'If I crown her to-day, she will crown me to-morrow.'

"'Now I will dance,' said the Fire-tongs, and accordingly she did dance; and oh! it was wonderful to see how high she threw one of her legs up into the air; the old Chair-cover in the corner tore with horror at seeing her. 'Am not I to be crowned too?' asked the Tongs, and she was crowned forthwith.

"'These are the vulgar rabble!' thought the Matches.

"The Tea-urn was now called upon to sing, but she had a cold, she said, she could only sing when she was boiling; however, this was all her pride and affectation, the fact was she never cared to sing except when she was standing on the parlour-table before company.

"On the window-ledge lay an old Quill-pen, with which the maids used to write; there was nothing remarkable about her, except that she had been dipped too low in the ink; however she was proud of that. 'If the Tea-urn does not choose to sing,' quoth she, 'she may let it alone; there is a Nightingale in the cage hung just outside, he can sing; to be sure, he has never learnt the notes,—never mind, we will not speak evil of any one this evening!'

"'I think it highly indecorous,' observed the Tea-kettle, who was the vocalist of the kitchen, and a half-brother of the Tea-urn's, 'that a foreign bird should be listened to. Is it patriotic? I appeal to the Turf-basket.'

"'I am only vexed,' said the Turf-basket; 'I am vexed from my inmost soul that such things are thought of at all. Is it a becoming way of spending the evening? Would it not be much more rational to reform the whole house, and establish a totally new order of things, rather more according to nature? Then every one would get into his right place, and I would undertake to direct the revolution. What say you to it? That would be something worth the doing!'

"' Oh, yes, we will make a grand commotion!' cried they all. Just then the door opened—it was the servant-maid. They all stood perfectly still, not one dared stir, yet there was not a single kitchen-utensil among them all but was thinking about the wonderful things he could have done, and how great was his superiority over the others. 'Ah, if I had chosen it,' thought each of them, 'what a merry evening we might have had!'

"The maid took the Matches and struck a light—oh, how they sputtered and blazed up!

"' Now every one may see,' thought they, 'that we are of highest rank; what a splendid, dazzling light we give, how glorious!'—and in another moment they were burnt out."

"That is a capital story," said the Queen! "I quite felt myself transported into the kitchen;—yes, thou shalt have our daughter!"

"With all my heart," said the King; "on Monday thou shalt marry our daughter." They said "Thou" to him now, since he was so soon to become one of the family. The wedding was a settled thing; and on the evening preceding the whole city was illuminated; cakes, buns, and sugar-plums, were thrown out among the people; all the little boys in the streets stood upon tip-toes, shouting " Hurrah!" and whistling through their fingers—it was famous!

"Well, I suppose I ought to do my part too," thought the merchant's son; so he went and bought sky-rockets, squibs, Catherine-wheels, Roman-candles, and all kinds of fireworks conceivable; put them all into his trunk, and flew up into the air, letting them off as he flew.

Hurrah! what a glorious sky-rocket was that?

All the Turks jumped up to look, so hastily that their slippers flew about their ears, such a meteor they had never seen before. Now they might be sure that it was indeed the Prophet who was to marry their Princess.

As soon as the merchant's son had returned in his trunk to the wood, he said to himself, "I will now go into the city and hear what people say about me, and what sort of figure I made in the air." And, certainly, this was a very natural idea.

Oh what strange accounts were given! Every one whom

he accosted had beheld the bright vision in a way peculiar to himself, but all agreed that it was marvellously beautiful.

"I saw the great Prophet with my own eyes," declared one; "he had eyes like sparkling stars, and a beard like foaming water."

"He flew enveloped in a mantle of fire," said another; "the prettiest little cherubs were peeping forth from under its folds."

Yes; he heard of many beautiful things, and the morrow was to be his wedding-day.

He now went back to the wood, intending to get into his trunk again, but where was it?

Alas! the trunk was burnt. One spark from the fireworks had been left in it, and set it on fire; the trunk now lay in ashes. The poor merchant's son could never fly again, could never again visit his bride.

She sat the live long day upon the roof of her palace expecting him; she expects him still; he, meantime, goes about the world telling stories, but none of his stories are so pleasant as that one which he related in the Princess's palace about the Brimstone Matches.

THE OLD STREET LAMP.

HAVE you never heard the history of the Old Street Lamp? Not that it is so extraordinarily entertaining, but I think it will bear telling just for once.

A decent, respectable Old Street Lamp was the one of which I speak; for many, many years she had done good service, but was now to be cashiered. For the very last evening she sat on the lamp-post, giving light to the street, and she felt very much as a superannuated ballet-dancer feels when she is dancing for the last time, and knows that to-morrow and ever after she will sit alone in her attic-chamber, morning, noon, and night, unthought of and uncared for by the generous public. Our Lamp felt just such a horror of the coming day, for she knew that she would then be taken, for the first time in her life, into the Council-room, to be surveyed by the "six-and-thirty men" of the Town-council, in order that they might decide whether she were or were not any longer fit for service. Then, too, would it be determined whether she should be sent out to one of the bridges to give light there, or, into the country, to one of the manufactories, or, perhaps, to an ironfoundry, to be melted down and made into something new. And this last probability was especially painful to her, for she feared that if she were made into something new she would retain no recollection of ever having been a Street Lamp. Besides, whatever became of her, she was sure to be separated from the watchman and his wife, whom she had known so long that she had learnt to consider herself quite one of their family. The watchman had been made a watchman just at the very same time that she was made a lamp. His wife was somewhat proud and finical in those days, only when she passed the Street Lamp of an evening did she deign to throw a glance up at her—never by day. Now, on the contrary, in these latter years, when all three, watchman, wife, and Lamp, had grown old, the wife had become more friendly, had often cleaned out the Lamp and given her fresh oil. Very honourable people were this man and wife, they had never cheated the Lamp of a single drop that was her due.

It was her last night in the street, and to-morrow she must go into the Council-room; these were two gloomy thoughts for the Lamp, and, naturally enough, she burned with a dimmed and feeble light. But other thoughts besides these passed across her; she had shone upon so many things, she had seen so much, perhaps as much as "the six-and-thirty men;" although she never would have said so, for she was a really modest, decorous Old Lantern, and would on no account have given offence to any one, least of all to her superiors. She remembered so much, and in the midst of her recollections her flame suddenly blazed up high as though she were thinking, "Yes, and there are a few, too, who will remember me. There was, for instance, that handsome young man—ah! it is many years ago now—who came with a letter in his hand, it was written on rose-coloured paper, so pretty, so delicate, and with gilt edges, and it was in a lady's hand-writing; he read the letter twice over, and then kissed it, and looked up at me, and his two eyes seemed to say, 'I am the very happiest man in the world!' Ah, none but he and I knew what was written in that first letter from his betrothed bride. And I remember well seeing two other eyes; it is strange how thoughts spring up in one. There was a splendid funeral passing through the street, such a beautiful young lady lay in her coffin inside the carriage, wreaths of flowers were thrown upon the coffin, and so many bright torches were there in the procession, that my dim light was quite put out by them; a great crowd of people followed the procession; but after they were all passed by, and the torches out of sight, and I looked around me, I saw some one standing by the post weeping: never shall I forget those two sorrowful eyes that then glanced up at me!"

Thus many different thoughts passed across the Old Street Lamp, on her last evening of public service. The sentinel upon guard, when he is relieved, at least knows his successor, and can exchange a few words with him, but the Lamp knew not who was to take her place, and thus could not, as otherwise she might have done, give him one or two useful hints concerning rain and sleet, or show how far the moonlight was wont to spread over the pavement, or from what side the wind blew.

On the gutter-board stood three candidates for the vacant office; they had presented themselves to the Lamp, under the idea that she would have to appoint her own successor. The first of these was a herring's head, which, you know, shines in the dark, and this herring's head was of opinion that his being elevated to the lamp-post would be a great saving of oil. The second was a piece of tinder, which, as it declared, shone brighter in the dark than a stock-fish even; besides, it was a fragment from a tree that had once been the glory and pride of the forest. The third candidate was a glow-worm; how she had got there the Lamp could not conceive; however, there she was, and glittering very prettily, but the herring's head and the piece of tinder were both ready to take their oaths that she could only shine at certain times, and that, consequently, she was quite out of the question.

The Old Lamp explained that not one of them gave sufficient light to be fit to take her place, but this none of the three would believe; and so, when they heard that it was not for the Lamp to choose her successor, they said that they were very glad of it, for that she was too much decayed to be able to choose with judgment.

Just then the Wind came rushing round the corner of the street; he blew through the smoke-cowl upon the Old Lantern, exclaiming, "What is this that I hear? that thou wilt really leave us to-morrow? Is this actually the last evening that I shall meet thee here? Well, if it must be so, I will at least make thee a parting gift — I will blow into thy brain-pan, so that not only shalt thou remember clearly and plainly whatever thou hast seen and heard, but whenever anything is told or read aloud in thy presence, thou shalt be so clear-headed as to see it as in a picture!"

"Ah, that is a valuable gift, indeed!" replied the Old Street Lamp. "Many thanks!—if only I am not melted down——"

"We must hope that will not happen," said the Wind. "And now I blow this faculty into thee; if thou canst get many such gifts thou mayest still enjoy a comfortable old age."

"If only I am not melted down!" sighed the Lamp. "Or canst thou, perhaps, even in that case, secure me my memory?"

"Old Lantern, be reasonable!" exhorted the Wind, and again he blew. And now the Moon stepped forth from the clouds. "What will you give?" inquired the Wind.

"I shall give just nothing at all!" was her reply. "I am now on the wane, and lanterns have never shone for me, long as I have shone for lanterns." And accordingly the Moon retired behind the clouds again, for she was determined not to be plagued into giving anything.

Presently a drop of Water fell down upon the cover of the Lamp; it was like a drop from a roof, but it declared that it came from the grey clouds, and was sent as a gift, perhaps the very best gift imaginable. "I penetrate into thee, so as to enable thee in one night, if thou shouldst wish it, to become rusty, and thus fall to pieces and return to dust." But to the Lamp this seemed a miserable gift, and so seemed it to the Wind. "Has no one a better—has no one a better to offer?" whistled he as loud as he could, and in that moment there fell a bright shooting-star, glittering in a long trail down the air.

"What was that?" cried the Herring's Head. "Was that a star falling down? I verily believe it went into the Lamp! Well, to be sure, if the office is sought by people of such very high station as that, we had best give up the idea of it!" and so he did, and the two other candidates did the same. But the Lamp suddenly flared up so high and bright: "That was a charming gift!" said she. "The brilliant stars above, whom I have always delighted in so much, and who shine so beautifully, as I have never been able to shine, although it has been the grand aim and effort of my life so to do,—those brilliant, beaming stars have taken heed of me, a poor old lantern, and one of them has come down to me with a rare gift,—so that in future all that I can myself remember and see so plainly shall also be seen by those whom I love!—a precious gift, indeed, for every enjoyment that cannot be shared with another is only half an enjoyment."

"Very rightly thought; the sentiment does thee honour!" said the Wind. "It seems, though, thou dost not know that unless a wax-candle is lighted inside thee, no one will be able to see any pictures through thy means. But the stars never thought of that, they imagine that everything that shines here below has at least one wax-candle in it. But now I am right weary," added the Wind; "I will lay myself down to rest a little while." And so he lay down to rest.

Next day—but we may as well pass over the next day;—next evening the Lamp lay in an arm-chair—and where? In the old watchman's room. He had begged of the "six-and-thirty-men," in consideration of his long and faithful services to be allowed to keep the Old Lamp for his own; they laughed at his odd request and gave it him; and so now the Lamp lay in the arm-chair, close by the warm stove, and she seemed to have grown so much larger as nearly to fill the great arm-chair. And the old people were sitting at supper, and every now and then they threw a kind, friendly glance at the Old Lamp, as though they would gladly have given her a place at the table. The room wherein they dwelt was properly a cellar; however, it was tolerably warm and comfortable, and very clean and neat; the door was bound round with list, there were curtains to the bedstead and the little windows, and on the window-ledges stood two such strange-looking flower-pots! Neighbour Christian, the sailor, had brought them home from the Indies—whether from the East or the West the old people did not know,—they were two earthenware elephants, without backs, and hollow inside, and out of the mould with which they were filled sprang up from one of them the most delicate young leeks—that was their kitchen-garden: from the other, a large geranium full of blossoms—that was their flower-garden. On the wall hung a large coloured print of "The Congress at Vienna,"—there were seen

Kings and Emperors both, all so grand! A clock, with heavy leaden weights, kept up an incessant "tick, tick;" it always went too fast, but that was better than going too slow,—at least so said the old folks. And they ate their evening meal; and the Old Street Lamp, as before said, lay in the arm-chair close by the warm stove, and she felt as though she were ruthlessly tossed hither and thither amid the wide world. But when the old watchman looked at her, and began to talk of what they two had lived through together, in moonlight and darkness, in rain and in mist, in the bright, brief summer nights, and in the long, severe hours of winter, when the snow-flakes drifted thickly about them, and he was so glad to get back to the shelter of his cellar-home,—then, while he talked thus, all was right again with the Old Lamp, for she saw all he spoke of, and she knew that the Wind had not deceived her.

They were so brisk and busy, those old people, not a single hour of theirs was ever dozed or dawdled away. On Sunday afternoons some book or other was always brought forward, generally a book of travels, and the old man would read aloud about Africa, about its vast forests and the wild elephants that roamed at large among them, and the old woman would listen so attentively, and cast a look at the earthenware elephants that served her as flower-pots. "Yes, I can almost fancy that!" she would say. And the Lamp wished so fervently that a wax-candle were lighted and put inside her, for then the good old woman would actually see the whole scene pictured visibly before her, just as the Lamp saw it—the tall trees, with their thickly-leaved, intertwining boughs, the naked black men on horseback, and whole herds of elephants, reeds and underwood breaking and crackling under their broad feet.

"What can all my rare gifts avail when no wax-candle is lit within me?" sighed the Lamp. "They have nothing but train-oil and tallow-candles, and neither of those will do."

One day, however, a number of wax-candle ends were brought into the cellar; the larger pieces were burnt out in the candlestick, and the smaller ones the old woman used to wax her thread with when she was at work. This was worse than ever! Here were wax-candles in plenty, and no one ever thought of putting one little piece into the Lamp

"So here I stand with all my rare gifts!" thought the Lamp. "I see so many charming pictures pass before me, but I may never share the enjoyment with you, my friends! Alas, you do not know that I can change these bare white walls to the richest tapestry, to glorious, leafy woods, to everything that you can desire to see,— alas, you know it not!"

The Lamp was continually being rubbed clean, and in the corner where it stood it was so placed that every one's eyes fell upon it; people, truly enough, called it a piece of old rubbish, but the old couple cared nothing for that — they loved it.

One day — it was the old watchman's birthday — his wife came up to the Lamp, saying, with a smile, "I will get up a little illumination in his honour;" and the Lamp's iron hat cracked, for she thought, "Now, then, I shall have a wax-candle!" But oil, not wax, was given her; she burned all the evening long, and she now felt sure that the gift the stars had given her, the best gift of all, must needs remain a hidden treasure, as far as this present life was concerned. Then she dreamt,— for a Lamp so highly gifted as she was must surely be able to dream,— she dreamt that the old people were dead, and that she herself had been carried to an ironfoundry to be melted down. Very much frightened was she, as frightened as when she was taken into the Council-room to be examined by "the six-and-thirty men:" and yet, although she knew she had the power of becoming rust and dust if she chose, she did not choose it; and so it came to pass that she was cast into the furnace, and became a most beautiful little iron candlestick, intended to hold wax-tapers, and wax-tapers only; it was in the form of an angel holding a bouquet of flowers, and in the centre of the bouquet the wax-candle was placed, and the candlestick itself was set on a green writing-desk. And the room around it was such a pretty room; books were scattered about, and beautiful pictures hung upon the walls — it was a poet's room, and all that he imagined and wrote about seemed whirling round — the chamber becoming now a deep, gloomy forest,— now a sun-lit plain, scattered with hamlets, the stork striding about on his long legs,— now a stately ship, tossing nigh on the waves of the heaving ocean!

"O! what rare gifts are mine!" thought the Old Lamp,

when she awoke. "Almost could I long to be melted down!—but no, that must not be while the old folks live. They love me for my own sake, I am like their child to them, and they have rubbed me clean, and given me fresh oil for so many years, and I am as well off here, and as honoured as 'The Congress at Vienna.' I ought certainly to be contented with my lot!"

And from henceforth she had more inward peace: and surely this respectable Old Street Lamp deserved to be at peace—don't you think she did?

THE LITTLE MATCH-GIRL.

IT was dreadfully cold, it was snowing fast, and almost dark; the evening—the last evening of the old year—was drawing in. But, cold and dark as it was, a poor little girl, with bare head and feet, was still wandering about the streets. When she left her home she had slippers on, but they were much too large for her—indeed, properly, they belonged to her mother—and had dropped off her feet whilst she was running very fast across the road, to get out of the way of two carriages. One of the slippers was not to be found; the other had been snatched up by a little boy, who ran off with it, thinking it might serve him as a doll's cradle.

So the little girl now walked on, her bare feet quite red and blue with the cold. She carried a small bundle of matches in her hand, and a good many more in her tattered apron. No one had bought any of them the live-long day—no one had given her a single penny. Trembling with cold and hunger crept she on, the picture of sorrow: poor little child!

The snow-flakes fell on her long, fair hair, which curled in such pretty ringlets over her shoulders; but she thought not of her own beauty, or of the cold. Lights were glimmering through every window, and the savour of roast goose reached her from several houses; it was New Year's eve, and it was of this that she thought.

In a corner formed by two houses, one of which projected beyond the other, she sat down, drawing her little feet close under her, but in vain—she could not warm them. She dared not go home, she had sold no matches, earned not a single penny, and perhaps her father would beat her; besides, her home was almost as cold as the street—it was an attic; and, although the larger of the many chinks in the roof were stopped up with straw and rags, the wind and snow often penetrated through. Her hands were nearly dead with cold; one little match from her bundle would warm them, perhaps, if she dared light it. She drew one out, and struck it against the wall: bravo! it was a bright, warm flame, and she held her hands over it. It was quite an illumination for that poor little girl,—nay, call it rather a magic taper,—for it seemed to her as though she were sitting before a large iron-stove with brass ornaments, so beautifully blazed the fire within! The child stretched out her feet to warm them also: alas! in an instant the flame had died away, the stove vanished, the little girl sat cold and comfortless, with the burnt match in her hand.

A second match was struck against the wall; it kindled and blazed, and wherever its light fell the wall became transparent as a veil—the little girl could see into the room within. She saw the table spread with a snow-white damask cloth, whereon were ranged shining china-dishes; the roast goose stuffed with apples and dried plums stood at one end, smoking-hot, and—which was pleasantest of all to see—the goose, with knife and fork still in her breast, jumped down from the dish, and waddled along the floor right up to the poor child. The match was burnt out, and only the thick, hard wall was beside her.

She kindled a third match. Again shot up the flame;—and now she was sitting under a most beautiful Christmas-tree, far larger, and far more prettily decked out, than the one she had seen last Christmas-eve through the glass doors of the rich merchant's house. Hundreds of wax-tapers lighted up the green branches, and tiny painted figures, such as she had seen in the shop-windows, looked down from the tree upon her. The child stretched out her hands towards them in delight, and in that moment the light of the match was quenched; still, however, the Christmas candles burned higher and higher — she beheld them beaming like stars in heaven: one of them fell, the lights streaming behind it like a long, fiery tail.

"Now some one is dying," said the little girl, softly, for she had been told by her old grandmother — the only person who had ever been kind to her, and who was now dead — that whenever a star falls an immortal spirit returns to the God who gave it.

She struck yet another match against the wall; it flamed up, and, surrounded by its light, appeared before her that same dear grandmother, gentle and loving as always, but bright and happy as she had never looked during her lifetime.

"Grandmother!" exclaimed the child, "oh, take me with you! I know thou wilt leave me as soon as the match goes out — thou wilt vanish like the warm fire in the stove, like the splendid New Year's feast, like the beautiful large Christmas-tree!" and she hastily lighted all the remaining matches in the bundle, lest her grandmother should disappear. And the matches burned with such a blaze of splendour, that noon-day could scarcely have been brighter. Never had the good old grandmother looked so tall and stately, so beautiful and kind; she took the little girl in her arms, and they both flew together — joyfully and gloriously they flew — higher and higher, till they were in that place where neither cold, nor hunger, nor pain, is ever known — they were in Paradise.

But in the cold morning hour, crouching in the corner of the wall, the poor little girl was found — her cheeks glowing, her lips smiling — frozen to death on the last night of the Old Year. The New Year's sun shone on the lifeless child; motionless she sat there with the matches in her lap, one bundle of them quite burnt out.

"She has been trying to warm herself, poor thing!" the people said; but no one knew of the sweet visions she had beheld, or how gloriously she and her grandmother were celebrating their New Year's festival.

THE NEIGHBOURS.

ANY one might have supposed that something very extraordinary had happened in the duck-pond, there was such a commotion. All the ducks—some swimming, some standing in the pond with their heads downwards—suddenly jumped on land, leaving the traces of their feet in the wet clay, and sending forth a loud startled cry. The water too, which had hitherto been smooth as a mirror, was now troubled. Just before, it had so calmly and clearly reflected everything around—every tree, every bush, the peasant's cottage with its gable-end full of holes, the swallow's nest beneath, and especially the large rose-tree with its branches and flowers covering the wall, and hanging almost into the water,—all these had been painted on the clear surface and looked like a picture, only with every object reversed, *i.e.* upside down; but now that the water was troubled, colours and forms seemed to run into each other, and the picture was spoiled. Two feathers from the ducks' wings, which had hitherto been calmly wafted hither and thither, now took flight, as though carried away by a gust of wind, and yet not a breath was stirring. Presently they lay still, and the water also became tranquil and smooth, again reflecting, as before, the peasant's gable-roof, the swallow's nest, and the large rose-tree. Each single Rose beheld itself therein; all were beautiful, but they knew it not, for no one had ever told them so. The sun shone through their delicate petals so full of fragrance, and every Rose felt just as we do when our hearts are full of untold happiness.

"How delightful it is to live here!" said each Rose to herself; "the only thing I can find to wish for is, that I could kiss the sun, because he is so warm and bright. Ah, and then, too, the Roses down in the water! I would kiss them also; they are exactly like us. And I should like to kiss those dear little birds in the nest just below them; there are some others, too, above us; they pop out their tiny heads and twitter so prettily; they have no feathers, as their father and mother have. Ours are certainly pleasant neighbours, both above and below. Oh, how charming it is to live here!"

Now the young birds above—those below were but the reflection in the water—were sparrows. Their father and mother were sparrows also; they had taken possession of the empty swallow's nest the year before, and were now perfectly at home in it.

"Are those the ducks' children swimming down there?" asked the young Sparrows, as soon as they had spied out the two feathers skimming over the water.

"If you must ask questions, at least let there be some sense in them!" returned the mother. "Don't you see that they are feathers—live clothes, such as I wear, and as you will some day? Only, ours are of a finer quality. I wish, however, that we had those feathers up here in the nest, for they would make it warm and comfortable. I should like to know what it was that frightened the ducks just now! it must have been something in the water, for it could not be my calling to you, though I did say 'Twit,' rather loudly. Those thick-headed Roses might have found out what was the matter! but they know nothing and do nothing but look at themselves and scent the air. I am so heartily weary of these neighbours of ours!"

"Listen to the sweet little birds up there!" said the Roses; "they are actually trying to sing; they cannot yet, but they will in time; how pleasant that must be! It is quite amusing to have such merry neighbours!"

Now came galloping up to the water two horses with a peasant-boy upon one of them; the boy had taken off his outer garment, and wore a large broad-brimmed black hat on his head. He whistled as though he too had been a little bird, and rode through the deepest part of the pond. When he came up to the rose-tree he tore off one of the Roses and stuck it in his hat, then, fancying himself very smart, off he rode again. The other Roses looked after their lost sister, and asked each other, "Where is she gone?" but that none of them knew.

"I should like to go out into the world," said one of the Roses, "but it is very pleasant here at home in our own green branches. All day long the sun is so warm, and at night-time the sky is still more beautiful; we can then look into those little holes which it is so full of."

By the holes in the sky she meant the stars, for Roses know no better.

"We are the life of the house!" said the mother of the Sparrows, "and people say that a swallow's nest brings luck, so they are glad enough to have us. But as to our neighbours, such a great rose-bush as that by the wall only makes the place damp; I should think it will be rooted up soon, and then, perhaps, corn may grow there. Roses are good for nothing but for people to look at and smell, or, at most, to stick in their hats. And this I have heard from my mother: every year they fall to pieces, the peasant's wife collects them and strews salt over them; then a French name is given to them, which I cannot pronounce, nor care to do so, and afterwards they are thrown into the fire to perfume the room. Such is their life; they live only to please the eyes and nose. Now you know all about them!"

As the evening advanced, and the gnats were dancing merrily in the warm atmosphere, and the clouds above looking so red and bright, the nightingale came and sang to the Roses. He sang that beauty was like sunshine in the world, and that the beautiful shall live for ever. But the Roses believed that the nightingale was singing about himself, which, indeed, might have been true. As to the song being addressed to them, of that they would never have thought; still they were pleased with it, and wondered whether all the young Sparrows would not become nightingales also in due time.

"I understand quite well what that bird was singing about," said one of the young Sparrows; "there was only one word that was not clear to me; what does he mean by the beautiful?"

"It is nothing," said the mother-bird; "it is only an appearance. At the Hall, where the doves have a house of their own, and peas and grains of corn are strewn for them every day — I have dined with them, and so shall you some time or other — tell me who are thy companions, and I will tell thee who thou art — at the Hall, as I said before, there are two birds with green necks and a tuft on their heads; they can spread out the tail as though it were a large wheel, and it has so many colours that one's eyes are dazzled by looking at it; that is 'the beautiful.' The birds are called peacocks; they should just be stripped of their feathers, and then they would not look different from us and everybody else. I would have plucked them myself, had they not been so large."

"Never mind; I will pluck them, depend upon it!" said the youngest of the Sparrows, who had not yet a single feather of his own.

In the cottage dwelt two young, married people, — they were cheerful and industrious, and loved each other, so everything went on pleasantly with them. On Sunday morning the young woman went out, gathered a handful of the loveliest among the roses, put them in a glass of water, and placed the glass upon the chest.

"Now I can see that it is Sunday," said the husband. He kissed his fair young wife, and they sat down, hand in hand, and read a Psalm, while the sun shone brightly through the windows upon the fresh roses and the happy young couple.

"I am weary of looking at this," said the mother of the Sparrows, as she peeped from her nest into the room; and away she flew.

Every Sunday fresh roses were gathered to adorn the room, and yet the rose-tree blossomed none the less. The young Sparrows at last had feathers of their own, and wanted to fly away with their mother. But this she would not allow; so they were obliged to remain in the nest. And well it was for them that they did; for one day, not looking where she was going, she flew right into a net made of horse-hair, which some boys had fastened to a bough. The net pressed so closely round her leg that it was almost ready to break. Oh, what pain, what terror, she suffered! The boys sprang forward to secure their prey,—their grasp was cruelly hard. "It is nothing but a sparrow!" said they; but they would not let her fly again,—they took her home, and, every time she cried out, they struck her on the beak.

There was an old man in the yard, who used to make soap, and sell it made up into balls and pieces for hands and beards,—a merry, careless old fellow he was, and a merry, wandering life he led; and when he saw the poor sparrow which the boys had caught, and which they said they did not care about, he said to them, "Suppose we make the ugly bird beautiful!" Mother-sparrow shivered from head to foot on hearing this, and she well might. Out of his box, which was provided with the brightest colours, the old man took a quantity of shining leaf-gold, and, having sent the boys for an egg, he smeared the white of it all over the bird, and then laid upon it the leaf-gold. Thus Mother-sparrow was gilt; but she took no pleasure in her finery,—her limbs shook with fear. And the old soap-maker tore off a piece of red cloth from his jacket, cut it and clipped it to look like a cock's-comb, and then stuck it on the poor bird's head.

"Now you shall see the gold bird fly," said he, letting Mother-sparrow loose; and away she flew in deadly terror. Oh, how she sparkled in the sunshine! All the Sparrows, even a large full-grown Crow, who at her age ought to have been surprised at nothing, flew back quite startled and shocked at the unwonted sight. But they all soon returned, eager to discover what sort of strange bird this might be.

"Whence, and whither? whence, and whither?" screamed the Crow.

"Wait a bit! wait a bit!" cried the Sparrows. But she would not wait; in terror and anguish she flew homewards. She was ready to sink down upon the earth; and the crowd of birds, both small and great, increased every moment,—some even flew at her to peck her. "Only look! only look!" cried they all.

"Only look, only look!" squeaked out the young ones, as she flew towards the nest. "Surely that is a young peacock, for peacocks are of all manner of colours,—they hurt the eyes, mother said. Twit! that is the beautiful." And then they attacked her with their little beaks, so that she could not possibly get into the nest, and she was so overcome with fright that she could not even say "twit," far less tell them that she was their mother. And now all the other birds pecked her—not a single feather was left; wounded and bleeding, she sank into the rose-bush.

"Poor creature!" said the Roses; "we will hide thee. Come, rest thy little head upon us."

Once more the suffering bird tried to unfold her wings, then closed them again, and died among her neighbours— the fresh, lovely Roses.

"Twit, twit!" quoth one of the young Sparrows in the nest; "I can't imagine where mother is staying; perhaps this is a trick of hers to teach us to shift for ourselves. She has left us the house for an inheritance; but I should like to know which of us is to have it when we have families."

"Ah, I can tell you that!" said the youngest; "I shall not let you all stay here when I have a mate and children of my own."

"But I shall have more wives and children than you," said another.

"But I am the eldest," cried a third; and then all began to scold, flap their wings, and peck with their beaks, till one after another was thrown out of the nest. There they lay full of anger and spite; they held their heads on one side and winked with their eyes: this was their fashion of sulking.

They could already fly a little, and through practice they improved; and at last, having agreed to separate, they settled a mode of salutation, whereby they might recognise each other if they should chance to meet in the wide world before them. This was to say "twit," and scrape the ground three times with the left leg.

The youngest Sparrow who remained in the nest made himself as big as he could. He was now a householder. However, his dignity did not last long. One night, red lightning flashed through the window-panes, flames of fire burst forth from under the roof, the dry straw was immediately in a blaze, the house was burnt, and with it the Sparrow and his nest. The young married pair happily escaped.

When the sun rose next morning, and everything seemed

refreshed as after a gentle nightly slumber, nothing was found remaining of the cottage, except a few blackened beams attached to the chimney, which stood among the ruins quite its own master. There was a strong smell of burning all around, but the rose-tree flourished still as blooming as ever, and the peaceful water of the pond reflected every single bough and flower just as before.

"How pretty those Roses look blossoming close to the ruined cottage!" exclaimed a passer-by; "it is the most charming little picture imaginable,—I must have it!" And he took out of his pocket a little book with blank leaves, for he was an artist, and sketched the blackened, smoking ground, the half-burnt planks, the chimney which seemed to lean on one side, more and more every moment, as though about to fall, and, in the foreground, the large, beautiful rose-tree, whose beauty, indeed, had been the cause of the little picture being sketched.

Later in the day, two of the former inmates of the nest hopped by. "Where is the cottage?" said they; "where is the nest? twit, it is all burnt, and our strong little brother is burnt also! that is because he turned us out of the nest. Those Roses have had a narrow escape; there they are still with their cheeks as red as ever; they care not a grain for their neighbours' misfortunes. Well, I shall not speak to them, and this is a horrible place—that is my opinion!" And away they flew.

In the course of the autumn there was one beautiful, sun-shiny day,—such a day as one never expects to meet with except in the height of summer. The court-yard in front of the grand flight of steps leading up to the hall-door was swept unusually dry and clean, and there flitted to and fro a multitude of doves, some black, some white, some violet-colour; their plumage glittered in the sunshine, and the ancient and respectable matrons of the Dove-family bustled about with much stateliness, crying out to their children, "Stand in groups! stand in groups!" for this was the best way of showing themselves off to advantage.

"Who are those little grey birds hopping about amongst us?" asked an old Dove with red and green eyes. "Little grey birds, little grey birds!" repeated she

"They are Sparrows, respectable creatures; we have always had the credit of being good-natured, so we allow them to pick up a few of our grains. They never talk to us, and they scrape so neatly with their legs!"

They did scrape; three times they scraped with their left legs, and then said, "Twit!" and thus they recognised each other; they were, in fact, three Sparrows from the nest in the roof of the burnt cottage.

"Provisions are uncommonly good here!" said the Sparrows. Meanwhile the Doves hopped round, ruffled their plumes, and made their private observations.

"Just look at the Crop-pigeon!" said one Dove to another; "do but look at her, see how she snaps up the peas! She gets too many, she gets the best; coo! coo! look what an ugly, wicked creature she is; coo! coo!" And the Dove's eyes sparkled with malice. "Join the group, join the group, little grey birds! little grey birds! coo! coo! coo!" And then their beaks went to work, and so it will be a hundred years hence.

The Sparrows ate heartily and listened attentively, nay, they even joined the group, but were soon weary, so they left the Doves to themselves, and, after indulging in a few remarks on their late companions, hopped under the garden-fence, and finding the door of the summer-house open, one of them ventured upon the threshold. "Twit," said he; "see what I dare to do!" "Twit," said another; "I will do more!" whereupon he hopped into the room. Nobody was there, and the third Sparrow perceiving this, flew boldly in, crying out, "Either do a thing thoroughly, or not at all! what a ridiculous human nest this is! and how is this? what do I see?"

Plainly set before the eyes of every Sparrow were their old neighbours the Roses; they mirrored themselves in the water, and the blackened beams of the cottage rested slantingly upon the falling chimney. Well might the Sparrows exclaim, "How is this? how came all this in the apartments of the great?" And they all tried to fly over the chimney, but their wings were repulsed by a flat wall, for the whole scene was in reality a large splendid picture which the artist had made from his little sketch.

"Twit," said the Sparrows, "it is nothing at all, it is only an appearance; twit, that is the beautiful! can you understand it, for I can't?" And they flew away, for people came into the room.

Days passed, years passed, many times had the Doves cooed and wooed; nay, they quarrelled too, malicious birds that they were! The Sparrows lived luxuriously in summer, and were half-frozen in winter; most of them were either betrothed or married; they had young ones, and each, of course, thought his own the handsomest and cleverest of all the sparrows in the world; they flew hither and thither, and when they chanced to meet they greeted each other with a "twit!" and three scrapes of the left leg. The eldest of them was now much advanced in years; she had lived a single life, she had neither nest nor young ones, and wishing once more to visit a large town, she one day flew to Copenhagen.

Here she saw a large handsome house standing close by the palace and the canal, wherein lay vessels heavily laden with fruits and wine. The windows of the house were wider below than above, and, on peeping through, every apartment appeared to Miss Sparrow's eyes like a tulip, so rich and varied were the hues that adorned the walls. In the midst of all these gay apartments stood a number of white figures, some of marble, some only of plaster, but, marble or plaster, it was all the same to Miss Sparrow. On the roof of the house was a metal car, with metal horses, and the Goddess of Victory, likewise of metal, guiding them. It was Thorwaldsen's Museum.

"How it shines! how it shines!" quoth the ancient Sparrow-maiden, "why, this must be the 'beautiful.' Twit! it is much larger than a peacock!" for she still remembered what her mother told her formerly about the largest specimen of the beautiful known to her.

And she flew down into the court; this also was splendid, palm-branches and fresh green foliage were painted on the walls, and in the centre was a large rose-tree in full blossom, its fresh, green branches, laden with flowers, drooping over a grave—one solitary grave.

She flew to the spot, for many other Sparrows were there; "Twit!" said she, and scraped the ground three times with her left leg. This greeting she had practised again and again that year, and no one had understood it, for friends once parted do not meet every day; the salute had become a mere matter of form: but now, to her surprise, two old Sparrows and one young one said, "Twit!" in return, and likewise scraped with their left legs.

"Ah, good morning, good morning!" Here had met together no less than three of the old Sparrows from the swallow's nest in the cottage-roof, and one of their descendants. "To think that we should all meet here!" said they. "This is a very fine place, but there is not much to eat; it is the beautiful, you know! Twit!"

Several persons now came into the court from one of the rooms where stood the marble figures, and they went up to the grave which held the remains of the great master whose skill had formed them.

All stood with glistening eyes round Thorwaldsen's grave, and some picked up the scattered rose-leaves to carry home with them. There were travellers from distant lands; from mighty England, from Germany and from France; and the fairest lady in the company plucked one of the Roses, and wore it near her heart. This made the Sparrows believe that the Roses reigned here, and that this magnificent mansion had been built for them alone; it seemed to them rather too much honour; nevertheless, as mankind was evidently so intent upon showing respect to the Roses, they determined to do the same. "Twit!" said they; and swept the ground with their tails, winking with one eye upon the Roses the while. Long did they look at them before they could quite make up their minds whether these Roses were or were not their old neighbours: yes, such most assuredly they were; the artist who had sketched the rose-bush growing near the blackened remains of the cottage had afterwards gained permission to transplant it, and had then given it to the architect of the Museum. Nowhere could Roses be found more lovely or more fragrant than those borne by this tree, so it was planted close by Thorwaldsen's grave, and there, a living symbol of the beautiful, it blossomed year after year, and gave its bright-hued, delicate leaves to be carried away as remembrances to foreign lands.

"So you have got an establishment in this town!" said the Sparrows. And the Roses nodded assent; they had recognised their neighbours and were very glad to see them.

"How delightful it is to live and blossom here! to see old

neighbours. Ah, I remember the time when they lived by the duck-pond; twit, how droll it is that they should attain such a high station. Some folks come to honour while they are sleeping. And what there is so wonderful in a great red rag like that I can't think! Ah, there is a withered leaf, that I can see!"

And they pecked at it till the leaf fell off, but the tree looked all the fresher and greener, and the Roses gave forth their perfume to the sunbeams even after they had fallen on Thorwaldsen's grave, with whose long-enduring name the memory of their fleeting beauty thus became linked.

THE BELL.

EVERY evening, when the sun disappeared and the clouds glistened like gold among the high chimneys of the town, there was heard, sometimes by one, sometimes by another, a strange deep sound like the pealing of a church bell. Only for a moment could it be heard, for there was such an incessant rumbling of carts and carriages, such a bustle of coming and going, such a noise of singing and shouting as well-nigh bewildered people, and at times quite drowned the distant chime. "Hark! there is the evening bell," they used to say; "the sun is just setting."

If you went beyond the town into the suburbs, where the houses stood farther apart, with gardens and meadows lying between them, you would behold the evening sky arrayed in colours still more bright and beautiful, and the tones of the unknown Bell might be heard ringing far more loudly and sweetly. It seemed as though the sound must proceed from some church deep within the still, fragrant forest in the distance, and you could not help casting a glance thitherwards, and feeling impressed with pious awe.

Time passed on, the Bell still pealed regularly as ever; at

last people said, "Can there be a church in the forest? The tones of the Bell are indeed strange, and beautiful exceedingly; why should not we go and search into this mystery?" And, accordingly, the rich drove thither in their carriages and the poor walked on foot, but they found the distance longer than they had expected, and when they reached the willow-grove that skirted the forest, they were tempted to sit down to rest in the shade, and then they would look up into the branches overhead and fancy themselves already in the forest. And soon the chief confectioner in the town came out and spread his tent there, and this excited a rival confectioner to do the like, and he must needs hang up a bell right over his tent. This bell was covered with tar to preserve it from the rain, but it had no clapper. So when the people returned home, they declared that they had enjoyed themselves extremely, and that it was quite a romantic excursion, quite a gipsy party.

There were three persons who boasted of having penetrated right through as far as the other side of the forest, and they asserted that there also they had heard the singular tones of the supposed Bell; but that the sound then seemed to proceed from the town. And one man wrote a long poem about the Bell, wherein he likened it to the voice of a mother speaking to a beloved and loving child, and declared that no melody might compare in depth and sweetness with that thrilling, unearthly chime.

The poem aroused the attention of the Emperor of that country, and he promised that whoever should discover the cause of this mysterious sound, should bear the title of "Universal Bell-ringer," even though it should turn out that there was no bell at all.

So in hopes of obtaining this distinction, several persons went rambling all over the forest, but only one returned with any pretence to an explanation. Not that he had penetrated much deeper than the others; however, he asserted, that the bell-like tones came from a very large owl in a hollow-tree — it was the Owl of Wisdom, he said, and she was incessantly striking her head against the tree; but whether the sound proceeded from her head or from the hollow trunk, he owned frankly he could not decide. Nevertheless, he was appointed "Universal Bell-ringer," and published every year a short treatise "On the Owl of Wisdom." For all this, people were just about as wise as they were before.

It was a confirmation-day; the bishop had addressed the children so kindly and earnestly, bidding them remember that this day was for them a most important day, that the blessing of God had been invoked upon their heads, they had all at once ceased to be children, and become full-grown men and women; that their childish minds, therefore, must now unfold into the maturity of reason. The glorious sun-light shone around them, as the newly confirmed walked all together out of the town, when suddenly the marvellous, incomprehensible Bell was heard pealing loudly from the distant forest. Immediately the young Christians were seized with a longing to go and search into the cause of the sound. All agreed to set out forthwith in search of the mystery, except three; one of these wanted to go home and try on her ball-dress—and, indeed, had it not been for the ball, she would not have cared about being confirmed that year; another was a poor boy who had borrowed his confirmation coat and boots from the innkeeper's son, and had promised to return them within a fixed time; and as for the third, he declared that he never went to any strange place without his parents; he had always been a good child, and intended to be so still, although he was confirmed, and they ought not to laugh at him for it! Laugh, however, they did, and that right heartily.

So three went back to the town, whilst the rest sped merrily on their way. The sun shone, the birds sang, and the newly-confirmed sang with them, all holding each other by the hands. They had none of them yet entered upon the business of life; they were like brothers and sisters—all equal—all children of the good God above them.

But very soon two of the youngest became weary, and turned back, and two little girls sat down by the wayside to weave garlands; they stayed so long that it seemed of no use trying to overtake the rest. And when the party reached the willow-grove, where stood the confectioner's tent, they said to each other, "See, here we are at last! After all, there is really no such thing as the Bell,—it is only a fancy of ours."

However, in that same moment the Bell was heard to peal from out the forest-depths, in tones so sweet and solemn, that four or five determined to seek it farther.

The trees grew close together, many-branched and thickly-leaved. It was no easy task to make a path through,—anemones and the sweet-scented wood-roof grew almost too high; honeysuckles and wild convolvuluses hung in long wreaths from tree to tree; the nightingales sang, and the joyous sunbeams peeped in here and there through the boughs. Oh, the forest was most beautiful, though certainly it was no place for girls,—they would have torn their frocks among the brambles! Several large blocks of stone, covered with lichens of every colour, formed a basin, whence shot up a fountain of fresh spring water; merrily gushed it forth, with a strange, gurgling noise, like "Cluck, cluck!"

"And what if this should be the Bell?" suggested one of the young adventurers; and he crouched down on the ground to listen. "I must examine into this thoroughly." So there he stayed examining, and let the others go on without him.

They came to a cottage built with bark and boughs,—a large tree, bearing wild crab-apples, leaned over it, as though to shower down its rich blessing over the roof; a rose-bush was trained up the front wall, its green leaves and bright-red flowers clustering thickly round the gable-end, and just under this gable-end hung a little bell. Could this be the Bell they sought? Yes, all agreed that it was, excepting one, who said that it was far too small, and its tones too low to have been heard at such a distance, and that the chimes which had stirred the hearts of all men so powerfully were indeed very different. He who spoke thus was a King's son; so the others said, "This is always the way; these grand folks must needs be wiser than all the rest of the world put together."

So they suffered him to pursue his way alone; and as he wandered on he felt his spirit more and more impressed with the silent beauty of the forest. He could still hear the ringing of the little bell, the sight of which had so delighted his comrades, and at times, too, the wind bore over to him the tones of the confectioner's bell, as it rang the holiday-makers to tea; but the deep, solemn strokes that had called him forth from the town sounded above them all, growing louder and louder, and more and more like the music of an organ. And he fancied this singular music proceeded from some place to his left—from the side where the heart beats.

Suddenly there was a rustling among the bushes; the King's son turned round, and saw beside him a little boy, wearing wooden shoes, and a jacket with sleeves so short as to leave his wrists quite bare. The King's son recognised him immediately,—it was the boy who could not come with the rest in search of the Bell, because he must first restore his borrowed confirmation clothes. This he had done, and had then followed alone in his own wooden shoes and miserable patched garments; for the Bell rang with a melody so clear and deep, that he felt he must come and seek it.

"Well, then, we can go on together," said the King's son. But the poor youth in the wooden shoes was very bashful; he tugged at his short jacket-sleeves, and said he feared he could not walk so quickly; besides, he thought that the Bell must be sought towards the right, because the right-hand side was always the place of honour.

"Certainly, then, we shall not agree at all," replied the King's son; and he nodded a friendly farewell to the poor boy, who went on into the deepest, thickest recesses of the wood, where the thorns tore his clothes to pieces, and made his face, hands, and feet, bleed terribly. The King's son, on his part, did not escape without a few sharp scratches; but the sun shone full on his path, and he it is whom we shall follow. A royal heart, indeed, had this King's son.

"The Bell I must and will find," said he, "even should I go to the end of the world after it!"

Hideous, grinning monkeys sat chattering and grinding their teeth among the branches. "Shall we cudgel him?" cried they, "shall we thrash him? he is a King's son!"

But, nothing daunted, on he passed, deeper and deeper, into the forest shades, where grew the loveliest and strangest flowers. Large white lilies with blood-red stamens, and sky-blue tulips waving to and fro in the wind, sprang up at his feet, and apple-trees extended to him their tempting fruit, shining like great glistening soap-bubbles in the dazzling sunbeams. Here and there were seen clear spots of the freshest greensward, where hart and hind sported together under the shade of magnificent oaks and beeches; and if the trunks of some of these were riven asunder, grass and long creepers covered the cleft. Calm, glassy lakes, too, he saw, white swans swimming upon their bosom, and continually flapping their long snowy wings. The King's son often stood still to look and listen, often he fancied that the bell-like tones must issue from the depths of one of these unruffled lakes; however, he was soon convinced of his mistake; he still heard the pealing of the Bell, but still, as ever, it came from some distant region of the forest.

At last the sun set, the firmament glowed as if on fire, the forest seemed more silent, more sacred than ever; he sank upon his knees, sang his evening hymn, and when it was ended, said to himself, "Never shall I find that which I seek! the sun is setting; night, dark night, is coming on. I would fain see the round, red sun once more, before it sinks beneath the earth; I will climb up yonder group of rocks, the centre peak is as high as the tallest tree in the forest."

And, seizing hold of roots and shrubs, he clambered over the moist stones, where water-snakes lay writhing their long smooth coils, and toads sat croaking at him. Up he clambered, and gained the peak just before the sun, as seen from that height, had quite disappeared. Oh, what a scene now burst upon his eyes! The sea, the great, glorious sea, was spread before him, dashing its foaming billows on the coast; and the half-set sun shone like a rich golden altar in the place where sea and sky met, melting into each other, into the same glowing hues. The forest sang, the sea sang, and his heart sang with them; all nature seemed one vast and holy church, wherein the trees, crowned by light, hovering clouds, formed the arched pillars, flowers and grass being woven into a soft velvet carpet at his feet, while heaven itself hung like a spacious dome overhead. And as he gazed, the bright red hues faded rapidly away, the sun had quite vanished, but, one by one, millions of stars burst out, just as though millions of diamond lamps had been suddenly kindled. The King's son raised his arms in grateful rapture towards sky, sea, and forest—and just at that moment the poor youth, in wooden shoes and short jacket, came forward from the right-hand side; following his own path, he had in the end been brought to the same spot. They ran to meet each other, and stood together, hand in hand, in the vast Church of Nature and Poetry, whilst above them pealed the holy, invisible Bell, and blessed Spirits hovered round, singing in chorus their own triumphant Hallelujah!

THE DARNING-NEEDLE.

THERE was once a Darning-needle so fine that she fancied herself a Sewing-needle.

"Now take care, and hold me fast!" said the Darning-needle to the Fingers that took her up. "Don't lose me, pray! If I were to fall down on the floor, you would never be able to find me again, I am so fine!"

"That's more than you can tell!" said the Fingers, as they took hold of her.

"See, I come with a train!" said the Darning-needle, drawing a long thread, without a single knot in it, after her.

The Fingers guided the Needle to the cook-maid's slippers; the upper leather was torn, and had to be sewn together.

"This is vulgar work!" said the Darning-needle; "I shall never get through; I break, I am breaking!" And break she did. "Did I not say so?" continued she; "I am too fine!"

"Now she is good for nothing," thought the Fingers; however, they must still keep their hold; the cook-maid dropped sealing-wax upon the Darning-needle and then stuck her into her neckerchief.

"See, now I am a Breast-pin!" said the Darning-needle; "I knew well that I should come to honour; when one is something, one always becomes something." And at this she laughed, only inwardly, of course, for nobody has ever seen or heard a Darning-needle laugh; there sat she now at her ease, as proud as if she were driving in her carriage, and looking about her on all sides.

"May I take the liberty of asking if you are of gold?" inquired she of the pin that was her neighbour. "You have a pleasing exterior, and a very peculiar head; it is but small, though. You must take care that it grows, for it is not every one that can have sealing-wax dropped upon her!" And the Darning-needle drew herself up so proudly that she fell off from the neckerchief into the sink, where the cook was engaged just then in washing up.

"Now for our travels!" said the Darning-needle; "but I hope I shall not go very far." However, she did travel far, very far.

"I am too fine for this world," said she, as at last she sat still in the gutter. "However, I know who I am, and there is always some little pleasure in that." And so the Darning-needle held herself erect, and did not lose her good-humour.

All sorts of things sailed past her; splinters of wood, straws, scraps of old newspapers. "See how they sail along!" said the Darning-needle. "They do not know what is sticking under them! It is I. I stick, I sit here. There goes a splinter, he thinks of nothing in the world but himself, splinter as he is. There floats a straw,—to see how it turns round and round! Nay, think not so much of thyself, thou mightest easily float against one of the stones. There swims a newspaper—everything in it is forgotten, yet how it spreads itself out!—I sit patiently and quietly! I know what I am, and that I shall always be the same!"

One day there chanced to be close by her something that glittered so charmingly that the Darning-needle felt persuaded it must needs be a diamond; it was, in reality, only a splinter of glass, but delighted with its appearance, the Darning-needle addressed it, introducing herself as a Breast-pin. "Surely, you are a diamond?" "Why, yes, something of the sort!" was the reply; so now each believed the other to be some very rare and costly trinket; and they both began to complain of the extraordinary haughtiness of the world.

"Yes, I have dwelt in a box belonging to a young lady," said the Darning-needle: "and this young lady was a cook-maid; she had five fingers on each hand, and anything so arrogant, so conceited, as these five fingers I have never known, and, after all, what were they good for? For nothing but to hold me, to take me out of the box and lay me in the box!"

"And were they at all bright,—did they shine?" asked the Glass-splinter.

"Shine!" repeated the Darning-needle, "not they, but conceited enough they were, notwithstanding! They were five brothers: 'Finger' was the family name; they held themselves so erect, side by side, although they were not all of the same height. The first, Thumbkin he was called, was short and thick; he generally stood out of the rank rather before the others; he had only one bend in his back, so that he could only bow once, but he used to say that if he were cut off from a man, that man would no longer be fit for military service. Foreman, the second, would put himself forward everywhere, meddled with sweet and with sour, pointed at sun or moon, and he it was who pressed upon the pen whenever the fingers wrote. Middleman was so tall that he could look over the others' heads; Ringman wore a gold belt round his body; and as for Littleman, he did nothing at all, and was proud of that, I suppose. Proud they were, and proud they would be, therefore I took myself off into the gutter!"

"And now we sit together and shine!" quoth the Glass-splinter. Just then, some more water was poured into the gutter, it overflowed its boundaries, and carried the Glass-splinter along with it.

"So now he has advanced farther," observed the Darning-needle. "I stay here—I am too fine—but such it is my pride to be,—it is respectable." So still she sat there erect, enjoying her own thoughts.

"I could almost believe I was born of a sunbeam, I am so fine; and yet the sunbeams do not seem to seek me out under the water. Alas, I am so fine that even my mother cannot find me! Had I still my old eye which broke, I believe I could weep—I would not, though—it is not refined to weep."

One day some boys were raking about in the gutter, hunting for old nails, pennies, and such like. This was very dirty, certainly, but such was their pleasure.

"Halloo!" cried one, pricking himself with the Darning-needle; "there's a fellow for you!"

"Do not call me a fellow,—I am a young lady," said the Darning-needle; but no one heard it. The sealing-wax had worn off, and she had become quite black; black, however, makes a person look thin, so she fancied herself finer than ever.

"There sails an egg-shell," said the boys; and they stuck the Darning-needle into the shell.

"White walls and a lady in black!" said the Darning-needle, "that is very striking! Now every one can see me! But I hope I shall not be sea-sick, for then I shall break." Her fear was needless; she was not sea-sick, neither did she break.

"Nothing is so good to prevent sea-sickness as being of steel, and then, too, never to forget that one is a little more than man. Now my trial is over; the finer one is, the more one can endure."

"Crash!" went the egg-shell; a waggon rolled over it. "Ugh, what a pressure!" sighed the Darning-needle; "now I shall be sea-sick after all! I shall break! I shall break!" But she broke not, although the wheel had passed over her; long did she lie there—and there let her lie!

LITTLE TUK.

A DROLL name, to be sure, is Tuk! however, it was not the little boy's real name,—his real name was Carl—but when he was so young he could hardly speak, he used to call himself Tuk—why, it would be difficult to say, for Tuk is not at all like Carl. However, the boy was still called Little Tuk by all who knew him.

Little Tuk had to take care of his sister Gustava, who was smaller even than himself, and he had also to learn his lesson; here were two things to be done, and the difficulty was, how to do them both at once. The poor boy sat with his little sister in his lap, singing to her all the pretty songs he knew, yet every now and then casting a side-long glance at his geography-book, which lay open beside him; by to-morrow morning he must not only be able to repeat without book the names of all the towns in the diocese of Zealand, but to tell about them all that could be told.

At last his mother came home and took little Gustava; Tuk then ran to the window, and read and read till he had nearly read his eyes out, for it was growing darker every minute, and his mother could not afford to buy candles.

"There goes the old washerwoman home through the street," said the mother, looking out of window; "she can hardly carry herself, poor thing! and she has the weight of

THE NEW YORK
PUBLIC LIBRARY
ASTOR, LENOX AND
TILDEN FOUNDATIONS.

LITTLE TUK.

Page 349.

that great heavy pail of water from the pump to bear besides. Jump up, like a good boy, little Tuk; go and help the poor old creature!"

And little Tuk immediately jumped up and ran to help her. When he came back it was quite dark, it was of no use to wish for a candle, he must go to bed. There he lay, still thinking of his geography-lesson, of the diocese of Zealand, and all that his master had told him. It should have been all read over again by rights, but that he could not do now. His geography-book he put under his pillow, for somebody had told him that would help him wonderfully to remember his lesson. However, he had never yet found that this sort of help was at all to be depended upon.

So there he lay, thinking and thinking, till all at once he felt as though some one were gently sealing his eyes and mouth with a kiss. He slept, and yet he slept not, for he seemed to see the old washerwoman's mild eyes fixed upon him, and to hear her say:—

"It would be a sin and a shame, little Tuk, if you were not to know your lesson. You helped me, now I will help you, and then our Lord will help us both."

And then the leaves of the book under little Tuk's head began to rustle, and to turn over and over.

"Cluck, cluck, cluck!" cried a hen—she came from the town of Kiöge. "I am a Kiöge hen," said she; and she told little Tuk how many inhabitants the town contained, and about the battle that had once been fought there, and how it was now a place of no consequence at all.

"Kribbley krabbley, kribbley krabbley!"—and here a great wooden bird bounced down upon the bed; it was the popinjay from the shooting-ground at Prestoe. It declared that there were as many inhabitants in Prestoe as it had nails in its body; it was a proud bird.

"Thorwaldsen lived in one corner of Prestoe! Am not I a pretty bird—a merry popinjay?"

And now little Tuk no longer lay in bed,—he was on horseback—on he went, gallop, gallop! A magnificently-clad knight—a knight of the olden time—wearing a bright helmet and a waving plume, held him on his own horse, and on they rode together, through the wood, to the ancient city of Vordingborg; and it was once again full of life and bustle, as in the days of yore; the high towers of the King's castle rose up against the sky, and bright lights were seen gleaming through the windows. Within were song, and dance, and merriment; King Waldemar was leading out the noble young ladies of his court to tread stately measures with him. Suddenly the morning dawned, the lamps grew pale, the sun rose, and the outlines of the buildings gradually faded away, one high form after another seemed blotted out of the clear morning sky, till at last one tower alone remained to mark the spot where that royal castle had stood. And the vast city had shrunk up into a poor, mean-looking, little town; and the school-boys came out of school, their books under their arms, and they said, " Two thousand inhabitants." But that was not true,—there were not near so many.

And little Tuk lay in his bed again: he knew not whether he had been dreaming or not. Again there was somebody close by his side.

"Little Tuk! little Tuk!" cried a voice,—it was the voice of a young sailor-boy. "I come to salute you from Corsöer. Corsöer is a new town—a living town—it has steam-ships and stage-coaches of its own; once people used to call it a low, vulgar place, but that is an old, worn-out prejudice. 'I dwell by the sea-side,' says Corsöer; 'I have broad high-roads and pleasure-gardens, and I have given birth to a poet—a very amusing one, too, which is more than all poets are. I once thought of sending a ship all round the world; I did not send it, but I might just as well have done so—and I dwell so pleasantly, close by the port—the loveliest roses are blossoming round about me!'"

And little Tuk could see the roses,—their soft, blushing red petals, and their fresh, green leaves, gleamed before his eyes. But in a moment the flowers had vanished, and the green leaves spread and thickened; a perfect grove had grown up above the bright waters of the fiord, and above the grove towered the two high-pointed steeples of a glorious old church; from the grass-grown side of the hill gushed forth, as in clear rainbow-hued streams of light, a fountain,—a merry, musical voice it had—and close beside it sat a king, wearing a gold crown upon his long, dark hair. This was King Hroar sitting by the fountain, and hard by was the town now called Roeskilde (Hroar's Fountain). And beyond the hill, on a broad highway, advanced all Denmark's kings and queens, all wearing their gold crowns; hand in hand they passed on into the church, and the organ's deep tones mingled with the clear rippling of the fountains. And little Tuk saw and heard it all.

All at once this scene too had vanished! What had become of it? it was just like turning over the leaves of a book. Now he saw an old woman; she was a weeder, she came from Soroe, where grass grows in the very market-place. Her grey linen apron was thrown over her head and back; the apron was wet, it must have been raining. "Yes, so it has," said she; and then she began to repeat something very funny out of Holberg's comedies; nor were they all she knew — she could recite old ballads about Waldemar and Absalon. But all of a sudden she shrunk up together, and rocked her head, just as if she were going to jump.

"Croak," said she, "it is wet, it is wet: it is still as the grave in Soroe!" She had become a frog. "Croak!" and again she was an old woman. "One must dress to suit the weather," says she; "it is wet, it is wet; my town is like a flask — one goes into it through the cork, and through the cork one must get out again. But I have healthy, rosy-cheeked boys at the bottom of the flask; there they learn wisdom — Greek, Greek! Croak, croak, croak!"

Her voice was like frog-music, or like the noise one makes in walking through a marsh in great boots; always the same tone, so monotonous, so dull, that little Tuk fell into a sound sleep, and a very good thing it was for him.

But even in this sleep a dream visited him; his little sister Gustava, with her blue eyes and curling flaxen hair, had, it seemed, all at once grown up into a beautiful girl; and, though she had no wings, she could fly, and they flew together over all Zealand — over its green woods and blue waters.

"Listen to the cock crowing, little Tuk! Cock-a-doodle-doo! — look at the hens scraping away in the town of *Kiöge!* There thou shalt have such a famous poultry-yard; thou shalt no longer suffer hunger and want; thou shalt shoot at the popinjay, and reach the mark; thou shalt be a rich and happy man; thy house shall rise as proudly as King Waldemar's castle at *Vordingborg,* and shall be decked so splendidly with marble statues, like those that Thorwaldsen sculptured at *Prestoe*. Thy good name shall be borne round the world like the ship which should have gone out from *Corsöer*, and in the town of *Roeskilde* thou shalt speak and give counsel, wisely and well, like King Hroar—and then at last, little Tuk, when thou shalt lie in thy peaceful grave, thou shalt sleep as quietly——"

"As if I lay sleeping in *Soroe!*" said little Tuk, and hereupon he awoke. It was bright morning, and he remembered nothing of all his dreams; they were to him as though they had never been.

He jumped out of bed and sought for his book, he knew the names of all the towns in his lesson perfectly well. And the old washerwoman put her head in at the door, and nodded to him, saying;—

"Thanks for yesterday's help, thou dear, sweet child! may the angels bring thy best dream to pass!"

But little Tuk had forgotten what he had dreamt—it mattered not, though, the angels knew it.

THE SHADOW.

IN hot countries the sun's rays burn with a vengeance; People have their complexions dyed a mahogany brown colour, and in the very hottest regions of all are scorched into negroes. Our story, however, relates, not to these very sultry climes, but to one of the moderately hot countries, which was visited, once upon a time, by a learned man from the cold, cold north. This learned man at first imagined that he might run about as freely as he had been used to do at home. But he was soon undeceived, and, like all other reasonable people, he remained in his house all day long, keeping the doors and window-shutters closed, just as though everybody were asleep or away from home.

The narrow street of high-built houses where he dwelt was so situated, that the sunbeams fell full upon it from dawn of day till evening; it was positively unbearable! and the learned man from the cold country felt as though sitting in a heated oven; he was a young as well as a wise man, and the sun injured his health, he became quite thin, his shadow also—for the sun affected that as well as himself—was, during the day-time, considerably smaller than it had used to be. However, at night, after the sun had set, both man and Shadow constantly revived.

A A

It was really a pleasure to see the change! As soon as lights were brought into the room, the Shadow stretched itself up the wall, nay, even as far as the ceiling; it seemed stretching itself to the utmost in order to recover its original size. The learned man used to go out on the balcony, that was *his* place for stretching, and when the stars shone forth in the clear, balmy atmosphere, he felt a new life breathing through his limbs. Figures of men and women then made their appearance on all the balconies in the street, and in hot countries no single window is without a balcony, for people must have air, even though they are accustomed to be mahoganized. Above and below, everything became full of life; butchers and bakers, cobblers and tailors, flitted about the streets, chairs and tables were brought out, and lamps, nay, thousands of lamps, were lighted; one shouted, another sang, some walked, some drove, some rode on asses — *klinge-lingeling*, the little bells on their harness tinkled merrily as they passed, — little boys let off squibs and crackers, the church-bells pealed, psalms were sung, and many a solemn funeral procession moved along. Yes, the street was then thoroughly alive!

Only in one house — it was that which stood exactly opposite the one in which dwelt the northern student, — there was silence, and yet it could not be uninhabited, for flowers adorned the balcony, — beautifully they flourished amid the sun's burning heat, and flourish they could not, unless constantly watered, and watered they could not be without hands. Besides, every evening the balcony-window used to open; and, although it was quite dark within, at least in the foremost chamber, from some deeper recess the notes of music were heard, incomparably delicious, at least so thought our stranger; but this might very possibly be only a fancy, as, according to him, everything in this hot country was incomparably delicious, always excepting the sun. The stranger's landlord declared that he did not know who occupied the house opposite, no one had ever been seen there, and as for the music, it seemed to him dreadfully tedious. "It is," said he, "just like a person sitting and practising a piece which he cannot play, — always the same piece. 'I shall play it at last', he keeps on saying, but it is plain that he never will, with all his practising."

One night the stranger was sleeping. He slept close to the open window; the curtains were waved aside by the wind, and the opposite balcony was discovered wrapped in a wondrous splendour; all the flowers shone like flames of the loveliest and most varied hues, and amid the flowers stood a tall, graceful maiden, surrounded by a glory which dazzled his eyes—indeed, in his eagerness he opened them so fearfully wide that he awoke. With one spring he was on the floor, crept softly behind the curtain, but the lady was gone, the glory which had dazzled his eyes was gone, the flowers shone no longer, but looked exactly as they had been wont to look; the door was half open, and deep from within sounded music so soft and plaintive! Surely this was sorcery, for who could be living there?

One evening the stranger was sitting in his balcony, lights were burning in the apartment behind him, and consequently, as was quite natural, his Shadow fell upon the opposite wall; there it seemed to sit among the flowers of the balcony, and whenever its master moved, the Shadow moved also, as a matter of course.

"I verily believe my Shadow is the only thing stirring to be seen over there," said the learned stranger. "See, how comfortably it sits among the flowers, the door within is half-open, I do wish my Shadow would but have the sense to walk in, look about, and then return to tell me what it had seen there. Ah! it might be of great advantage to thee!" continued he, jestingly; " be so kind as to step forward! Well, wilt thou go?" And he nodded to the Shadow, and the Shadow nodded again in return. "Well, then, go, but don't stay!" And forthwith the stranger arose, and his Shadow on the opposite balcony rose also; the stranger then turned round, whereupon the Shadow likewise turned round, and any close observer might have seen that the Shadow passed through the half-opened door into the apartment in the opposite house, just as the stranger retired into his own room, closing the long curtains behind him.

Next morning the learned man went out to drink coffee and read the journals. "How is this?" he exclaimed, as he came out into the sunshine; "why, I have no Shadow! Then it really did pass over into the opposite house yesterday evening, and has not returned! Now, on my word, this is the most provoking thing ever heard of!"

He was vexed, not so much because his Shadow was gone, as because he knew that there was already a story about a man without a Shadow, which was well known to all the people in his own country, so that now, if he were to tell his story, everybody would call him a plagiarist, and that would not please him at all. So he determined to say nothing about it, and this was certainly a wise resolve.

In the evening he went again into the balcony, first placing the candles so as to be just behind his back, for he knew that a Shadow always requires its master to act as its screen, but he could by no means entice it forth,—he stretched himself, he contracted himself, but no Shadow made its appearance. He said, "Hem, hem!" but that was of no avail either.

All this was vexatious; however, in hot countries everything grows very fast; accordingly, after eight days had elapsed, on going into the sunshine, he observed, to his great delight, that a new Shadow was beginning to spring out from under his feet,—the root must have remained there,—and in three weeks' time he had once more a very tolerable Shadow, which, as he was now travelling homewards, increased rapidly in size during the journey, until at last it became so long and so broad that half of it might have sufficed him.

So this same learned man now returned to his cold fatherland, and he wrote books about all that was true, and good, and beautiful, in the world. Days passed on, and weeks passed on, and years passed on — many years.

One evening, when he was sitting alone in his room, he heard a low tapping at the door.

"Come in!" he said; but no one came in, so he arose and opened the door. Before him stood a man so unaccountably thin and meagre that the sight quite startled him. This stranger was, however, exceedingly well dressed, and appeared a person of rank.

"With whom have I the honour of speaking?" inquired the Scholar.

"Ah! I thought as much!" replied the thin gentleman. "I expected that you would not recognise me. I have gained so much body lately,—I have gained both flesh and clothes,—I dare say you never thought to see me in such excellent condition. Do you not recollect your old Shadow? Ah! you must have fancied I never meant to return at all. Things have gone so well with me since I was last with you, I have become quite wealthy! I can easily ransom myself, if it be necessary!" And with these words he passed his hand over the heavy gold watch-chain which he wore round his neck, and rattled the large bunch of costly seals which hung from it, and oh! how his fingers glittered with the diamonds encircling them! And all this was real!

"No, I cannot recover my senses!" exclaimed the Scholar; "what can all this mean?"

"Certainly, it is rather extraordinary," said the Shadow. "But then you yourself are by no means an ordinary man; and, as you know, I have trod in your steps from childhood. As soon as you thought me capable of going alone, I went my own way in the world. My circumstances are most brilliant, nevertheless a sort of yearning came over me to see you once more before you die. You must die, you know! Besides, I felt a wish to see this country again, for one cannot help feeling love for one's own fatherland. I know that you have now another Shadow; have I to pay you anything for it? Be so kind as to tell me how much?"

"Is it really and truly thyself?" cried the Scholar, "this is, indeed, most extraordinary! Never could I have believed that my old Shadow would return to me a man!"

"Tell me what I am to pay," repeated the Shadow; "for on no account would I remain in any one's debt."

"How canst thou speak so?" said the Scholar. "Why talk about debts? Thou art perfectly free, and I am exceedingly rejoiced to hear of thy good fortune. Come, old friend, sit down, and tell me how it has all come to pass, and what thou didst see in that mysterious house just opposite mine in the hot country."

"Well, I will tell you," said the Shadow, sitting down as requested; "but then you must first promise that you will never let any one in this town, where, perchance, you may meet me again, know that I was once your Shadow. I have some thoughts of matrimony,—I have the means for supporting more than one family."

"Have no fear," replied the Scholar; "I will not reveal to any one what thou really art. Here is my hand,—upon my honour as a gentleman, I promise it!"

"And I will speak truly,—upon my honour as a Shadow!" rejoined the mysterious visitor; of a truth, he could hardly express himself otherwise.

It was, certainly, quite wonderful to see how much of a man he had become. He was dressed completely in black, the finest black cloth, with shining boots, and a hat which could be squeezed together, so as to be only crown and brim,— not to speak of things we have already mentioned, gold chain, seals, and diamond rings. Yes, indeed, the Shadow was uncommonly well dressed, and, in fact, it was his dress which made him appear so completely a man.

"Well then, now I will tell you all about it," said the Shadow; and he planted his legs, with the shining boots, as firmly as he could upon the arm of the Scholar's new shadow, which lay like a poodle at its master's feet. This was done, perhaps, out of pride, but more probably under the idea that he might, perchance, seduce it into cleaving to himself for the future. And the recumbent shadow kept its place on the ground, still and motionless, lest it should lose a word; for it was naturally anxious to learn how it might, in its turn, free itself and become its own master.

"Can you guess who proved to be dwelling in the opposite house?" asked the Shadow, triumphantly. "It was Poesy, —most beautiful, most charming Poesy! I was there three weeks, and that is as good as if I had lived there three thousand years, and had read all that was imagined and written during that time. This I declare to you, and it is true; I have seen all, and I know all!"

"Poesy!" cried the Scholar; "ah, yes! she often dwells, a hermitess, in the very heart of a bustling city. Poesy!— yes. I, too, have seen her, but it was only for one moment, when sleep had charmed my eyes; she stood at the balcony, radiant and glorious as the northern lights. Oh, tell me,— pray tell me! Thou wert in the balcony, thou didst enter by the door, and then ——"

"Why, then—I was in the ante-chamber," said the Shadow; "you recollect you used to sit looking across into the ante-chamber. It was not lighted up, it was in a kind of twilight; but door after door, all open, led through a long suite of rooms and saloons, and in the distance there were lights in plenty—quite an illumination; indeed, the glare would have killed me, had I passed on into the lady's apartment. But I was prudent; I took my time and was patient, as every one should be."

"And what didst thou see?" inquired the Scholar.

"I saw everything; and I would tell you all about it, only—it is not pride, by any means, but as a free man, and a man of education and science, not to speak of my high position and circumstances—I do wish you would treat me with more respect. Cannot you give up that way of continually *thou*-ing me, and call me *you?*"

"I beg pardon," said the Scholar; "it is an old habit, and therefore difficult to cure oneself of. You are quite right, and I will try to remember. But now tell me all you saw."

"All, indeed," returned the Shadow; "for I have seen all, and I know all."

"What were the inner chambers like?" again inquired the Scholar. "Seemed they like fresh, balm-breathing groves? Seemed they like a holy church? Were those chosen halls like the starry heavens, when beheld from a mountain height?"

"Everything beautiful was there," said the Shadow. "I did not exactly go in—I remained in the twilight of the outer room; but that was an excellent position! I saw everything, and I know everything! I have been at Poesy's Court; I have been in the ante-chamber."

"But what did you see? Did all the ancient divinities pass through spacious halls? Did not bold heroes and chivalrous knights do battle there as in olden time? Were there not pretty, fairy-like children, gambolling together, and telling each other their dreams?"

"I repeat that I was there, and I beg you to understand that I saw everything which was to be seen, and I became a man!—had you gone over, possibly you might have become something more—but thus was it with me. I gained the knowledge of my inmost nature, my properties, and the relationship I bore to Poesy. During the time I spent with you, I thought little of these matters. Whenever the sun rose or set, as you know, I became wonderfully tall,—indeed, by moonlight, I might have been thought more noticeable even than yourself; but I did not then understand my own nature. In that ante-chamber all was made plain—I became a man! I left the place completely altered. You were no longer in the hot country, and I was ashamed to go about as a man in my then condition. I wanted boots and clothes: in short, all that human garnish which distinguishes a man, or, rather, makes him known to be such. I took my way—yes, I think I may trust you with my secret, you must not put it into a book—I took my way under the cook-maid's cloak, I hid myself in it—she little thought whom she was sheltering. It was evening when I first ventured out; I ran along the street in the moonlight, I stretched myself up along the wall —that is so pleasant and cooling to one's back! I ran up and I ran down; I peeped into rooms through the uppermost, even through the attic windows; I peeped where no one else could peep; I saw what no one else could see. After all, this is but a poor, miserable affair of a world! I would not be a man, but for the imaginary honour of the thing. I saw the most incredible, unheard-of things among all ranks and classes. I saw," continued the Shadow, emphatically, " what none must know, but all would so much like to know,— *their neighbours' secret evil deeds*. Had I published a new journal, would not people have read it? But, instead of this, I wrote to the individuals themselves, whose private doings I had spied out; and thus I raised wonder and fear in every town I visited. They were so afraid of me! and they loved me so much! Professors made me a professor; tailors gave me new clothes—you will observe I am well provided; coiners struck coin for me; and women declared I was so handsome! And thus I became the man you see me! And now I must bid you farewell. Here is my card; I dwell on the sunny side of the way, and am always at home in rainy weather."

And the Shadow took his departure.

"Strange, certainly, very strange!" said the Scholar.

Days and years passed away,—the Shadow came again.

"How is it with you?" he inquired.

"Alas!" sighed the Scholar, " I still write of what is true, and good, and beautiful, but no one seems to care to hear of such things. I am quite in despair. I suppose I take it to heart too much."

"That I never do," returned the Shadow. "I am growing fat, as every one should try to be. Ah, you don't understand the world, and thus you suffer yourself to be disgusted by it. You should travel; I intend to make a tour this summer; suppose you come with me? I should like to have a companion — will you travel with me as my shadow? It would be a great pleasure to me to have you with me; I will pay your expenses."

"An odd proposal, certainly!" and the Scholar smiled at the idea.

"What matter, when it suits both of us? Travelling will do wonders for you. Be my shadow, and you shall have everything you want."

"This is too absurd,—you are mad!"

"If I am, all the rest of the world is mad, too, and mad it will be to the end." And with this the Shadow went his way.

Meantime the Scholar's affairs grew worse and worse; sorrow and care pursued him, and as for his writing about the true, and the good, and the beautiful, all this was for the multitude about just as much use as it would be to scatter roses at the feet of a cow. At last he became downright ill.

"Actually, you look like a shadow!" so said his friends, and a shiver thrilled through the Scholar's frame on hearing the words.

"You must go to the baths," said the Shadow, at his next visit; "there is nothing else for you. I will take you with me for old acquaintance' sake. I will pay the expenses of the journey, and you shall write descriptions and entertain me on the way. I want to go to the baths myself; my beard does not grow quite as it should do, and that is as bad as a disease; for one cannot do without a beard. Now, be reasonable, and accept my offer; we shall travel as comrades."

And so they travelled: the Shadow was now the master, and the master was the shadow; they drove, they rode, they walked, always together, sometimes side by side, sometimes before or behind one another, according to the position of the sun.

The Shadow always took care to secure the place of honour for himself; but for this the Scholar cared little, he was really a kind-hearted man, and of an exceedingly mild and placid temper. One day, however, he said to the Shadow, "As we are now fellow-travellers, not to speak of having grown up together from childhood, why should we not call each other 'thou?' it sounds so much more affectionate and familiar."

"There is something in what you say," replied the Shadow, or rather the master, for such he was, to all intents and purposes. "It is kindly and honestly said, I will be no less honest and kind. You, as a man of learning, must know well what strange and unaccountable whims nature is subject to at times. Some men there are who cannot endure the smell of brown paper—it makes them quite ill; others shiver all over whenever any one scratches a pane of glass with a nail. And in like manner, I have a most painful feeling whenever I hear you say 'thou' to me. I feel myself, as it were, pressed to the earth—reduced to my former servile position. You see, it is a delicacy of feeling: certainly it is not pride—at any rate, I cannot suffer you to say 'thou' to me, but I will willingly call you 'thou,' and thus your wish will be half fulfilled."

So, henceforth, the Shadow called its former master "thou."

"This is rather cool," thought the latter, "I to address him as 'you' and he to say 'thou' to me." But there was no help for it.

They arrived at one of the Spas. Many strangers were there, and amongst them a king's daughter, marvellously beautiful. Her malady consisted in this, that she was too sharp-sighted; so much so that it rendered her quite uncomfortable.

She, of course, perceived at once that the new comer was quite a different sort of person from all the other visitors. "They say," observed she, "that he comes here because his beard will not grow, but I see well the real cause,—he cannot cast a shadow."

Her curiosity was excited. Accordingly, one day, meeting him on her walk, she took the opportunity of accosting him. Being a king's daughter, it was not necessary for her to use much ceremony; so she said at once, "Your malady is that you cannot cast a shadow."

"I am delighted to find that your Royal Highness is so much better!" was the Shadow's reply. "I am aware that it has been your misfortune to be too keen-sighted; but that disease must be entirely cured, for the fact is, that I have a very unusual shadow! Do you not see the person who always walks close to me? Other men have mere common shades for their shadows; but I do not like anything that is common. You may have observed that people often give their servants finer clothes for their liveries than they wear themselves; in like manner, I have allowed my shadow to dress himself up like a man, and, in fact, as you see, I have even given him a shadow of his own. This has been rather expensive, certainly; but I love to be peculiar."

"Hem!" thought the Princess, "am I actually recovered? There is nothing like these baths, the waters have of late years had powers almost miraculous. But I shall not leave the place at present, it is only just beginning to grow amusing; this stranger pleases me exceedingly; it is to be hoped that his beard will not grow, for, if it does, I suppose he will go away."

That evening, in the grand assembly-room, the king's daughter danced with the Shadow. She was very light, but he was still lighter; such a partner she had never had before. She told him what country she came from, and he knew the country; he had been there, though at a time when she was not at home; he had peeped in at both upper and lower windows of the palace; he had seen many curious things, so that he could answer the questions of the Princess and make revelations to her that were positively startling. Surely, he must be the wisest man living! She was struck with wonder and awe, and by the time they had danced the second dance, she was fairly in love with him. Of this the Shadow soon became aware; her eyes were continually piercing him through and through. They danced a third time, and she was very near telling him what she thought; but, very prudently, she restrained herself, remembering her land and heritage, and the multitude of beings over whom she would reign at some future period.

"He is a wise man," thought she, "that is well! and he dances charmingly, that is well too; but has he solid acquirements? they are of no less importance. I must try him." And she began to propound to him various questions, so difficult that she could not have answered them herself; and the Shadow made up a very strange face.

"Then you cannot answer me?" said the King's daughter.

"Oh, I have learned all that in the days of my childhood," replied her new acquaintance; "I believe that my shadow, even, now standing at the door yonder, could answer you."

"Your shadow? that would be rather remarkable!"

"Mind, I do not say decidedly that he can, but I should think so — he has followed me and listened to all I have said for so many years — yes, really I should think he could answer you. But your Royal Highness must first permit me to warn you that he especially prides himself upon passing for a man, so that to keep him in good-humour — and without that you will get nothing out of him — he must be treated quite as if he were a man."

"Oh, with all my heart!" said the Princess. So she went up to the learned man standing at the door, and began conversing with him about the sun and moon, and different nations, both far and near; and he answered her in such a manner as fully proved his wisdom and learning.

"What a wonderful man must he be who has so wise a shadow!" thought the Princess; "it would be a positive blessing to my kingdom and people if I were to choose him for my consort. And I will do it!"

And they were soon agreed, the King's daughter and the Shadow, but no one was to know of their engagement before the Princess returned to her own country.

"No one shall know, not even my shadow!" declared the intended bridegroom, and for this arrangement, no doubt, he had his own reasons.

So they went forthwith to the country of the Princess.

"Listen to me, my good friend!" said the Shadow to the Scholar; "I have now arrived at the height of happiness and power, — I must think of doing something for thee! Thou shalt always live with me at the palace, drive out with me in the royal carriage, and receive an annuity of a hundred thousand rix-dollars; but in return, thou must suffer every one to call thee a shadow; thou must never tell any one that thou hast been a man; and once every year, when I sit publicly in the balcony in the sunshine, thou must lie meekly at my feet, as every shadow should lie. For know this! I am going to marry the King's daughter; this very evening the nuptials will be celebrated."

"No, this is too bad!" exclaimed the Scholar, "this shall never be; I will not do it! It would be deceiving the whole country, not to speak of the King's daughter. I will make everything public! how, that I am the man, and thou the shadow,—that thou art only dressed like a man!"

"No one will believe you," returned the Shadow; "be reasonable, pray, or I shall call the guard."

"I am going straight to the King's daughter!" cried the Scholar.

"But I am going first," said the Shadow; "and thou art going to prison."

And to prison he went, for of course the guard obeyed him whom they knew their Princess had chosen as her consort.

"Thou tremblest!" observed the Princess, when the Shadow entered her apartment, "has anything happened? thou must not be ill this evening, our bridal evening!"

"I have lived to see the most fearful thing," said the Shadow; "you would never believe it—ah! a poor shadow's brain cannot bear much—just imagine it; my shadow has become crazy; he actually believes that he is a man, and that I—only think—that I am his shadow!"

"This is shocking indeed!" said the Princess; "I hope he is locked up?"

"Of course; I am much afraid he will never recover himself."

"Poor shadow! he is truly unfortunate; it would really be a charity to free him from the little life he possesses; and, indeed, when I consider how ready people are in these days to take part with the lower classes against the great, it seems to me that the best thing we can do will be to make away with him privately."

"It is hard, very hard, for he has been a faithful servant." And the Shadow made as though he sighed.

"You are a noble character!" exclaimed the King's daughter.

That evening the whole city was illuminated; cannons were fired—*boom!* and the soldiers presented arms. All this was in honour of the royal wedding. The King's daughter and the Shadow went out on the balcony to show themselves and hear " Hurrah!" shouted again and again.

The Scholar heard nothing of all these grand doings, for they had already taken his life.

THE OLD HOUSE.

THERE stood in a street a very, very old house; it was, indeed, almost three hundred years old, as might be known by looking at the beam, whereon the date of its building was carved out among fantastic tulips and curling hop-tendrils; whole texts, too, were cut in the time-worn wood, after the fashion of days by-gone; and over every window peered a human face—such curious, wry faces were those! The first-floor of this house projected a good way beyond the ground-floor, and immediately under the roof ran a leaden gutter with a dragon's head to it; the rain-water was meant to run out from the dragon's mouth; but there being a hole in the gutter, it generally chose in preference to pour down through this hole.

All the other houses in the street were so new and so neat, and so spruce, with their large window-panes and flat smooth walls; it was quite plain that they would have nothing to do with the Old House; you could see so well that they were saying within themselves, "How much longer is that heap of rubbish to stand here, a disgrace to the street? Why, the upper story puts itself so forward, that no one from our windows can see what is being done underneath it! And just look at the steps too, they are as broad as if they belonged to a castle, and as high—one would suppose they led up to a church-steeple; the iron balustrade looks for all the world just like the entrance to an old tomb, and it must needs have brass knobs too. So stupid, so tasteless!"

On the opposite side of the street all the houses were new, neat, and spruce; and they were all of the same way of thinking as the other houses. But at one of the windows, looking straight at the Old House, used to sit a little boy with fresh rosy cheeks and bright sparkling eyes; and he thought better of this despised old building; he loved it, both in sunshine and moonshine. And when he sat there, looking at the mouldering wall, from which all the mortar had worn away, he could fancy such strange pictures! he could image to himself how the street looked three centuries back, when all the houses had flights of steps, projecting upper stories, and pointed gable-ends; he could see soldiers walking about with halberds in their hands, and gutters running down in the shapes of dragons and griffins. Yes, that was just the house to please him! and in it, he knew, dwelt an old gentleman who wore large brass buttons on his coat, and such a wig! you could be sure it was a real wig. Every morning a servingman as old as his master came to him, to clean up his rooms and go on errands; at other times, the old gentleman in brass buttons was quite alone in the Old House. Sometimes he came and looked out from his window, and then the little boy nodded to him, and he nodded again to the little boy, and thus they became friends and acquaintances, although they had never yet spoken to each other. But that might come in time. The little boy heard his parents say, "The old gentleman opposite is very well off; but it is terrible to be so quite alone as he is."

So next Sunday the little boy was very busy wrapping something up in paper; he then went down to the door and watched till the old man who went on errands came by, and said to him, "Please to take this to the old gentleman up there from me; I have two Tin-soldiers, this is one of them; I want him to have it, because I know that he is so terribly lonely."

And the old man looked quite pleased, nodded, and took the Tin-soldier into the Old House. By-and-by he came back to ask whether the little boy would not like to come himself and pay the old gentleman a visit. And the child got leave of his parents, and then went over the way into the Old House.

And the brass knobs on the balustrades shone much brighter than usual, he thought, as though they had been fresh rubbed in honour of his visit; and the carved trumpeters rising out of the tulips on the door blew with all their might; their cheeks, he was sure, were much more puffed out than ever they had been before. Yes, they blew their trumpets, " Tararara! See, the little boy comes, Tararara!" and then the door opened. The whole length of the passage was hung with portraits of knights in armour and ladies in full silk robes; and the armour rattled and the silk robes rustled so pleasantly! And then there was a staircase; the stairs first went a good way up, and then a little way down; and next the little boy and his conductor stood in a balcony, a very decayed balcony, with many a large chink and crevice in it. grass and weeds sprouting thickly out of all these gaps, and making the place look as green as if it had been a garden instead of a balcony. Antique flower-pots, all having human faces and asses' ears, were ranged here; the plants in them grew exactly as suited their own pleasure and convenience. In one pot were seen some straggling gilliflowers; the green leaves and shoots— there were no blossoms yet —had spread out over the edges, as though in very great glee; you could see that the plant meant to say, " The breeze has fanned me, the sun has kissed me, and promised me a little flower on Sunday, a little flower on Sunday!"

And then his guide led the little boy into a chamber where the walls were covered with leather hangings with gold flowers stamped upon them.

> " Gilding wears out, with time and bad weather,
>   But leather endures, there's nothing like leather!"

sang the Walls.

And here stood such high-backed arm-chairs, carved all over, and with arms on either side. "Sit down, sit down," cried they. "Ugh! how I am cracking inside! I have got the rheumatism in my back like the old cabinet. Rheumatism in my back, ugh!"

At last the little boy entered the room which fronted the street, and where the old gentleman sat.

"Thanks for the Tin-soldier, my little friend," said the old gentleman. "And thanks, too, for coming over to see me."

"Thanks, thanks!" or "Crack, crack!" said all the pieces of Furniture in the room; there were so many of them, and they stood in each other's way to see the little boy.

On the middle panel of the wall hung the picture of a beautiful lady; very young and very happy she looked; but she was clad quite after the fashion of the olden time. She had powder in her hair, and her clothes stood out stiffly round her. She said neither "thanks" nor "crack," but she looked with her gentle eyes upon the little boy, who immediately asked the old gentleman, "Where did you get her from?"

"From the pawnbroker's," replied the old gentleman. "There are so many pictures to be had there, nobody knows or cares anything about them; for the people they were meant for were all buried long ago, but I happened to know that lady in past times — she is dead, too; dead and gone these fifty years."

And under the portrait hung a bouquet of faded flowers, carefully preserved behind glass; they must have been fifty years old too, they looked so very antique. And the pendulum of the great clock swung backwards and forwards, and the hand went round and round, and everything in the room grew older and older every moment, but they never thought of that.

"They say at home," said the little Boy, "that you are so terribly lonely."

"Oh, no!" was the reply. "The old thoughts and the memories and scenes they bring with them come and visit me continually; and now you are come too! I am very happy."

And then the old gentleman took down from the bookcase a picture-book — such pictures were those! There were long, endless processions; the strangest carriages, such as are never seen now-a-days; soldiers not unlike knaves of clubs, and peaceable citizens bearing the banners of different companies; the tailors' flag showed a pair of scissors held between two lions; the shoemakers' ought to have had boots for their device, but they had not — they carried an eagle with two heads, for everything belonging to shoemakers, you know, must be so that they may say, "It is a pair." Ah, a rare picture-book was that!

And presently the old gentleman went into an adjoining room to fetch out sweetmeats, nuts, and apples; the Old House was rich in stores of these, it seemed.

Then spoke the Tin-soldier, who stood on the chest of drawers: "I cannot stand this, indeed! It is so sad and lonely here, no one who has ever been used to live in a family can accustom himself to such a life as is led here. No, I cannot bear it! The day is so long and wearisome, and the evenings are still longer; it is not as over the way with you, where your father and mother used to talk so pleasantly and sensibly, while you and all the other sweet children played at your merry games. This old gentleman is quite a hermit! Do you think there are any kind eyes watching him? do you think he ever has kisses given him? or a pretty Christmas-tree? Nothing will ever be given to him, except his funeral! No, I cannot bear it!"

"You must not take it in that way," said the little boy. "For my part, I think it is very pleasant to be here; and did you not hear him say how that all his old thoughts and memories came to visit him?"

"That may be; but I don't see them, and I know nothing about them," replied the Tin-soldier. "I tell you I cannot bear it!"

"But you must bear it," insisted the little boy.

Here the old gentleman came back, a bright smile on his face, and the most delicious fruits and sweetmeats in his hand. And the little boy quite forgot the Tin-soldier.

Happy and pleased the little boy returned home. Days and weeks passed away; often and often did the little boy stand at the window to nod at the Old House; often and often did the old gentleman nod to him in return; often and often did the little boy go to pay a visit over the way.

And every time the carved Trumpeters blew, "Trararara! see the little boy comes; tra-ra-ra-ra!" and the Swords and the Armour in the old knightly portraits rattled, and the Ladies' Silk Robes rustled; the Leather Hangings chanted

> " Gilding wears out, with time and bad weather,
> But leather endures, there's nothing like leather!"

and the old Arm-chairs cracked, because of the rheumatism in their backs. It was always exactly as the first time the little boy had been there; for in the Old House every day — every hour even — passed like the foregoing.

"I cannot bear it!" again declared the Tin-soldier; "it is so very sad, it makes me weep tin tears! Rather let me go to the wars, and lose my arms and legs; that will be a change at least. I cannot bear this life; I know now what it is to be visited by one's old thoughts and memories, for mine have been paying visits to me, and I assure you there is no pleasure in it at all; I have many a time been nearly jumping down off the chest of drawers. I saw all of you as plainly as if you had been here; it was Sunday morning again, and all you children were standing before the table and singing your hymns, as you always used to sing them. There you stood, looking so earnest, and with your hands clasped; and your father and mother were listening so gravely! And then the door opened, and your little sister Maria, who is not yet two years old, and who always begins to dance whenever she hears music or singing, of whatever kind it may be, came in. She had better have stayed away, for she immediately began to dance; but she could not make out the time at all, because the tune was so slow; and so she stood first on one foot, with her head drooping down over it, and then on the other foot, leaning her head quite on the opposite side. But still she could not hit upon the right time. You all of you stood so grave, though it was really very difficult to be serious any longer; I could not — I laughed inwardly — and therefore I fell down from the table and lamed myself. I am lame still in consequence; it was wrong of me to laugh. And all this happens over again within me,— and so does everything else that I have lived through and seen; and this is what the old gentleman means by ' his old thoughts, and the memories and scenes they bring with them.' But tell

THE NEW YORK
PUBLIC LIBRARY

ASTOR, LENOX AND
TILDEN FOUNDATIONS.

THE OLD HOUSE.

Page 373.

me, do you still sing on Sundays? Tell me something about little Maria, and about my comrade, the other Tin-soldier — ah, he is a lucky fellow! I cannot bear this life!"

"You are given away," said the little boy; "you must stay here. I wonder you don't see that!"

And the old gentleman brought out a drawer, wherein were kept many things wonderful to see — money-boxes, and balm-boxes, and packs of old-fashioned cards. Very large gilt cards were they, such as are never met with now. And other drawers, full of old curiosities, were opened, and the harpsichord, too, was opened; there was a landscape painted on the inside of the lid, and the instrument was very hoarse when the old gentleman played upon it. He began to hum a tune.

"Ah, yes, she used to sing that!" said he; and he looked up at the portrait he had bought at the pawnbroker's. So brightly the old gentleman's eyes sparkled as he looked at it!

"I will go to the wars! I will go to the wars!" cried the Tin-soldier, as loud as ever he could; and down he fell upon the floor.

What could have become of him? The old gentleman hunted in vain, the little boy hunted in vain. "Never mind, I shall be sure to find him," said the old gentleman; however, he never could find him. The floor was full of cracks and crevices; the Tin-soldier had fallen through one of these crevices, and there he lay buried alive.

Evening came, and the little boy went home; weeks passed away, — many weeks passed away. The windows were now quite frozen over; the little boy had to breathe hard upon them before he could make a tiny peep-hole, through which he could look at the Old House, and then he saw that the snow had drifted into all the wooden carving-work and quaint devices, and lay quite thick upon the steps, just as though no one were at home. And no one was at home: the old gentleman was dead.

On the evening of that day a carriage drove up to the door of the Old House, and a coffin was carried down the steps; the old gentleman was to be buried far out in the country. The carriage drove away. No one followed it, — all his friends were dead. The little boy kissed his hand to the coffin; then he saw it disappear.

A few days afterwards there was a sale at the Old House; the little boy looked out from his window, watching to see the different pieces of furniture as they were carried out. The old knights and ladies, the flower-pots, with the long asses' ears, the old chairs and cabinets, all his acquaintances, he saw taken away, some to one place, some to another; the portrait bought at the pawnbroker's returned to the pawnbroker's again, and there it was left undisturbed, for no one living now knew anything of that sweet, gentle-eyed face, and no one cared about such an old, dusty, musty picture.

Next spring the House itself was pulled down, for " it was a disgrace to the street," people said. One could now look from the street right into the room where were the leathern hangings, all torn and gashed, and the green weeds of the balcony clung wildly round the falling planks. By degrees all was cleared away.

" A very good thing, too!" declared the neighbouring Houses.

* * * * * * * * *

And a pleasant new house with large windows, and smooth, white walls was built in its stead, and the space in front, where the Old House had stood, was made into a little garden, vines grew clustering up over the neighbour's walls, so as to shelter it on either side, and it was shut out from the street by a large, iron grating, with a trellis-gate. That looked quite grand; people stood outside, and tried to peep in through the iron trellis. And the sparrows, too, clustered by dozens and dozens among the vines, chirping as loud and as fast as they could; not about the Old House, though, for that they could none of them have known. Many years had elapsed, so many, that the little boy we spoke of had grown up to be a man; yes, and a good and clever man he was, and his parents took great pride and pleasure in him. He had just married, and had removed with his fair young bride into this new house with the garden to it; and he stood by her side in the garden whilst she was planting a little field-flower that had taken her fancy. She planted it with her own pretty white hand, and smoothed down the earth round it with her fingers. " Oh, dear, what was that?" She had pricked herself. There was something sharp and pointed among the soft mould.

It was—only think!—it was the Tin-soldier, the very same one which the old gentleman had lost, and which, after being tumbled and tossed about hither and thither, had now lain for many years quietly in the earth.

And the young bride wiped the Tin-soldier dry, first with a green leaf, and then with her own pocket-handkerchief,—it was perfumed so deliciously! and the Tin-soldier felt as though awakening from a trance.

"Let me look at him," said the young man, and he smiled and shook his head. "No, it cannot possibly be the very same Tin-soldier, but it reminds me so of one that I had when I was a little boy." And then he told his wife about the Old House, and the old gentleman, and the Tin-soldier that he had given him, because he was so terribly lonely. He told it exactly as it had been, and tears came into his young wife's eyes at thinking of the solitary life the old gentleman must have lived.

"I don't see why this should not be the very same Tin-soldier," said she; "I will keep it just to put me in mind of all you have told me. And you must show me the old gentleman's grave."

"I wish I knew it," was the reply. "I believe nobody knows it. All his friends were dead, nobody cared about the matter, and I was such a little boy then!"

"He must have been terribly lonely, poor old gentleman!" remarked she.

"Yes, terribly lonely!" said the Tin-soldier; "but it is charming to find that one is not forgotten!"

"Charming, indeed!" cried something close by,—no one but the Tin-soldier recognised the thing that spoke; it was a shred from the old leather hangings, the gilding was all worn off, and it looked like a clod of moist earth: still it held by its former good opinion of itself, and asserted it too:

> "Gilding wears out, with time and bad weather,
> But leather endures, there's nothing like leather!"

However, the Tin-soldier believed nothing of such vain boasting.

THE FLAX.

THE Flax was in full bloom. Its pretty blue blossoms were as soft as the wings of a moth, and still more delicate. And the sun shone on the flax-field, and the rain watered it; and that was as good for the flax-flowers as it is for little children to be washed and kissed by their mother,— they look so much fresher and prettier afterwards. Thus it was with the Flax-flowers.

"People say I am so fine and flourishing," observed the Flax; "and that I am growing so charmingly tall, a splendid piece of linen will be got from me. Oh, how happy I am! how can any one be happier? Everything around me is so pleasant, and I shall be of use for something or other. How the sun cheers one up, and how fresh and sweet the rain tastes! I am incomparably happy; I am the happiest vegetable in the world!"

"Ah, ah, ah!" jeered the Stakes in the hedge; "you don't know the world, not you, but we know it, there are **knots in us!**" and then they cracked so dolefully:

"Snip, snap, snurre,
Bassilurre,
And so the song is en-ded-ded-ded."

"No, it is not ended," replied the Flax; "the sun shines every morning, the rain does me so much good, I can see myself grow; I can feel that I am in blossom—who so happy as I?"

However, one day people came, took hold of the Flax, and pulled it up, root and all; that was exceedingly uncomfortable; and then it was thrown into water, as though intended to be drowned, and, after that, put before the fire, as though to be roasted. This was most cruel!

"One cannot always have what one wishes!" sighed the Flax; "it is well to suffer sometimes, it gives one experience."

But matters seemed to get worse and worse. The Flax was bruised and broken, hacked and hackled, and at last put on the wheel—snurre rur! snurre rur!—it was not possible to keep one's thoughts collected in such a situation as this.

"I have been exceedingly fortunate," thought the Flax, amid all these tortures. "One ought to be thankful for the happiness one has enjoyed in times past. Thankful, thankful, oh yes!" and still the Flax said the same when taken to the loom. And here it was made into a large, handsome piece of linen; all the Flax of that one field was made into a single piece.

"Well, but this is charming! Never should I have expected it. What unexampled good fortune I have carried through the world with me! What arrant nonsense the Stakes in the hedge used to talk with their

'Snip, snap, snurre,
Bassilurre.'

The song is not ended at all! Life is but just beginning It is a very pleasant thing, too, is life; to be sure I have suffered, but that is past now, and I have become something through suffering. I am so strong, and yet so soft! so white and so long! this is far better than being a vegetable; even during blossom-time nobody attends to one, and one only gets water when it is raining. Now, I am well taken care of— the girl turns me over every morning, and I have a shower-bath from the water-tub every evening; nay, the parson's wife herself came and looked at me, and said I was the finest piece of linen in the parish. No one can possibly be happier than I am!"

The Linen was taken into the house, and cut up with scissors. Oh, how it was cut and clipped, how it was pierced and stuck through with needles! that was certainly no pleasure at all. It was at last made up into twelve articles of attire, such articles as are not often mentioned, but which people can hardly do without; there were just twelve of them.

"So this, then, was my destiny. Well, it is very delightful; now I shall be of use in the world, and there is really no pleasure like that of being useful. We are now twelve pieces, but we are still one and the same—we are a dozen! Certainly, this is being extremely fortunate!"

Years passed away,—at last the Linen could endure no longer.

"All things must pass away some time or other," remarked each piece. "I should like very much to last a little while longer, but one ought not to wish for impossibilities." And so the Linen was rent into shreds and remnants numberless; they believed all was over with them, for they were hacked, and mashed, and boiled, and they knew not what else—and thus they became beautiful, fine, white paper!

"Now, upon my word, this is a surprise! And a most delightful surprise too!" declared the Paper. "Why, now I am finer than ever, and I shall be written upon! I wonder what will be written upon me. Was there ever such famous good fortune as mine!" And the Paper was written upon; the most charming stories in the world were written on it, and they were read aloud! and people declared that these stories were very beautiful and very instructive; that to read them would make mankind both wiser and better. Truly, a great blessing was given to the world in the words written upon that same Paper.

"Certainly, this is more than I could ever have dreamt of, when I was a wee little blue flower of the field! How could I then have looked forward to becoming a messenger destined to bring knowledge and pleasure among men? I can hardly understand it even now. Yet, so it is, actually. And, for my own part, I have never done anything, beyond the little that in me lay, to strive to exist, and yet I am carried on from one state of honour and happiness to another; and every time that I think within myself, 'Now, surely, the song is en-ded-ded-ded,' I am converted into something new something far higher and better. Now, I suppose I shall be sent on my travels, shall be sent round the wide world, so that all men may read me. I should think that would be the wisest plan. Formerly I had blue blossoms, now for every single blossom I have some beautiful thought, or pleasant fancy — who so happy as I?"

But the Paper was not sent on its travels, it went to the printer's instead, and there all that was written upon it was printed in a book; nay, in many hundred books: and in this way an infinitely greater number of people received pleasure and profit therefrom than if the written Paper itself had been sent round the world, and perhaps got torn and worn to pieces before it had gone half way.

"Yes, to be sure, this is much more sensible," thought the Paper. "It never occurred to me, though. I am to stay at home and be held in as great honour as if I were an old grandfather. The book was written on me first, the ink flowed in upon me from the pen and formed the words. I shall stay at home, while the books go about the world, to and fro — that is much better. How glad I am! how fortunate I am!"

So the Paper was rolled up and laid on one side. "It is good to repose after labour," said the Paper. "It is quite right to collect oneself, and quietly think over all that dwelleth within one. Now, first, do I rightly know myself. And to know oneself, I have heard, is the best knowledge, the truest progress. And come what will, this I am sure of, all will end in progress — always is there progress!"

One day the roll of Paper was thrown upon the stove to be burnt — it must not be sold to the grocer to wrap round pounds of butter and sugar. And all the children in the house flocked round; they wanted to see the blaze, they wanted to count the multitude of tiny red sparks which seem to dart to and fro among the ashes, dying out, one after another, so quickly — they call them "the children going out of school," and the last spark of all is the schoolmaster; they often fancy he is gone out, but another and another spark flies up unexpectedly, and the schoolmaster always tarries a little behind the rest.

And now all the Paper lay heaped up on the stove

"Ugh!" it cried, and all at once it burst into a flame. So high did it rise into the air, never had the Flax been able to rear its tiny blue blossoms so high, and it shone as never the white Linen had shone; all the letters written on it became fiery red in an instant, and all the words and thoughts of the writer were surrounded with a glory.

"Now, then, I go straight up into the sun!" said something within the flames. It was as though a thousand voices at once had spoken thus; and the Flame burst through the chimney, and rose high above it; and brighter than the Flame, yet invisible to mortal eyes, hovered little tiny beings, as many as there had been blossoms on the Flax. They were lighter and of more subtle essence than even the Flame that bore them; and when that Flame had quite died away, and nothing remained of the Paper but the black ashes, they once again danced over them, and wherever their feet touched the ashes, their footprints, the fiery red sparks, were seen. Thus "the children went out of school, and the schoolmaster came last;" it was a pleasure to see the pretty sight, and the children of the house stood looking at the black ashes and singing—

>' Snip, snap, snurre,
>Bassilurre,
>And now the song is en-ded-ded-ded.'

But the tiny invisible beings replied every one, "The song is never ended; that is the best of it! We know that, and therefore none are so happy as we are!"

However, the children could neither hear nor understand the reply; nor would it be well that they should, for children must not know everything.

THE DROP OF WATER.

SURELY you know what a microscope is—that wonderful glass which makes everything appear a hundred times larger than it really is. If you look through a microscope at a single drop of ditch-water, you will perceive more than a thousand strange-shaped creatures, such as you never could imagine dwelling in the water. It looks not unlike a plateful of shrimps, all jumping and crowding upon each other; and so ferocious are these little creatures, that they will tear off each other's arms and legs without mercy; and yet they are happy and merry after their fashion.

Now there was once an old man, whom all his neighbours called Cribbley Crabbley,—a curious name to be sure! He always liked to make the best of everything, and, when he could not manage it otherwise, he tried magic.

So one day he sat with his microscope held up to his eye, looking at a drop of ditch-water. Oh, what a strange sight was that! All the thousand little imps in the water were jumping and springing about, devouring each other, or pulling each other to pieces.

"Upon my word, this is too horrible!" quoth old Cribbley Crabbley; "there must surely be some means of making them live in peace and quiet." And he thought and thought but still could not hit on the right expedient. "I must give them a colour," he said at last, "then I shall be able to see them more distinctly;" and accordingly he let fall into the water a tiny drop of something that looked like red wine, but in reality it was witches' blood; whereupon all the strange little creatures immediately became red all over, not unlike the Red Indians; the drop of water now seemed a whole townful of naked wild men.

"What have you there?" inquired another old magician, who had no name at all, which made him more remarkable even than Cribbley Crabbley.

"Well, if you can guess what it is," replied Cribbley Crabbley, "I will give it you; but I warn you, you'll not find it out so easily."

And the magician without a name looked through the microscope. The scene now revealed to his eyes actually resembled a town where all the inhabitants were running about without clothing; it was a horrible sight! But still more horrible was it to see how they kicked and cuffed, struggled and fought, pulled and bit each other. All those that were lowest must needs strive to get uppermost, and all those that were highest must be thrust down. "Look, look!" they seemed to be crying out, "his leg is longer than mine; pah! off with it! And there is one who has a little lump behind his ear,—an innocent little lump enough, but it pains him, and it shall pain him more!" And they hacked at it, and seized hold of him and devoured him, merely because of this little lump. Only one of the creatures was quiet, very quiet, and still: it sat by itself, like a little modest damsel, wishing for nothing but peace and rest. But the others would not have it so; they pulled the little damsel forward, cuffed her, cut at her, and ate her.

"This is most uncommonly amusing," remarked the nameless magician.

"Do you think so? Well, but what is it?" asked

Cribbley Crabbley. "Can you guess, or can you not?—that's the question."

"To be sure I can guess," was the reply of the nameless magician, "easy enough. It is either Copenhagen or some other large city; I don't know which, for they are all alike. It is some large city."

"It is a drop of ditch-water!" said Cribbley Crabbley

THE HAPPY FAMILY.

THE largest green leaves that you can find in the country are the burdock-leaves; if a little girl take one of them and hold it in front of the skirt of her frock, it serves her as an apron; and if she place it on her head, it is almost as good a shelter against the rain as an umbrella—so very, very large are these leaves. Never is one burdock-leaf found growing alone, wherever one grows, a whole colony of them grow also; they are sociable leaves, and beautiful, too, but all their beauty is food for the snails. Those large white Snails, of which the grand folks used, in olden time, to make fricassees, dine off the burdock-leaves; and greedily they eat of them, saying all the while, "Hum, how nice! how exquisite!" for they think the food quite delicious; they live upon burdock-leaves, and for their sakes, they imagine, the burdock-leaves have been sown.

Now there was an old-fashioned manor-house; snails were no longer cooked and eaten there, for not only had the custom died away, but the last owners of the house had also died, and no one lived in it at all. But burdock-leaves grew near this house, and they had not died away; they still grew, and thrived, and multiplied; and as there was no one to weed them up, they spread over all the paths and all the beds, till the garden at last became a perfect wilderness of burdock-leaves. Here and there, indeed, might still be seen a solitary apple or plum-tree, otherwise no one could possibly have guessed that this place had ever been a garden; on all sides you saw burdock-leaves, nothing but burdock-leaves. And among them dwelt two old Snails, the last of their race.

Even they themselves could not tell how old they were; but they could remember perfectly that their family had once been very numerous; that they belonged to a colony from a foreign land; and that for them and theirs the whole grove had been planted. Beyond the burdock-grove they had never been, but they knew that there was another place in the world called the Manor-house, and that there snails were cooked, and then became black, and were laid upon silver dishes; but what happened afterwards they could not divine. Nor could they at all imagine how they would feel when cooked and laid on silver dishes; but that it was very delightful, and a very great honour and distinction—of that they were certain. Neither the Cockchafer, the Toad, or the Earthworm, all of whom they had questioned on the subject, could give them any correct information, for not one of these had ever been cooked or laid in a silver dish.

No creatures in the world were held in such high honour as these old white Snails; they were quite sure of that: the burdock-wood had grown up solely on their account, and the Manor-house stood beyond merely that they might some day be taken there, cooked, and laid in silver dishes.

They now lived a very lonely, and yet a very happy life, and as they had no children of their own, they had taken a liking to a little common Snail, and brought it up as their own child. Unfortunately, this little Snail, being of a different species, could not grow larger, so as to become like its foster-parents; however, old Mother Snail insisted that she could perceive he was growing fast; and she begged Father Snail, since he could not see it as she did, to touch the little Snail's house and feel it. And old Father Snail felt the house, and acknowledged that the mother was in the right.

One day there came a heavy shower of rain. "Only listen, what a drum-drum-drumming there is on the burdock-leaves!" remarked Father Snail.

"It is the drops that make that drumming," rejoined Mother Snail. "Look, now they are running straight down the stalk; you will see it quite wet presently. I am glad we have our own good house; and the little one too, he is safe in his. Certainly, it cannot be denied, that more is done for us than for all other creatures put together; it is easily seen that we are of the first importance in the world. We have houses provided for us from our birth, and the burdock-wood is planted for our sakes! I should rather like to know, though, how far it extends, and what is beyond it."

"There is nothing beyond it!" quoth Father Snail. "And if there were any other places, what would it signify? No place can be better than this; we have nothing to wish for."

"I cannot say that, for my part," replied Mother Snail. "I own I should like to go up to the Manor-house, and there be cooked and laid in a silver dish. All our forefathers went there, and only think what an honour it must be!"

"Most probably the Manor-house has fallen to pieces," said Father Snail, "or else the burdock-grove has grown over it, so that the human beings cannot now get out to fetch us. However, there is no need to be in such haste, but you are always in such a violent hurry about everything; and the little one, too, he begins to take after you. Why, he has crept all up the stalk in less than three days; it makes my head turn quite dizzy to look at him!"

"Don't scold him," said Mother Snail, "he crawls so cleverly! we shall have great pride and pleasure in him, and what else have we old folks got to live for? But there is one thing we ought to think of now; how are we to get him a wife? Don't you think that far out in the burdock-grove there may, perhaps, be a few more of our family left?"

"Black Snails, no doubt, there are in plenty," replied the other; "Black Snails without houses; but they are so low, so vulgar! I'll tell you what we can do; we can commission the Ants to look about for us, they are always running backwards and forwards, as if all the business in the world had to be done by them; they must certainly be able to find a wife for our little Snail."

"To be sure, we know where is the loveliest little creature imaginable!" exclaimed five or six Ants, who were passing by just then. "But, perhaps, she may not choose to listen to the proposal, for she is a Queen."

"What does that matter?" returned the two old Snails. "Has she a house? that is much more to the purpose!"

"A house!" repeated the Ants; "she has a palace! the most magnificent ant-palace, with seven hundred passages!"

"Oh, thank you!" said Mother Snail; "if you fancy our son is going to live in an ant-hill, you are very much mistaken, that's all. If you have no better proposal to make than that, we can give the commission to the white Gnats; they flutter about in rain and in sunshine; they know every corner of the burdock-grove quite intimately."

"Ah, yes, we know the wife for him!" declared the Gnats, on being appealed to. "A hundred human paces off there sits, on a gooseberry-bush, a little Snail with a house; she lives so solitary, poor thing! like a hermitess, and she is quite old enough to marry. It is only the distance of a hundred human paces."

"Well, then, let her come to him," said the old Snails; "that will be most fitting; he has a burdock-grove, she has only a gooseberry-bush."

And so the Gnats fluttered away to make the offer to little Miss Snail. Eight days passed before she made her appearance; so much the better, that showed she came of the right breed.

And now the bridal solemnities were held. Six Glow-worms shone as brightly as they could; otherwise, the whole affair passed off very quietly, for neither of the two old Snails could endure merriment and rioting. Indeed, Father Snail was too much moved to be able to say a word; but Mother Snail made a most beautiful and affecting speech, giving to the two young people the whole burdock-grove for their inheritance, and declaring, as she always had declared, that it was the best, if not the only place in the world; moreover, she promised that if they lived together peaceably and honestly, and multiplied in the grove, they and their children should at last be taken to the Manor-house, there to be cooked till they were black, and then be laid on silver dishes.

And after this speech was ended, the two old Snails crept back into their houses, and never came out again; there they slept. And the young Snails reigned in the burdock-wood in their stead, and had a numerous posterity. But they never had the good fortune to be cooked, or to be put in silver dishes; and so they decided that the Manor-house must have fallen to pieces, and that all the human beings in the world must be dead; no one ever contradicted them in this opinion, and therefore it must needs be true. And for their sakes the rain-drops beat upon the burdock-leaves, and made drum music, and for their sakes the sun shone on the burdock-leaves, giving them a bright green colour; and they were very happy, and the whole Snail family were very happy.

THE FALSE COLLAR.

THERE was once a fine gentleman whose toilet-table displayed nothing but a boot-jack and a comb, but he possessed the most charming false Collar in the world, and it is the history of this Collar that the following pages would relate. The Collar was so old that he began to think of marriage; it so chanced that one day in the wash he and the Garter were thrown together.

"Well, upon my honour!" quoth the False Collar, "never have I seen anything so slender and delicate, so pretty and soft! May I take the liberty of asking your name?"

"Certainly not; and if you do ask, I shall not tell you," replied the Garter.

"Where do you live?" inquired the Collar.

But the Garter was very modest and shy, and seemed to think that even this was too impertinent a question.

"Surely you must be a waistband," said the Collar; "a Queen's waistband, perhaps! I see you are useful as well as ornamental, pretty lady!"

"You must not speak to me," returned the Garter; "I do not think I have given any encouragement to such behaviour."

"Yes, indeed," insisted the False Collar; "beauty like yours may encourage one to anything."

"You are not to come so near me," said the Garter; "you look as if you belonged to a man."

"I am a fine gentleman," retorted the False Collar proudly; "I have a boot-jack and a comb, all to myself." But this was mere boasting, they belonged to his master, not to himself.

"Don't come so near me, I tell you," repeated the Garter; "I am not accustomed to such familiarities."

"So you're a prude, are you?" quoth the discomfited False Collar, and just then he was taken out of the wash-tub. He was starched, and next he was hung across a chair in the sunshine, and at last laid upon the ironing-board. And now the hot iron approached him.

"Lady!" cried the False Collar; "pretty widow lady! I am growing so warm — I am burning hot! I am becoming quite another creature, the wrinkles are all taken out of me; you will burn a hole in me — ugh! Pretty widow, suffer me to pay my addresses to you!"

"Stuff!" exclaimed the Iron, as she passed haughtily over the Collar; for she imagined herself to be a steam-engine, and that she was meant, some day or other, to be put on a railroad to draw carriages.

"Stuff!" said she again.

The Collar was a little unravelled at the edges, so a pair of scissors was brought to clip off the loose threads.

"Oh!" cried the False Collar, "surely you must be a ballet-dancer! How cleverly you can throw out your limbs! Never have I seen anything half so charming. I am sure that no human being in the world could do anything at all like it!"

"You need not tell me that, I know it already," replied the Scissors.

"You deserve to be a Countess," said the False Collar. "Alas! I am only a fine gentleman; to be sure I have a boot-jack and a comb,— if I had but an earldom!"

"Does he really mean this for courtship?" said the Scissors. "I wonder what next!" and forthwith she *cut* him, for she was very indignant. So he had his third dismissal.

"I can still address the Comb. It is quite delightful to see how long you have kept all your teeth, fair lady!" Thus spoke the False Collar to the Comb. "Have you never thought of betrothing yourself?"

"Why, yes," replied the Comb; "if you particularly wish to know, I will tell you a secret. I am engaged to the Boot-jack."

"Engaged to the Boot-jack?" repeated the False Collar, in consternation. There was now no one left to whom he could pay his addresses, accordingly he began to despise the fair sex altogether.

A long, long time passed away. At last the Collar found himself in a box at the paper-mill. The box harboured a large community of rags and tatters, and this community formed itself into snug coteries, the fine keeping by themselves, and the coarse by themselves, just as it ought to be. Every one of them had a great deal to say, but the False Collar most of all, for he was a perfect braggadocio.

"I have had so many sweethearts!" declared the False Collar; "they would not let me have any peace,—that was because I was such a fine gentleman, and so well starched; I had both a Boot-jack and a Comb, neither of which I ever used. You should have seen me when I lay down,—I looked so charming then. Never shall I forget my first love. She was a Waistband, so delicate, so soft, and pretty! she threw herself into a tub of water, in her despair of winning my love. Then there was the widow-lady, who grew red with passion because I slighted her; however, I left her to stand and cool at her leisure. Cool she did, no doubt, and black she turned; but that does not matter. There was the ballet-dancer, too; she gave me the cut direct. I shall never forget how furious she was. Why, even my own Comb was in love with me; she lost all her teeth through care and anxiety. Yes, indeed, I have lived to make many experiences of this sort; but I suffer most remorse on account of the Garter—I mean the Waistband—who threw herself into the tub of water. I have a great deal on my conscience; I wish I could become pure white paper!"

And white paper the Collar became—all the rags were made into white paper, but the False Collar was made into this very identical sheet of white paper now before you, gentle reader,—the sheet upon which this history is printed. And this was the punishment for his shameless boasting and falsehood. And it is well that we should all read the story, and think over it, that we may beware how we brag and boast as the False Collar did; for we can hardly make sure that we may not, some unlucky day, get into a rag-chest, too, and be made into white paper, and have our whole history, even our most secret thoughts and doings, printed upon us, and thus be obliged to travel about the world, and make our misdeeds known everywhere, just like the False Collar

STORY OF A MOTHER

A MOTHER sat watching her little child; she was so sad, so afraid lest it should die. For the child was very pale; its eyes had closed, its breathing was faint: and every now and then it fetched a deep sigh, and the mother's face grew sadder and sadder as she watched the little tiny creature.

There was a knock at the door, and a poor old man, wrapped up in a great horse-cloth, came in. He had need of warm clothing, for it was a cold winter's night; the ground outside the house was covered with ice and snow, and the wind blew keen and cutting into the wanderer's face.

And as the old man was shivering with cold, and the little child seemed just at that moment to have fallen asleep, the mother rose up and fetched some beer in a little pot, placing it inside the stove to warm it for her guest. And the old man sat rocking the cradle; and the mother sat down on a chair beside him, still gazing on her sick child, listening anxiously to its hard breathing, and holding its tiny hand.

"I shall keep him, do not you think so?" she inquired. "God is good, He will not take my darling away from me!"

And the old man—it was Death himself—bowed his head so strangely, you could not tell whether he meant to say "yes" or "no." And the mother cast down her eyes, and tears streamed over her cheeks. She felt her head growing so heavy; for three whole days and nights she had not closed her eyes, and now she slept,—but only for a minute; presently she started up, shivering with cold. "What is this?" she exclaimed, and she looked around her. The old man was gone, and her little child was gone; he had taken it with him. And yonder, in the corner, the old clock ticked and ticked; the heavy leaden pendulum swung lower and lower, till at last it fell on the floor, and then the clock stood still also.

But the poor bereaved mother rushed out of the house, and cried for her child.

Outside, amidst the snow, there sat a woman clad in long black garments, who said, "Death has been in thy room; I saw him hurry out of it with thy little child; he strides along more swiftly than the wind, and never brings back anything that he has taken away."

"Only tell me which way he has gone!" entreated the mother. "Tell me the way, and I will find him."

"I know the way," replied the woman in black robes; "but before I show it thee, thou must first sing to me all the songs thou hast ever sung to thy child. I am Night, and I love these songs; I have heard thee sing them many a time, and have counted the tears thou hast shed whilst singing them."

"I will sing them all, every one!" said the mother; "but

do not keep me low, let me hasten after Death, let me recover my child!"

But Night made no reply; there she sat, mute and unrelenting. Then the mother began to sing, weeping and wringing her hands the while. Many were the songs she sung, but many more were the tears she wept! And at last Night said, "Turn to the right, and go through the dark fir-grove, for thither did Death wend his way with thy child."

But deep within the grove several roads crossed, and the poor woman knew not in which direction she should turn. Here grew a thorn-bush, without leaves or flowers, for it was winter, and icicles clung to the bare branches.

"Oh! tell me, hast thou not seen Death pass by, bearing my little child with him?"

"Yes, I have," was the Thorn-tree's reply; "but I will not tell thee which way he has gone, unless thou wilt first warm me at thy bosom. I am freezing to death in this place, I am turning into ice."

And she pressed the Thorn-bush to her breast so closely as to melt all the icicles. And the thorns pierced into her flesh, and the blood flowed in large drops. But the Thorn-bush shot forth fresh green leaves, and was crowned with flowers in that same bitter-cold winter's night;—so warm is the heart of a sorrowing mother! And the Thorn-bush told her which path she must take.

And the path brought her on to the shore of a large lake, where neither ship nor boat was to be seen. The lake was not frozen hard enough to bear her weight, not shallow enough to be waded through, and yet cross it she must, if she would recover her child. So she lay down, thinking to drink the lake dry. That was quite impossible for one human being to do, but the poor unhappy mother imagined that perchance a miracle might come to pass.

"No, that will never do!" said the Lake. "Rather let us see if we cannot come to some agreement. I love to collect pearls, and never have I seen any so bright as thine eyes; if thou wilt weep them into my bosom, I will bear thee over to the vast conservatory where Death dwells, and tends his trees and flowers—each one of them a human life."

"Oh, what would I not give to get to my child!" cried the mother. And she wept yet again, and her eyes fell down into the Lake, and became two brilliant pearls. And the Lake received her, and its bosom heaved and swelled, and its current bore her safely to the opposite shore, where stood a wondrous house, many miles in length. It were hard to decide whether it were really a house and built with hands, or whether it were not rather a mountain with forests and caverns in its sides. But the poor mother could not see it at all; she had wept out her eyes.

"Where shall I find Death, that I may ask him to restore to me my little child?" inquired she.

"He has not yet returned," replied a hoary-haired old woman who was wandering to and fro in Death's conservatory, which she had been left to guard in his absence. "How didst thou find thy way here? who has helped thee?"

"Our Lord has helped me," she answered; "He is merciful, and thou, too, wilt be merciful. Where shall I find my little child?"

"I do not know," said the old woman; "and thou, I perceive, canst not see. Many flowers and trees have withered during this night; Death will come very soon to transplant them. Thou must know that every human being has his tree or flower of life, as is appointed for each. They look like common vegetables, but their hearts beat. So be of good cheer, perchance thou mayest be able to distinguish the heart-beat of thy child; but what wilt thou give me, if I tell thee what else thou must do?"

"I have nothing to give," said the mourning mother. "But I will go to the end of the world at thy bidding."

"I want nothing from the end of the world," said the old woman; "but thou canst give me thy long black hair. Thou must know well that it is very beautiful; it pleases me exceedingly! And thou canst have my white hair in exchange: even that will be better than none."

"Desirest thou nothing further?" returned the mother; "I will give it thee right willingly." And she gave away her beautiful hair, and received instead the thin snow-white locks of the old woman.

And then they entered Death's vast conservatory, where flowers and trees grew in wonderful order and variety. There were delicate hyacinths, protected by glasses, and great healthy peonies. There grew water-plants, some looking quite fresh, some sickly, water-snakes were clinging about them, and black crabs clung fast by the stalks. Here were seen magnificent palm-trees, oaks, and plantains; yonder clustered the humble parsley and fragrant thyme. Not a tree, not a flower, but had its name; each corresponded with a human life; the persons whose names they bore lived in all countries and nations on the earth; one in China, another in Greenland, and so forth. There were some large trees planted in little pots, so that their roots were contracted, and the trees themselves ready to break out from the pots; on the other hand, there was many a weakly tiny herb set in rich mould, with moss laid over its roots, and the utmost care and attention bestowed upon its preservation.

And the grieving mother bent down over all the tiniest plants; in each one she heard the pulse of human life; and out of a million others she distinguished the heart-throb of her child.

"There it is!" cried she, stretching her hand over a little blue crocus-flower which was hanging down on one side, sickly and feeble.

"Touch not the flower!" said the old woman. "But place thyself here; and when Death shall come—I expect him every minute—then suffer him not to tear up the plant; but threaten to do the same by some of the other flowers—that will terrify him! For he will have to answer for it to our Lord; no plant may be rooted up before the Almighty has given permission."

Suddenly an icy-cold breath swept through the hall, and the blind mother felt that Death had arrived.

"How hast thou found the way hither?" asked he. "How couldest thou arrive here more quickly than I?"

"I am a mother!" was her answer.

And Death extended his long hand towards the tiny delicate crocus-flower; but she held her hands clasped firmly round it, so closely, so closely! and yet with such anxious care lest she should touch one of the petals. Then Death breathed upon her hands, and she felt that his breath was more chilling than the coldest, bitterest, winter wind; and her hands sank down, numbed and powerless.

"Against me thou hast no strength!" said Death.

"But our Lord has, and He is merciful" replied she.

"I do but accomplish His will!" said Death. "I am His gardener. I take up all His plants and trees, one by one, and transplant them into the glorious Garden of Paradise, into the Unknown Land. Where that lies, and how they thrive there, that I dare not tell thee!"

"Oh, give me back my child!" cried the mother, and she wailed and implored. All at once she seized firm hold of two pretty flowers, one with each hand, exclaiming, "I will tear off all thy flowers, for I am in despair!"

"Touch them not!" commanded Death. "Thou sayest that thou art very unhappy; and wouldest thou therefore make another mother as unhappy as thyself?"

"Another mother!" repeated the poor woman, and she immediately loosed her hold of both the flowers.

"There are thine eyes again," said Death. "I fished them out of the lake, they glistened so brightly; but I did not know that they were thine. Take them back; they are now even brighter than before; now look down into this deep well. I will tell thee the names of the two flowers which thou wert about to pluck, and thou shalt see pictured in the water their whole future, the entire course of their human lives. Thou shalt see all that thou hast yearned to destroy."

And she gazed into the well; and a lovely sight it was to see how one of these lives became a blessing to the whole world, to see what a sunshine of joy and happiness it diffused around it. And she beheld the life of the other, and there was sin and sorrow, misfortune and utter misery.

"Both are God's will!" said Death.

"Which of them is the flower of unhappiness, and which the blessed and blessing one?" inquired she.

"That I will not tell thee," returned Death; "but this shalt thou learn from me, that one of those two flowers was the flower of thine own child. Thou hast seen the destiny, the future of thine own child!"

Then the mother shrieked out with terror, "Which of the two is my child? Tell me that! Save the innocent child! Release my child from all this misery! Rather bear it away—bear it into God's kingdom! Forget my tears; forget my entreaties, and all that I have done!"

"I do not understand thee," said Death. "Wilt thou

have thy child back again, or shall I carry him away to that place which thou knowest not?"

And the mother wrung her hands, fell upon her knees, and prayed to the All-wise, All-merciful Father, "Hear me not when I pray for what is not Thy will — Thy will is always best! Hear me not, Lord! hear me not!"

And her head drooped down upon her breast.

And Death departed, and bore away her child to the Unkrown Land.

THE HISTORY OF THE YEAR.

IT was last January; there was a terrible snow-storm, the snow drifted like a whirlwind through lane and street, encrusted the window-panes, and lay heaped up on the roofs. The people who chanced to be out of doors sped along as though some one were in chase of them, ran up against each other, fell into each other's arms, and then kept fast hold for a moment, fearing to lose their footing if they let go again. Horses and carriages were all well powdered, footmen stood with their backs to the carriages to escape the wind beating against their faces, foot-passengers kept steadily in the lee of the vehicles, which rolled slowly on through the deep snow; and when at last the storm was laid and a narrow path had been swept in front of the houses, the folks came to a dead stop whenever they met, neither party liking to step aside into the snow to give room for the other to pass. Silently they would stand, facing each other, till at last, tacitly arriving at a mutual compromise, either would sacrifice one foot, setting it into the snow-drift.

Towards evening came a lull; the heavens looked as if they had been swept, and seemed higher and more transparent; the stars might have been taken to be spick-and-span new, they were so dazzlingly bright, and some few glistened with such a soft blue light. The air was very keen, so much so, that the uppermost layer of snow was frozen quite hard. And now, in the early morning hour, came forth the little gray sparrows; they hopped up and down wherever the snow had been shovelled away, but there was not much to be found to eat, and the poor things were half starved, as well as half frozen.

"Twit!" said one, "this is what folks call the New Year! Why, it is worse than the Old! I am very discontented, and no wonder. We might just as well have kept the Old Year!"

"Yes, and all the world has been running about, making such a fuss with proclaiming the New Year," said a stiff, frost-bitten little Sparrow. "They were quite wild with joy because the Old Year was gone and done with; and I was glad, too, for I expected we should now get some warm days, but it has turned out a regular take-in—it freezes worse than ever. Men must have made a mistake in their reckoning."

"That's just it—so they have," rejoined a third, an old Sparrow, hoary-white on the crest. "They have something which they call an almanack—it is all their own invention—and they want to make everything go on as that goes on; but they can't do it, after all. When spring comes, that is the real beginning of the year; that is the course of nature, and that is my way of reckoning."

"But when will spring come?" asked the others.

"Spring comes when the stork comes; but he is very unpunctual, and here in the town there is no one who understands anything about the matter,—they know better in the country. Suppose we fly thither and wait? We shall be nearer spring there than here."

"All very well for you," remarked another Sparrow, who had kept on twittering for a long time without saying anything intelligible; "but, for my part, I have many conveniences here in the town which I fear I should miss in the country. In a house up yonder lives a human family, who, very sensibly, have contrived to set in the wall three or four flower-pots, with the large opening turned inside and the bottom outside, and in the bottom a hole is cut large enough for me to fly in and out; it is there that my mate and I have our nest, and thence have all our young ones taken their first flight. The human family have, of course, arranged all this that they may have the pleasure of looking at us, else why should they have done it? And they strew crumbs of bread about,—all for their own amusement,—and that's the way we get our living; and thus we are provided for. So I believe I shall stay here, and my mate will stay here, although we are very discontented;—yes, we shall stay here."

"And we will fly away into the country, to see if Spring is coming." And so away they flew.

In the country it was winter with a vengeance; the frost was some degrees keener than in the town; the cutting, icy wind blew pitilessly over the snow-covered fields. The peasant, sitting in his sledge, swathed in thick woollen wraps, let his whip lie in his lap, and beat himself with his arms to get something like life into them, while the snow crackled under the hoofs of his lean, steaming horses, and the half-frozen Sparrows hopped about in the tracks left by the sledge-wheels. "Twit! will Spring never be coming? We have been waiting so long!"

"So long!" The words were wafted far over the fields from the highest of the snowy banks. Perhaps it was Echo who repeated them, perhaps it was the strange old man who sat up there, exposed to wind and weather, on the highest snow-drift. He was perfectly white, like a peasant in his mantle of coarse white wool; he had long white hair, and a white beard, and large bright eyes glittered in his wan face.

"And who's that old man up there, I wonder?" quoth the Sparrows.

"I know," replied a grave old Raven, perched upon a paling hard by, who was condescending enough to acknowledge that we are all small birds in the sight of Him who made us, and therefore did not disdain to converse even with Sparrows, and enlighten their ignorance with his superior wisdom. "I know who the old man is. He is Winter, the old man of last year,—he is not dead, as the almanack says; no, he is a sort of Regent for the young Prince Spring, who is coming. Yes, Winter rules the roast, and will for some time to come. Ugh! do ye comprehend it now, you little ones?"

"Yes, that is just what I say," answered the least and youngest of the Sparrows. "The almanack is a mere human invention—it is not founded upon nature. They should have let us make it,—us Sparrows, whose organs are so much finer and more delicate than theirs."

One week passed, the second had nearly passed; the wood was black, the frozen lake looked dark and heavy as lead, the clouds,—nay, clouds they were not, they were damp, icy-cold vapours,—brooded in dull stillness over the landscape, flocks of great black crows flew by, but silently; not so much as a single "Caw!" was heard. It seemed as though all Nature were sleeping. Suddenly a sunbeam glided over the lake, whereupon it smiled and shone like molten tin, and the snowy mantle on field and bank glittered with countless, unwonted sparkles. But the hoary white form, even Winter, still sat motionless, gazing steadily towards the South, seemingly unobservant that his carpet of snow was, as it were, sinking into the earth, and that here and there a tiny, grass-green spot gleamed forth, all alive with busy, twittering Sparrows.

"Quivit! Quivit! Surely he has come at last, has Spring!"

"Spring!" the joyous sound re-echoed over field and meadow, and through the dusky groves, where the bright moss clung, fresh and green, to trunk and stem. And now, from the sunny South, came flying through the air the two first storks, each bearing on its back a beautiful little child; one was a boy, the other a girl. They kissed the earth on alighting, and wherever they set their feet, white flowers sprang forth from under the snow. Hand in hand they went up to the old ice-man, Winter, lovingly nestling upon his breast, and, behold! they all three vanished from sight, the landscape vanishing with them, a thick wet mist enveloping the whole. Gradually the air lightened again, the wind rushed furiously past, driving the mist before him, the sun shone out so warmly! Winter, old Winter, was gone, and Spring's lovely children were seated on the throne of the Year

"Ah, this is what I call New Year's Day!" declared the Sparrows. "Now we shall have our rights and liberties again, now we shall have compensation for the inclemency of that severe old Winter."

Wherever the two children turned, green buds shot forth from bush and tree, the grass grew higher, the young green corn darkened in hue. And the little maiden scattered flowers around her: she had such abundance of them that, however zealously she might throw them away, still her lap was full; in her haste she shook a perfect shower of snow-white blossoms over apple and peach-trees, so now they stood arrayed in glorious apparel, although as yet they had no leafy garment. And she clapped her hands, and the boy clapped his, and then the birds flew forth, they knew not why, and one and all twittered, and chirped, and sang, " Spring is come ! "

It was a lovely sight to see ! Many an old, old dame tottered over the threshold of her door in the glad sunshine, looked at the golden blossoms that starred the meadow, just as in the days of her youth, and felt that the world had become young again. " It is glorious to be out to-day ! " quoth she then.

And the wood was still half-brown, half-green, bud after bud slowly expanding, but the wood-ruff, so fresh and fragrant, was abroad already, violets clustered together in tufts, anemones, cowslips, and oxlips raised their heads, and every single blade of grass had a grace and glory of its own. A splendid enamelled carpet was the turf, and on it sate the two sweet children of Spring, holding fast each other's hands, singing, smiling, and growing ever more and more.

A soft rain fell from heaven upon them, but they marked it not, the gentle rain-drops mingled with their own tears of joy. And bride and bridegroom kissed each other, and, behold! the wood burst at that moment into fulness of life. When the sun rose next, all the woods were clothed in green.

And hand in hand passed the bridal pair under the fragrant canopy of leafy bowers, where only the sunbeams and the shadows cast by the clouds gave variety to the changeless green. A virgin purity, a balmy perfume, dwelt in those delicate leaves ; clear, bright, and lively rippled the silver brooklet between reeds of velvet green, over a mosaic of sparkling pebbles. " Beautiful for ever, never dying, never failing!"—such seemed the song of Nature. And the cuckoo and the lark sang of Spring, joyous Spring ; and yet all this time the Willow-trees kept their blossoms veiled up in woolly sheaths, so detestably cautious, so calculating were they!

Days and weeks passed away, and now an intense sultriness seemed to have fallen from the sky upon the earth; no waves of air breathed through the corn, which was now changing from green to golden. On the woodland lakes the lotus of the North, the white water-lily, spread out its large leaves flatly on the watery mirror, and the fishes sought shelter under their shade. And on the very hottest side of the wood, where the sun burned on the cottage-wall and heated through and through the petals of the roses that had burst open to greet him, where the cherry-trees were laden with juicy, sun-ripened black berries,—there sate a beautiful woman, the same whom we saw as a merry child, as a happy bride. She was gazing on the slowly drifting clouds, mountain-like in form and colour; heavy, dark-blue clouds, from three sides they drifted, heaving themselves ever higher and higher over the arch of the sky, till at last, not unlike a sea of huge, turbulent waves spell-bound and petrified, they closed over the wood, where everything was hushed into a charmed stillness. Not a breath of air stirred, not a leaf rustled, not a bird dared to raise his voice; all Nature seemed, as it were, waiting with awed expectation; meantime roads and footpaths were quickly cleared, every passenger by carriage, horse, or foot, hurrying under cover. All at once it lightened; it was as though the sun had burst forth for one second, dazzling, blinding, scorching; darkness followed, and a deep, rolling crash; water gushed down in torrents, night and light, calmed stillness and the roar of thunder, alternated in rapid succession. Grass and corn lay beaten to the ground, as though they never could rise again. Suddenly the rain abated, falling only in single drops, the sun shining, and blade and leaf glittering with hundreds and thousands of diamonds; the birds sang, the fishes darted up to the surface of the water, the gnats danced, and yonder, on the stone washed by the current, sate Summer himself, in his prime of manhood, with his vigorous limbs and dripping wet hair; as though renewed by his fresh-water bath, he sate basking in the warm sunshine. And, in very truth, all things were renewed, all creatures were joyful, healthful, and beautiful; it was summer-time, warm, luxuriant summer-time.

And sweet and reviving was the fragrance wafted from the clover-field, and the bees hovered and hummed over the spot where Danish kings, warriors, and sages had been wont to meet in olden time; the bramble had now twined round the altar-stone which, washed by the rain, shone brightly in the sunshine, and thither flew the Queen Bee with her swarm, stored her wax, and made sweet honey. None saw it save Summer and his wife; they, strong and healthful, loved the noon-day heat; to them that old heathen altar, once stained with human blood, stood now enriched with the pure, sinless offerings of Nature to her God.

And the evening sky glowed like gold, no cathedral dome was ever half so rich and glorious, and the pale moon reigned in her beauty during the hours between evening-red and morning-red. It was summer-time!

Days and weeks went by again. And now the keen scythes of the reapers gleamed in the corn-fields, the apple-boughs lowered their red and yellow freightage, the hops sent out their pleasant perfume and hung down their large cups; and under the hazel-bushes, heavy with nuts, sate Summer and his wife, looking grave and weary.

"What wealth!" said she; "blessing and prosperity on every side, everything home-like and pleasant, and yet—I know not what is wanting to me—I yearn for rest, perfect rest—I cannot tell why. See, they are already ploughing the fields, more and more riches will these men be ever striving for!—And oh, look at the storks, flying yonder in a stream, as though following the plough, the birds of Egypt, who bore us hither through the air! rememberest thou not how we were brought together into this Northern land, when children?—Flowers we brought with us, warm sunshine, and green leaves—beautiful leaves, but the Wind has touched them with his rough hand; the trees are now turning brown and dark like the trees of the South, but they bear no golden fruits like theirs!"

"Is that what thou longest for?" asked Summer; "look up then, and rejoice!" And he lifted his arm, and immediately the foliage was dyed in hues of crimson and gold, all the woods around standing arrayed in a costly festive garb. The rose-hedge grew bright with blood-red hips, the elder-boughs hung heavy with large brownish-black berries, the wild chestnuts dropped ripe from their dark-green calyces, and again, on the woodland-banks, blossomed violets.

Meantime, the Queen of the year grew yet more pale and languid. "What a cold wind!" sighed she; "there are such wet mists at night—oh, I long for my childhood's home!"

And she saw the storks fly away, every one! and she stretched her hands after them. And she glanced at the empty nests: in one grew a long-stalked corn-flower; it looked just as if the nest was meant as a hedge to fence it round. The Sparrows hopped up and peeped in, "Twit! so master and mistress are off! they can't bear, not they, that the wind should blow upon their nobility, so they have taken themselves off. Good riddance!"

Yellower and yellower grew the foliage, leaf after leaf fell, boisterous storms went abroad; it was late Autumn. And on a bed of yellow leaves lay the Queen of the year, her gentle eyes fixed on the glittering stars, and her husband stood beside her. A gust shook the trees, again the leaves fell,— behold! she was gone, but a fair butterfly, the latest of the year, fluttered through the cold air.

Now came damp mists, icy blasts, and dark, long nights. The hair of the Monarch of the year was hoary-white, but he noticed it not, or perhaps fancied it was so from the snow-flakes that fell from the sky. And a thin shroud of snow already covered the green fields.

And the church-bells rang in the merry Christmas-tide.

"Bells ringing, bells ringing!" said the Monarch of the year; "yes, they ring for a birth! Soon will be born the new royal pair, and I shall have rest, like my beloved. Rest in yon glistening stars with her!"

And in the ever-fresh, ever-green pine-wood, stood amid the snow the Angel of Christmas, consecrating the young trees that should be chosen to celebrate the holy, happy festival.

"Joy to you with your green boughs! go ye, and bring joy with you into the warm dwellings of the children of men!" said the King of the year, whom a few weeks had worn into a snow-white bearded, weary old man. "It is nearly time for me to rest; the young sovereigns of the year will now take my crown and sceptre."

"But the rule is yet thine," spake the Angel of Christmas, "rule, and not rest! See that the snow lies warm over the young seed; learn to bear that homage and honour should be paid to another, whilst thou art still ruler, learn to be forgotten, and yet to live and work. Thine hour of release will come in good time, as soon as Spring comes."

"When will Spring come?" asked Winter.

"Spring will come when the stork comes."

And so with thin locks and flowing beard, both alike hoary-white, bowed with age, but strong as the storm, strong as the ice, sate Winter on the high snow-drift, gazing southwards, just as the Winter before him had sat and gazed. And the ice crackled, the snow crisped, the skaters fleeted over the smooth lakes, and crows and ravens were seen standing out in bold relief upon the white ground. Not a wind was stirring; Winter clasped his hands in the still air, and the ice grew fathoms deep between land and land.

Then out came the Sparrows from the town, and asked again, "Who is the old man up there?" And the Raven, or a son of his, which comes to the same, was ready at hand, and prompt to answer, "It is Winter, the old man of last year. He is not dead, as the almanack says; he is Regent for the young Prince Spring, who is coming."

"When Spring comes," said the Sparrows, "we shall have good times, and a better government; the old is fit for nothing!"

And in silent thought Winter bowed his head towards the black, leafless groves, where every tree displayed the delicate curves and archings of its boughs. Ice-cold vapours darkened the sky during Winter's slumber. And the weary old Monarch dreamed pleasantly of his youth and his manhood, and at day-dawn all the woods stood gemmed with glittering hoar-frost; this was Winter's dream of Summer. But the sun soon kissed the hoar-frost from the branches.

"When is Spring coming? I wish it were Spring!" quoth the Sparrows.

"Spring!" it re-echoed from the snow-covered banks. And the sun shone warmer and warmer, the snow melted, the birds carolled, "Spring is coming!"

And high through the air flew the earliest stork, the second following; on the back of each rode a lovely child. And the children sprang down on the open field, and they kissed the earth, and they kissed the still old man, and he vanished, borne away in mists.

The history of the year was ended.

"It is all very fine," quoth the Sparrows; "and all very pleasant, but it is not according to the almanack; so one or the other must be quite in the wrong."

THE WORLD'S FAIREST ROSE.

THERE was once a great Queen, whose gardens abounded with the loveliest flowers of every season and every clime, but of all flowers she loved roses best. Of these she had an infinite number of different varieties, from the fragrant dog-rose of the hedges, with its wild grace and sprays of smooth green leaves, to the rarest Provençal beauty, the lady of the garden. The Queen's roses grew in unchecked luxuriance up the palace-walls, twined their branches round window-sill and balcony, flung them in through the passages, and spread along the ceilings of the saloons, one and all vying with each other in perfume, delicacy of tint, and perfect beauty of form.

But sorrow and anguish dwelt within those rose-embowered halls; the Queen lay on her sick-bed, and the physicians declared she must die.

"There is yet a remedy that may bring her life," said the wisest among them. "Bring her the World's Fairest Rose, that which is the expression of the highest and purest love; let but her gaze be fixed upon that before her eye-strings break, and she will not die."

And old and young came round her, bringing roses,—all brought the loveliest treasure of their gardens. But this was not what the sage had meant. From the Garden of Love must the wonder-working flower be gathered; but who could tell which rose in that mystic garden was the expression of the highest and purest love?

And minstrels sang the praise of the World's Fairest Rose, each extolling his own chosen favourite. And heralds were sent out far and wide to every loving heart of every age and rank throughout the land.

"No one has yet named the flower," said the Sage. "No one yet has pointed to the spot whence it sprang in its glory. It is not the rose that blossomed in the dark sepulchre of Romeo and Juliet, nor that which scattered its pale-tinted leaves on Valborg's grave, albeit the perfume of those roses shall live for ever in song and saga; it is not the rose that shot forth from Winkelried's bleeding veins, though no death is sweeter than that which meets him who fights for his fatherland, no rose redder than the blood that gushes from a hero's breast. Neither is it that wondrous blossom for whose sake men give away the strength and freshness of their lives, tending it in some lonely chamber through weary days and sleepless nights—the magic Rose of Science."

"I know where it blossoms," said a happy mother, who had come to the Queen's bed-side, her tiny infant in her arms. "I know where to find the World's Fairest Rose, the rose that is the expression of the highest and purest love. It blooms on the blushing cheeks of my sweet child when, strengthened by sleep, he opens his eyes and smiles on me with all his innocent and confiding love."

"Beautiful is that rose, but another there is more beautiful," replied the Sage.

"Yes, far more beautiful!" exlaimed another woman. "I have seen it, a rose more holy or more pure cannot be; but it was pale, pale as the frail rose of China. I saw it blossoming on the Queen's own cheeks; she had laid aside her royal crown, and went to spend the long sad night with her sick child; she wept over it, kissed it, and breathed to Heaven a prayer for it, a prayer such as only mothers, in their hour of extremest anguish, can breathe."

"Holy and marvellous in its power is the white Rose of

Sorrow, but the one I speak of is holier and more powerful still."

"Aye, the World's Fairest Rose I have seen at the altar of the Lord," said the pious old Bishop. "I have seen it beaming forth, manifesting itself, as it were the presence of an angel. A band of young maidens went up to the Holy Table to renew their baptismal covenant, the roses blushing and paling alternately on their fresh cheeks; there was one young girl standing among her companions; I saw her look up to her God with all the purity and loving devotion of her virgin soul;—then saw I the expression of the highest and purest love!"

"Blessed, thrice blessed is Piety," said the Sage; "still hast not even thou discovered the World's Fairest Rose."

Then entered the chamber a child, the Queen's little son; his eyes were glistening, and his cheeks wet with tears; open in his hands he carried a large book bound in velvet, and having large silver clasps.

"Mother!" cried the child, "oh, listen to what I have read here!"—and he sat down by the bed-side and read aloud from the book. He read of Him who "so loved the world" that he gave Himself up to death, even the death of the cross, to save sinners. "Greater love hath no man than this!"

And a faint rosy gleam passed over the Queen's cheek, the glance of her eye grew stronger and brighter, for from the leaves of that book she felt wafted to her the fragrance of the World's Fairest Rose, the Rose that sprang forth from the sacred Blood that was shed on Calvary.

"I see it!" she exclaimed. "Never can he die who looks upon that Rose, the fairest of the earth, the Rose of Sharon!"

A PICTURE FROM THE CASTLE RAMPARTS.

It is autumn; we stand on the Castle ramparts and look out across the sea with its many ships to the Swedish coast rising beyond, bright in the evening sunshine. Behind us the rampart descends abruptly; magnificent trees, whose yellow leaves are falling fast, grow below, and behind them are certain close-built, dull-looking houses with wooden palisades; a dreary walk has the sentinel who paces to and fro among them, but still drearier and darker must it be within those grated windows, for there dwell convict slaves, the worst of criminals.

A beam from the setting sun strays into the bare chamber, for the sun shines alike on the evil and on the good. The sullen, savage felon gazes gloomily on the cold sunbeam. A little bird flies upon the grating; his song, too, is for the evil as for the good. "Quirrevit!" his song is a brief one, but he remains perched on the grating; he flaps his wings, plumes his feathers, one tiny feather falls off, the others he ruffles up round his neck. And the chained criminal looks on, and a softer expression passes over his hard coarse features, a feeling he is scarcely conscious of springs up within his heart, a feeling in some way akin to the sunbeam that has darted through the trellis, and the fragrance of the violets that in the spring cluster so abundantly outside his prison But now sounds the horn of some home-bound huntsman; clear, strong, and lively are the notes. Away from the grating flies the bird, from the bare wall fades away the sunbeam, and all is dark again within the chamber, dark again in the convict's heart. But, thank Heaven! the sun has shone therein, the bird's song has been heard, though but for one minute.

Die not away so soon, ye sweet, clear tones from the huntsman's horn! The evening is mild, the sea calm and smooth as a mirror.

"QUITE TRUE!"

"IT is a shocking story!" said the Hen who was telling it. "A most shocking story!" repeated she; "I really could not bear to sleep alone to-night; it is a good thing there are so many of us here to roost together." And she told the tale again and again, till the Hens, her companions, felt their feathers standing on end, and the Cock lowered his comb for very horror. " Quite true, quite true ! "

But we will begin at the beginning, and relate what took place in a hen-house at the opposite end of the town. The sun went down, and the Hens flew up ; one of them, she was white-feathered and short-limbed, laid her eggs regularly, as was expected of her, and comported herself in every way as a respectable Hen should ;—as she flew up to roost she plumed herself with her beak. A tiny little feather fell off.

" Let it go ! " said she ; " the more I plume myself, the handsomer I shall grow." And this was said in innocent light-heartedness, for, despite her extreme respectability, she was a sort of wag among the Hens. And in her innocence she fell asleep.

It was darkness all around ; Hen sate close to Hen ; one of them could not sleep that night ; the speech of her white-feathered companion she had heard and yet not heard, as often happens in this world of ours. Sleepless and restless, she turned the words over and over in her mind, till at last she could keep silence no longer; she must needs arouse her next neighbour and whisper to her, " Did you hear what was said a while ago ? I will not mention names, but there is a Hen who intends to pluck herself, just to make herself look well ; now, if I were the Cock, I should despise her ! "

Just over the hen-house dwelt a family of Owls, who, according to their custom, were wide awake that night. All of that family are known to have sharp ears ; they heard the words of the second Hen, and they rolled their great eyes, and Mother Owl fanned herself with her wings. " Don't listen, pray ! But you must have heard what was said ? I heard it with my own ears ; well, wonders will never cease ! There is one of the Hens who has to such a degree forgotten what becomes her as a Hen that she is sitting there plucking off her feathers before the eyes of the Cock ! "

" *Prenez garde aux enfants !* " interposed Father Owl ; " it is not fit that children should know of such things."

" I must just go and tell our esteemed neighbour ; it is a real privilege, the society of so respectable and sagacious an Owl as he is ! "— and away flew Mother Owl with the tale.

" Tu-whit, tu-whoo ! tu-whit, tu-whoo ! " They hooted between them a fine duet at the nearest dove-cot. " Have ye heard, have ye heard? tu-whoo!—there is a Hen who has plucked herself of all her feathers to please the Cock; she must be freezing to death, if, indeed, she be not dead already, tu-whoo!"

"Where? where?" cooed the Doves in chorus.

"At neighbour's farm. I have as good as seen it myself! The story is scarcely fit to be told, but it is quite true!"

"True, true, true! every word of it true, true, true!" cooed the Doves, and they bore the report down to their owner's poultry-yard. "There is a Hen, nay, some say there are two, who have plucked off all their feathers, in order to look different from the rest, and thus attract the Cock's attentions. It is a dangerous game to play; one might easily catch cold and die; and they are dead already, both of them!"

"Wake up! wake up!" crowed the Cock, as he flew upon the post; he was still half asleep, and his eyes were but half open, but he crowed all the same. "Three Hens have died of unrequited love for a Cock! They had stripped themselves of all their feathers! It is a scandalous tale; I will not help to hush it up; let it be known, let it go farther!"

"Let it go farther!" shrieked the Bats; "Let it go farther!" clucked the Hens; "Let it go farther!" crowed the Cocks; and thus the story was handed round from hen-house to hen-house, till at last it was carried back to the very same spot whence it had started.

"There are five Hens," now ran the tale, "who have plucked off all their feathers, to show which of them had most wasted away through unhappy love to their Cock; and then they pecked each other till all five fell bleeding and dead, to the shame and scandal of their families, and to the great loss of the proprietor!"

And the original Hen who had lost one innocent little white feather, naturally enough did not recognise her own history, and being, as was said before, a respectable, orderly Hen, she exclaimed, "How disgraceful! I despise such creatures! Such things should be known, and I will do my best to get the story into the newspaper, so that it shall spread far and wide; the Hens have richly deserved it, and the family too, and they shall not be spared!"

And the story did get into the newspaper; and this, at least, is "quite true," viz. that "one little feather may grow into five hens!"

THE SWANS' NEST.

BETWEEN the Baltic and the North Seas lies an old Swans' Nest,—it is called Denmark; in it have been born, and will be born hereafter, Swans whose names shall never die.

In the olden time, a flock of Swans flew thence over the Alps to Milan's lovely green plains. There they lighted down and dwelt, for right pleasant was it there to dwell. These Swans were called Lombards.

Another flock, with bright shining plumage, and clear, truthful eyes, lighted down at Byzantium, nestled round the Emperor's throne, and spread out their broad white wings as shields to protect him. These were known as Varangians.

From the coasts of France arose a cry of anguish and terror — terror at the bloody Swans who, with fire under their wings, flew thither from the north. Loud was the prayer of village and town, "God save us from the wild Normans!"

On England's fresh meadow-turf, near the shore, wearing a triple crown on his kingly head, his golden sceptre stretching far over the land, stood the royal Swan, Canute the Dane.

And on Pomerania's shores the heathens bowed the knee,

for thither, too, with drawn swords, and bearing the standard of the cross, had flown the Danish Swans

"But this was in the days of old."

In times nearer our own, then, have mighty Swans been seen to fly out from the Nest. A flash of lightning cleft the air — lightning that shone over all Europe — for a Swan had flapped his strong wings and scattered the twilight mist, and the starry heavens became more visible — were brought, as it were, nearer the earth. The Swan's name was Tycho Brahe.

"Yes, just that once," it will be said; "but now, in our own generation?"

Well, in our own generation we have beheld Swans soaring in a high and glorious flight.

One we saw gently sweep his wings over the golden chords of the harp, whereupon sweet music thrilled through the northern lands, the wild Norwegian mountains lifted their proud crests higher in the full sunlight of the olden time, pine and birch bowed their heads and rustled their leaves, the "Gods of the North" — the heroes and noble women of Scandinavian history — lived and breathed again, their tall, stately figures standing out from the dark background of deep forests.

A second Swan we saw strike his pinions upon the hard marble rock till it cleft asunder, and new forms of beauty, hitherto shut up in the stone, were revealed to the light of day, and the nations of Europe gazed in wonder and admiration at the glorious statuary.

A third Swan we have seen weaving threads of thoughts that spun and spread around the earth, so that words can fly with lightning speed from land to land.

Dear to the protecting heavens above is the old Swans' Nest between the Baltic and the North Sea. Let mighty birds of prey, if they will, speed thither to tear it down. It shall not be! Even the unfledged, unplumed young ones will press forward to the margin of the Nest — we have seen it — will fight desperately with beak and claw, will offer their bleeding breasts in defence of their home.

Centuries will pass away, and Swans will still fly forth from the Nest, and make themselves seen and heard far over the world; long will it be before the time shall come when in sad truth it may be said, "Behold the last Swan! — Listen to the last sweet song from the Swans' Nest!"

GOOD HUMOUR.

FROM my father I have inherited that best inheritance— Good Humour.—" And who was my father?" it will be asked. Now what signifies who he was? He was a thriving, lively, happy, little man, his exterior and interior equally at variance with his office. " And what was his office, his position in the community?"—That will be the next question; and it strikes me that if the answer to it were written and printed right at the beginning of a book, most people would lay the book down almost as soon as they had opened it, saying, " That is enough, I don't want anything of this kind." And yet my father was neither hangman nor headsman; on the contrary, his office often brought him into communication with the most honourable men of the state; and in such cases he invariably took precedence of them, even of bishops and princes of the blood royal, for—to confess the truth—he was the driver of a hearse!

Now the worst is said!—and it must be added that when my father was seen sitting up on high, his face, despite the garnish of the long black mantle and crape-bordered, three-cornered hat, ever benign, contented, and placid, no one could help feeling that either he, or the great, heavy, dismal hearse, with its unseemly and melancholy pomp, was strangely out of place. But enough of this; suffice it to say that, from my father, besides my good humour, I have inherited two habits, first, that of paying frequent visits to the churchyard, secondly, that of reading all the newspapers, but especially the advertisement sheets.

I am not exactly young; I have neither wife, children, nor ibrary to entertain me, but, as I have already said, I read all the advertisements through, and they supply me with a fund of ever-varying amusement. From them I know who preaches in the churches and who preaches in the new books; I know where I may get houses, servants, well-fitting clothes, and delicacies for the table—when I want them: I know who is selling off and who is buying in. Then, too, I hear of so many deeds of pure, disinterested benevolence! I read so many such innocent verses! their author may have intended them to convey cutting sarcasms, but they are quite guiltless of offence to any one. I become, by dint of patient study, and at the cost of a little imagination, initiated into so many interesting family mysteries;—all this through reading the advertisement sheets.

Every one, of course, is free to read the newspapers at pleasure; but as for my second amusement, my walks in the churchyard, if anybody would like to share it, let him come with me some day when the sun shines and the trees are green; then let us ramble together among the graves; each one is like a closed book with the back set out towards you, so that you can just read the title which tells you what the book contains. Too often, though, the title is a complete misnomer: no matter, I know all about it, I have it all in a book I have written for my own especial benefit and instruction, and I will impart some of its contents to my companion.

Now we are in the churchyard.

Here, behind this white-painted trellis-work, within which once grew a rose-tree,—it is dead now from neglect, but a stray bit of evergreen from the neighbouring grave stretches a long green arm over the sod, as though to compensate for the loss and make a little show,—here rests a man who was singularly unhappy. Yet no one would have called him unfortunate; he had a sufficient income, and was never visited by any great calamity. His unhappiness was, in fact, of his own making; according to the common phrase, he took everything too much to heart. Thus, if he went one evening to the theatre, it was sufficient to spoil his enjoyment that the machinist had put too strong a light into the moon, or that the scene-painter had been guilty of some such mistake as introducing a palm-tree into a home-landscape, cactuses among the plains of Tyrol, or beech-trees on the Norwegian mountains. If the play and the actors were right, the audience was sure to be wrong, applauding too much or too little, or laughing when they had no business to laugh; and this was enough to vex him thoroughly. Petty mischances, minor misunderstandings, made the misery of his life; an especially unhappy man was he.

Here rests a very fortunate man, a man of extremely high birth, wherein, in fact, consisted his good fortune, for, had he not been high-born, nothing could ever have been made of him. But everything is so wisely arranged, and so it was in this case. He went to and fro in state, he was introduced into the saloons of great people, very much as a fine embroidered bell-rope is introduced into a room,—behind the handsome show bell-rope is always a good strong cord which really does all the service required. And this man had his good cord behind him, who now pulls the wires behind a new embroidered bell-rope. Is it not so? everything is so wisely arranged that it is easy enough to keep up one's good humour.

Here rests—nay, now this is really sad!—here rests a man who during threescore-and-seven years worried himself and worked his brains to hit upon a happy idea. For the sake of this happy idea he lived alone all his days, and when at last he had persuaded himself that he had succeeded, he was so overcome that he died of joy,—died of joy at having found it,—died before he had time to announce it to the world. I can almost fancy that he has no rest in his grave, because of the happy idea at last conceived, but which no one but himself has rejoiced over, or ever can rejoice over. For, look you, this was an idea such as to produce a sensation should it be brought out before a merry breakfast-party. Now it is universally received that ghosts can only walk at midnight; should this ghost, therefore, come forth at the appointed hour and appear among his friends, his idea will be a total failure; no one will laugh, for jesting comes unseasonably at midnight, and so the ill-fated ghost will return disappointed to his grave. It really is very sad.

Here reposes a lady noted for her thriftiness; during her life-time she was wont to get up at night and mew, that her neighbours might imagine she kept a cat, which she did not—there was thriftiness for you!

And here a young lady of good family; in society she was always called upon to sing, and when she sang, "Mi manca la voce!" that was the sole and only truth in her life.

And here rests another young girl, a very different nature. Alas! when the heart's canary-bird begins to sing, too often will Reason put her finger in her ears. Poor girl, so young, so lovely!—it is an old story; may she rest in peace!

Here lies a widow lady who had the sweetness of the dove on her lips, and the gall of the owl in her heart. Like a bird of prey, she went about from one family to another, feeding upon her neighbours' faults.

This is a family vault; every member of the race to which it belonged lived in the faith that whatever the world and the newspaper said must needs be true. If the youngest grandson of that house came home from school and said, "So have I heard it said;" whatever the news might be was received as unquestionable. And certain it is that if the cock belonging to that house had taken it into his head to crow at midnight, the whole family would have believed that morning had dawned, whatever the sky and the sun might have maintained to the contrary.

The great Goethe concluded his "Faust" with the words, "it may be continued;" in like manner I will conclude our walk in the churchyard. My visits are frequent, for whenever any one of my friends, or unfriends, gives me reason to suppose that he wishes to be the same as dead to me, I go thither, seek out an unoccupied spot of green turf, and dedicate it to him. Thus I have buried many of my acquaintances: there they lie, powerless to hurt me; and meanwhile, I look forward to the time when they may return to life again, better and wiser than they were before. Their life and history, as seen from my point of view, I write down in my book. And here let me recommend others to do as I do, viz. when they have received a slight or wound from any one, to bury the offender out of sight and out of mind, and whatever evil chances befall, to keep constant to Good Humour.

GRIEF OF HEART.

THIS story that I am about to tell consists by rights of two parts; the first part, to be sure, one could do almost as well without, but then it is of use to explain what comes afterwards.

We were staying at a pleasant country-house, my sister and I, and it so chanced that our host and hostess spent one day from home. During their absence arrived, her pug in her lap, a widow lady from the nearest town, who wanted, it seemed, to get people to take shares in a certain tannery of hers. She had brought her papers with her, so we advised her to enclose them in a cover, and write on it our host's name and title, "General-Commissioner of War, Knight, &c." She took up the pen, hesitated, and then begged us to repeat the title more slowly; we did so, and she wrote, but while writing the word "General" she paused again, sighed, and said, "I am only a woman!" Pug, whom she had set down on the floor while she wrote, now began to growl; he had been brought out for health and amusement's sake, and there was no amusement, he evidently thought, in being set down on the floor. A flat nose, a fat back, these were Pug's characteristics.

"He won't bite you, he has no teeth," said his mistress. "He is quite like one of the family, faithful old Pug — cross enough certainly; but then he is so teased by my grandchildren; whenever they play at having a wedding, they make him act as bridesmaid, and that excites him so much, poor old fellow!"

And giving up her papers to our care, she took Pug in her arms and went her ways. This is the first part, as you see, quite unimportant.

Now for the second part.

A week afterwards we went to the town, and took up our quarters at an inn. Our windows here looked out on a yard which was divided into two parts by a fence; in the one hung skins and leather, raw and tanned — it was, in fact, the widow's tan-yard — in the other sported a troop of children, the widow's grandchildren, who were now high busy preparing poor Pug's grave. For Pug had died that very morning, and they were bent upon laying him in a pretty and picturesque grave, such as it might be a real pleasure to lie in.

So they hedged it in with bits of broken crockery, and strewed it over with sand, and at the head they set a broken beer-bottle with the neck upwards. This was quite a mistake; they should have reversed it, and then the device would have been allegorical.

And the children danced round the grave, and the eldest of the boys, a practical youth, seven years of age, proposed that Pug's grave should be turned into an exhibition, and that the price of admission should be one button, that being a possession which every boy in the street might boast of. The proposition was received with great applause, and all the children of that street and the street that ran behind it came and paid their button: many of them had to wear shoes or trousers half-loose all the afternoon in consequence, but, at all events, they had seen Pug's grave, and that was worth the sacrifice.

But outside the tan-yard, close to the wicket-gate, stood a little ragged girl — such a tiny, delicate creature, with the sunniest curly hair, and eyes so blue and clear! she spoke not a word, she shed not a tear, but every time the wicket opened she looked eagerly forward. She had not a single button in her possession; she knew it, and stood sorrowfully there, waiting till all had seen and all were gone away; then she sate down, held her little brown hands before her eyes and burst into tears; she alone had not seen Pug's grave! It was real anguish, grief of heart, as real, keen, and bitter as grown-up people can suffer.

We stood at our window and looked on, and as seen from above — like our own and our fellows' sorrows, throughout the world — this little tragedy seemed laughable enough. Well! this is the whole story, and he who comprehendeth it not may go and take shares in the widow's tan-yard.

"EVERYTHING IN ITS PLACE!"

'TIS more than a hundred years since. Near the large lake behind the wood stood an old baronial Hall, deep moats, half choked up with reeds and rushes, surrounding it. Close by the bridge leading over the moat to the carriage-entry stood a venerable willow-tree, bending protectingly over the reeds.

The merry noise of horns and hoof-tramps came nearer and nearer from the high-road beyond, and the little goose-girl hurried her geese on one side to make room for the hunting-party; on they galloped, and the girl had to jump up on one of the high stones of the bridge, to escape being run over. She was scarcely more than a child, slight and delicate as a fairy, with the sweetest expression in her face, and such sparkling hazel eyes! But the hunters took no note either of her graceful form or her bright eyes; on they galloped, and one of them, the Lord of the Hall, as he passed, in pure wantonness striking her on the breast with the handle of his whip, pushed her over the bridge.

"Everything in its place!" cried he, "so down with thee into the mud!" and he laughed at his own stupid jest, and his comrades all laughed in chorus. And with their loud laugh and the yet louder bark of the hounds, the whole party swept past.

The poor little goose-girl, as she fell, had seized hold of one of the over-hanging willow-boughs; clinging by it she held herself above the slough of the moat, and as soon as hunters, horses, hounds, and horns, were safe within the Hall-gates, she laboured to clamber up on the bridge again. But the willow-bough she held broke off from the trunk, and she was on the point of falling heavily among reeds when a strong hand from above seized and saved her. A wandering hosier had been witness to the little scene, and hurried up to help the poor girl.

"Everything in its place!" repeated he, laughing, as he lifted her up and set her upon terra firma; and he tried to set the cracked willow-bough straight again, but he could not succeed, it stubbornly refused to return to "its right place," so he stuck it into the soft earth, saying, "Grow there if thou canst, and supply the folks at the hall with a flute, if they mend their manners; with a cane, if they don't!" And, gathering up his chattels, the pedlar passed on through the gates, to display them in the servants' hall. Meantime, up-roarious tumult reigned in the banqueting-room, unseemly songs, coarse jests, and rude laughter mingling with the many-toned bark of dogs, for the hounds had been called in to share the day's sport to the end; wine and ale foamed in pitcher and glass, and the dogs were made to drink with their masters. The pedlar was soon summoned to bring in his pack, but only as a jest; the wine was in and the sense was out; ale was poured into a stocking, and he was bidden to swallow it down quickly. But in another moment the humour of the party took another turn; whole herds of cattle, broad lands and peasants' cottages, were set upon one card, were lost and won.

"Everything in its place!" repeated the pedlar, when he was safe out of Sodom and Gomorrah, as he called the banquet-room. "The open road, the King's highway, that is my proper place; in that Hall I am quite out of my element." And the little goose-girl, standing behind a stile, nodded to him a grateful farewell.

Days and weeks passed away, and the broken willow-bough that the pedlar had stuck into the soft mould of the moat was still fresh and green, and even thrust out new shoots; the little goose-girl saw that it must have taken root, and she quite rejoiced over it; it was her tree, she thought. But while the willow-sprig throve so well, at the Hall everything throve ill; drinking and gambling, these were the two notes on which the Lord of the Hall rang the changes, and six years had not fully passed away when he wandered with scrip and staff, a ruined man, banished the home of his fathers; and that home was purchased by a hosier, the very same who had been made a laughing-stock in his banquet-room, and made to drink ale out of a stocking. Thrift and honesty, that had been his rule of life; and now the pedlar was Lord of the Hall, and from that hour a card was never seen in it. "Paper was meant for something better," he was wont to say, "but when the Evil One first saw God's Book, he determined he would have his Bible too, and so he invented cards."

The new Lord of the Hall hastened to take to himself a wife, and who should she be but the little goose-girl, then grown up into a good, pious, and modest maiden! Her gentle nature stood her in stead of gentle blood, and in her new attire she moved as refined, courteous, and noble as any high-born lady in the land. And now came happy and peaceful times for the Old Hall, the lady ruling all within, and her husband all without, and blessing seemed to rest on all their labours. The moats were drained, and fruit-trees planted in their place; the rooms were all kept clean, the floors bright as a mirror, and in the state saloon sate Madam, with her daughters and her maidens, the long winter evenings through, spinning wool and flax. And every Sunday evening the Bible was read aloud to the whole assembled household, read by the Councillor himself, for a Councillor was the pedlar in his old age. And children grew up around him, and children's children, and all were well brought up, though not all were gifted with an equal portion of sense,—that could not be expected in any family.

And all this time the willow-bough without had grown, and spread, and flourished, a large, magnificent tree. "It is our genealogical tree," the old folks were wont to say; and they bade their children hold it in all honour, and especially they impressed this upon those among them who, as aforesaid, were not over-burdened with brains.

And now the hundred years are gone and past, our own generation has succeeded. The lake has become a marsh, an oblong strip of water encased in stone is all that remains of the moat, and over it a splendid old tree droops its branches, a willow-tree; it stands there as though to prove how beautiful a willow-tree may be, if it is but left alone and suffered to grow in its own way. Storms have at times handled it roughly, the trunk is cleft asunder from the crown almost to the root, and grass and flowers grow in all the crevices, especially near the crown, where the great boughs are parted; wind and weather have conveyed mould enough to supply a perfect little hanging garden, chickweed, raspberries, nay, even a tiny little service-shrub has taken root there, and, slender and delicate, grows embedded in the old willow-tree, reflecting itself in the black water whenever the wind drives the duck-weed aside into a corner of the stream. A little foot-path leads past the tree over the fields.

And high on the bank near the wood, commanding a charming prospect, stands the New Hall: the old one has been razed to the ground, wiped out of the landscape, as it were. The New Hall is large and splendid, the broad steps leading up to the door look like a bower of roses and large-leaved plants; the window-panes are marvellously bright, and the lawn on which they open is as smoothly green as though it were swept morning and evening. The saloons within are rich with costly paintings, and with chairs and couches of splendid velvet and silk, and so cleverly constructed that they can almost walk on their own legs: there are tables with marble slabs, books bound in morocco with gilt edges. For rich people dwell here now, and grand people too, with the title of Baron!

"Everything in its place!" is still the family motto, and accordingly the pictures that had once hung in all glory and honour on the walls of the Old Hall have been banished to the gallery leading to the servants' room. Among the "old rubbish," as they were called, were two quaint old portraits, one of a grave-looking man wearing a wig and a crimson coat, the other of a lady fair, her hair powdered and combed back after the antique fashion, and holding a red rose in her hand. Both pictures were encircled with a wreath of willow-boughs; they are portraits of the old Councillor and his wife, from whom the present occupants of the Hall claim descent. The pictures are in tolerable preservation, except that they are pierced with small round holes innumerable, the juvenile Barons having used them as targets when they were trying their skill with the cross-bow.

"But they are not really of our family," remarked one of the young Barons. "He was a pedlar and she was a goose-girl. They were not like our papa and mamma!"

"Mere rubbish" were these old pictures! "Everything in its place!" so the great-grand-parents were sent to the servants' gallery.

The little Barons have a tutor; he is a clergyman's son, and lives at the Hall. One day the tutor, his pupils, and their eldest sister, who had lately been confirmed, went out for a walk; they took the path leading past the old willow-tree, and as they went the young girl made herself a bouquet of wild-flowers and green sprays. "Everything in its place!" and out among the green fields, in the fresh morning air, these children of Danish soil looked as fair as any bouquet of rich-hued exotics. But while her fingers were busy, her ears were open to hear every word the tutor was saying; it pleased her right well to hear him speak of the beauty of Nature, and of that beauty more excellent than Nature's, moral beauty,—to hear him tell of the gallant deeds and heroic lives of the great men and noble women of history. For hers was a thoroughly happy and healthful mind; noble and elevated thoughts were natural to her, and she had a heart large enough to embrace and love all that God has created.

The party stopped at the old willow-tree; the youngest of

the young Barons wanted to have a flute cut for him out of it; his tutor broke off a bough for the purpose.

"Oh, don't do it, pray!" cried the young Baroness, but her protest came too late, it was done. "Oh, you should not touch our famous old tree, I love it so much! they all laugh at me at home about it, but I don't care for that. There is a legend about this tree——"

And she went on to relate what we have heard already about the Old Hall, the goose-girl and the pedlar who met there for the first time, the ancestors of the family at the New Hall, and of the young Baroness herself.

"They would not be ennobled, those good honest, old folks," added she. "They were fond of the proverb, 'Everything in its place!' and they never would buy themselves a title to higher rank then they could claim by birth. It was their son, my grandfather, who was made a Baron; he was a very learned man, was much respected and beloved by Princes and Princesses, and used to go to all their grand festivities. He was his parents' favourite, too; I don't know why, but I do love those old folks so much; I always think there must have been something so homelike, so patriarchal, about that Old Hall, with the mistress of the house sitting spinning among her maidens, and the old Councillor reading the Bible aloud."

"Yes, they were excellent people, right-minded people!" replied the tutor; and he forthwith fell into a discourse upon the difference between the aristocracy and the burgher-families; no one who heard his enthusiasm for the old nobility could have imagined that he himself was plebeian-born.

"It is glorious to belong to a race that has made itself illustrious! glorious to know that the blood that flows in one's own veins is the same that has glowed like living fire in the good cause of old! glorious to claim as one's own rightful heritage a name that is, as it were, a passport everywhere. So long as the nobles are noble, who shall deny them honour and precedence? I know that the fashion of the time is to decry respect for our old nobility as a stupid, worn-out prejudice, and to assume that the lower we descend into the mud of poverty and obscurity, the brighter will be the gems of true goodness to be found glistening among the rubbish. But that is not my way of thinking, for it is perfectly mad, utterly false. Many examples of true nobility of soul may be found among the nobly born; I could cite several, but I will instance only one, which I learnt from my mother. She was staying at a great house, my grandmother had been nurse, or some such thing, to its mistress; my mother was in the parlour with the old lord when he noticed a poor old woman hobbling, upon crutches, into the court-yard: she used to come once every week for a small pension. 'Poor thing!' said he, 'it is too bad for her to have to walk up here,' and almost as he spoke he was out of the door and down the steps—he, the old lord, nearly eighty years of age, himself hurried down to the poor woman, to spare her the labour of walking upstairs to fetch her money. This may seem a trivial anecdote enough, but, trivial as it is, it reveals a truly kindly and noble character. Honour to all such! honour to the courtesy and gentleness that smooth down the harsh barriers between rank and rank, that acknowledge the same human nature everywhere, whether it be clothed in woollen, or in purple and fine linen! But as for those gentry who prate of their 'blood,' and pride themselves on their pedigrees, with less of right and of reason than high-mettled Arab steeds, and who arch their necks and eye-brows in scorn at the rest of the world,—such as these disgrace the nobility they are too often supposed to represent; they have, of their own accord, put on the ridiculous mask given them by Thespis, and are rightly handed over to the satirist."

Such was the tutor's oration; it was rather too long for the occasion, but then he was busy making the flute the while.

There was a large party at the Hall that evening; the grand saloon was crowded with guests, some from the neighbourhood, some from the capital, a bevy of ladies richly dressed, with and without taste, a group of the clergy from the adjoining parishes standing in a corner together, as grave as though met for a funeral. A funeral party it certainly was not; it was meant for a party of pleasure, but the pleasure was yet to come. Music and song went on, first one of the party volunteering, then another; but it was mostly music of that sort which is more delightful to the performer than to the audience. The little Baron brought out his flute, but neither he nor his papa, who tried it after him, could make anything of it; it was pronounced a perfect failure.

"But you are a performer too, surely," quoth a witty fine

gentleman, addressing the tutor; "you are, of course, a flute-player as well as a flute-maker. You are a universal genius, I hear, and genius is quite the rage now-a-days—nothing like genius. Come now, I am sure you will be so good as to entrance us by playing on this little instrument." And he handed it over, announcing in a loud voice that the tutor was going to favour the company with a solo on the flute.

It was easy to see that these people wanted to make game of him, and he refused to play; but they pressed him so long and so urgently that at last, in very weariness, he took the flute and raised it to his lips.

It was a strange flute! A sound issued from it, loud, shrill, and vibrating as that sent forth by a steam-engine, nay, louder far; it thrilled right through the house, through garden and woodland, miles out into the country, and with the sound came also a strong, rushing wind, its stormy breath clearly uttering the words, "Everything in its place!"

Forthwith the Baron, the master of the Hall, caught up by the storm-wind, flew out at the window, and was shut up in the porter's lodge in a trice; and the porter himself was borne up, not into the drawing-room, no, for that he was not fit, but into the servants' hall, where the proud, finical flunkeys, in their silk stockings, shook with horror to see such a low person sit down at table with them.

But, in the grand saloon, the young Baroness was wafted up to the seat of honour, where she was right worthy to sit,—and the tutor's place was beside her. There they sat together, for all the world like bride and bridegroom. An old Count, descended from one of the noblest houses in the land, retained his seat, not so much as a breath of air disturbing him. For the flute was strictly just. And the witty young gentleman who had been the occasion of all this tumult was whirled out head foremost to join geese and gander in the poultry-yard.

Half a mile out in the country, the flute wrought wonders. The family of a rich merchant, who drove with four horses, were all precipitated from the carriage-window, and two farmers, who had of late grown too wealthy to know their nearest relations, were puffed into a ditch. It was a dangerous flute. Lucky that at the first sound it uttered it cracked in twain, and was then put safely by in the tutor's pocket. "Everything in its place!"

Next day no more was said about the adventure than if it had never happened. The affair was hushed up, and all things were in the same order as before, save that the two old portraits of the pedlar and the goose-girl continued to hang on the walls of the saloon, whither the storm-wind had blown them. Here some connoisseur chanced to see them, and, as he pronounced them to be painted by a master-hand, they were cleaned and restored, and ever after held in honour. Their value had not been known before.

"Everything in its place!" so shall it be all in good time, never fear!—not in this world, though, that would be expecting rather too much.

THE NISSE AT THE GROCER'S.

THERE was once a Student—a proper Student; he lived in an attic, and possessed just nothing at all. There was also a Grocer—a proper Grocer; he lived in a comfortable room, and possessed the whole house. So the Nisse clung to the Grocer, for the Grocer could give him, every Christmas-eve, a bowl of gruel, with such a great lump of butter in it! The Student could not afford him that; so the Nisse dwelt in the shop, and was right comfortable there.

One evening the Student came by the back-door into the shop to buy candles and cheese; he had no servant to fetch these things for him. They gave him what he wanted, he paid the money, and the Grocer, and Madam, his wife—she was a woman! she had uncommon gifts of speech!—both nodded "Good evening" to him. The Student nodded in return, and was turning away, when his eye fell upon something that was printed on the paper in which his cheese was wrapped, and he stood still to read it. It was a leaf torn out of an old book, a book that ought never to have been torn up, a book full of rare old poetry.

"Plenty more, if you like it," quoth the Grocer; "I gave an old woman some coffee-beans for it; you shall have the whole for eightpence."

"Thank you," said the Student, "let me have it instead of the cheese, I can very well sup off bread and butter, and it would be a sin and a shame for such a book as this to be torn up into scraps. You are an excellent man, a practical man, but as for poetry, you have no more taste for it than that tub!"

Now this speech sounded somewhat rudely, but it was spoken in jest, the Student laughed, and the Grocer laughed too. But the Nisse felt extremely vexed that such a speech should be made to a Grocer who was a householder and sold the best butter.

So when night was come, the shop shut up, and all, except the Student, were gone to bed, the Nisse stole away Madam's tongue,—she did not want it while she slept. And now whatever object he put it upon not only received forthwith the faculty of speech, but was able to express its thoughts and feelings to the full as well as Madam herself. Fortunately the tongue could be in only one place at a time, otherwise there would have been a rare tumult and talkation in the shop, all speaking at once.

And the Nisse put the tongue on the tub wherein all the old newspapers lay. "Is it really true," he asked, "that you do not know what poetry is?"

"Don't I know!" replied the Tub; "it is something that is put into the newspapers to fill them up. I should think I have more of it in me than the Student has, though I am only a Tub at the Grocer's!"

And the Nisse put the tongue on the coffee-mill,—oh, how bravely it worked then!—and he put it on the money-box and on sundry other articles, and he asked them all the same question, and all gave much the same answer; all were of the same opinion, and the opinion of the multitude must be respected.

"Now for the Student!" and the Nisse glided very softly up the back-stairs leading to the Student's attic. There was light within, and the Nisse peeped through the key-hole to see what the Student was about. He was reading in his new-found treasure, the torn old book. But oh, how glorious

A bright sunbeam, as it were, shot out from the book, expanding itself into a mighty, broad-stemmed tree, which raised itself on high and spread its branches over the Student. Every leaf on the tree was fresh and green, every flower was like a graceful, girlish head, the faces of some lit up with eyes dark, thrilling, and passionate, and others animated by serene blue orbs, gentle as an angel's. And every fruit was like a glittering star, and such delicious melody was wafted around!

No, such glory and beauty as this never could the little Nisse have imagined. And, mounted on tip-toe, he stood peeping and peeping, till at last the bright light within died away, till the Student blew out his lamp and went to bed. Nor even then could little Nisse tear himself away, for soft, sweet music still floated around, lulling the Student to rest.

"This is beyond compare!" exclaimed the little Nisse; "this could I never have anticipated! I believe I will stay with the Student henceforth." But he paused, and reflected, and reasoned coolly with himself, and then he sighed, "The Student has no gruel to give me." So down he went; yes, back he went to the Grocer's; and it was well that he did, for the Tub had, meantime, nearly worn out Madam's tongue, by giving out through one ring all that was rumbling within it, and was just on the point of turning in order to give out the same through the other ring when the Nisse came and took the tongue back to Madam. But from that time everything in the shop was always of the same opinion as the Tub, and all trusted it implicitly, and respected it to such a degree, that when of an evening the Grocer read his newspaper aloud, the whole shop invariably believed it was the Tub holding forth.

But the little Nisse was no longer content to stay quietly in the shop, listening to all the wit and wisdom to be gathered there; no, as soon as ever the lamp gleamed from the attic-chamber he was gone; that slight thread of lamp-light issuing from under the Student's door acted upon him as it were a strong anchor-rope drawing him upward; he must away to peep through the key-hole. And then he felt a tumult of pleasure within him, a feeling such as we all have known while gazing on the glorious sea when the Angel of the

Storm is passing over it; and then he would burst out weeping, he knew not why, but they were happy, blessed tears. Oh. delightful beyond conception would it have been to sit with the Student under the tree! but that would be too much happiness; content was he and right glad of the key-hole. And there he would stand for hours in the draughty passage, with the bleak autumn-wind blowing down from the trap-door in the roof full upon him; but the enthusiastic little spirit never heeded the cold, nor, indeed, felt it at all until the light in the attic had been extinguished, and the sweet music had died away in the mournful night-wind. Ugh! then he did shake and shiver, and crept back into his comfortable warm corner. And when Christmas-eve came, and the great lump of butter in his gruel—ah! then he felt that the Grocer was his master, after all!

But one midnight the Nisse was awaked by a terrible rat-tat upon the window-shutters; a crowd of people outside were shouting with all their might and main; the watchman was sounding his alarum; the whole street was lit up with a blaze of flame. Fire! where was it? at the Grocer's, or next door? The tumult was beyond description. Madam, in her bewilderment, took her gold ear-rings off her ears and put them in her pocket, by way of saving something; the Grocer was in a state of excitement about his bonds, the maid wild for her silk mantilla. Every one would fain rescue whatsoever he deemed most precious; so would the little Nisse. In two bounds he was upstairs, in the attic. The Student was standing at the open window, calmly admiring the fire, which was in the neighbour's house, not theirs; the marvellous book lay on the table, the little Nisse seized it, put it into his red cap, and held it aloft with both hands; the most precious thing the house possessed was saved! Away he darted with it, sprang upon the roof, and in a second was seated on the chimney-pot, the glorious raging flames like a halo around him, both hands grasping firmly the little red cap wherein lay his treasure. And now he knew where his heart was, felt that the Student was really his master; but when the fire was extinguished, and he recovered his senses,—what then? "I will divide my allegiance between them," quoth he; "I cannot quite give up the Grocer, because of my bowl of gruel."

Now this was really quite human, though it was a spirit who said it. Don't we all of us cleave to the Grocer,—for the love of his butter and his grits?

A THOUSAND YEARS HENCE.

YES, a thousand years hence they will cross the wide ocean, wafted through the air on the wings of steam. A thousand years hence will the rising generation of America come to pay our poor old Europe a visit of curiosity and compliment. They will make the tour of our antique monuments and dust-buried cities, just as we, in our own present time, travel hence to gaze on the crumbling glories of South Asia.

Yes, a thousand years hence!

Still will the Thames, the Danube, and the Rhine flow on; still will Mont Blanc rear his majestic, hoary forehead to the clouds; still will the Northern Lights dance and flash above the snowy plains of Scandinavia. But generation upon generation will be dust, whole armies of the mighty will have sunk into oblivion, even as now the sages and warriors of the olden time slumber forgotten beneath many a green mound where the wealthy corn-grower sets up a bench, that he may sit and overlook his waving fields of wheat.

"To Europe!" the watchword passes from one young American to another; "to Europe, the home of our fathers, the continent dear to memory and to fancy,—to Europe!"

And now the air-ship is freighted and sped; it is crowded with passengers, for the air-voyage is so much more rapid than that by sea, and the electro-magnetic thread has telegraphed far and wide the advantages of this mighty air-caravan. And now it hovers over Europe; the coasts of Ireland are visible first, but the passengers are asleep, and do not care to be waked till they reach England; they would fain tread the earth where Shakespeare trod—so say the intellectual among them; others refer to it as the land of politics, of commerce, and manufactures.

So they sojourn here throughout one whole day; so much and so little time has this very fast generation to devote to England and Scotland.

And now for France, the land of Charlemagne and Napoleon. Molière, too, is mentioned, the learned have a little talk about the classical and romantic schools, such as they were in the far-off days of old, and a little enthusiasm is got up for heroes, bards, and men of science unknown to us, to whom Paris has yet to give birth.

Again flies the air-steamer over the country whence Columbus sailed, where Cortes first saw the light, and where Calderon sang dramas in melodious verse; beautiful women, black-eyed, and graceful in motion as a wave of the sea, still dwell and make their bowers among those blooming valleys, and the Cid and the Alhambra still live in their old wild songs.

And now through the air to Italy, where Rome once sat as a Queen on her Seven Hills. Alas! the Eternal City is wiped out from the world, the Campagna is a desert; one solitary fragment of wall is shown to the traveller as a relic of St. Peter's; but there are strong doubts as to its being genuine.

Hence to Greece, to sleep one night in the grand hotel on the top of Mount Olympus. That is enough for Greece; now away to the Bosphorus, there to alight for a few hours and see the spot where Byzantium stood; a few poor fishermen are found spreading their nets; they have legends to tell of the fair gardens of the harem that bloomed here in the time of the Ottomans.

There are vestiges of once proud cities to be traced on the shores of the Danube; cities whereof we know nought are glanced at as the air-ship flies on. Here and there the mighty caravan is lowered, and the passengers alight, but only for an hour or two, and then the steamer again bounds upwards.

See, yonder lies Germany, which was once intertwined with a thick net of railroads and canals; here are the lands where Luther spoke, where Goethe sang, where Mozart bore the sceptre as the master of sweet sounds. One day must be given to Germany, one day also to Scandinavia, the birth-land of Linnæus and Oersted, the home of the old heroes, whence swarmed forth those restless, colonising young Normans. Iceland is taken on the way home; the Geysers have given up their habit of boiling over, Hecla has spent itself, but, like the saga's eternal Runic stone, sternly stands forth the bleak, rocky island amid the dashing breakers.

"There is a good deal to see in Europe," remarks the young travelled American, "and we saw it thoroughly in our eight days; for that, you know, is quite time enough, as the great traveller"—here is mentioned the name of some contemporary writer—"has shown in his celebrated work, 'Europe Seen in Eight Days.'"

UNDER THE WILLOW-TREE

DOWN by Kiöge the country is somewhat barren the town lies close by the shore—a neat little town, but prettier it might be easily; a flat plain surrounds it, and the woods are in the far distance. But when a place is thoroughly familiar and home-like to us, we may often find in it a secret charm, an undefined beauty, the memory whereof will excite a sigh and a longing thought even amid the loveliest scenes this world can show us. Also, it must be allowed that in the outskirts of Kiöge, just where a cluster of cottage gardens run down to the little brooklet, which, rippling past them, makes its way to the sea, it is really very pleasant in summer-time. As for those two little playmates, Kanute and Joanna, they thought the spot quite beautiful. They were neighbours' children; in the garden of Kanute's parents stood an elder-tree, in that of Joanna's an old willow; and the children used to creep under the gooseberry-bush hedge that sundered the gardens, and play together. Their favourite haunt was the willow-tree; there they would play for hours: it was somewhat dangerous, for the tree leant forward over the brook, and they were often near falling into the water, but our Lord takes care for little children; were it not so, there would be small chance of their living to be grown men and women. However, these children were uncommonly prudent; as for the boy, he was so shy of the water that not even in summer, when all the other children took such delight in dabbling about in wet places, could he be got down to the shore; he was well laughed at, but he cared not for that. And one night little Joanna dreamt that she was sailing in a boat in Kiöge bay, and that Kanute came out through the sea after her, and that the water first washed over his neck, and at last closed over his head; she told this dream to Kanute, and after that he would no longer bear being called a coward patiently; he would insist that he had good reason to shun the water, and would refer triumphantly to Joanna's dream. He was quite proud of that dream, and with the water would Kanute have nought to do.

Not only in their parents' gardens did Kanute and Joanna play together; sometimes they rambled along the highroads, where alongside of the ditches stood a whole row of willow-trees, by no means handsome, certainly, they were so cut and hewed about the crowns; but then they were planted for use, not for ornament. The old willow-tree in the children's garden was much more picturesque.

There is a large open space in the town of Kiöge, where in market-time used to stand rows of booths, with silk ribands, boots and shoes and all possible things; and what was best of all, nice cakes of gingerbread. Now the man who sold these last always lodged, during market-time, with the parents of little Kanute, and thus came into his hands many a goodly piece of gingerbread, which was, of course, honestly shared with Joanna. But there was one thing they enjoyed still more, and that was, that the gingerbread-seller could tell stories about everything in the world, even about his own gingerbread; nay, concerning this he one evening related a wonderful history, that made a strong impression upon the two children, for which reason we give it here; it is short enough:—

"There once lay upon the counter two cakes of gingerbread," so began the story; "the one had the form of a man, with a hat on; the other, that of a damsel without a hat, but with a bit of leaf-gold on her head, and both had faces on the side that was turned uppermost. The gingerbread man had a bitter almond for a heart, a little to the left. They were left as samples on the counter; they lay there so long that at last they fell in love with each other; but neither spoke of it, which was a pity, for silent love can never come to any good. 'He is a man, he must speak the first word,' thought the gingerbread damsel, but she would have been so glad to know that her affection was returned. As for the other, he grew hotter and hotter internally; at last he dreamt he was a living, moving, greedy street-boy, possessed of four farthings, and that he bought the little damsel and ate her up. And thus they lay for days and weeks together on the counter, and grew quite dry, and the damsel's sentiments became finer and more feminine still. 'It is happiness enough for me that I am beside him on the counter,' she thought, and as she thought thus she cracked in half. 'Had she known my love, she would have held out longer,' thought he.

"That is the story, and here are the two identical cakes," concluded the gingerbread-seller. "They are remarkable on account of their history and their silent love, which came to no good. Look! here you have them;" and he gave to Joanna the whole cake, and to Kanute the cracked little damsel. But the children were so taken with the story, they did not like to eat the hero and heroine of it. The next day, however, they went to walk in Kiöge churchyard, where the old wall is overgrown with ivy, that winter and summer hangs over it like a rich green carpet, and they set up the two cakes among the green leaves, in full sunshine, and they told the story of these silent lovers to a flock of other children. All admired the story; but when, at the end of it, all eyes turned again to the gingerbread pair, behold, a great big boy had seized the poor little damsel and eaten her! The children shed tears of dismay; and then, lest the poor forsaken cake should feel himself alone in the world, they ate the man too. But they never forgot the story.

While these children were continually together, at the elder-bush or under the willow-tree, the little girl used to sing the prettiest songs in a voice clear as silver bells; Kanute had no such tones in his throat, but he always knew the words of her songs. All the Kiöge folk who passed by when Joanna was singing would stop to listen, and say, "What a sweet voice that little creature has!"

Those were blessed days; they were not to last for ever. The little girl's mother died; her father removed to Copenhagen, and married again. The neighbours parted with tears, especially the children, but the elders promised to write to each other at least once a-year. And Kanute was apprenticed to a shoemaker; he was now too big to be suffered to idle away his time; and then he was confirmed.

Oh, how he longed to go to Copenhagen to see little Joanna! Copenhagen is only five miles from Kiöge; in clear weather Kanute could see the towers beyond the bay; on his confirmation-day he could plainly distinguish the gold cross gleaming on the summit of Frue Kirke.

But did Joanna remember him? Yes! At Christmas-time came a letter from her father to his; they were thriving in Copenhagen, and Joanna's beautiful voice had been taken notice of; she was being trained to sing in public; and she herself sent one whole rix-dollar to her old neighbours at Kiöge, that they might drink her health on Christmas-day; and her own hand had added a postscript to the letter, and in it she said, "Kind greetings to Kanute!"

He wept for joy. Every day had Joanna been in his thoughts, and now he knew that she, too, was not unmindful of him. The older he grew, the more he grew fixed in one idea, viz. that she must be his little wife. When he thought this, a smile would steal over his face, and he would sew on so energetically he nearly sewed his finger to his shoe-soles;

but that mattered not. He would not be mute, like the two gingerbread cakes; he had learned wisdom from that story.

At last came the time when he was to go to Copenhagen He had a master there. How glad Joanna would be, and how surprised! She was now seventeen years of age, he nineteen. He would have bought a wedding-ring before he started, but he bethought him that he could get it better in Copenhagen. He took a hasty leave of his parents; quickly he trudged away through autumn rain and mist, the yellow leaves falling around him; wet to the skin he reached Copenhagen, and went straight to his new master.

The following Sunday he had destined for paying his visit to Joanna's father. He had on his best clothes, and his new hat from Kiöge. He found the house, and walked up staircase after staircase; it almost made him giddy to think how folk were crowded above each other in this great city. He entered a pleasant, well-furnished room, and was kindly received by Joanna's father; madam, her step-mother, was a stranger to him, but she gave him her hand and a cup of coffee.

"Joanna will be pleased to see thee," said her father; "ah! I have great joy and pride in that girl, thank God! She has her own chamber, and pays us for it." And he knocked at his daughter's door, as ceremoniously as though she had been a stranger, and they were bidden come in. Well, this was charming! the Queen herself could not have a prettier room, Kanute thought. There were curtains down to the ground, there was a real velvet arm-chair, there were flowers, and pictures, and a looking-glass one might almost run into; it was as big as a door. Kanute saw all this at a glance, and yet he hardly seemed to see anything but Joanna; and she was so altered, Kanute had never imagined she was so beautiful! so graceful too! there was not a girl like her in Kiöge. For a moment she looked with a startled glance at Kanute, but only one moment; then she ran up to him almost as though she would have kissed him; she did not kiss him, but she was very near doing it. Oh, she was indeed glad to see the friend of her childhood! Did not tears stand in her eyes? And then she had so many questions to ask about everything, from Kanute's parents down to the old elder-bush and willow, which last she called "Mother Elder" and "Father Willow."

She recollected everything, even the story of the two gingerbread cakes that lay together on the counter, and then she laughed so heartily! But Kanute's cheeks burned and his heart beat so fast! One thing was certain, she had not grown proud. He saw that it was to please her that her father invited him to stay for the rest of the evening, and she poured out the tea, and her own hand offered him a cup. And after tea she took a book and read aloud, and then she sang, and the tears ran down Kanute's cheeks the while. He was ashamed of himself, and felt thoroughly stupid, and yet she pressed his hand and seemed pleased. It was an incomparable evening, such an evening as spoils one's sleep for the night; and we may be sure Kanute did not sleep. And at leave-taking, Joanna's father said, "Ah, you won't quite forget us, then? Don't let the winter go away without seeing us again."

He resolved he would soon go again. But meanwhile, after his day's work was ended, Kanute used to walk through the town, and his walk always took him through the street where Joanna lived, and he would look up at her window, which was usually lighted, and once he could discern the shadow of her face on the window-curtain; that was a fortunate evening! "In a few days I shall see her again, and then I will tell her what is on my mind—that she must be my little wife! Certainly, I am only a poor journeyman shoemaker, but I will become a master; I will work and strive so hard." And he paid his second visit, but, how unlucky! they were going out. But Joanna pressed his hand, and promised to send him on the following Wednesday a ticket for a concert at which she was going to sing; she wanted him to hear her How kind that was of her! and on Wednesday the ticket came, and he went. She looked and sang beautifully; even the King smiled at her, as though it were a pleasure to him to see her, and the people clapped and applauded her, and Kanute with them. How small, how insignificant he felt! but it mattered not, he loved her so unspeakably; and she? she certainly loved him, and he was the man—he must speak the first word.

He went to see her the third time; he felt as solemn as though he were going to church. Joanna received him alone; this was just what he wished.

"I am so glad you are come!" she said; "I had half a

mind to send my father to you, but I had a fancy that you would come this evening of your own accord. And I have something to tell you; next Friday I am going to France."

The room whirled round before Kanute's eyes as she spoke, his heart seemed ready to burst, but no tears came into his eyes. But Joanna's grew moist, for she saw that he was grieved. "You dear, faithful fellow!" she said, and at this Kanute's tongue was loosed, and he told her how passionately he loved her. But as he spoke, Joanna turned deadly pale; she let go his hand, and replied in a grave, sad voice, "Don't make yourself and me unhappy, Kanute! I will always be a good sister to you, but nothing more," and she stroked his burning forehead with her soft hand. "God gives us all the strength we need, if we do but will it," she added. At this moment her step-mother entered. "Kanute is quite beside himself because we are going away," said Joanna to her. And she patted his arm as if he were a child, "Now, do be a man! be good and rational, as in the old times under the willow-tree, when we both were children."

The old people thought they had only been talking about Joanna's journey; they were very kind to Kanute, but he was utterly bewildered; his thoughts seemed like a broken thread, carried to and fro by the wind. Joanna handed him his tea, and sang, as before, but all seemed changed. When he rose to go, Kanute did not offer his hand, but she took it, saying, "Won't you give your sister your hand at parting, my old playmate, my brother?" And her tears fell as she repeated the word "brother,"—but that did him little good. And so they parted.

And Joanna sailed to France, Kanute remained in Copenhagen. His comrades asked what made him so silent and moody, and bade him enjoy himself while his youth lasted But Kanute could not share in their pleasures; they would have taken him to places where, he felt, he could not take Joanna, and she was always with him in thought. So he spent the evenings in wandering alone, past the house where she had dwelt: her little window was now dark, dreary, and empty. So seemed all the world to Kanute. The winter came on and the waters froze, but when spring followed, the ice broke up, and the first steamer started, a longing for travel came over him; out into the world would he go, only not too near France.

So he buckled on his knapsack, and wandered through Germany, from town to town; not till he reached the famous old city of Nuremberg did he rest. Nuremberg is a wonderful town, as quaint as if it had been cut out of an old picture. The streets run on according to their own sweet will; the houses don't seem to trouble themselves about standing evenly in rows; balconies with tiny towers, scroll-work, and statues spring forward over the pavement, and high up from the strangely-formed roofs run out into the middle of the streets gutters shaped like dragons or wonderfully long-bodied dogs.

On the market-place stood Kanute with his knapsack on his back, near him splashed one of those old fountains, where the curious old images representing personages in the Bible or in history stand amid the sparkling streams of water. A pretty servant-lassie was just fetching water from the fountain; she offered her pitcher to Kanute, and pitying the poor lad's weary looks, gave him a rose out of her posy. This seemed to him a good omen. And now the tones of the organ reached his ears; it sounded so home-like, reminding him of Kiöge church. He entered the great cathedral; the sun shone through its coloured window-panes, and threw brilliant lights among the tall slender pillars; he felt happier —calm peace and pious trust filled his soul.

He resolved to sojourn at Nuremberg; he sought out a good master, abode with him, and learned the language of the country.

The old graves round the town have been converted into tiny kitchen-gardens, but the high walls with their heavy towers still remain; the rope-maker twists his ropes on the wooden gallery along the wall towards the town, and here and here, from holes and crevices, spring forth elder-bushes, which hang their branches over the small, lowly dwellings beneath. In one of these houses dwelt Kanute's master, and close over the little attic-chamber where he slept the elder drooped its boughs. He remained here through the summer and the following winter, but, when spring came, he could bear it no longer. The elder was in full blossom, and the scent of the flowers brought back to him so vividly his own garden at Kiöge, and therefore Kanute left his master, and sought out another farther in the town, where elder-trees grew not.

Close by one of the old walled bridges, opposite a water-mill, he found his next resting-place. The river flowed on, hemmed in by houses decorated with old tumble-down balconies; one could almost fancy the houses had a mind to shake them down into the water. Here grew no fragrant elder-bushes, here scarce even could a flower-pot be seen; but here, nevertheless, stood a withered old willow-tree, clinging fast to the house nearest it, as though to escape being torn away by the stream, and stretching its boughs over the water, just like the willow-tree in Joanna's old garden at Kiöge. So he had fled from "Mother Elder" to "Father Willow," and the old tree looked so home-like on bright moonlight evenings! He could not endure it. Why not? Ask the Willow, ask the fragrant Elder! He bade his master goodbye, and quitted Nuremberg.

To no one did he ever speak of Joanna, he kept his grief within him, and many a strange fancy he had. It seemed to him that the strap of his knapsack tightened him so that he could hardly breathe; he loosened it, but felt no difference. Only half his world was without him, the other lay within, deep in his heart.

But when he saw mountains there came some relief; tears swelled to his eyes, and he breathed more freely. The Alps seemed to him like the folded wings of the earth, glorious wings, which, when spread open, displayed pictures of black woods, foaming waters, clouds, and snow. "At the last day the earth will lift up its great wings, fly into the bosom of its Maker, and burst like a bubble in the beams of His unapproachable light! When will that day come?" he sighed.

Silently he wandered through a land that seemed to him like a verdant fruit-garden; pretty lacemakers nodded to him from the wooden balconies of the houses, the mountain-tops glowed in the red evening sun, and still lakes lay gleaming amid the dark trees; then he thought of the shore at Kiöge bay, but it was with quiet sadness, no longer with agony. And when he beheld the Rhine rushing forward, rolling, roaring, and breaking into wreaths of snow-white foam, the rainbow fluttering like a loose riband above it, he remembered the noisy, riotous water of the mill at Kiöge. He loved the Rhine, and would have tarried in its neighbourhood, but he could not; there were too many elders and willows. So he crossed the Alps: over thistles, Alpine roses, and snow, he passed out into the warm summer sun. He had bidden farewell to the northern lands, and was now among chestnut groves and vineyards, the mountains standing up like a wall between him and his past. This was as it should be.

He abode at Milan, working under a German master, who, with his good old wife, took a great liking to the quiet foreign lad, who spoke so little, laboured so diligently, and bore himself always as a pious Christian. And now it seemed as though the heavy burden had been lifted from off his heart. He loved to mount to the roof of that splendid marble dome; he could have fancied the fairies had shapen it out of northern snow, and carved and fretted it into its numberless bas-reliefs, its one-hundred-and-four tapering spires, its two thousand statues. From every corner, every arch, every pinnacle, those white statues smiled upon him; above him extended the blue sky, below him lay the city and the wide green plains of Lombardy, shut in towards the north by the high mountains with their eternal snow. He often thought of the old church at Kiöge, and the ivy wreaths trailing over the red walls; but he longed not for them, here, behind the mountains, would he be buried.

He had lived for a year at Milan; it was now three years since he had left his home. One day his master treated him to the opera. From the floor to the roof, in seven rows of curtained boxes, sat ladies with bouquets in their hands, as though it were a ball; the light was as dazzling as the brightest sunshine, the music was so loud and beautiful, far more beautiful than that he had heard at Copenhagen,—but then Joanna was there. Surely it was magic! the curtain rose, and before his eyes stood Joanna herself, clad in silk and gold, and with a crown on her head; she sang, she smiled, as only Joanna could sing and smile, and she looked straight at Kanute.

Poor fellow! he seized his master's hand and shouted "Joanna!" but the music drowned his voice, and his master nodded and answered, "To be sure it is Joanna;" and he took out a printed paper, and showed Kanute her name at full length on it. No, it was not a dream! and every one applauded, and flung flowers and wreaths at her feet. And when the performance was over, the people crowded round her carriage, and drew it, and Kanute was among the foremost; and when they had reached her house, he stood close by the carriage-door. The light shone on her gentle face as she stepped out, and smiled, and spoke her thanks so sweetly, and Kanute looked full at her, and she looked direct at him, but she did not recognise him. A grand gentleman with a star on his breast gave her his arm as she entered the house; he was her betrothed.

Kanute heard this repeated from one to another; he went straight home, and began packing his knapsack. No entreaties could detain him; he was told winter was coming on, the snow was already falling up in the mountains; it mattered not, wherever the slow, heavy waggon had a path made for it, he could follow, his knapsack on his back, his staff in hand.

He had wandered till late in the evening, he was weary, and saw neither village nor hostel near; the stars twinkled above, his knees tottered, his head was dizzy; down in the valley below him stars were gleaming out also; it was as though the sky was spread below as well as above him. Brighter and brighter grew these stars of the earth; at last he comprehended that a little town glittering with lights lay beneath; he collected all his strength, walked on, and reached a miserable inn.

Four-and-twenty hours he tarried here, he needed rest so much, and the valleys were full of half-melted snow. But a poor wandering minstrel came that way, and he played an old Danish melody, and then Kanute could rest no longer, he must fain hasten back to Denmark. Never had he confessed his home-sickness, no one knew his inmost soul. In the only letter his parents had written to him during the last twelve months, he read these words, "Thou art hardly a true Dane! Thou lovest foreign lands, and we love our own home." So thought his parents, and he had never gainsayed it.

It was evening, he was trudging along on the open high-road; it was freezing, and the country grew flatter and less sheltered as he walked on; by the way-side stood an old willow-tree; the whole scene looked quite Danish and home-like. Weak and way-worn, he seated himself under the willow-tree, his head drooped, his eyes closed. He felt that the willow bowed its branches towards him; nay, the tree had become a vigorous old man—Father Willow himself—and lifted him, the weary son, upon his arms, and bore him back to his Danish home near the open shore—to Kiöge bay, to the garden of his childhood. Yes, it was actually the Willow-tree from Kiöge, that had gone out into the world to seek him, and now he was found, and borne home to the tiny garden by the brook-side; and there stood Joanna, in her splendid array, and with the gold crown on her head, as he had seen her last, and she said, "Welcome!" And close in front of him stood two wondrous figures, and these were the two celebrated Gingerbread cakes, man and woman; but they looked far more human, far more life-like, than in his childhood, and they spoke to him too. "Thanks!" said they both. "Thou hast loosed our tongues; thou hast taught us freely to speak our thought, else it can never come to good. Ours has come to good at last; we are betrothed!" And the two figures went hand in hand through the streets of Kiöge, up to the church, and Kanute and Joanna followed, hand in hand likewise; and the church stood there as of old time, with its red walls and beautiful green ivy, and both the leaves of the great church-door opened, and the organ sent forth solemn sound, and the two figures walked up the aisle. "We are bridesmaid and bridesman," said they, and then they stepped apart, to make room for Kanute and Joanna between them. And he and Joanna knelt down side by side, and she drooped her head over his face, and ice-cold tears dropped from her eyes; that was because the ice about her heart had melted beneath the warmth of his strong love, and the tears fell on his burning cheeks, and—he awoke.

There he sate, that cold winter evening, in a foreign land, under the old Willow-tree; it was hailing, and the hard-frozen lumps beat against his face.

"That was the happiest hour of my life," he muttered, "but it was a dream. Oh, let me dream again!" and he again closed his eyes; he slept, he dreamt.

Next morning there was a fall of snow, it tossed and whirled softly over his feet. The country-folk passed by on their way to church; they stopped to see who it was. There sate the young wanderer, dead, frozen to death—under the Willow-tree!

A VISION OF THE LAST DAY.

OF all the days of our life the greatest and most solemn is the day on which we die. Hast thou ever tried to realise that most sure, most portentous hour, the last hour we shall spend on earth?

There was a certain man, an upholder of truth and justice, a Christian man and orthodox, so the world esteemed him. And, in sooth, it may be that some good thing was found in him, since in sleep, amid the visions of the night, it pleased the Father of spirits to reveal him to himself, making manifest to him what he was in truth, viz. one of those who trust in themselves that they are righteous and despise others.

He went to rest, secure that his accounts were right with all men, that he had paid his dues and wrought good works that day; of the secret pride of his heart, of the harsh words that had passed his lips, he took no account at all. And so he slept, and in his sleep Death stood by his bed-side, a glorious Angel, strong, spotless, beautiful, but unlike every other angel, stern, unsmiling, pitiless of aspect.

"Thine hour is come, and thou must follow me!" spake Death. And Death's cold finger touched the man's feet, whereupon they became like ice, then touched his forehead, then his heart. And the chain that bound the immortal soul to clay was riven asunder, and the soul was free to follow the Angel of Death.

But during those brief seconds, while yet that awful touch thrilled through feet, and head, and heart, there passed over the dying man, as in great, heaving, ocean-waves, the recollection of all that he had wrought and felt in his whole life; just as one shuddering glance into a whirlpool suffices to reveal in thought rapid as lightning, the entire unfathomable depth; just as in one momentary glance at the starry heavens we can conceive the infinite multitude of that glorious host of unknown orbs.

In such a retrospect the terrified sinner shrinks back into himself, and finding there no stay by which to cling, must feel shrinking into infinite nothingness; while the devout soul raises its thoughts to the Almighty, yielding itself up to Him in child-like trust, and praying, "Thy will be done in me!"

But this man had not the child-like mind, neither did he tremble like the sinner; his thoughts were still the self-praising thoughts in which he had fallen asleep. His path, he believed, must lead straight heavenwards, and Mercy, the promised Mercy, would open to him the gates.

And, in his dream, the Soul followed the Angel of Death, though not without first casting one wistful glance at the couch where lay, in its white shroud, the lifeless image of clay, still, as it were, bearing the impress of the soul's own individuality. And now they hovered through the air, now glided along the ground. Was it a vast, decorated hall they were passing through, or a forest? It seemed hard to tell; Nature, it appeared, was formally set out for show, as in the artificial old French gardens, and amid its strange, carefully arranged scenes, passed and re-passed troops of men and women, all clad as for a masquerade.

"Such is human life!" said the Angel of Death.

The figures seemed more or less disguised; those who swept by in the glories of velvet and gold were not all among the noblest or most dignified-looking, neither were all those who wore the garb of poverty insignificant or vulgar. It was a strange masquerade! But most strange it was to see how one and all carefully concealed under their clothing something they would not have others perceive, but in vain, for each was bent upon discovering his neighbour's secret, and they tore and snatched at one another till, now here, now there, some part of an animal was revealed. In one was found the grinning head of an ape, in another the cloven foot of a goat, in a third the poison-fang of a snake, in a fourth the clammy fin of a fish.

All had in them some token of the animal, the animal which is fast rooted in human nature, and which here was seen struggling to burst forth. And, however closely a man might hold his garment over it, the others would never rest till they had rent the hiding veil, and all kept crying out, "Look here! look now! here he is! there she is!"—and every one mockingly laid bare his fellow's shame.

"And what was the animal in me?" inquired the disembodied Soul; and the Angel of Death pointed to a haughty form, around whose head shone a bright, wide-spread glory of rainbow-coloured rays, but at whose heart might be seen lurking, half hidden, the feet of the peacock; the glory was, in fact, merely the peacock's gaudy tail.

And as they passed on, large, foul-looking birds shrieked out from the boughs of the trees; with clear, intelligible, though harsh, human voices they shrieked, "Thou that walkest with Death, dost remember me?" All the evil thoughts and desires that had nestled within him from his birth until his death now called after him, "Rememberest thou me?"

And the Soul shuddered, recognising the voices; it could not deny knowledge of the evil thoughts and desires that were now rising up in witness against it.

"In our flesh, in our evil nature, dwelleth no good thing," cried the Soul; "but, at least, thoughts never with me ripened into actions; the world has not seen the evil fruit." And the

Soul hurried on to get free from the accusing voices; but the great black fowls swept in circles round, and screamed out their scandalous words louder and louder, as though they would be heard all over the world. And the Soul fled from them like the hunted stag, and at every step stumbled against sharp flint stones that lay in the path. "How came these sharp stones here? They look like mere withered leaves lying on the ground."

"Every stone is for some incautious word thou hast spoken, which lay as a stumbling-block in thy neighbour's path, which wounded thy neighbour's heart far more sorely and deeply than these sharp flints now wound thy feet."

"Alas! I never once thought of that," sighed the Soul.

And those words of the Gospel rang through the air, "Judge not, that ye be not judged."

"We have all sinned," said the Soul, recovering from its momentary self-abasement. "I have kept the Law and the Gospel, I have done what I could, I am not as others are!"

And in his dream this man now stood at the gates of Heaven, and the Angel who guarded the entrance inquired, "Who art thou? Tell me thy faith, and show it to me in thy works."

"I have faithfully kept the Commandments, I have humbled myself in the eyes of the world, I have preserved myself free from the pollution of intercourse with sinners, I have hated and persecuted evil, and those who practise it, and I would do so still, yea, with fire and sword, had I the power."

"Then thou art one of Mohammed's followers?" said the Angel.

"I? a Mohammedan?—never!"

"'He who strikes with the sword shall perish by the sword,' thus spake the Son; His religion thou knowest not. It may be that thou art one of the children of Israel, whose maxim is, 'An eye for an eye, a tooth for a tooth,'—art thou such?"

"I am a Christian."

"I see it not in thy faith or in thine actions. The law of Christ is the law of forgiveness, love, and mercy."

"Mercy!" The gracious echo of that sweet word thrilled

through infinite space, the gates of heaven opened, and the Soul hovered towards the realms of endless bliss.

But the flood of light that streamed forth from within was so dazzlingly bright, so transcendently white and pure, that the Soul shrank back as from a two-edged sword, and the hymns and harp-tones of Angels mingled in such exquisite celestial harmony as the earthly mind has not power either to conceive or to endure. And the Soul trembled and bowed itself deeper and deeper, and the heavenly light penetrated it through and through, and it felt to the quick, as it had never truly felt before, the burden of its own pride, cruelty, and sin.

"What I have done of good in the world, that did I because I could not otherwise, but the evil that I did—that was of myself!"

This confession was wrung from him; more and more the man felt dazzled and overpowered by the pure light of heaven; he seemed falling into a measureless abyss, the abyss of his own nakedness and unworthiness. Shrunk into himself, humbled, cast out, unripe for the kingdom of heaven, shuddering at the thought of the just and holy God,—hardly dared he to gasp out, "Mercy!"

And the face of the Angel at the portal was turned towards him in softening pity. "Mercy is for them who implore it, not claim it; there is Mercy also for thee. Turn thee, child of man, turn thee back the way thou camest to thy clayey tabernacle; in pity is it given thee to dwell in dust yet a little while. Be no longer righteous in thine own eyes, copy Him who with patience endured the contradiction of sinners, strive and pray that thou mayest become poor in spirit, and so mayest thou yet inherit the Kingdom."

"Holy, loving, glorious for ever shalt thou be, oh erring human spirit!"—thus rang the chorus of Angels. And again overpowered by those transcendent melodies, dazzled and blinded by that excess of purest light, the Soul again shrank back into itself. It seemed to be falling an infinite depth; the celestial music grew fainter and fainter, till common earthly sights and sounds dispelled the vision. The rays of the early morning sun falling full on his face, the cheerful crow of the vigilant cock, called the sleeper up to pray.

Inexpressibly humbled, yet thankful, he arose and knelt beside his bed. "Thou, who hast shown me to myself, help me now, that I may not only do justly, but love mercy, and walk humbly with my God. Thou, who hast convicted me of sin, now purify me, strengthen me, that, though ever unworthy of Thy presence, I may yet, supported by Thy Love dare to ascend into Thine everlasting light!"

The Vision was his; be the lesson, the prayer, also ours.

AN ALPHABETICAL LIST

OF BOOKS CONTAINED IN

BOHN'S LIBRARIES.

Detailed Catalogue, arranged according to the various Libraries, will be sent on application.

ADDISON'S Works. With the Notes of Bishop Hurd, Portrait, and 8 Plates of Medals and Coins. Edited by H. G. Bohn. 6 vols. 3s. 6d. each.

ÆSCHYLUS, The Dramas of. Translated into English Verse by Anna Swanwick. 4th Edition, revised. 5s.

—— **The Tragedies of.** Newly translated from a revised text by Walter Headlam, Litt.D., and C. E. S. Headlam, M.A. 3s. 6d.

—— **The Tragedies of.** Translated into Prose by T. A. Buckley, B.A. 3s. 6d.

ALLEN'S (Joseph, R. N.) Battles of the British Navy. Revised Edition, with 57 Steel Engravings. 2 vols. 5s. each.

AMMIANUS MARCELLINUS. History of Rome during the Reigns of Constantius, Julian, Jovianus, Valentinian, and Valens. Translated by Prof. C. D. Yonge, M.A. 7s. 6d.

ANDERSEN'S Danish Legends and Fairy Tales. Translated by Caroline Peachey. With 120 Wood Engravings. 5s.

ANTONINUS (M. Aurelius), The Thoughts of. Trans. literally, with Notes and Introduction by George Long, M.A. 3s. 6d.

APOLLONIUS RHODIUS. 'The Argonautica.' Translated by E. P. Coleridge, B.A. 5s.

APPIAN'S Roman History. Translated by Horace White, M.A., LL.D. With Maps and Illustrations. 2 vols. 6s. each.

APULEIUS, The Works of. Comprising the Golden Ass, God of Socrates, Florida, and Discourse of Magic. 5s.

ARGYLL (Duke of). The Life of Queen Victoria. Illustrated. 3s. 6d.

ARIOSTO'S Orlando Furioso. Translated into English Verse by W. S. Rose. With Portrait, and 24 Steel Engravings. 2 vols. 5s. each.

ARISTOPHANES' Comedies. Translated by W. J. Hickie. 2 vols. 5s. each.

ARISTOTLE'S Nicomachean Ethics. Translated, with Introduction and Notes, by the Venerable Archdeacon Browne. 5s.

—— **Politics and Economics.** Translated by E. Walford, M.A., with Introduction by Dr. Gillies. 5s.

—— **Metaphysics.** Translated by the Rev. John H. M'Mahon, M.A. 5s.

—— **History of Animals.** Trans. by Richard Cresswell, M.A. 5s.

—— **Organon;** or, Logical Treatises, and the Introduction of Porphyry. Translated by the Rev. O. F. Owen, M.A. 2 vols. 3s. 6d. each.

—— **Rhetoric and Poetics.** Trans. by T. Buckley, B.A. 5s.

ARRIAN'S Anabasis of Alexander, together with the Indica. Translated by E. J. Chinnock, M.A., LL.D. With Maps and Plans. 5s.

ATHENÆUS. The Deipnosophists; or, the Banquet of the Learned. Trans. by Prof. C. D. Yonge, M.A. 3 vols. 5s. each.

BACON'S Moral and Historical Works, including the Essays, Apophthegms, Wisdom of the Ancients, New Atlantis, Henry VII., Henry VIII., Elizabeth, Henry Prince of Wales, History of Great Britain, Julius Cæsar, and Augustus Cæsar. Edited by J. Devey, M.A. 3s. 6d.

—— **Novum Organum and Advancement of Learning.** Edited by J. Devey, M.A. 5s.

BASS'S Lexicon to the Greek Testament. 2s.

BAX'S Handbook of the History of Philosophy. for the use of Students. By E. Belfort Bax. 5s.

BEAUMONT and FLETCHER, their finest Scenes, Lyrics, and other Beauties, selected from the whole of their works, and edited by Leigh Hunt. 3s. 6d.

BECHSTEIN'S Cage and Chamber Birds, their Natural History, Habits, Food, Diseases, and Modes of Capture. Translated, with considerable additions on Structure, Migration, and Economy, by H. G. Adams. Together with SWEET BRITISH WARBLERS. With 43 coloured Plates and Woodcut Illustrations. 5s.

BEDE'S (Venerable) Ecclesiastical History of England. Together with the ANGLO-SAXON CHRONICLE. Edited by J. A. Giles, D.C.L. With Map. 5s.

BELL (Sir Charles). The Anatomy and Philosophy of Expression, as connected with the Fine Arts. By Sir Charles Bell, K.H. 7th edition, revised. 5s.

BERKELEY (George), Bishop of Cloyne, The Works of. Edited by George Sampson. With Biographical Introduction by the Right Hon. A. J. Balfour, M.P. 3 vols. 5s. each.

BION. *See* THEOCRITUS.

BJÖRNSON'S Arne and the Fisher Lassie. Translated by W. H. Low, M.A. 3s. 6d.

BLAIR'S Chronological Tables Revised and Enlarged. Comprehending the Chronology and History of the World, from the Earliest Times to the Russian Treaty of Peace, April 1856. By J. Willoughby Rosse. Double vol. 10s.

BLEEK'S Introduction to the Old Testament. By Friedrich Bleek. Edited by **Johann** Bleek and Adolf Kamphausen. Translated by G. H. Venables, under the supervision of the Rev. Canon Venables. 2 vols. 5s. each.

BOETHIUS'S Consolation of Philosophy. King Alfred's Anglo-Saxon Version of. With a literal English Translation on opposite pages, Notes, Introduction, and Glossary, by Rev. S. Fox, M.A. 5s.

BOHN'S Dictionary of Poetical Quotations. 4th edition. 6s.

BOHN'S Handbooks of Games. New edition. In 2 vols., with numerous Illustrations 3s. 6d. each.
   Vol. I.—TABLE GAMES :—Billiards, Bagatelle, Chess, Draughts, Backgammon, Dominoes, Solitaire, Reversi, Go-Bang, Rouge et Noir, Roulette, E.O., Hazard, Faro.
   Vol. II.—CARD GAMES:—Whist, Solo Whist, Poker, Piquet, Ecarté, Euchre, Bézique, Cribbage, Loo, Vingt-et-un, Napoleon, Newmarket, Pope Joan, Speculation, &c., &c.

BOND'S A Handy Book of Rules and Tables for verifying Dates with the Christian Era, &c. Giving an account of the Chief Eras and Systems used by various Nations; with the easy Methods for determining the Corresponding Dates. By J. J. Bond. 5s.

BONOMI'S Nineveh and its Palaces. 7 Plates and 294 Woodcut Illustrations. 5s.

BOSWELL'S Life of Johnson, with the TOUR IN THE HEBRIDES and JOHNSONIANA. Edited by the Rev. A. Napier, M.A. With Frontispiece to each vol. 6 vols. 3s. 6d. each.

BRAND'S Popular Antiquities of England, Scotland, and Ireland. Arranged, revised, and greatly enlarged, by Sir Henry Ellis, K.H., F.R.S., &c., &c. 3 vols. 5s. each.

BREMER'S (Frederika) Works. Translated by Mary Howitt. 4 vols. 3s. 6d. each.

BRIDGWATER TREATISES.
Bell (Sir Charles) on the Hand. With numerous Woodcuts. 5s.

Kirby on the History, Habits, and Instincts of Animals. Edited by T. Rymer Jones. With upwards of 100 Woodcuts. Vol. I., 5s. Vol. II. out of print.

Kidd on the Adaptation of External Nature to the Physical Condition of Man. 3s. 6d.

Chalmers on the Adaptation of External Nature to the Moral and Intellectual Constitution of Man. 5s.

BRINK (B. ten) Early English Literature. By Bernhard ten Brink. Vol. I. To Wyclif. Translated by Horace M. Kennedy. 3s. 6d.

   Vol. II. Wyclif, Chaucer, Earliest Drama Renaissance. Translated by W. Clarke Robinson, Ph.D. 3s. 6d.

   Vol. III. From the Fourteenth Century to the Death of Surrey. Edited by Dr. Alois Brandl. Trans. by L. Dora Schmitz. 3s. 6d.

—— Five Lectures on Shakespeare. Trans. by Julia Franklin. 3s. 6d.

BROWNE'S (Sir Thomas) Works. Edited by Simon Wilkin. 3 vols. 3s. 6d. each.

BURKE'S Works. 8 vols. 3s. 6d. each.

   I.—Vindication of Natural Society—Essay on the Sublime and Beautiful, and various Political Miscellanies.

   II.—Reflections on the French Revolution — Letters relating to the Bristol Election—Speech on Fox's East India Bill, &c.

   III.—Appeal from the New to the Old Whigs—On the Nabob of Arcot's Debts—The Catholic Claims, &c.

   IV.—Report on the Affairs of India, and Articles of Charge against Warren Hastings.

   V.—Conclusion of the Articles of Charge against Warren Hastings—Political Letters on the American War, on a Regicide Peace, to the Empress of Russia.

   VI.—Miscellaneous Speeches—Letters and Fragments—Abridgments of English History, &c. With a General Index.

   VII. & VIII.—Speeches on the Impeachment of Warren Hastings; and Letters. With Index.

—— Life. By Sir J. Prior. 3s. 6d.

BURNEY. The Early Diary of Fanny Burney (Madame D'Arblay), 1768-1778. With a selection from her Correspondence and from the Journals of her sisters, Susan and Charlotte Burney. Edited by Annie Raine Ellis. 2 vols. 3s. 6d. each.

—— Evelina. By Frances Burney (Mme. D'Arblay). With an Introduction and Notes by A. R. Ellis. 3s. 6d.

BURNEY'S Cecilia. With an Introduction and Notes by A. R. Ellis. 2 vols. 3s. 6d. each.

BURN (R.) Ancient Rome and its Neighbourhood. An Illustrated Handbook to the Ruins in the City and the Campagna, for the use of Travellers. By Robert Burn, M.A. With numerous Illustrations, Maps, and Plans. 7s. 6d.

BURNS (Robert), Life of. By J. G. Lockhart, D.C.L. A new and enlarged Edition. Revised by William Scott Douglas. 3s. 6d.

BURTON'S (Robert) Anatomy of Melancholy. Edited by the Rev. A. R. Shilleto, M.A. With Introduction by A. H. Bullen, and full Index. 3 vols. 3s. 6d. each.

BURTON (Sir R. F.) Personal Narrative of a Pilgrimage to Al-Madinah and Meccah. By Captain Sir Richard F. Burton, K.C.M.G. With an Introduction by Stanley Lane-Poole, and all the original Illustrations. 2 vols. 3s. 6d. each.

*** This is the copyright edition, containing the author's latest notes.

BUTLER'S (Bishop) Analogy of Religion, Natural and Revealed, to the Constitution and Course of Nature; together with two Dissertations on Personal Identity and on the Nature of Virtue, and Fifteen Sermons. 3s. 6d.

BUTLER'S (Samuel) Hudibras. With Variorum Notes, a Biography, Portrait, and 28 Illustrations. 5s.

—— or, further Illustrated with 60 Outline Portraits. 2 vols. 5s. each.

CÆSAR. Commentaries on the Gallic and Civil Wars. Translated by W. A. McDevitte, B.A. 5s.

CAMOENS' Lusiad; or, the Discovery of India. An Epic Poem. Translated by W. J. Mickle. 5th Edition, revised by E. R. Hodges, M.C.P. 3s. 6d.

CARLYLE'S French Revolution. Edited by J. Holland Rose, Litt.D. Illus. 3 vols. 5s. each.

—— Sartor Resartus. With 75 Illustrations by Edmund J. Sullivan. 5s.

CARPENTER'S (Dr. W. B.) Zoology. Revised Edition, by W. S. Dallas, F.L.S. With very numerous Woodcuts. Vol. I. 6s. [*Vol. II. out of print.*]

CARPENTER'S Mechanical Philosophy, Astronomy, and Horology. 181 Woodcuts. 5s.

—— Vegetable Physiology and Systematic Botany. Revised Edition, by E. Lankester, M.D., &c. With very numerous Woodcuts. 6s.

—— Animal Physiology. Revised Edition. With upwards of 300 Woodcuts. 6s.

CASTLE (E.) Schools and Masters of Fence, from the Middle Ages to the End of the Eighteenth Century. By Egerton Castle, M.A., F.S.A. With a Complete Bibliography. Illustrated with 140 Reproductions of Old Engravings and 6 Plates of Swords, showing 114 Examples. 6s.

CATTERMOLE'S Evenings at Haddon Hall. With 24 Engravings on Steel from designs by Cattermole, the Letterpress by the Baroness de Carabella. 5s.

CATULLUS, Tibullus, and the Vigil of Venus. A Literal Prose Translation. 5s.

CELLINI (Benvenuto). Memoirs of, written by Himself. Translated by Thomas Roscoe. 3s. 6d.

CERVANTES' Don Quixote de la Mancha. Motteaux's Translation revised. 2 vols. 3s. 6d. each.

—— Galatea. A Pastoral Romance. Translated by G. W. J. Gyll. 3s. 6d.

—— Exemplary Novels. Translated by Walter K. Kelly. 3s. 6d.

CHAUCER'S Poetical Works. Edited by Robert Bell. Revised Edition, with a Preliminary Essay by Prof. W. W. Skeat, M.A. 4 vols. 3s. 6d. each.

CHEVREUL on Colour. Translated from the French by Charles Martel. Third Edition, with Plates, 5s.; or with an additional series of 16 Plates in Colours, 7s. 6d.

CHINA. Pictorial, Descriptive, and Historical. With Map and nearly 100 Illustrations. 5s.

CHRONICLES OF THE CRUSADES. Contemporary Narratives of the Crusade of Richard Cœur de Lion, by Richard of Devizes and Geoffrey de Vinsauf; and of the Crusade at St. Louis, by Lord John de Joinville. 5s.

CHRONICLES OF THE TOMBS. A Collection of Epitaphs by T. J. Pettigrew, F.R.S. 5s.

CICERO'S Orations. Translated by Prof. C. D. Yonge, M.A. 4 vols. 5s. each.

CICERO'S Letters. Translated by Evelyn S. Shuckburgh. 4 vols. 5s. each.

—— **On Oratory and Orators.** With Letters to Quintus and Brutus. Translated by the Rev. J. S. Watson, M.A. 5s.

—— **On the Nature of the Gods,** Divination, Fate, Laws, a Republic, Consulship. Translated by Prof. C. D. Yonge, M.A., and Francis Barham. 5s.

—— **Academics,** De Finibus, and Tusculan Questions. By Prof. C. D. Yonge, M.A. 5s.

—— **Offices**; or, Moral Duties. Cato Major, an Essay on Old Age; Lælius, an Essay on Friendship; Scipio's Dream; Paradoxes; Letter to Quintus on Magistrates. Translated by C. R. Edmonds. 3s. 6d.

CLARK'S (Hugh) Introduction to Heraldry. 18th Edition, Revised and Enlarged by J. R. Planché, Rouge Croix. With nearly 1000 Illustrations. 5s. Or with the Illustrations Coloured, 15s.

CLASSIC TALES, containing Rasselas, Vicar of Wakefield, Gulliver's Travels, and The Sentimental Journey. 3s. 6d.

COLERIDGE'S (S. T.) Friend. A Series of Essays on Morals, Politics, and Religion. 3s. 6d.

—— **Aids to Reflection,** and the CONFESSIONS OF AN INQUIRING SPIRIT, to which are added the ESSAYS ON FAITH and the BOOK OF COMMON PRAYER. 3s. 6d.

—— **Lectures and Notes on** Shakespeare and other English Poets. Edited by T. Ashe. 3s. 6d.

COLERIDGE'S Biographia Literaria; together with Two Lay Sermons. 3s. 6d.

—— **Biographia Epistolaris.** Edited by Arthur Turnbull. 3s. 6d.

—— **Table-Talk and Omniana.** Edited by T. Ashe, B.A. 3s. 6d.

—— **Miscellanies, Æsthetic and Literary**; to which is added, THE THEORY OF LIFE. Collected and arranged by T. Ashe, B.A. 3s. 6d.

COMTE'S Positive Philosophy. Translated and condensed by Harriet Martineau. With Introduction by Frederic Harrison. 3 vols. 5s. each.

—— **Philosophy of the Sciences,** being an Exposition of the Principles of the *Cours de Philosophie Positive*. By G. H. Lewes. 5s.

CONDÉ'S History of the Dominion of the Arabs in Spain. Translated by Mrs. Foster. 3 vols. 3s. 6d. each.

COOPER'S Biographical Dictionary. Containing Concise Notices (upwards of 15,000) of Eminent Persons of all Ages and Countries. By Thompson Cooper, F.S.A. With a Supplement, bringing the work down to 1883. 2 vols. 5s. each.

CORNELIUS NEPOS.—*See* JUSTIN.

COXE'S Memoirs of the Duke of Marlborough. With his original Correspondence. By W. Coxe, M.A., F.R.S. Revised edition by John Wade. 3 vols. 3s. 6d. each.

—— **History of the House of Austria** (1218-1792). With a Continuation from the Accession of Francis I. to the Revolution of 1848. 4 vols. 3s. 6d. each.

CRAIK'S (G. L.) Pursuit of Knowledge under Difficulties. Illustrated by Anecdotes and Memoirs. Revised edition, with numerous Woodcut Portraits and Plates. 5s.

CUNNINGHAM'S Lives of the Most Eminent British Painters. A New Edition, with Notes and Sixteen fresh Lives. By Mrs. Heaton. 3 vols. 3s. 6d. each.

DANTE. Divine Comedy. Translated by the Rev. H. F. Cary, M.A. New Edition, by M. L. Egerton-Castle. 3s. 6d.

—— Translated into English Verse by I. C. Wright, M.A. 3rd Edition, revised. With Portrait, and 34 Illustrations on Steel, after Flaxman.

DANTE. The Inferno. A Literal Prose Translation, with the Text of the Original printed on the same page. By John A. Carlyle, M.D. 5s.

DE COMMINES (Philip), Memoirs of. Containing the Histories of Louis XI. and Charles VIII., Kings of France, and Charles the Bold, Duke of Burgundy. Together with the Scandalous Chronicle, or Secret History of Louis XI., by Jean de Troyes. Translated by Andrew R. Scoble. With Portraits. 2 vols. 3s. 6d. each.

DEFOE'S Novels and Miscellaneous Works. With Prefaces and Notes, including those attributed to Sir W. Scott. 7 vols. 3s. 6d. each.

    I.—Captain Singleton, and Colonel Jack.

    II.—Memoirs of a Cavalier, Captain Carleton, Dickory Cronke, &c.

    III.—Moll Flanders, and the History of the Devil.

DEFOE'S NOVELS AND MISCELLANEOUS WORKS—*continued.*

    IV.—Roxana, and Life of Mrs. Christian Davies.

    V.—History of the Great Plague of London, 1665; The Storm (1703); and the True-born Englishman.

    VI.—Duncan Campbell, New Voyage round the World, and Political Tracts.

    VII.—Robinson Crusoe. 3s. 6d. Also with 86 Illustrations. 5s.

DEMMIN'S History of Arms and Armour, from the Earliest Period. By Auguste Demmin. Translated by C. C. Black, M.A. With nearly 2000 Illustrations. 7s. 6d.

DEMOSTHENES' Orations. Translated by C. Rann Kennedy. 5 vols. Vol. I., 3s. 6d.; Vols. II.-V., 5s. each.

DE STAËL'S Corinne or Italy. By Madame de Staël. Translated by Emily Baldwin and Paulina Driver. 3s. 6d.

DICTIONARY of Latin and Greek Quotations; including Proverbs, Maxims, Mottoes, Law Terms and Phrases. With all the Quantities marked, and English Translations. With Index Verborum (622 pages). 5s.

DICTIONARY of Obsolete and Provincial English. Compiled by Thomas Wright, M.A., F.S.A., &c. 2 vols. 5s. each.

DIDRON'S Christian Iconography: a History of Christian Art in the Middle Ages. Translated by E. J. Millington and completed by Margaret Stokes. With 240 Illustrations. 2 vols. 5s. each.

DIOGENES LAERTIUS. Lives and Opinions of the Ancient Philosophers. Translated by Prof. C. D. Yonge, M.A. 5s.

DOBREE'S Adversaria. Edited by the late Prof. Wagner. 2 vols. 5s. each.

DODD'S Epigrammatists. A Selection from the Epigrammatic Literature of Ancient, Mediæval, and Modern Times. By the Rev. Henry Philip Dodd, M.A. Oxford. 2nd Edition, revised and enlarged. 6s.

DONALDSON'S The Theatre of the Greeks. A Treatise on the History and Exhibition of the Greek Drama. With numerous Illustrations and 3 Plans. By John William Donaldson, D.D. 5s.

DRAPER'S History of the Intellectual Development of Europe. By John William Draper, M.D., LL.D. 2 vols. 5s. each.

DUNLOP'S History of Fiction. A new Edition. Revised by Henry Wilson. 2 vols. 5s. each.

DYER'S History of Modern Europe, from the Fall of Constantinople. 3rd edition, revised and continued to the end of the Nineteenth Century. By Arthur Hassall, M.A. 6 vols. 3s. 6d each.

DYER'S (Dr T. H.) Pompeii: its Buildings and Antiquities. By T. H. Dyer, LL.D. With nearly 300 Wood Engravings, a large Map, and a Plan of the Forum. 7s. 6d.

DYER (T. F. T.) British Popular Customs, Present and Past. An Account of the various Games and Customs associated with Different Days of the Year in the British Isles, arranged according to the Calendar. By the Rev. T. F. Thiselton Dyer, M.A. 5s.

EBERS' Egyptian Princess. An Historical Novel. By George Ebers. Translated by E. S. Buchheim. 3s. 6d.

EDGEWORTH'S Stories for Children. With 8 Illustrations by L. Speed. 3s. 6d.

ELZE'S William Shakespeare. —See SHAKESPEARE.

EMERSON'S Works. 5 vols. 3s. 6d. each.
   I.—Essays and Representative Men.
   II.—English Traits, Nature, and Conduct of Life.
   III.—Society and Solitude—Letters and Social Aims — Addresses.
   IV.—Miscellaneous Pieces.
   V.—Poems.

EPICTETUS, The Discourses of. With the ENCHEIRIDION and Fragments. Translated by George Long, M.A. 5s.

EURIPIDES. A New Literal Translation in Prose. By E P. Coleridge, M.A. 2 vols. 5s. each.

EUTROPIUS.—See JUSTIN.

EUSEBIUS PAMPHILUS, Ecclesiastical History of. Translated by Rev. C. F. Cruse, M.A. 5s.

EVELYN'S Diary and Correspondence. Edited from the Original MSS. by W. Bray, F.A.S. With 45 engravings. 4 vols. 5s. each.

FAIRHOLT'S Costume in England. A History of Dress to the end of the Eighteenth Century. 3rd Edition, revised, by Viscount Dillon, V.P.S.A. Illustrated with above 700 Engravings. 2 vols. 5s. each.

FIELDING'S Adventures of Joseph Andrews and his Friend Mr. Abraham Adams. With Cruikshank's Illustrations. 3s. 6d.

—— **History of Tom Jones,** a Foundling. With Cruikshank's Illustrations. 2 vols. 3s. 6d. each.

—— **Amelia.** With Cruikshank's Illustrations. 5s.

FLAXMAN'S Lectures on Sculpture. By John Flaxman, R.A. With Portrait and 53 Plates. 6s.

FOSTER'S (John) Essays: on Decision of Character; on a Man's writing Memoirs of Himself; on the epithet Romantic; on the aversion of Men of Taste to Evangelical Religion. 3s. 6d.

—— **Essays on the Evils of Popular Ignorance;** to which is added, a Discourse on the Propagation of Christianity in India. 3s. 6d.

—— **Essays on the Improvement of Time.** With NOTES OF SERMONS and other Pieces. 3s. 6d.

GASPARY'S History of Italian Literature to the Death of Dante. Translated by Herman Oelsner, M.A., Ph.D. 3s. 6d.

GEOFFREY OF MONMOUTH, Chronicle of.—*See Old English Chronicles.*

GESTA ROMANORUM, or Entertaining Moral Stories invented by the Monks. Translated by the Rev. Charles Swan. Revised Edition, by Wynnard Hooper, B.A. 5s.

GILDAS, Chronicles of.—*See Old English Chronicles.*

GIBBON'S Decline and Fall of the Roman Empire. Complete and Unabridged, with Variorum Notes. Edited by an English Churchman. With 2 Maps and Portrait. 7 vols. 3s. 6d. each.

GILBART'S History, Principles, and Practice of Banking. By the late J. W. Gilbart, F.R.S. New Edition (1907), revised by Ernest Sykes. 2 vols. 5s. each.

GIL BLAS, The Adventures of. Translated from the French of Lesage by Smollett. With 24 Engravings on Steel, after Smirke, and 10 Etchings by George Cruikshank. 6s.

GIRALDUS CAMBRENSIS' Historical Works. Translated by Th. Forester, M.A., and Sir R. Colt Hoare. Revised Edition, Edited by Thomas Wright, M.A., F.S.A. 5s.

GOETHE'S Faust. Part I. German Text with Hayward's Prose Translation and Notes. Revised by C. A. Buchheim, Ph.D. 5s.

GOETHE'S Works. Translated into English by various hands. 14 vols. 3s. 6d. each.

    I. and II.—Poetry and Truth from My Own Life. New and revised edition.

    III.—Faust. Two Parts, complete. (Swanwick.)

    IV.—Novels and Tales.

    V.—Wilhelm Meister's Apprenticeship.

    VI.—Conversations with Eckermann and Soret.

    VIII.—Dramatic Works.

    IX.—Wilhelm Meister's Travels.

    X.—Tour in Italy, and Second Residence in Rome.

    XI.—Miscellaneous Travels.

    XII.—Early and Miscellaneous Letters.

    XIII.—Correspondence with Zelter (out of print).

    XIV.—Reineke Fox, West-Eastern Divan and Achilleid.

GOLDSMITH'S Works. A new Edition, by J. W. M. Gibbs. 5 vols. 3s. 6d. each.

GRAMMONT'S Memoirs of the Court of Charles II. Edited by Sir Walter Scott. Together with the BOSCOBEL TRACTS, including two not before published, &c. New Edition. 5s.

GRAY'S Letters. Including the Correspondence of Gray and Mason. Edited by the Rev. D. C. Tovey, M.A. Vols. I. and II. 3s. 6d. each. (Vol. III. in the Press.)

GREEK ANTHOLOGY. Translated by George Burges, M.A. 5s.

GREEK ROMANCES of Heliodorus, Longus, and Achilles Tatius—viz., The Adventures of Theagenes & Chariclea; Amours of Daphnis and Chloe; and Loves of Clitopho and Leucippe. Translated by Rev. R. Smith, M.A. 5s.

GREENE, MARLOWE, and BEN JONSON. Poems of. Edited by Robert Bell. 3s. 6d.

GREGORY'S Letters on the Evidences, Doctrines, & Duties of the Christian Religion. By Dr. Olinthus Gregory. 3s. 6d.

GRIMM'S TALES. With the Notes of the Original. Translated by Mrs. A. Hunt. With Introduction by Andrew Lang, M.A. 2 vols. 3s. 6d. each.

—— **Gammer Grethel**; or, German Fairy Tales and Popular Stories. Containing 42 Fairy Tales. Trans. by Edgar Taylor. With numerous Woodcuts after George Cruikshank and Ludwig Grimm. 3s. 6d.

GROSSI'S Marco Visconti. Translated by A. F. D. The Ballads rendered into English Verse by C. M. P. 3s. 6d.

GUIZOT'S History of the English Revolution of 1640. From the Accession of Charles I. to his Death. Translated by William Hazlitt. 3s. 6d.

—— **History of Civilisation**, from the Fall of the Roman Empire to the French Revolution. Translated by William Hazlitt. 3 vols. 3s. 6d. each.

HALL'S (Rev. Robert) Miscellaneous Works and Remains. 3s. 6d.

HAMPTON COURT: A Short History of the Manor and Palace. By Ernest Law, B.A. With numerous Illustrations. 5s.

HARDWICK'S History of the Articles of Religion. By the late C. Hardwick. Revised by the Rev. Francis Procter, M.A. 5s.

HAUFF'S Tales. The Caravan—The Sheik of Alexandria—The Inn in the Spessart. Trans. from the German by S. Mendel. 3s. 6d.

HAWTHORNE'S Tales. 4 vols. 3s. 6d. each.
- I.—Twice-told Tales, and the Snow Image.
- II.—Scarlet Letter, and the House with the Seven Gables.
- III.—Transformation [The Marble Faun], and Blithedale Romance.
- IV.—Mosses from an Old Manse.

HAZLITT'S Table-talk. Essays on Men and Manners. By W. Hazlitt. 3s. 6d.

HAZLITT'S Lectures on the Literature of the Age of Elizabeth and on Characters of Shakespeare's Plays. 3s. 6d.

—— Lectures on the English Poets, and on the English Comic Writers. 3s. 6d.

—— The Plain Speaker. Opinions on Books, Men, and Things. 3s. 6d.

—— Round Table. 3s. 6d.

—— Sketches and Essays. 3s. 6d.

—— The Spirit of the Age; or, Contemporary Portraits. Edited by W. Carew Hazlitt. 3s. 6d.

—— View of the English Stage. Edited by W. Spencer Jackson. 3s. 6d.

HEATON'S Concise History of Painting. New Edition, revised by Cosmo Monkhouse. 5s.

HEGEL'S Lectures on the Philosophy of History. Translated by J. Sibree, M.A.

HEINE'S Poems, Complete. Translated by Edgar A. Bowring, C.B. 3s. 6d.

—— Travel-Pictures, including the Tour in the Harz, Norderney, and Book of Ideas, together with the Romantic School. Translated by Francis Storr. A New Edition, revised throughout. With Appendices and Maps. 3s. 6d.

HELIODORUS. Theagenes and Chariclea. — See GREEK ROMANCES.

HELP'S Life of Christopher Columbus, the Discoverer of America. By Sir Arthur Helps, K.C.B. 3s. 6d.

—— Life of Hernando Cortes, and the Conquest of Mexico. 2 vols. 3s. 6d. each.

HELP'S Life of Pizarro. 3s. 6d.

—— Life of Las Casas the Apostle of the Indies. 3s. 6d.

HENDERSON (E.) Select Historical Documents of the Middle Ages, including the most famous Charters relating to England, the Empire, the Church, &c., from the 6th to the 14th Centuries. Translated from the Latin and edited by Ernest F. Henderson, A.B., A.M., Ph.D. 5s.

HENFREY'S Guide to English Coins, from the Conquest to 1885. New and revised Edition by C. F. Keary, M.A., F.S.A. 6s.

HENRY OF HUNTINGDON'S History of the English. Translated by T. Forester, M.A. 5s.

HENRY'S (Matthew) Exposition of the Book of the Psalms. 5s.

HERODOTUS. Translated by the Rev. Henry Cary, M.A. 3s. 6d.

—— Analysis and Summary of. By J. T. Wheeler. 5s.

HESIOD, CALLIMACHUS, and THEOGNIS. Translated by the Rev. J. Banks, M.A. 5s.

HOFFMANN'S (E. T. W.) The Serapion Brethren. Translated from the German by Lt.-Col. Alex. Ewing. 2 vols. 3s. 6d. each.

HOLBEIN'S Dance of Death and Bible Cuts. Upwards of 150 Subjects, engraved in facsimile, with Introduction and Descriptions by Francis Douce and Dr. Thomas Frognall Dibdin. 5s.

HOMER'S Iliad. A new translation by E. H. Blakeney, M.A. Vol. I. containing Books I.-XII. 3s. 6d. (Vol. II. in the Press.)

—— Translated into English Prose by T. A. Buckley, B.A. 5s.

HOMER'S Odyssey. Hymns, Epigrams, and Battle of the Frogs and Mice. Translated into English Prose by T. A. Buckley, B.A. 5s.

—— *See also* POPE.

HOOPER'S (G.) Waterloo: The Downfall of the First Napoleon: a History of the Campaign of 1815. By George Hooper. With Maps and Plans. 3s. 6d.

—— **The Campaign of Sedan:** The Downfall of the Second Empire, August–September, 1870. With General Map and Six Plans of Battle. 3s. 6d.

HORACE. A new literal Prose translation, by A. Hamilton Bryce, LL.D. 3s. 6d.

HUGO'S (Victor) Dramatic Works. Hernani—Ruy Blas—The King's Diversion. Translated by Mrs. Newton Crosland and F. L. Slous. 3s. 6d.

—— **Poems, chiefly Lyrical.** Translated by various Writers, now first collected by J. H. L. Williams. 3s. 6d.

HUMBOLDT'S Cosmos. Translated by E. C. Otté, B. H. Paul, and W. S. Dallas, F.L.S. 5 vols. 3s. 6d. each, excepting Vol. V. 5s.

—— **Personal Narrative** of his Travels to the Equinoctial Regions of America during the years 1799-1804. Translated by T. Ross. 3 vols. 5s. each.

—— **Views of Nature.** Translated by E. C. Otté and H. G. Bohn. 5s.

HUMPHREYS' Coin Collector's Manual. By H. N. Humphreys. with upwards of 140 Illustrations on Wood and Steel. 2 vols. 5s. each.

HUNGARY: its History and Revolution, together with a copious Memoir of Kossuth. 3s. 6d.

HUNT'S Poetry of Science. By Richard Hunt. 3rd Edition, revised and enlarged. 5s.

HUTCHINSON (Colonel). Memoirs of the Life of. By his Widow, Lucy: together with her Autobiography, and an Account of the Siege of Lathom House. 3s. 6d.

INGULPH'S Chronicles of the Abbey of Croyland, with the CONTINUATION by Peter of Blois and other Writers. Translated by H. T. Riley, M.A. 5s.

IRVING'S (Washington) Complete Works. 15 vols. With Portraits, &c. 3s. 6d. each.

   I.—Salmagundi, Knickerbocker's History of New York.

   II.—The Sketch-Book, and the Life of Oliver Goldsmith.

   III.—Bracebridge Hall, Abbotsford and Newstead Abbey.

   IV.—The Alhambra, Tales of a Traveller.

   V.—Chronicle of the Conquest of Granada, Legends of the Conquest of Spain.

   VI. & VII.—Life and Voyages of Columbus, together with the Voyages of his Companions.

   VIII.—Astoria, A Tour on the Prairies.

   IX.—Life of Mahomet, Lives of the Successors of Mahomet.

   X.—Adventures of Captain Bonneville, U.S.A., Wolfert's Roost.

   XI.—Biographies and Miscellaneous Papers.

   XII.-XV.—Life of George Washington. 4 vols.

IRVING'S (Washington) Life and Letters. By his Nephew, Pierre E. Irving. 2 vols. 3s. 6d. each.

ISOCRATES, The Orations of. Translated by J. H. Freese, M.A. Vol. I. 5s.

JAMES'S (G. P. R.) Life of Richard Cœur de Lion. 2 vols. 3s. 6d. each. (Vol. I. out of print.)

JAMESON'S (Mrs.) Shakespeare's Heroines. Characteristics of Women: Moral, Poetical, and Historical. By Mrs. Jameson. 3s. 6d.

JESSE'S (E.) Anecdotes of Dogs. With 40 Woodcuts and 34 Steel Engravings. 5s.

JESSE'S (J. H.) Memoirs of the Court of England during the Reign of the Stuarts, including the Protectorate. 3 vols. With 42 Portraits. 5s. each.

—— Memoirs of the Pretenders and their Adherents. With 6 Portraits. 5s.

JOHNSON'S Lives of the Poets. Edited by Mrs. Alexander Napier, with Introduction by Professor Hales. 3 vols. 3s. 6d. each.

JOSEPHUS (Flavius), The Works of. Whiston's Translation, revised by Rev. A. R. Shilleto, M.A. With Topographical and Geographical Notes by Colonel Sir C. W. Wilson, K.C.B. 5 vols. 3s. 6d. each.

JULIAN, the Emperor. Containing Gregory Nazianzen's Two Invectives and Libanus' Monody, with Julian's extant Theosophical Works. Translated by C. W. King, M.A. 5s.

JUNIUS'S Letters. With all the Notes of Woodfall's Edition, and important Additions. 2 vols. 3s. 6d. each.

JUSTIN, CORNELIUS NEPOS, and EUTROPIUS. Translated by the Rev. J. S. Watson, M.A. 5s.

JUVENAL, PERSIUS, SULPICIA and LUCILIUS. Translated by L. Evans, M.A. 5s.

KANT'S Critique of Pure Reason. Translated by J. M. D. Meiklejohn. 5s.

—— Prolegomena and Metaphysical Foundations of Natural Science. Translated by E. Belfort Bax. 5s.

KEIGHTLEY'S (Thomas) Mythology of Ancient Greece and Italy. 4th Edition, revised by Leonard Schmitz, Ph.D., LL.D. With 12 Plates from the Antique. 5s.

KEIGHTLEY'S Fairy Mythology, illustrative of the Romance and Superstition of Various Countries. Revised Edition, with Frontispiece by Cruikshank. 5s.

LA FONTAINE'S Fables. Translated into English Verse by Elizur Wright. New Edition, with Notes by J. W. M. Gibbs. 3s. 6d.

LAMARTINE'S History of the Girondists. Translated by H. T. Ryde. 3 vols. 3s. 6d. each.

—— History of the Restoration of Monarchy in France (a Sequel to the History of the Girondists). 4 vols. 3s. 6d. each.

—— History of the French Revolution of 1848. 3s. 6d.

LAMB'S (Charles) Essays of Elia and Eliana. Complete Edition. 3s. 6d.

LAMB'S (Charles) Specimens of English Dramatic Poets of the Time of Elizabeth. 3*s.* 6*d.*

—— Memorials and Letters of Charles Lamb. By Serjeant Talfourd. New Edition, revised, by W. Carew Hazlitt. 2 vols. 3*s.* 6*d.* each.

—— Tales from Shakespeare. With Illustrations by Byam Shaw. 3*s.* 6*d.*

LANE'S Arabian Nights' Entertainments. Edited by Stanley Lane-Poole, M.A., Litt.D. 4 vols. 3*s.* 6*d.* each.

LAPPENBERG'S History of England under the Anglo-Saxon Kings. Translated by B. Thorpe, F.S.A. New edition, revised by E. C. Otté. 2 vols. 3*s.* 6*d.* each.

LEONARDO DA VINCI'S Treatise on Painting. Translated by J. F. Rigaud, R.A., With a Life of Leonardo by John William Brown. With numerous Plates. 5*s.*

LEPSIUS'S Letters from Egypt, Ethiopia, and the Peninsula of Sinai. Translated by L. and J. B. Horner. With Maps. 5*s.*

LESSING'S Dramatic Works, Complete. Edited by Ernest Bell, M.A. With Memoir of Lessing by Helen Zimmern. 2 vols. 3*s.* 6*d.* each.

—— Laokoon, Dramatic Notes, and the Representation of Death by the Ancients. Translated by E. C. Beasley and Helen Zimmern. Edited by Edward Bell, M.A. With a Frontispiece of the Laokoon group. 3*s.* 6*d.*

LILLY'S Introduction to Astrology. With a GRAMMAR OF ASTROLOGY and Tables for Calculating Nativities, by Zadkiel. 5*s.*

LIVY'S History of Rome. Translated by Dr. Spillan, C. Edmonds, and others. 4 vols. 5*s.* each.

LOCKE'S Philosophical Works. Edited by J. A. St. John. 2 vols. 3*s.* 6*d.* each.

LOCKHART (J. G.)—*See* BURNS.

LODGE'S Portraits of Illustrious Personages of Great Britain, with Biographical and Historical Memoirs. 240 Portraits engraved on Steel, with the respective Biographies unabridged. 8 vols. 5*s.* each.

[*Vols. II. IV. and VII. out of print.*]

LOUDON'S (Mrs.) Natural History. Revised edition, by W. S. Dallas, F.L.S. With numerous Woodcut Illus. 5*s.*

LOWNDES' Bibliographer's Manual of English Literature. Enlarged Edition. By H. G. Bohn. 6 vols. cloth, 5*s.* each. Or 4 vols. half morocco, 2*l.* 2*s.*

LONGUS. Daphnis and Chloe.—*See* GREEK ROMANCES.

LUCAN'S Pharsalia. Translated by H. T. Riley, M.A. 5*s.*

LUCIAN'S Dialogues of the Gods, of the Sea Gods, and of the Dead. Translated by Howard Williams, M.A. 5*s.*

LUCRETIUS. A Prose Translation. By H. A. J. Munro. Reprinted from the Final (4th) Edition. With an Introduction by J. D. Duff, M.A. 5*s.*

—— Literally translated. By the Rev. J. S. Watson, M.A. With a Metrical Version by J. M. Good. 5*s.*

LUTHER'S Table-Talk. Translated and Edited by William Hazlitt. 3s. 6d.

—— **Autobiography.** — See MICHELET.

MACHIAVELLI'S History of Florence, together with the Prince, Savonarola, various Historical Tracts, and a Memoir of Machiavelli. 3s. 6d.

MALLET'S Northern Antiquities, or an Historical Account of the Manners, Customs, Religions and Laws, Maritime Expeditions and Discoveries, Language and Literature, of the Ancient Scandinavians. Translated by Bishop Percy. Revised and Enlarged Edition, with a Translation of the PROSE EDDA, by J. A. Blackwell. 5s.

MANZONI. The Betrothed: being a Translation of 'I Promessi Sposi.' By Alessandro Manzoni. With numerous Woodcuts. 5s.

MARCO POLO'S Travels; the Translation of Marsden revised by T. Wright, M.A., F.S.A. 5s.

MARRYAT'S (Capt. R.N.) Masterman Ready. With 93 Woodcuts. 3s. 6d.

—— **Mission**; or, Scenes in Africa. Illustrated by Gilbert and Dalziel. 3s. 6d.

—— **Pirate and Three Cutters.** With 8 Steel Engravings, from Drawings by Clarkson Stanfield, R.A. 3s. 6d.

—— **Privateersman.** 8 Engravings on Steel. 3s. 6d.

—— **Settlers in Canada.** 10 Engravings by Gilbert and Dalziel. 3s. 6d.

MARRYAT'S (Capt. R.N.) Poor Jack. With 16 Illustrations after Clarkson Stansfield, R.A. 3s. 6d.

—— **Peter Simple.** With 8 full-page Illustrations. 3s. 6d.

MARTIAL'S Epigrams, complete. Translated into Prose, each accompanied by one or more Verse Translations selected from the Works of English Poets, and other sources. 7s. 6d.

MARTINEAU'S (Harriet) History of England, from 1800-1815. 3s. 6d.

—— **History of the Thirty Years' Peace**, A.D. 1815-46. 4 vols. 3s. 6d. each.

—— See *Comte's Positive Philosophy*.

MATTHEW OF WESTMINSTER'S Flowers of History, from the beginning of the World to A.D. 1307. Translated by C. D. Yonge, M.A. 2 vols. 5s. each.

MAXWELL'S Victories of Wellington and the British Armies. Frontispiece and 5 Portraits. 5s.

MENZEL'S History of Germany, from the Earliest Period to 1842. 3 vols. 3s. 6d. each.

MICHAEL ANGELO AND RAPHAEL, their Lives and Works. By Duppa and Quatremere de Quincy. With Portraits, and Engravings on Steel. 5s.

MICHELET'S Luther's Autobiography. Trans. by William Hazlitt. With an Appendix (110 pages) of Notes. 3s. 6d.

—— **History of the French Revolution** from its earliest indications to the flight of the King in 1791. 3s. 6d.

MIGNET'S History of the French Revolution, from 1789 to 1814. 3s. 6d. New edition, reset.

MILL (J. S.). Early Essays by John Stuart Mill. Collected from various sources by J. W. M. Gibbs. 3s. 6d.

MILLER (Professor). History Philosophically Illustrated, from the Fall of the Roman Empire to the French Revolution. 4 vols. 3s. 6d. each.

MILTON'S Prose Works. Edited by J. A. St. John. 5 vols. 3s. 6d. each.

—— **Poetical Works**, with a Memoir and Critical Remarks by James Montgomery, an Index to Paradise Lost, Todd's Verbal Index to all the Poems, and a Selection of Explanatory Notes by Henry G. Bohn. Illustrated with 120 Wood Engravings from Drawings by W. Harvey. 2 vols. 3s. 6d. each.

MITFORD'S (Miss) Our Village Sketches of Rural Character and Scenery. With 2 Engravings on Steel. 2 vols. 3s. 6d. each.

MOLIÈRE'S Dramatic Works. A new Translation in English Prose, by C. H. Wall. 3 vols. 3s. 6d. each.

MONTAGU. The Letters and Works of Lady Mary Wortley Montagu. Edited by her great-grandson, Lord Wharncliffe's Edition, and revised by W. Moy Thomas. New Edition, revised, with 5 Portraits. 2 vols. 5s. each.

MONTAIGNE'S Essays. Cotton's Translation, revised by W. C. Hazlitt. New Edition. 3 vols. 3s. 6d. each.

MONTESQUIEU'S Spirit of Laws. New Edition, revised and corrected. By J. V. Pritchard, A.M. 2 vols. 3s. 6d. each.

MORE'S Utopia. Robinson's translation, with Roper's 'Life of Sir Thomas More,' and More's Letters to Margaret Roper and others. Edited, with Notes, by George Sampson. Introduction and Bibliography by A. Guthkelch. 5s.

MORPHY'S Games of Chess. Being the Matches and best Games played by the American Champion, with Explanatory and Analytical Notes by J. Löwenthal. 5s.

MOTLEY (J. L.). The Rise of the Dutch Republic. A History. By John Lothrop Motley. New Edition, with Biographical Introduction by Moncure D. Conway. 3 vols. 3s. 6d. each.

MUDIE'S British Birds; or, History of the Feathered Tribes of the British Islands. Revised by W. C. L. Martin. With 52 Figures of Birds and 7 Coloured Plates of Eggs. 2 vols.

NEANDER (Dr. A.) Life of Jesus Christ. Translated by J. McClintock and C. Blumenthal. 3s. 6d.

—— **History of the Planting and Training of the Christian Church by the Apostles.** Translated by J. E. Ryland. 2 vols. 3s. 6d. each.

—— **Memorials of Christian Life in the Early and Middle Ages**; including Light in Dark Places. Trans. by J. E. Ryland. 3s. 6d.

NIBELUNGEN LIED. The Lay of the Nibelungs, metrically translated from the old German text by Alice Horton, and edited by Edward Bell, M.A. To which is prefixed the Essay on the Nibelungen Lied by Thomas Carlyle. 5s.

NICOLINI'S History of the Jesuits: their Origin, Progress, Doctrines, and Designs. With 8 Portraits. 5s.

NORTH (R.) Lives of the Right Hon. Francis North, Baron Guildford, the Hon. Sir Dudley North, and the Hon. and Rev. Dr. John North. By the Hon. Roger North. Together with the Autobiography of the Author. Edited by Augustus Jessopp, D.D. 3 vols. 3s. 6d. each.

NUGENT'S (Lord) Memorials of Hampden, his Party and Times. With a Memoir of the Author, an Autograph Letter, and Portrait. 5s.

OLD ENGLISH CHRONICLES, including Ethelwerd's Chronicle, Asser's Life of Alfred, Geoffrey of Monmouth's British History, Gildas, Nennius, and the spurious chronicle of Richard of Cirencester. Edited by J. A. Giles, D.C.L. 5s.

OMAN (J. C.) The Great Indian Epics: the Stories of the RAMAYANA and the MAHABHARATA. By John Campbell Oman, Principal of Khalsa College, Amritsar. With Notes, Appendices, and Illustrations. 3s. 6d.

OVID'S Works, complete. Literally translated into Prose. 3 vols. 5s. each.

PASCAL'S Thoughts. Translated from the Text of M. Auguste Molinier by C. Kegan Paul. 3rd Edition. 3s. 6d.

PAULI'S (Dr. R.) Life of Alfred the Great. Translated from the German. To which is appended Alfred's ANGLO-SAXON VERSION OF OROSIUS. With a literal Translation interpaged, Notes, and an ANGLO-SAXON GRAMMAR and GLOSSARY, by B. Thorpe. 5s.

PAUSANIAS' Description of Greece. Newly translated by A. R. Shilleto, M.A. 2 vols. 5s. each.

PEARSON'S Exposition of the Creed. Edited by E. Walford, M.A. 5s.

PEPYS' Diary and Correspondence. Deciphered by the Rev. J. Smith, M.A., from the original Shorthand MS. in the Pepysian Library. Edited by Lord Braybrooke. 4 vols. With 31 Engravings. 5s. each.

PERCY'S Reliques of Ancient English Poetry. With an Essay on Ancient Minstrels and a Glossary. Edited by J. V. Pritchard, A.M. 2 vols. 3s. 6d. each.

PERSIUS.—See JUVENAL.

PETRARCH'S Sonnets, Triumphs, and other Poems. Translated into English Verse by various Hands. With a Life of the Poet by Thomas Campbell. With Portrait and 15 Steel Engravings. 5s.

PICKERING'S History of the Races of Man, and their Geographical Distribution. With AN ANALYTICAL SYNOPSIS OF THE NATURAL HISTORY OF MAN by Dr. Hall. With a Map of the World and 12 coloured Plates. 5s.

PINDAR. Translated into Prose by Dawson W. Turner. To which is added the Metrical Version by Abraham Moore. 5*s*.

PLANCHÉ. History of British Costume, from the Earliest Time to the Close of the Eighteenth Century. By J. R. Planché, Somerset Herald. With upwards of 400 Illustrations. 5*s*.

PLATO'S Works. Literally translated, with Introduction and Notes. 6 vols. 5*s*. each.

 I.—The Apology of Socrates, Crito, Phædo, Gorgias, Protagoras, Phædrus, Theætetus, Euthyphron, Lysis. Translated by the Rev. H. Carey.

 II.—The Republic, Timæus, and Critias. Translated by Henry Davis.

 III.—Meno, Euthydemus, The Sophist, Statesman, Cratylus, Parmenides, and the Banquet. Translated by G. Burges.

 IV.—Philebus, Charmides, Laches, Menexenus, Hippias, Ion, The Two Alcibiades, Theages, Rivals, Hipparchus, Minos, Clitopho, Epistles. Translated by G. Burges.

 V.—The Laws. Translated by G. Burges.

 VI.—The Doubtful Works. Translated by G. Burges.

—— Summary and Analysis of the Dialogues. With Analytical Index. By A. Day, LL.D. 5*s*.

PLAUTUS'S Comedies. Translated by H. T. Riley, M.A. 2 vols. 5*s*. each.

PLINY. The Letters of Pliny the Younger. Melmoth's translation, revised by the Rev. F. C. T. Bosanquet, M.A. 5*s*.

PLOTINUS, Select Works of. Translated by Thomas Taylor. With an Introduction containing the substance of Porphyry's Plotinus. Edited by G. R. S. Mead, B.A., M.R.A.S. 5*s*.

PLUTARCH'S Lives. Translated by A. Stewart, M.A., and George Long, M.A. 4 vols. 3*s*. 6*d*. each.

—— **Morals.** Theosophical Essays. Translated by C. W. King, M.A. 5*s*.

—— **Morals.** Ethical Essays. Translated by the Rev. A. R. Shilleto, M.A. 5*s*.

POETRY OF AMERICA. Selections from One Hundred American Poets, from 1776 to 1876. By W. J. Linton. 3*s*. 6*d*.

POLITICAL CYCLOPÆDIA. A Dictionary of Political, Constitutional, Statistical, and Forensic Knowledge; forming a Work of Reference on subjects of Civil Administration, Political Economy, Finance, Commerce, Laws, and Social Relations. 4 vols. (1848.) 3*s*. 6*d*. each.

   [*Vol. I. out of print.*

POPE'S Poetical Works. Edited, with copious Notes, by Robert Carruthers. With numerous Illustrations. 2 vols. 5*s*. each.

   [*Vol. I. out of print.*

—— Homer's Iliad. Edited by the Rev. J. S. Watson, M.A. Illustrated by the entire Series of Flaxman's Designs. 5*s*.

—— Homer's Odyssey, with the Battle of Frogs and Mice, Hymns, &c., by other translators. Edited by the Rev. J. S. Watson, M.A. With the entire Series of Flaxman's Designs. 5*s*.

—— Life, including many of his Letters. By Robert Carruthers. With numerous Illustrations. 5*s*.

POUSHKIN'S Prose Tales: The Captain's Daughter—Doubrovsky—The Queen of Spades—An Amateur Peasant Girl—The Shot—The Snow Storm—The Postmaster—The Coffin Maker—Kirdjali—The Egyptian Nights—Peter the Great's Negro. Translated by T. Keane. 3s. 6d.

PRESCOTT'S Conquest of Mexico. Copyright edition, with the notes by John Foster Kirk, and an introduction by G. P. Winship. 3 vols. 3s. 6d. each.

—— Conquest of Peru. Copyright edition, with the notes of John Foster Kirk. 2 vols. 3s. 6d. each.

—— Reign of Ferdinand and Isabella. Copyright edition, with the notes of John Foster Kirk. 3 vols. 3s. 6d. each.

PROPERTIUS. Translated by Rev. P. J. F. Gantillon, M.A., and accompanied by Poetical Versions, from various sources. 3s. 6d.

PROVERBS, Handbook of. Containing an entire Republication of Ray's Collection of English Proverbs, with his additions from Foreign Languages and a complete Alphabetical Index; in which are introduced large additions as well of Proverbs as of Sayings, Sentences, Maxims, and Phrases, collected by H. G. Bohn. 5s.

POTTERY AND PORCELAIN, and other Objects of Vertu. Comprising an Illustrated Catalogue of the Bernal Collection of Works of Art, with the prices at which they were sold by auction, and names of the possessors. To which are added, an Introductory Lecture on Pottery and Porcelain, and an Engraved List of all the known Marks and Monograms. By Henry G. Bohn. With numerous Wood Engravings, 5s.; or with Coloured Illustrations, 10s. 6d.

PROUT'S (Father) Reliques. Collected and arranged by Rev. F. Mahony. New issue, with 21 Etchings by D. Maclise, R.A. Nearly 600 pages. 5s.

QUINTILIAN'S Institutes of Oratory, or Education of an Orator. Translated by the Rev. J. S. Watson, M.A. 2 vols. 5s. each.

RACINE'S (Jean) Dramatic Works. A metrical English version. By R. Bruce Boswell, M.A. Oxon. 2 vols. 3s. 6d. each.

RANKE'S History of the Popes, during the Last Four Centuries. Translated by E. Foster. Mrs. Foster's translation revised, with considerable additions, by G. R. Dennis, B.A. 3 vols. 3s. 6d. each.

—— History of Servia and the Servian Revolution. With an Account of the Insurrection in Bosnia. Translated by Mrs. Kerr. 3s. 6d.

RECREATIONS in SHOOTING. By 'Craven.' With 62 Engravings on Wood after Harvey, and 9 Engravings on Steel, chiefly after A. Cooper, R.A. 5s.

RENNIE'S Insect Architecture. Revised and enlarged by Rev. J. G. Wood, M.A. With 186 Woodcut Illustrations. 5s.

REYNOLDS' (Sir J.) Literary Works. Edited by H. W. Beechy. 2 vols. 3s. 6d. each.

RICARDO on the Principles of Political Economy and Taxation. Edited by E. C. K. Gonner, M.A. 5s.

RICHTER (Jean Paul Friedrich). Levana, a Treatise on Education: together with the Autobiography (a Fragment), and a short Prefatory Memoir. 3s. 6d.

RICHTER (Jean Paul Friedrich). Flower, Fruit, and Thorn Pieces, or the Wedded Life, Death, and Marriage of Firmian Stanislaus Siebenkaes, Parish Advocate in the Parish of Kuhschnapptel. Newly translated by Lt.-Col. Alex. Ewing. 3*s*. 6*d*.

ROGER DE HOVEDEN'S Annals of English History, comprising the History of England and of other Countries of Europe from A.D. 732 to A.D. 1201. Translated by H. T. Riley, M.A. 2 vols. 5*s*. each.

ROGER OF WENDOVER'S Flowers of History, comprising the History of England from the Descent of the Saxons to A.D. 1235, formerly ascribed to Matthew Paris. Translated by J. A. Giles, D.C.L. 2 vols. 5*s*. each.
[*Vol. II. out of print.*

ROME in the **NINETEENTH CENTURY.** Containing a complete Account of the Ruins of the Ancient City, the Remains of the Middle Ages, and the Monuments of Modern Times. By C. A. Eaton. With 34 Steel Engravings. 2 vols. 5*s*. each.

—— *See* BURN.

ROSCOE'S (W.) Life and Pontificate of Leo X. Final edition, revised by Thomas Roscoe. 2 vols. 3*s*. 6*d*. each.

—— **Life of Lorenzo de' Medici,** called 'the Magnificent.' With his poems, letters, &c. 10th Edition, revised, with Memoir of Roscoe by his Son. 3*s*. 6*d*.

RUSSIA. History of, from the earliest Period, compiled from the most authentic sources by Walter K. Kelly. With Portraits. 2 vols. 3*s*. 6*d*. each.

SALLUST, FLORUS, and **VELLEIUS PATERCULUS.** Trans. by J. S. Watson, M.A. 5*s*.

SCHILLER'S Works. Translated by various hands. 7 vols. 3*s*. 6*d*. each:—

I.—History of the Thirty Years' War.

II.—History of the Revolt in the Netherlands, the Trials of Counts Egmont and Horn, the Siege of Antwerp, and the Disturbances in France preceding the Reign of Henry IV.

III.—Don Carlos, Mary Stuart, Maid of Orleans, Bride of Messina, together with the Use of the Chorus in Tragedy (a short Essay).

These Dramas are all translated in metre.

IV.—Robbers (with Schiller's original Preface), Fiesco, Love and Intrigue, Demetrius, Ghost Seer, Sport of Divinity.

The Dramas in this volume are translated into Prose.

V.—Poems.

VI.—Essays, Æsthetical and Philosophical.

VII.—Wallenstein's Camp, Piccolomini and Death of Wallenstein, William Tell.

SCHILLER and GOETHE. Correspondence between, from A.D. 1794–1805. Translated by L. Dora Schmitz. 2 vols. 3*s*. 6*d*. each.

SCHLEGEL'S (F.) Lectures on the Philosophy of Life and the Philosophy of Language. Translated by the Rev. A. J. W. Morrison, M.A. 3*s*. 6*d*.

—— **Lectures on the History of Literature,** Ancient and Modern. Translated from the German. 3*s*. 6*d*.

—— **Lectures on the Philosophy of History.** Translated by J. B. Robertson. 3*s*. 6*d*.

SCHLEGEL'S Lectures on Modern History, together with the Lectures entitled Cæsar and Alexander, and The Beginning of our History. Translated by L. Purcell and R. H. Whitelock. 3s. 6d.

—— **Æsthetic and Miscellaneous Works.** Translated by E. J. Millington. 3s. 6d.

SCHLEGEL'S (A. W.) Lectures on Dramatic Art and Literature. Translated by J. Black. Revised Edition, by the Rev. A. J. W. Morrison, M.A. 3s. 6d.

SCHOPENHAUER on the Fourfold Root of the Principle of Sufficient Reason, and On the Will in Nature. Translated by Madame Hillebrand. 5s.

—— **Essays.** Selected and Translated. With a Biographical Introduction and Sketch of his Philosophy, by E. Belfort Bax. 5s.

SCHOUW'S Earth, Plants, and Man. Translated by A. Henfrey. With coloured Map of the Geography of Plants. 5s.

SCHUMANN (Robert). His Life and Works, by August Reissmann. Translated by A. L. Alger. 3s. 6d.

—— **Early Letters.** Originally published by his Wife. Translated by May Herbert. With a Preface by Sir George Grove, D.C.L. 3s. 6d.

SENECA on Benefits. Newly translated by A. Stewart, M.A. 3s. 6d.

—— **Minor Essays and On Clemency.** Translated by A. Stewart, M.A. 5s.

SHAKESPEARE DOCUMENTS. Arranged by D. H. Lambert, B.A. 3s. 6d.

SHAKESPEARE'S Dramatic Art. The History and Character of Shakespeare's Plays. By Dr. Hermann Ulrici. Translated by L. Dora Schmitz. 2 vols. 3s. 6d. each.

SHAKESPEARE (William). A Literary Biography by Karl Elze, Ph.D., LL.D. Translated by L. Dora Schmitz. 5s.

SHARPE (S.) The History of Egypt, from the Earliest Times till the Conquest by the Arabs, A.D. 640. By Samuel Sharpe. 2 Maps and upwards of 400 Illustrative Woodcuts. 2 vols. 5s. each.

SHERIDAN'S Dramatic Works, Complete. With Life by G. G. S. 3s. 6d.

SISMONDI'S History of the Literature of the South of Europe. Translated by Thomas Roscoe. 2 vols. 3s. 6d. each.

SMITH'S Synonyms and Antonyms, or Kindred Words and their Opposites. Revised Edition. 5s.

—— **Synonyms Discriminated.** A Dictionary of Synonymous Words in the English Language, showing the Accurate signification of words of similar meaning. Edited by the Rev. H. Percy Smith, M.A. 6s.

SMITH'S (Adam) The Wealth of Nations. Edited by E. Belfort Bax. 2 vols. 3s. 6d. each.

—— **Theory of Moral Sentiments.** With a Memoir of the Author by Dugald Stewart. 3s. 6d.

SMITH'S (Pye) Geology and Scripture. 2nd Edition. 5s.

SMYTH'S (Professor) Lectures on Modern History. 2 vols. 3s. 6d. each.

SMOLLETT'S Adventures of Roderick Random. With short Memoir and Bibliography, and Cruikshank's Illustrations. 3s. 6d.

—— **Adventures of Peregrine Pickle.** With Bibliography and Cruikshank's Illustrations. 2 vols. 3s. 6d. each.

—— **The Expedition of Humphry Clinker.** With Bibliography and Cruikshank's Illustrations. 3s. 6d.

SOCRATES (surnamed 'Scholasticus'). The Ecclesiastical History of (A.D. 305-445). Translated from the Greek. 5s.

SOPHOCLES, The Tragedies of. A New Prose Translation, with Memoir, Notes, &c., by E. P. Coleridge, M.A. 5s.

SOUTHEY'S Life of Nelson. With Portraits, Plans, and upwards of 50 Engravings on Steel and Wood. 5s.

—— **Life of Wesley,** and the Rise and Progress of Methodism. 5s.

—— **Robert Southey.** The Story of his Life written in his Letters. Edited by John Dennis. 3s. 6d.

SOZOMEN'S Ecclesiastical History. Translated from the Greek. Together with the ECCLESIASTICAL HISTORY OF PHILOSTORGIUS, as epitomised by Photius. Translated by Rev. E. Walford, M.A. 5s.

SPINOZA'S Chief Works. Translated, with Introduction, by R. H. M. Elwes. 2 vols. 5s. each.

STANLEY'S Classified Synopsis of the Principal Painters of the Dutch and Flemish Schools. By George Stanley. 5s.

STAUNTON'S Chess-Player's Handbook. 5s.

STAUNTON'S Chess Praxis. A Supplement to the Chess-player's Handbook. 5s.

—— **Chess-player's Companion.** Comprising a Treatise on Odds, Collection of Match Games, and a Selection of Original Problems. 5s.

STOCKHARDT'S Experimental Chemistry. Edited by C. W. Heaton, F.C.S. 5s.

STOWE (Mrs. H. B.) Uncle Tom's Cabin. Illustrated. 3s. 6d.

STRABO'S Geography. Translated by W. Falconer, M.A., and H. C. Hamilton. 3 vols. 5s. each.

STRICKLAND'S (Agnes) Lives of the Queens of England, from the Norman Conquest. Revised Edition. With 6 Portraits. 6 vols. 5s. each.

—— **Life of Mary Queen of Scots.** 2 vols. 5s. each.

—— **Lives of the Tudor and Stuart Princesses.** With Portraits. 5s.

STUART and REVETT'S Antiquities of Athens, and other Monuments of Greece. With 71 Plates engraved on Steel, and numerous Woodcut Capitals. 5s.

SUETONIUS' Lives of the Twelve Cæsars and Lives of the Grammarians. Thomson's translation, revised by T. Forester. 5s.

SWIFT'S Prose Works. Edited by Temple Scott. With a Biographical Introduction by the Right Hon. W. E. H. Lecky, M.P. With Portraits and Facsimiles. 12 vols. 5s. each.

I.—A Tale of a Tub, The Battle of the Books, and other

SWIFT'S PROSE WORKS (*continued*).
early works. Edited by Temple Scott. With a Biographical Introduction by W. E. H. Lecky.
II.—The Journal to Stella. Edited by Frederick Ryland, M.A. With 2 Portraits and Facsimile.
III. & IV.—Writings on Religion and the Church.
V.—Historical and Political Tracts (English).
VI.—The Drapier's Letters. With facsimiles of Wood's Coinage, &c.
VII.—Historical and Political Tracts (Irish).
VIII.—Gulliver's Travels. Edited by G. R. Dennis, B.A. With Portrait and Maps.
IX.—Contributions to Periodicals.
X.—Historical Writings.
XI.—Literary Essays.
XII.—Full Index and Bibliography, with Essays on the Portraits of Swift by Sir Frederick Falkiner, and on the Relations between Swift and Stella by the Very Rev. Dean Bernard.

SWIFT'S Poems. Edited by W. Ernst Browning. 2 vols. 3*s.* 6*d.* each.

TACITUS. The Works of. Literally translated. 2 vols. 5*s.* each.

TASSO'S Jerusalem Delivered. Translated into English Spenserian Verse by J. H. Wiffen. With 8 Engravings on Steel and 24 Woodcuts by Thurston. 5*s.*

TAYLOR'S (Bishop Jeremy) Holy Living and Dying. 3*s.* 6*d.*

TEN BRINK.—See BRINK.

TERENCE and PHÆDRUS. Literally translated by H. T. Riley, M.A. To which is added, Smart's Metrical Version of Phædrus. 5*s.*

THEOCRITUS, BION, MOSCHUS, and TYRTÆUS. Literally translated by the Rev. J. Banks, M.A. To which are appended the Metrical Versions of Chapman. 5*s.*

THEODORET and EVAGRIUS. Histories of the Church from A.D. 332 to A.D. 427; and from A.D. 431 to A.D. 544. Translated. 5*s.*

THIERRY'S History of the Conquest of England by the Normans. Translated by William Hazlitt. 2 vols. 3*s.* 6*d.* each.

THUCYDIDES. The Peloponnesian War. Literally translated by the Rev. H. Dale. 2 vols. 3*s.* 6*d.* each.

—— An Analysis and Summary of. By J. T. Wheeler. 5*s.*

THUDICHUM (J. L. W.) A Treatise on Wines. Illustrated. 5*s.*

URE'S (Dr. A.) Cotton Manufacture of Great Britain. Edited by P. L. Simmonds. 2 vols. 5*s.* each.

—— Philosophy of Manufactures. Edited by P. L. Simmonds. 7*s.* 6*d.*

VASARI'S Lives of the most Eminent Painters, Sculptors, and Architects. Translated by Mrs. J. Foster, with a Commentary by J. P. Richter, Ph.D. 6 vols. 3*s.* 6*d.* each.

VIRGIL. A Literal Prose Translation by A. Hamilton Bryce, LL.D. With Portrait. 3*s.* 6*d.*

VOLTAIRE'S Tales. Translated by R. B. Boswell. Containing Bebouc, Memnon, Candide, L'Ingénu, and other Tales. 3*s.* 6*d.*

WALTON'S Complete Angler. Edited by Edward Jesse. With Portrait and 203 Engravings on Wood and 26 Engravings on Steel. 5*s.*

WALTON'S Lives of Donne, Hooker, &c. New Edition revised by A. H. Bullen, with a Memoir of Izaak Walton by Wm. Dowling. With numerous Illustrations. 5s.

WELLINGTON, Life of. By 'An Old Soldier.' From the materials of Maxwell. With Index and 18 Steel Engravings. 5s.

—— Victories of. *See* MAXWELL.

WERNER'S Templars in Cyprus. Translated by E. A. M. Lewis. 3s. 6d.

WESTROPP (H. M.) A Handbook of Archæology, Egyptian, Greek, Etruscan, Roman. Illustrated. 5s.

WHEATLEY'S A Rational Illustration of the Book of Common Prayer. 3s. 6d.

WHITE'S Natural History of Selborne. With Notes by Sir William Jardine. Edited by Edward Jesse. With 40 Portraits and coloured Plates. 5s.

WIESELER'S Chronological Synopsis of the Four Gospels. Translated by the Rev. Canon Venables. 3s. 6d.

WILLIAM of MALMESBURY'S Chronicle of the Kings of England. Translated by the Rev. J. Sharpe. Edited by J. A. Giles, D.C.L. 5s.

XENOPHON'S Works. Translated by the Rev. J. S. Watson, M.A., and the Rev. H. Dale. In 3 vols. 5s. each.

YOUNG (Arthur). Travels in France during the years 1787, 1788, and 1789. Edited by M. Betham Edwards. 3s. 6d.

—— Tour in Ireland, with General Observations on the state of the country during the years 1776-79. Edited by A. W. Hutton. With Complete Bibliography by J. P. Anderson, and Map. 2 vols. 3s. 6d. each.

YULE-TIDE STORIES. A Collection of Scandinavian and North-German Popular Tales and Traditions. Edited by B. Thorpe. 5s.

BOHN'S LIBRARIES.

A SPECIAL OFFER.

MESSRS. BELL have made arrangements to supply selections of 100 or 50 volumes from these famous Libraries, for £11 11s. or £6 6s. net respectively. The volumes may be selected without any restriction from the full List of the Libraries, now numbering nearly 750 volumes.

WRITE FOR FULL PARTICULARS.

THE YORK LIBRARY

A NEW SERIES OF REPRINTS ON THIN PAPER.

With specially designed title-pages, binding, and end-papers.

Fcap. 8vo. in cloth, 2s. net;
In leather, 3s. net.

'The York Library is noticeable by reason of the wisdom and intelligence displayed in the choice of unhackneyed classics. . . . A most attractive series of reprints. . . . The size and style of the volumes are exactly what they should be.'—*Bookman.*

The following volumes are now ready:

CHARLOTTE BRONTË'S JANE EYRE.

BURNEY'S EVELINA. Edited, with an Introduction and Notes, by ANNIE RAINE ELLIS.

BURNEY'S CECILIA. Edited by ANNIE RAINE ELLIS. 2 vols.

BURTON'S ANATOMY OF MELANCHOLY. Edited by the Rev. A. R. SHILLETO, M.A., with Introduction by A. H. BULLEN. 3 vols.

BURTON'S (SIR RICHARD) PILGRIMAGE TO AL-MADINAH AND MECCAH. With Introduction by STANLEY LANE-POOLE. 2 vols.

CALVERLEY. THE IDYLLS OF THEOCRITUS, with the Eclogues of Virgil. Translated into English Verse by C. S. CALVERLEY. With an Introduction by R. Y. TYRRELL, Litt.D.

CERVANTES' DON QUIXOTE. MOTTEUX'S Translation, revised. With LOCKHART'S Life and Notes. 2 vols.

CLASSIC TALES: JOHNSON'S RASSELAS, GOLDSMITH'S VICAR OF WAKEFIELD, STERNE'S SENTIMENTAL JOURNEY, WALPOLE'S CASTLE OF OTRANTO. With Introduction by C. S. FEARENSIDE, M.A.

COLERIDGE'S AIDS TO REFLECTION, and the Confessions of an Inquiring Spirit.

COLERIDGE'S FRIEND. A series of Essays on Morals, Politics, and Religion.

COLERIDGE'S TABLE TALK AND OMNIANA. Arranged and Edited by T. ASHE, B.A.

COLERIDGE'S LECTURES AND NOTES ON SHAKE-SPEARE, and other English Poets. Edited by T. ASHE, B.A.

DRAPER'S HISTORY OF THE INTELLECTUAL DEVELOPMENT OF EUROPE. 2 vols.

EBERS' AN EGYPTIAN PRINCESS. Translated by E. S. BUCHHEIM.

GEORGE ELIOT'S ADAM BEDE.

EMERSON'S WORKS. A new edition in 5 volumes, with the Text edited and collated by GEORGE SAMPSON.

FIELDING'S TOM JONES (2 vols.), AMELIA (1 vol.), JOSEPH ANDREWS (1 vol.).

THE YORK LIBRARY—*continued.*

GASKELL'S SYLVIA'S LOVERS.

GESTA ROMANORUM, or Entertaining Moral Stories invented by the Monks. Translated from the Latin by the Rev. CHARLES SWAN. Revised edition, by WYNNARD HOOPER, M.A.

GOETHE'S FAUST. Translated by ANNA SWANWICK, LL.D. Revised edition, with an Introduction and Bibliography by KARL BREUL, Litt.D., Ph.D.

GOETHE'S POETRY AND TRUTH FROM MY OWN LIFE. Translated by M. STEELE-SMITH, with Introduction and Bibliography by KARL BREUL, Litt.D.

HAWTHORNE'S TRANSFORMATION (THE MARBLE FAUN).

HOOPER'S WATERLOO: THE DOWNFALL OF THE FIRST NAPOLEON. With Maps and Plans.

IRVING'S SKETCH BOOK.

IRVING'S BRACEBRIDGE HALL, OR THE HUMOURISTS.

JAMESON'S SHAKESPEARE'S HEROINES.

LAMB'S ESSAYS. Including the Essays of Elia, Last Essays of Elia, and Eliana.

MARCUS AURELIUS ANTONINUS, THE THOUGHTS OF. Translated by GEORGE LONG, M.A. With an Essay on Marcus Aurelius by MATTHEW ARNOLD.

MARRYAT'S MR. MIDSHIPMAN EASY. With 8 Illustrations. 1 vol. PETER SIMPLE. With 8 Illustrations. 1 vol.

MIGNET'S HISTORY OF THE FRENCH REVOLUTION, from 1789 to 1814.

MONTAIGNE'S ESSAYS. Cotton's translation. Revised by W. C. HAZLITT. 3 vols.

MOTLEY'S RISE OF THE DUTCH REPUBLIC. With a Biographical Introduction by MONCURE D. CONWAY. 3 vols.

PASCAL'S THOUGHTS. Translated from the Text of M. AUGUSTE MOLINIER by C. KEGAN PAUL. Third edition.

PLUTARCH'S LIVES. Translated, with Notes and a Life by AUBREY STEWART, M.A., and GEORGE LONG, M.A. 4 vols.

RANKE'S HISTORY OF THE POPES, during the Last Four Centuries. Mrs. Foster's translation. Revised by G. R. DENNIS. 3 vols.

SWIFT'S GULLIVER'S TRAVELS. Edited, with Introduction and Notes, by G. R. DENNIS, with facsimiles of the original illustrations.

SWIFT'S JOURNAL TO STELLA. Edited, with Introduction and Notes, by F. RYLAND, M.A.

TROLLOPE'S BARSETSHIRE NOVELS.—THE WARDEN (1 vol.), BARCHESTER TOWERS (1 vol.), DR. THORNE (1 vol.), FRAMLEY PARSONAGE (1 vol.), SMALL HOUSE AT ALLINGTON (2 vols.), LAST CHRONICLE OF BARSET (2 vols.).

VOLTAIRE'S ZADIG AND OTHER TALES. Translated by R. BRUCE BOSWELL.

ARTHUR YOUNG'S TRAVELS IN FRANCE, during the years 1787, 1788, and 1789. Edited with Introduction and Notes, by M. BETHAM EDWARDS.

MASTERS OF LITERATURE

Crown 8vo. with portrait, 3s. 6d. net each.

This Series represents an attempt to include in a portable form the finest passages of our prose masters, with some apparatus for the intensive study of what is, by the consent of the specialists, the particular author's very best. The selection of passages has been entrusted to the best contemporary guides, who are also critics of the first rank, and have the necessary power of popular exposition. The editors have also been asked to adjust their introductions to the selection, and to write the connecting links which form a special feature of the series. These connections bring the excerpts together in one focus, and exhibit at the same time the unity and development of the given writer's work.

First List of Volumes:

SCOTT. By Professor A. J. GRANT.
THACKERAY. By G. K. CHESTERTON.
FIELDING. By Professor SAINTSBURY.
CARLYLE. By A. W. EVANS.
DEFOE. By JOHN MASEFIELD.
EMERSON. By G. H. PERRIS.
DE QUINCEY. By SIDNEY LOW.
DICKENS. By THOMAS SECCOMBE.
STERNE. By Dr. SIDNEY LEE.

A detailed prospectus will be sent on application.

BELL'S HANDBOOKS
OF
THE GREAT MASTERS
IN PAINTING AND SCULPTURE.

Edited by G. C. WILLIAMSON, Litt.D.

NEW AND CHEAPER REISSUE.

Post 8vo. With 40 Illustrations and Photogravure Frontispiece. 3s. 6d. net each.

The following Volumes have been issued:

BOTTICELLI. By A. Streeter. 2nd Edition.
BRUNELLESCHI. By Leader Scott.
CORREGGIO. By Selwyn Brinton, M.A. 2nd Edition.
CARLO CRIVELLI. By G. McNeil Rushforth, M.A. 2nd Edition.
DELLA ROBBIA. By the Marchesa Burlamacchi. 2nd Edition.
ANDREA DEL SARTO. By H. Guinness. 2nd Edition.
DONATELLO. By Hope Rea. 2nd Edition.
FRANCIA. By George C. Williamson, Litt.D.
GAUDENZIO FERRARI. By Ethel Halsey.
GERARD DOU. By Dr. W. Martin. Translated by Clara Bell.
GIORGIONE. By Herbert Cook, M.A. 2nd Edition.
GIOTTO. By F. Mason Perkins. 2nd Edition.
FRANS HALS. By Gerald S. Davies, M.A.
LEONARDO DA VINCI. By Edward McCurdy, M.A. 2nd Edition.
LUINI. By George C. Williamson, Litt.D. 3rd Edition.
MANTEGNA. By Maud Cruttwell. 2nd Edition.
MEMLINC. By W. H. James Weale. 2nd Edition.
MICHEL ANGELO. By Lord Ronald Sutherland Gower, M.A., F.S.A. 2nd Edition.
PERUGINO. By G C. Williamson, Litt.D. 2nd Edition.
PIERO DELLA FRANCESCA. By W. G. Waters, M.A.
PINTORICCHIO. By Evelyn March Phillipps.
RAPHAEL. By H. Strachey. 2nd Edition.
REMBRANDT. By Malcolm Bell. 2nd Edition.
RUBENS. By Hope Rea.
SIGNORELLI. By Maud Cruttwell. 2nd Edition.
SODOMA. By the Contessa Lorenzo Priuli-Bon.
TINTORETTO. By J. B. Stoughton Holborn, M.A.
VAN DYCK. By Lionel Cust, M.V.O., F.S.A.
VELASQUEZ. By R. A. M. Stevenson. 5th Edition.
WATTEAU. By Edgcumbe Staley, B.A.
WILKIE. By Lord Ronald Sutherland Gower, M.A., F.S.A.

Write for Illustrated Prospectus.

New Editions, fcap. 8vo. 2s. 6d. each net.

THE ALDINE EDITION

OF THE

BRITISH POETS.

'This excellent edition of the English classics, with their complete texts and scholarly introductions, are something very different from the cheap volumes of extracts which are just now so much too common.'—*St. James's Gazette.*

'An excellent series. Small, handy, and complete.'—*Saturday Review.*

Blake. Edited by W. M. Rossetti.

Burns. Edited by G. A. Aitken. 3 vols.

Butler. Edited by R. B. Johnson. 2 vols.

Campbell. Edited by His Son-in-law, the Rev. A. W. Hill. With Memoir by W. Allingham.

Chatterton. Edited by the Rev. W. W. Skeat, M.A. 2 vols.

Chaucer. Edited by Dr. R. Morris, with Memoir by Sir H. Nicolas. 6 vols.

Churchill. Edited by Jas. Hannay. 2 vols.

Coleridge. Edited by T. Ashe, B.A. 2 vols.

Collins. Edited by W. Moy Thomas.

Cowper. Edited by John Bruce, F.S.A. 3 vols.

Dryden. Edited by the Rev. R. Hooper, M.A. 5 vols.

Goldsmith. Revised Edition by Austin Dobson. With Portrait.

Gray. Edited by J. Bradshaw, LL.D.

Herbert. Edited by the Rev. A. B. Grosart.

Herrick. Edited by George Saintsbury. 2 vols.

Keats. Edited by the late Lord Houghton.

Kirke White. Edited, with a Memoir, by Sir H. Nicolas.

Milton. Edited by Dr. Bradshaw. 2 vols.

Parnell. Edited by G. A. Aitken.

Pope. Edited by G. R. Dennis. With Memoir by John Dennis. 3 vols.

Prior. Edited by R. B. Johnson. 2 vols.

Raleigh and Wotton. With Selections from the Writings of other COURTLY POETS from 1540 to 1650. Edited by Ven. Archdeacon Hannah, D.C.L.

Rogers. Edited by Edward Bell, M.A.

Scott. Edited by John Dennis. 5 vols.

Shakespeare's Poems. Edited by Rev. A. Dyce.

Shelley. Edited by H. Buxton Forman. 5 vols.

Spenser. Edited by J. Payne Collier. 5 vols.

Surrey. Edited by J. Yeowell.

Swift. Edited by the Rev. J. Mitford. 3 vols.

Thomson. Edited by the Rev. D. C. Tovey. 2 vols.

Vaughan. Sacred Poems and Pious Ejaculations. Edited by the Rev. H. Lyte.

Wordsworth. Edited by Prof. Dowden. 7 vols.

Wyatt. Edited by J. Yeowell.

Young. 2 vols. Edited by the Rev. J. Mitford.

THE ALL-ENGLAND SERIES.
HANDBOOKS OF ATHLETIC GAMES.

'The best instruction on games and sports by the best authorities, at the lowest prices.'—*Oxford Magazine.*

Small 8vo. cloth, Illustrated. Price 1s. each.

Cricket. By FRED C. HOLLAND.

Cricket. By the Hon. and Rev. E. LYTTELTON.

Croquet. By Lieut.-Col. the Hon. H. C. NEEDHAM.

Lawn Tennis. By H. W. W. WILBERFORCE. With a Chapter for Ladies, by Mrs. HILLYARD.

Tennis and Rackets and Fives. By JULIAN MARSHALL, Major J. SPENS, and Rev. J. A. ARNAN TAIT.

Golf. By H. S. C. EVERARD. Double vol. 2s.

Rowing and Sculling. By GUY RIXON.

Rowing and Sculling. By W. B. WOODGATE.

Sailing. By E. F. KNIGHT, dbl. vol. 2s.

Swimming. By MARTIN and J. RACSTER COBBETT.

Camping out. By A. A. MACDONELL. Double vol. 2s.

Canoeing. By Dr. J. D. HAYWARD. Double vol. 2s.

Mountaineering. By Dr. CLAUDE WILSON. Double vol. 2s.

Riding. By W. A. KERR, V.C. Double vol. 2s.

Ladies' Riding. By W. A. KERR, V.C.

Boxing. By R. G. ALLANSON-WINN. With Prefatory Note by Bat Mullins.

Fencing. By H. A. COLMORE DUNN.

Cycling. By H. H. GRIFFIN, L.A.C., N.C.U., C.T.C. With a Chapter for Ladies, by Miss AGNES WOOD. Double vol. 2s. [STRONG. New Edition.

Wrestling. By WALTER ARMSTRONG.

Broadsword and Singlestick. By R. G. ALLANSON-WINN and C. PHILLIPPS-WOLLEY. [Double vol. 2s.

Gymnastics. By A. F. JENKIN.

Gymnastic Competition and Display Exercises. Compiled by F. GRAF.

Indian Clubs. By G. T. B. COBBETT and A. F. JENKIN.

Dumb-bells. By F. GRAF.

Football — Rugby Game. By HARRY VASSALL. Revised Edition (1909)

Football—Association Game. By C. W. ALCOCK. Revised Edition.

Hockey. By F. S. CRESWELL. New Edition.

Skating. By DOUGLAS ADAMS. With a Chapter for Ladies, by Miss L. CHEETHAM, and a Chapter on Speed Skating, by a Fen Skater. Dbl. vol. 2s.

Baseball. By NEWTON CRANE.

Rounders, Fieldball, Bowls, Quoits, Curling, Skittles, &c. By J. M. WALKER and C. C. MOTT.

Dancing. By EDWARD SCOTT. Double vol. 2s.

THE CLUB SERIES OF CARD AND TABLE GAMES.

'No well-regulated club or country house should be without this useful series of books.'—*Globe.* Small 8vo. cloth, Illustrated. Price 1s. each.

Bridge. By 'TEMPLAR.'

Six-handed Bridge. By HUBERT STUART. 6d.

Whist. By Dr. WM. POLE, F.R.S.

Solo Whist. By ROBERT F. GREEN.

Billiards. By Major-Gen. A. W. DRAYSON, F.R.A.S. With a Preface by W. J. Peall.

Hints on Billiards. By J. P. BUCHANAN. Double vol. 2s.

Chess. By ROBERT F. GREEN.

The Two-Move Chess Problem. By B. G. LAWS.

Chess Openings. By I. GUNSBERG.

Draughts and Backgammon. By 'BERKELEY.'

Reversi and Go Bang. By 'BERKELEY.'

Dominoes and Solitaire. By 'BERKELEY.'

Bézique and Cribbage. By 'BERKELEY.'

Écarté and Euchre. By 'BERKELEY.'

Piquet and Rubicon Piquet. By 'BERKELEY.'

Skat. By LOUIS DIEHL.
. A Skat Scoring-book. 1s.

Round Games, including Poker, Napoleon, Loo, Vingt-et-un, &c. By BAXTER-WRAY.

Parlour and Playground Games. By Mrs. LAURENCE GOMME.

...LL'S CATHEDRAL SERIES.

Profusely Illustrated, cloth, crown 8vo 1s. 6d. net each.

...ISH CATHEDRALS. An Itinerary and Description. Compiled by JAMES G. ...LCHRIST, A.M., M.D. Revised and edited with an Introduction on Cathedral ...chitecture by the Rev. T. PERKINS, M.A., F.R.A.S. 2nd Edition, revised.

BANGOR. By P. B. IRONSIDE BAX.
BRISTOL. By H. J. L. J. MASSÉ, M.A. 2nd Edition.
CANTERBURY. By HARTLEY WITHERS. 6th Edition.
CARLISLE. By C. KING ELEY.
CHESTER. By CHARLES HIATT. 3rd Edition.
CHICHESTER. By H. C. CORLETTE, A.R.I.B.A. 2nd Edition.
DURHAM. By J. E. BYGATE, A.R.C.A. 4th Edition.
ELY. By Rev. W. D. SWEETING, M.A. 3rd Edition.
EXETER. By PERCY ADDLESHAW, B.A. 3rd Edition, revised.
GLOUCESTER. By H. J. L. J. MASSÉ, M.A. 5th Edition.
HEREFORD. By A. HUGH FISHER, A.R.E. 2nd Edition, revised.
LICHFIELD. By A. B. CLIFTON. 3rd Edition, revised.
LINCOLN. By A. F. KENDRICK, B.A. 4th Edition.
LLANDAFF. By E. C. MORGAN WILLMOTT, A.R.I.B.A.
MANCHESTER. By Rev. T. PERKINS, M.A.
NORWICH. By C. H. B. QUENNELL. 2nd Edition, revised.
OXFORD. By Rev. PERCY DEARMER, M.A. 2nd Edition, revised.
PETERBOROUGH. By Rev. W. D. SWEETING. 3rd Edition, revised.
RIPON. By CECIL HALLETT, B.A. 2nd Edition.
ROCHESTER. By G. H. PALMER, B.A. 2nd Edition, revised.
ST. ALBANS. By Rev. T. PERKINS, M.A.
ST. ASAPH. By P. B. IRONSIDE BAX.
ST. DAVID'S. By PHILIP ROBSON, A.R.I.B.A. 2nd Edition.
ST. PATRICK'S, DUBLIN. By Rev. J. H. BERNARD, M.A., D.D. 2nd Edition.
ST. PAUL'S. By Rev. ARTHUR DIMOCK, M.A. 4th Edition, revised.
ST. SAVIOUR'S, SOUTHWARK. By GEORGE WORLEY.
SALISBURY. By GLEESON WHITE. 4th Edition, revised.
SOUTHWELL. By Rev. ARTHUR DIMOCK, M.A. 2nd Edition, revised.
WELLS. By Rev. PERCY DEARMER, M.A. 4th Edition.
WINCHESTER. By P. W. SERGEANT. 4th Edition, revised.
WORCESTER. By E. F. STRANGE. 3rd Edition.
YORK. By A. CLUTTON-BROCK, M.A. 5th Edition.

Uniform with above Series. Now ready. 1s. 6d. net each.

...ABBEY, MALMESBURY ABBEY, and BRADFORD-ON-AVON CHURCH. ... the Rev. T. PERKINS, M.A.
...RLEY MINSTER. By CHARLES HIATT. 2nd Edition.
...CHURCHES OF COVENTRY. By FREDERICK W. WOODHOUSE.
...ERN PRIORY. By the Rev. ANTHONY C. DEANE. (*In the Press.*)
...EY ABBEY. By the Rev. T. PERKINS, M.A.
...ARTHOLOMEW'S, SMITHFIELD. By GEORGE WORLEY. [2nd Edition.
...ARTIN'S CHURCH, CANTERBURY. By the Rev. Canon C. F. ROUTLEDGE.
...FFORD-ON-AVON CHURCH. By HAROLD BAKER. 2nd Edition.
...TEMPLE CHURCH. By GEORGE WORLEY.
...ESBURY ABBEY. By H. J. L. J. MASSÉ, M.A. 4th Edition.
...ORNE MINSTER and CHRISTCHURCH PRIORY. By the Rev. T. ...RKINS, M.A. 2nd Edition.
...MINSTER ABBEY. By CHARLES HIATT. 3rd Edition.

...LL'S HANDBOOKS TO CONTINENTAL CHURCHES.

Profusely Illustrated. Crown 8vo, cloth, 2s. 6d. net each.

...NS. By the Rev. T. PERKINS, M.A.
...UX. By the Rev. R. S. MYLNE.
...TRES: The Cathedral and Other Churches. By H. J. L. J. MASSÉ, M.A.
... ST. MICHEL. By H. J. L. J. MASSÉ, M.A.
... (NOTRE-DAME). By CHARLES HIATT.
...N: The Cathedral and Other Churches. By the Rev. T. PERKINS, M.A.

New from Cover to Cover.

WEBSTER'S NEW INTERNATIONAL DICTIONARY.

MESSRS. BELL have pleasure in announcing an entirely new edition of Webster's International Dictionary. The fruit of ten years' work on the part of the large staff of Editors and Contributors is represented in this edition, which is in no sense a mere revision of 'The International,' but exceeds that book — in convenience, quantity, and quality — as much as it surpassed the 'Unabridged.'

Points of the New International.

400,000 WORDS AND PHRASES DEFINED. Half this number in old International.

2700 PAGES, every line of which has been revised and reset. (**400** pages in excess of old International, and yet the new book is practically the same size.)

6000 ILLUSTRATIONS, each selected for the clear explication of the term treated.

DIVIDED PAGE: important words above, less important below.

ENCYCLOPÆDIC INFORMATION on thousands of subjects.

SYNONYMS more skilfully treated than in any other English work.

GAZETTEER and BIOGRAPHICAL DICTIONARY are up to date.

MORE INFORMATION of MORE interest to MORE people than any other Dictionary.

GET THE BEST in Scholarship, Convenience, Authority, Utility.

WRITE NOW for full prospectus and specimen pages

LONDON: G. BELL & SONS, LTD.,
YORK HOUSE, PORTUGAL ST., KINGSWAY, W.C.

www.ingramcontent.com/pod-product-compliance
Lightning Source LLC
Chambersburg PA
CBHW031945290426
44108CB00011B/682